The Selected Letters of Yvor Winters

The Selected Letters of
Yvor Winters

Edited by R. L. Barth

Swallow Press / Ohio University Press

ATHENS

Swallow Press/Ohio University Press, Athens, Ohio 45701
© 2000 by Daniel Lewis Winters
Printed in the United States of America
All rights reserved. Published 2000

Swallow Press/Ohio University Press books are printed on acid-free paper ⊗ ™

09 08 07 06 05 04 03 02 01 00   5 4 3 2 1

Dear Miss Yamamoto: The Letters of Yvor Winters to Hisaye Yamamoto
(Fifth Season Press, 1999) and "Winters on Winters: Nine Letters to Allen Tate"
(*PN Review*) appeared previously.

All photographs not otherwise credited are from the collection of Daniel Lewis Winters.
Frontispiece photo courtesy of the News and
Publications Service, Stanford University

Library of Congress Cataloging-in-Publication Data

Winters, Yvor, 1900–1968.
   [Correspondence. Selections]
   The selected letters of Yvor Winters / ed., R.L. Barth.
     p. cm.
   Includes bibliographical references and index.
   ISBN 0-8040-1031-5 (alk. paper)
   1. Winters, Yvor, 1900–1968—Correspondence. 2. Poets, American
—20th century—Correspondence. 3. Critics—United States—
Correspondence. I. Barth, R. L. (Robert L.) II. Title.

PS3545.I765 Z48 2000
811'.52—dc21
  [B]   00-040655

CONTENTS

LETTERS

ILLUSTRATIONS

Holograph copy of Hart Crane's "To Emily Dickinson"

Mrs. Dodds, Dorothy and Howard Baker, and
Ford Madox Ford's daughter, and Ford, Paris
Yvor Winters in front of the goat shed, Oregon Avenue, Palo Alto, 1931
Caroline Gordon (Mrs. Allen Tate), her daughter Nancy,
and Robert Penn Warren's sister
Katherine Anne Porter, Mexico

Pearl Andelson Sherry and her son, Leonard, 1930s
Achilles "Tex" Holt, Palo Alto
J. V. Cunningham, Palo Alto, 1931–32
Coocoo (La Cucaracha)

Janet Lewis Winters and Yvor Winters with their daughter, Joanna, Los Altos
Yvor Winters and his son, Daniel, Los Altos, 1940

Yvor Winters and Champion Buckthorn Sal, 1946
Yvor Winters and Champion Buckthorn Black Jack, 1948

Yvor Winters receiving his lifetime membership in the NAACP, 1957
Yvor Winters in his Stanford University office

Yvor Winters in his Morris chair, Los Altos, 1962
Yvor and Janet Lewis Winters, Los Altos, 1962

ACKNOWLEDGMENTS

I would like to thank Dan Winters for asking if I would undertake this project. That bare statement, however, does not even begin to acknowledge adequately my debt to him. Without wishing to cause undue embarrassment, I must at least thank him for encouraging me, reading the manuscript and making corrections, willingly talking about his family whenever I imposed questions, and making available to me all the photos in his possession. I wish to thank Nancy Winters as well for providing many of the same offices, and particularly for her long-held belief that I should undertake this project.

In addition to Dan Winters, Dick Davis, David Leightty, Grosvenor E. Powell, and Gerald Wandio all read the manuscript of the letters, making suggestions, asking questions, and generally provoking me to additional thought. I am grateful to all of them, even if often enough I went my own obstinate way.

I also wish to thank David Sanders, the director of the Ohio University / Swallow Press for taking on this book, and for his encouragement. Nancy Basmajian's expert copyediting has saved me many an infelicity.

For checking a collection, providing material (even if I was ultimately unable to use it) or resources, or simply talking about Yvor Winters in general and this project in particular, I would like to thank the following people: Jeffrey Akard, Gus Blaisdell, Turner Cassity, Bradin Cormack, Robert Cowley, James Cummins, Mrs. Anthony DeSoto, Margaret Furbush, the late Charles Gullans, Thom Gunn, Donald Hall, Warren Hope, Joshua Odell, Timothy Steele, Victoria Steele, Helen Pinkerton Trimpi, and Thomas A. Zaniello.

I would also like to thank all the librarians who assisted me and the libraries who granted me permission to use materials from their collections, even when I was unable to use the letters provided. I cannot single out everyone, but there are some people whom I would like to mention. Patricia C. Willis of the Beinecke Library was of enormous assistance, and I came to look forward to Ellen Cordes's helpful and cheerful notes from that same library. William McPheron of Stanford University and Timothy Young of the Beinecke provided me, respectively, with uncatalogued material and material in the process of being catalogued.

Hardly least, I would also like to thank my wife, Susan, and my daughter, Ann.

INTRODUCTION

> I prefer to portray myself in my own
> writing.
>
> *Yvor Winters to Gus Blaisdell*
> *(July 5, 1967)*

Arthur Yvor Winters (1900–1968) is among the final major figures of his generation whose letters have not yet appeared in print. A clause in his will sealed the letters for twenty-five years after his death. In addition, he made a serious attempt during his lifetime to have his own letters either returned or destroyed. As for letters he received, they fell victim to his periodic bonfires, and this includes the love letters between Winters and his wife, Janet Lewis. Thus, two-sided correspondences with Winters are extremely rare and rely on his correspondent having kept carbons. There are two-sided correspondences with Lincoln Kirstein at the *Hound and Horn,* especially heavy during the years 1932–34 when Winters was the western editor for that journal, and with Harry Duncan. Another two-sided correspondence that would have survived complete was with Hart Crane: Winters carefully preserved his letters from Crane, but, ironically, his letters to Crane were either lost or destroyed.

On the other hand, a good many of Winters's correspondents refused either to destroy or return (for inevitable destruction) his letters. Certainly, in many cases, he knew they were being kept. Allen Tate (some letters to whom have the word "return" double underlined) informed Winters that he was keeping the letters for eventual deposit with his own papers. This led to an interesting and somewhat amusing incident, although it was hardly amusing to Winters or Tate at the time. When Leonard Greenbaum published *The Hound and Horn: The History of a Literary Quarterly* (1966), he illegally quoted substantial correspondence from various contributors and editors. One of those whose letters were quoted was Allen Tate. Another was Yvor Winters. Furious, Tate wrote Winters to say he was considering a lawsuit and wanted to know if Winters would join him. In response, Winters wrote:

> I have your recent letter and I understand the law on this point and the
> people involved are filthy bastards. But one can do nothing short of a lawsuit

or the threat of a lawsuit. I will not threaten anything that I cannot go through with. I have not the money, time, or energy for a lawsuit. I had intended to write the bastards and also the University of Michigan, but now I cannot do that. In a couple of days I undergo another operation, probably cancer again. . . .

A few years ago I asked you to destroy all of my letters and told you that I have always destroyed literary correspondence. You replied self-righteously that you were preserving my letters for posterity, or perhaps turning them over to some university. I don't remember. Your chickens have come home to roost. (November 30, 1966)

The reader who comes to these letters with the standard-issue caricature of Yvor Winters—cantankerous, dogmatic, Calvinistic—will not be disappointed. Like all caricatures, this one contains partial truth, but partial truth is ultimately more destructive than an outright lie. What these letters portray clearly is a complex individual: he can be cantankerous and dogmatic (he was never Calvinistic), but he is also generous in the extreme, egalitarian, sensitive (even sentimental), noble, and downright funny. The simple truth is that even in his published criticism Winters could be funny as well as witty, but his detractors, and some of his admirers, have either chosen to ignore the fact or simply do not see it.

It has seemed to me for many years that some of Winters's admirers and most of his detractors have misunderstood his essential character. The young Yvor Winters—the free-verse poet and the man—was romantic. To many readers, however, the standard picture is of the later Winters as a stern, combative classicist. There is a general knowledge that the young man, perceived at best as a kind of amorphous Modernist, was different in kind from the older man, and that the change coincided in the late 1920s with his abandonment of free verse for accentual-syllabic meters. The main problem with this view is that it posits two men. Nothing could be farther from the truth. J. V. Cunningham was correct when he called the later Winters a "congenital romantic," despite Winters's protestations to the contrary.

Let me put my understanding of Winters this way: the young romantic eventually understood (and the understanding was, to a great extent, derived from his reading and thinking, as these letters make abundantly clear) the limitations of his position and began to change himself. Now, this change was achieved only at great cost, and it was not total. Anyone who thinks such a change can be effected to the extent that early character traits and dispositions are annihilated fails to understand human nature. The "congenital romantic" must always struggle or simply succumb. In the letters such traits as Winters attempted to overcome are rendered more clearly than, say, in the later poems. There are the various temptations—to violence, sentimentality, the desire for victory (especially in argument), anger, impatience—that are sometimes mastered. Now, it is true that some of these traits do not seem inherently romantic, but what they all have in common is a temptation to self-indulgence and excess; and I have always taken the essence of romanticism to be self-indulgence and sentimentality (excess in all its forms). Most simply stated: Winters's struggle was ongoing. (See, for instance, the two letters to Donald Davie of April 10 and May 6, 1950.) It is precisely for this reason that his criticism and more especially his poetry convey such authority. He knew intimately about what he wrote.

I want to consider one recent hostile view of Winters—Paul Mariani's in *The Broken Tower: A Life of Hart Crane* (1999)—that is useful precisely because it simply repeats to a large extent elements of the caricature of Winters that has hung on for decades. Hart Crane seems always to bring out the worst in Winters's critics. In the first place, they all seem besotted with their subject, the misunderstood romantic genius as artist "betrayed" by figures such as Winters. It seems never to occur to them that the only "betrayal" involved was Crane's own—that is, his self-destructive pursuit of dissipation. The result is that this biography is simple-minded romantic hagiography. This would be bad enough, but such critics willfully distort Winters. Thus, for instance, of *The Bridge*, we are told "a failed epic was what Winters had called the poem" (Mariani, 352). Here, Mariani seems to follow Crane himself. However, this is what Winters wrote: "The book cannot be called an epic, in spite of its endeavor to create and embody a national myth, because it has no narrative framework and so lacks the formal unity of an epic" (*Uncollected Essays and Reviews,* ed. Francis Murphy [Chicago: Swallow Press, 1973], 73). I am not logic chopping. Winters's review of *The Bridge* opens with a taxonomy attempting to discover how the work is to be read. In fact, he concludes, "The structure we shall find is lyrical; but the poem is not a single lyric, it is rather a collection of lyrics on themes more or less related and loosely following out of each other. The model, in so far as there is one, is obviously Whitman, whom the author proclaims in this book as his master" (73). When Winters's final judgment is rendered, the "wreckage," we discover, is not of a failed epic but "the impossibility of getting anywhere with the Whitmanian inspiration" (82). I do not wish to belabor this point, but it is crucial for the reader who wants to understand Winters in all his complexity.

Furthermore, Mariani tells us that Winters's objection to emotionalism at the expense of intellect was "a return to Calvinism" (353). If there is one thing that Winters is not, it is a Calvinist, not if that term has any radical meaning whatever. It is true, as the letters delineate, that the young Winters held various mechanistic theories. Calvinism was never one of those theories. If Mariani means Winters is stoical, a term he does use, he might have something. But if he means Calvinist, his use of the word is simply absurd. The defining characteristic of Calvinism is its Protestant predestinarian element. In the first place, one can look at his letter taking Howard Baker to task for the predestinarian streak in his work: "your predestinarianism toward the close [of "Ode to Destiny"] is philosophically . . . unsatisfactory. . ." (April 16, 1941). (And for Winters's relation to Protestantism in general, see his letter to Howard Baker of December 27, 1931, among others.) In the second place, if there is anything that Winters stands for it is the idea of the free will. A Calvinist simply could not have written the review; nor could Crane have been criticized in the terms of the review. Indeed, Winters's struggle to overcome his own romanticism is more or less meaningless in a Calvinistic universe. Mariani's suggestion that Winters is perhaps the Professor X of his Crane essay is simply ludicrous and irresponsible. As these letters and Winters's published criticism and poetry make abundantly clear, he was the antithesis of Professor X (see "The Significance of *The Bridge* by Hart Crane, or What Are We to Think of Professor X?" in *In Defense of Reason* [1947]).

I have gone into this kind of detail on the matter of Hart Crane because it is important. Invariably, Winters's critics raise the subject; and Crane has always been allowed the final word, in part because Winters kept his letters. Winters's letters to Crane, on the other hand, as I have said, seem to have disappeared. For that reason, it is not possible to know with certainty what Winters actually wrote to Crane, despite Thomas Parkinson's attempt to reconstruct Winters's half of the correspondence from Crane's and certain of Allen Tate's letters. It is true that Crane blew up, in his final letter to Winters, over the review of *The Bridge*. At the same time, I am fairly certain that it is very risky indeed to assume Crane is doing anything like responding in an orderly fashion to Winters's letters on the book. What is certain, however, is that the letters in this volume demonstrate Winters's changing view of Crane's work. He became particularly concerned when he received the final sections of *The Bridge*. Furthermore, it is difficult to feel great sympathy for what some have called Crane's "betrayal" by Winters when it is only possible to view it as a "betrayal" by assuming Crane was so self-absorbed that he was wholly ignorant of Winters's change. (Had he been reading Winters's work carefully?) That self-absorption is not difficult to believe, of course, but it has to render somewhat ludicrous any objective notion of a betrayal. For the implication that Winters was callous toward Crane, the reader should consult his letters to Crane's mother included in this volume. Crane mattered to Winters throughout his lifetime. Along with portraits of Melville, Hardy, Valéry, and others hung in his study, there also hung the holograph copy of "To Emily Dickinson" given him by Crane, as well as the collage Crane made and inscribed to him.

These letters also detail aspects of Winters's life mentioned only in passing in his published writing. For instance, anyone who has read Winters knows he showed and bred Airedales; and his dogs appear in many of the letters. Airedales were an important part of his life from his adolescence until, as he says, the dogs simply became too powerful for him to control in the ring. As one would expect, he showed and bred his Airedales on his own, without the help of professional handlers. The activity was, as he insists in these letters, a real if minor art. He was good: his Buckthorn kennel produced champions. Furthermore, he was known and respected in Airedale circles. One example must suffice. "Probably everyone has heard the expression that a good Airedale head should be like a brick, but perhaps few know that Arthur was the one to first say so, and to give us the phrase" (*Airedale Terrier Club of America Newsletter*, August–September 1988, 18).

What I hope these letters demonstrate, and feel they must demonstrate for readers who come to them with an open mind, is Winters in all his complexity. If they achieve that end, everything else will take care of itself. For those who repeat the cliché that Winters's poems derive (sterilely, as is usually meant) from his criticism, the letters make it indisputably clear that he was a poet from the first. In fact, criticism was difficult for Winters, a genuinely unpleasant undertaking much of the time, and the letters register his complaints. Incidentally, his dogmatic statements on literature are interesting, especially in the early letters where the dogmatic statements obviously express tentative judgments. As he also acknowledges in the letters, his was a dogmatic temperament. However, the letters (and the life) also remind us that he was fundamentally a liberal. Early on, colleagues assumed he was a Red; in fact, he had an egalitarian sense of justice that led, for instance, to his memberships in the ACLU and the NAACP.

If any single theme predominates in these letters, it is Winters's generosity, a radical generosity that neither asked nor expected anything in return. I cite but a handful of examples: his efforts (with Caroline Gordon) to obtain needed money for Katherine Anne Porter (and his invitation to her to stay with his family should she not obtain adequate financial support); his financial contributions to Elizabeth Madox Roberts's stay in a sanatorium, and his overseeing the fund when the unofficial administrator was unable to continue; his letters to the Nisei writer Hisaye Yamamoto trying to get her to apply for a writing fellowship at Stanford simply because he had seen and been impressed by a story she published in *Furioso;* the letters of introduction he wrote for his students; the letters to obtain positions for his students; and the promotion of work he thought worth promoting, whether by students or not. (For those who accuse Winters of too vigorously promoting the work of his students, see his letter of June 1, 1950 to Harry Duncan about the contributors to his *Poets of the Pacific,* second series, as well as the letters generally.) Rather than overburden this edition with letters of the final three varieties, I have tried to choose letters that could stand as types. The complete record contains many more such letters.

Finally, the letters also clarify, and add to, our knowledge of Winters's bibliography. For instance, it is clear that Winters not only wrote a brief foreword to Maurine Smith's small collection of poems, *The Keen Edge,* but edited the book as well. The letters make it possible to pin down the publication date of *Diadems and Fagots* more narrowly than heretofore; and the letters also establish his essentially single authorship of *The Case of David Lamson.*

The letters in this edition present Winters's autobiography, both physical and intellectual, fairly completely, although they represent only about one-fourth of the material I gathered. The proportion of letters to decades in the book reflects, at least in a rough and ready manner, the proportions of the whole. Thus, while a large correspondence survives from the 1920s, the surviving correspondence from the 1940s is relatively slim. (I suspect this reflects the facts of his correspondence, not merely the accident of what survived.) The proportion is somewhat distorted by the early 1930s: he wrote roughly two hundred letters to the *Hound and Horn,* primarily to Lincoln Kirstein.

Winters's most important correspondent was Allen Tate. They carried on a correspondence beginning in 1926 and lasting until Winters's death, surviving a rift in the 1930s. (Roughly 125 of Winters's letters to Tate survive.) Winters admired Tate, argued with him, criticized him, instructed him. Although now almost completely destroyed, Tate's side of the correspondence was surely similar. Winters liked the give and take of serious argument and frankly admired worthy adversaries. (See, for instance, his letters to Harry Duncan on the subject of fine printing.) For a brief period of time, his correspondence with Hart Crane was perhaps almost as important to him. Even had Crane not exploded over the review of *The Bridge,* however, the correspondence would have lapsed. Winters had changed, abandoned as far as possible, his early beliefs and theories. Crane never did. There would have remained nothing to say, no common ground between them. There are other important letters and correspondents:

for instance, the early correspondence with Glenway Wescott. However, such correspondences were, for lack of a better term, outgrown. Other correspondences, like that conducted with Don Stanford, lasted longer but were, relatively, insubstantial. It seems obvious to me that Winters took correspondence seriously. He could be funny and witty, to be sure, but ultimately I believe he demanded of correspondence something like the specific density he demanded of poems. His own letters have a high level of specific density.

In this edition, small errors (misspellings and the like) have been silently corrected. Disliking excerpts, I have tried to keep them to a minimum. Omissions are noted by asterisks. (One exception to this rule is that I have occasionally omitted postscripts without noting the omissions when they added nothing to the letter.) I want to insist, however, that I have never omitted material to suppress anything that would show Winters in a negative manner. Generally, omitted passages were either repetitious or relatively dull and unimportant. On the other hand, excerpted letters had something or other that seemed to me too important to omit. Because of the wealth of material, I have, as I mentioned above, used certain letters as types, feeling that a few well-chosen examples would stand adequately for those not included. One type of letter I have generally eschewed: the letter detailing English departmental business at Stanford. Although I found such letters fascinating myself, I suspect that their interest for the general reader would be minimal. I regret the few people—no point in naming them—who would not respond to my requests to see material in their possession. I have kept to a minimum the notes, glosses (all material included in brackets is my own), and this introduction to allot as much space as possible to the letters themselves.

MANUSCRIPT SOURCE ABBREVIATIONS

Academy: American Academy of Arts and Letters, New York City. Used with permission.

Amherst: Special Collections, Amherst College Library: Louise Bogan Papers. Used with permission.

Boston: Eugene Burdick Collection, Department of Special Collections, Boston University. Used with permission.

Chicago: Special Collections, University of Chicago Library. Used with permission.

Columbia: Columbia University, Rare Book and Manuscript Library. Used with permission.

DeSoto: Mrs. Anthony DeSoto (Hisaye Yamamoto). Used with permission.

Duncan: Mrs. Harry Duncan. Used with permission.

Gullans: Turner Cassity and Mrs. Lorre Mehlinger: Charles Gullans Papers. Used with permission.

Gunn: Thom Gunn. Used with permission.

Harvard: Department of Manuscripts, Houghton Library, Harvard University. Used with permission.

Hopkins: Don Cameron Allen Papers, MS. 8, Special Collections, Milton S. Eisenhower Library, Johns Hopkins University. Used with permission.

Lilly: Special Collections, Lilly Library, Indiana University, Bloomington, Indiana. Used with permission.

Newberry: Malcolm Cowley Papers, The Newberry Library. Used with permission.

Odell: Joshua Odell. Used with permission.

Princeton: Manuscripts Division, Department of Rare Books and Special Collections, Princeton University Library. Published with permission of the Princeton University Library.

PSU: The Pennsylvania State University Libraries, Rare Books and Manuscripts Division, Special Collections Library. Used with permission.

Rosenbach: The Rosenbach Museum and Library: Marianne Moore Papers. Used with permission.

Stanford: Department of Special Collections, Stanford University Libraries. Used with permission.

SUNY: Poetry Collection, University at Buffalo, State University of New York. Used with permission.

Tulsa: Special Collections, McFarlin Library, University of Tulsa. Used with permission.

UC: August Vollmer Papers BANC MSS C-B 403, Box 34. The Bancroft Library, University of California, Berkeley. Used with permission.

UConn: Archives and Special Collections, Thomas J. Dodd Research Center, University of Connecticut Libraries: Seymour Gresser Papers. Used with permission.

UM: Special Collections, University of Maryland Libraries: Papers of Katherine Anne Porter. Used with permission.

UNH: Milne Special Collections and Archives, The University Library, University of New Hampshire. Used with permission.

UW: Special Collections, University of Washington Libraries: Theodore Roethke Papers. Used with permission.

Winters: Daniel Lewis Winters. Used with permission.

Yale: The Yale Collection of American Literature, Beinecke Rare Book and Manuscript Library, Yale University. Used with permission.

CHRONOLOGY

1900   Arthur Yvor Winters born October 17 in Chicago, Illinois, to Faith Evange-
        line Ahnefeldt and Harry Lewis Winters, a stockbroker.

1904   Moves with family to Eagle Rock, California, in the foothills north of Los
        Angeles (now part of Los Angeles). During this period, his grand-
        mother teaches him to read from the Bible and the works of Byron and
        Macauley.

1911   Family moves to Seattle.

1913   Returns to Eagle Rock.

1914   Joins family in Evanston, Illinois, and enters Evanston High School.

1915–17 Lives in Rogers Park, Illinois, and attends Nicholas Senn High School.

1917   Enrolls in the University of Chicago (attending four quarters); becomes a
        member (and secretary) of the Poetry Club.

1918   Works the summer at his uncle's dairy farm in Riverside, California. At the
        conclusion of the fall quarter returns to his uncle's farm to recuperate
        from suspected tuberculosis.

1919   Confirms diagnosis of tuberculosis in January and travels to Santa Fe,
        New Mexico. In February enters St. Vincent's Sanitorium, Santa Fe, and
        moves in October to Sunmount Sanitorium outside Santa Fe. Remains
        a patient, except for a few trips, until the fall of 1921.

1921   Returns to Chicago for a minor operation and meets Janet Lewis. In Oc-
        tober leaves Sunmount to teach grade school (grades 4–5) in Madrid,
        New Mexico. Publishes *The Immobile Wind.*

1922   Teaches high school in Cerrillos, New Mexico (replacing Maurice Lese-
        mann). Publishes *The Magpie's Shadow, Diadems and Fagots* (privately,
        with John Gaw Meem), and his edition of Maurine Smith's *The Keen
        Edge.*

1923   Becomes engaged to Janet Lewis in May; enrolls in the University of Col-
        orado at Boulder for the summer session.

1924   Publishes *The Testament of a Stone: Being Notes on the Mechanics of the Po-
        etic Image.*

1925   Graduates from the University of Colorado with B.A. and M.A. in Ro-
        mance Languages and minor in Latin; thesis: "A Method of Critical Ap-
        proach to Works of Literature Based Primarily upon a Study of the
        Lyric in French and English." Accepts position at the University of
        Idaho at Moscow to teach French and Spanish.

1926   Marries Janet Lewis on June 22; after honeymoon in Ranchos de Taos re-
        turns to Moscow while Janet Lewis remains at Sunmount, recuperating
        from tuberculosis.

1927	Resigns teaching position at the University of Idaho (for reasons of Janet Lewis's health); spends the summer with Janet Lewis in Santa Fe; in the fall they move to Palo Alto, where he enters Stanford University to begin work on a Ph.D. in English Literature. Publishes *The Bare Hills*.
1928	Becomes instructor in English at Stanford.
1929	Publishes the first issue of *Gyroscope*, a mimeographed little magazine that survives for a year and prints, as well as the "Gyroscope Group" (Winters, Lewis, Howard Baker, and others), such writers as Caroline Gordon and Katherine Anne Porter.
1930	Publishes *The Proof*.
1931	Joanna Winters born; YW publishes *The Journey and Other Poems*.
1932	Becomes Western editor for *The Hound and Horn* (in which capacity he will continue until the demise of the journal in 1934).
1934	Publishes *Before Disaster* and *The Case of David Lamson: A Summary*.
1935	Takes Ph.D. in English from Stanford University; dissertation: *A Study of the Post-Romantic Reaction in Lyrical Verse, and Incidentally in Certain Other Forms*.
1937	Publishes *Primitivism and Decadence: A Study of American Experimental Poetry* and his edition of *Twelve Poets of the Pacific*.
1938	Daniel Lewis Winters born; YW publishes *Maule's Curse: Seven Studies in the History of American Obscurantism*.
1940	Publishes *Poems*, printed by hand on his own press under the Gyroscope Press imprint.
1943	Turned down in March when he attempts to enlist in Army; becomes Citizens' Defense Corps Zone Warden for Los Altos; publishes *The Giant Weapon* and *The Anatomy of Nonsense*.
1946	Publishes *Edwin Arlington Robinson*.
1947	French translation of *Maule's Curse* by Georges Belmont, *Aspects de la littérature américaine;* publishes *In Defense of Reason*.
1948	Publishes his edition of Elizabeth Daryush's *Selected Poems*.
1949	Teaches at the Kenyon School of English during summer; publishes his edition of *Poets of the Pacific,* second series.
1950	Publishes *Three Poems*.
1952	Publishes *Collected Poems*.
1956	Elected to National Institute of Arts and Letters.
1957	Resigns membership in National Institute of Arts and Letters; publishes *The Function of Criticism: Problems and Exercises*.
1960	Awarded Brandeis University Creative Arts Award; publishes *Collected Poems,* revised edition.
1961	Awarded 1960 Bollingen Prize for *Collected Poems,* revised edition.
1966	Retires from Stanford University English Department.
1967	Publishes *Forms of Discovery*.
1968	Dies of cancer on January 25.

1918–1929

TO HARRIET MONROE

Chicago, / May 16 [1918?][1]

Dear Miss Monroe:

I am sending you the manuscripts of a number of our members, so that you will be able to look them over before the twenty-first if you desire to do so. Hoping that they do not put you to too much trouble, I am

Sincerely yours, / Arthur Y. Winters /
Secretary of The Poetry Club[2] of /
the University of Chicago.

MS: Chicago

Harriet Monroe (1860–1936): American poet, critic, and founder of *Poetry: A Magazine of Verse*, which she edited from its origin in 1912 until her death.

[1]Someone, perhaps later at the *Poetry* office, penciled in the year, which is, in terms of YW's biography, very likely correct.

[2]Among its members were YW, Pearl Andelson (Sherry), Maurice Lesemann, Elizabeth Madox Roberts, Maurine Smith, Glenway Wescott, and, after YW had gone to Santa Fe, Janet Lewis, Gladys Campbell, and Kathleen Foster Campbell. YW discusses briefly the Poetry Club and some of its poets in *Forms of Discovery* (336–38).

TO MAURICE LESEMANN

July 7, [1918?] / Riverside, Calif.

Dear Maurice,

After more or less delay, I decided to go out to my uncle's dairy[1] for the summer, and there I am now—and have been for almost a week. Something tells me I shan't read or write much this summer, although I did compose one arsenic poem on the milk route. My day's schedule runs something as follows: 3:30 A.M. get up; 4:00 A.M., milk; 5:00 A.M., bottle milk; 6:00 A.M., deliver milk; 8:00 A.M., eat breakfast; 8:30 A.M., wash bottles; 10:00 A.M., clean milking shed; 10:30 A.M., clean cow yard; 12:00, eat dinner; 12:00 to 3:00 P.M., do miscellaneous jobs and sleep; 3:00 P.M., milk; 4:30, bottle milk; 5:15, deliver milk; 7:30, eat supper; 8:30, go to bed. Now I know why Burns was a poor farmer.

The only way I can keep from becoming utterly bovine is to recite poetry and compose arsenic while I am working. I am getting some great material for the latter. I am also collecting material for a sonnet-sequence on hog raising.

Ezra [Pound] has some great poems in the May *Little Review*—did you see them? I hear he has some in the June number, too, although I have not gotten around to that yet. Paul [Jeans] would revel in the ones in the May number— in them Ezra rather out-"Gardens" "The Garden." There is some great scenery around here if I only had time to look at it. There are also some great sunrises, but I am always bottling milk when they occur. I will ask you, as I asked Paul, to please pardon the lack of "literary quality" in my correspondence, as I write bad prose instinctively, and just now I have time for nothing but instinct.

I am sending you the late arsenic poem[2] and a poem I composed shortly before I left. Tell me what you think of them.

Best of luck, / Arthur Winters

MS: Stanford

Maurice Lesemann (1899–1981): American poet and fiction writer and member of the University of Chicago Poetry Club. Although he did not give up writing, he published little in later years, earning his living as an advertising copy-writer. However, he won the Levinson Prize from *Poetry* in 1927; and from his retirement until his death, he wrote and revised *Stranger at Saddlerock* (alternatively titled *The Year of Orveille*), an unpublished novel based on his experiences in New Mexico in the 1920s.

[1]YW's uncle was Henry Ahnefeldt (1862–1929). YW paid tribute to him in the poem "The Last Visit."

[2]There are a few references to "arsenic" and "arsenic-ish" poems in the very early letters. The poem referred to here is the unpublished poem "Reincarnation": "My soul is livercolored / and oozes / viscous lusts . . . // Long slaughtered hecatombs, / dead men, / ghouleyed . . . / red eyes that burn / by night: lascivious murder-lights."

TO MAURICE LESEMANN

Feb. 8, 1919 / St. Vincent's Sanitorium / Santa Fe, N.M.

Dear Maurice:

We arrived several days ago & stopped at the principal hotel in town, but after several days' vain attempt to grow used to the dirt, damp, cold & what not, we moved over to the sanitorium, which, incidentally, is also a hospital & a hotel, & the only livable place in town. The only draw-back to it is that anyone with a fever of any sort is under doctor's orders. The orders just now are that I am to stay in bed. I have studied my own case, somewhat, however, & think that I shall be able to put one over on the authorities around here. I have noticed that if I sleep for about an hour my temperature comes down to normal —after a couple of hours awake it goes up two or three-fifths, or even more. They take one's temperature here at a regular time—hence my stunt is to roll over & go to sleep about an hour & a half before that time. It worked wonderfully today, & I think that inside of a day or two I shall have regained my liberty.

The other day—before we had moved in here—I met both Mrs. [Alice Corbin] Henderson & Marsden Hartley. Mrs. Henderson is quite charming & very interesting. Incidentally she is quite different from what I had imagined her to be—is quite free from the school-teacher sort of aggressiveness which I had always linked with her name in my mind. Hartley is the queerest thing ever. He was born in New England of English parents—facts which are very evident —& is a sort of wandering cosmopolite who can pass muster in almost any place or company & yet does not quite fit in anywhere. He is really quite a puzzle— even Mrs. Henderson admits he is one too many for her. I have seen a few of his paintings since I have been here & am utterly fascinated by them. Of course I know nothing about technique, or anything of that sort, but the man certainly has imagination. Most of his pieces are landscapes, & they have a sort of sensuous quality—in fact one of them is almost indecent. He is a post-Impressionist of course, & rather tends to symbolize his subjects. The one landscape I speak of—a New Mexico scene—seems to me to possess a sort of ominous physical mysticism, which I maintain is the principal characteristic of this country as opposed to the more ethereal & spiritual beauty of California. Said picture makes most of the blue-haze-in-the-distance pieces of Parsons & one or two other men around here seem watery & respectable. I have not seen any of Henderson's work yet.

Hardin Masters is staying with the Hendersons, & is really not a bad sort, though he will never, I fear, displace his two sisters in my estimation.

The town is a strange place. My mother detests it & I love it. It rather reminds me of a dilapidated hibiscus blossom—possesses the remnants of its erstwhile brilliance & picturesqueness, & is sort of set askew on the side of the mountains, as if it had been wandering in a drunken dream of orchids & dancing-girls, & had suddenly & unexpectedly sat down, & had not, as yet, quite ascertained its whereabouts.

If my requests, as embodied in my last letter, incommode you particularly, why forget them. Also in the [Poetry Club] membership list I sent you I omitted H. C. Huer. You & Glenway use your own judgment. I suppose Glenway received the records, etc.

Sincerely, / Arthur

P.S. Pardon scrawl. My Corona is unavailable, & I am writing, lying down.

MS: Stanford

March 4, 1919 / P.O. Box 306 / Riverside, Calif.

Dear Miss Monroe:

I am enclosing a slightly changed version of my Psychological poem, which I wish you would change for the version you have. I think this version clears up the rhythm in the third stanza a trifle. I am enclosing also a slightly abbreviated version of my "Shimmering Veil" poem—one of the group I sent you just before leaving Chicago. I think the poem can spare the lines I have cut out. And you would oblige me immensely if you would consign to the waste-basket the poem of the same group called "Drink." I have lately discovered its one good line in two other poems.

I am stranded here on the edge of the world's backwaters for the next five or six weeks, but hope to get to Santa Fe again about the middle of April. This is a great town in which to rest, though, so I suppose I ought to be satisfied. It looks a good deal like the folders they sell you on the train: "typical" California stuff: orange groves in the fore-ground, middle distance of pinetrees, and blue and white mountains beyond. If I had designed the place, however, I should have left out the palms. They march in single file down either side of the streets, parched and brown and dusty as the Sahara, with their hands clasped above their heads in an everlasting rain-prayer. I should call them a doubtful attraction to the real-estate agent's happy hunting ground. The town's chief attraction is an Airedale pup that lives about a block from where we are. He is the best specimen of his breed that I have ever seen—on a bench or off—this side the Mississippi. I shall cultivate his acquaintance.

I tried my hand as a propagandist today—converted my barber to Socialism while he was cutting my hair—and was really amazed at the talent I displayed. I merely guided his flow of conversation—which started Republican, and ended redder than Max Eastman. My technique was impeccable.

I wish I knew if Carlos Williams knew what he meant—if he meant anything—by that "Romance Moderne" poem in the last *Others*. I think it is almost the funniest thing *Others* has ever put forth. I have completed three parodies on it already.

Very sincerely, / A.Y. Winters

MS: Chicago

March 13, 1919 / P.O. Box 306 / Riverside, Calif.

Dear Maurice:

Your letter of the 6th inst. received and contents noted. Also your apologies are accepted, and I shall not expect you to answer this until the first day after exams. Please let me know, when you do write, how the [Conrad] Aiken affair comes off. L[ola] Ridge must have been interesting. Having read [Alfred] Kreymborg's review of her book [*The Ghetto, and Other Poems* (1918)], I suppose I shall have to read the book, but something tells me that I shall prefer [Maxwell] Bodenheim.

As you noted, Ezra would seem to have returned. The Propertius pieces, whether they are Propertius or not, come very close to my ideal of great poetry —particularly the last one. Much closer in fact than does Mr. Hueffer [Ford Madox Ford]—with all due respect for him. I have reached the conclusion that inasmuch as neither a poet nor a poem is a supremely serious thing, a poet ought not to take himself too seriously—especially when treating a tragic theme. It is too easy to run into gestures or even sentimentality. Which Hueffer does at times without a doubt. Ezra's casual "Marius and Jugurtha together, one tangle of shadows" means much more to me than "rivers and rivers of tears." There are many ways of course to effect the light touch. Wallace Stevens does it by a sort of meticulous delicacy, and by an equally meticulous sense of humor. Ezra does it by keeping his tongue in his cheek. Sandburg does it in such things as "Mammy Hums," "Handfuls," "Momus," etc., by a sort of wistful mysticism. His other poems, and I use "poems" advisedly, are largely poems of triumph or else of his somewhat exuberant sense of humor, and hence are safe from becoming sentimental. Even so, he almost always gives the impression of holding himself in. And Lawrence, although he sometimes tears loose, seldom goes as far as he might. And when he does tear loose his subject matter is usually sufficient excuse. Hardy is perhaps the best example of my theory. In his greatest work ("During Wind and Rain," etc.) he gives the impression of being a terrifyingly ominous force holding himself in check at great effort. Doubtless if he stated his case in full and played up his emotion most of the terror, having become visible, would not seem so terrible. "Prose," says Yeats, "is heard, Poetry overheard." Or in other words, almost any ankle is tantalizing, but most legs are vulgar. Which is—and here I get to my point—what I think you should keep in mind. I find upon rereading your "Lonely Woman" that I don't like it as well as I used to. It does verge on the melodramatic, and it takes itself too seriously.

In the same way, certain passages in "The Friend" go a little too far, I believe,—and verge on the sentimental. Though certain other passages (which are in the preponderance) more than overbalance them, I think. "The Last Day Out" seems to me about perfect in this respect. Also your late piece, which incidentally seems to me one of the best things you have done. "Woodwinds" is almost too taken up with being light. Though that may be a merely personal reaction. I hope you do not mind being criticized vigorously. You should really take it as a compliment. And please excuse my filling up my letter with rather unimportant opinions. An invalid in Riverside, Calif. has very little else with which to fill a letter.

I hope Glenway's illness is not due to the flu. The physicians all over the country are very nearly panic-stricken, at the results of the disease. There is an epidemic of tuberculosis sweeping Europe now as the result of it, and it is well underway in this country. In the past, you know, tuberculosis has been quite the usual thing after the flu, and conversely a great many tuberculosis cases started with the flu. I have been reading the literature on the subject lately and know what I am talking about. If one is running a temperature at any time in the day of two-fifths of a degree even one should see a physician—preferably a TB specialist, and take the tuberculin test. In the early stages a cure is a matter of a few months, after the cough and usual symptoms start it is a matter of several years, or may be incurable. Also, physical exercise even in the incipient stages is suicidal. I shall try to throw a scare into Glenway in my next letter. You should do the same.

Glenway told me about Maurine Smith.[1] I can't tell you how badly I feel about her. What is the matter with K.K.?

My mother and sister are going home about the middle of April, and I shall then return to Santa Fe—where I shall remain till about the early part of June. I hope to do some writing when I get there. I have a story in my head that has bothered me for some time, though I may make a poem of it. I have just about worked out the general system for a free verse narrative technique. I have definitely given up rhymed verse except for short excursions—find the other more interesting and more challenging. I truly believe that it can be used for practically anything for which one can use rhymed.

The first day after exams. Remem-bah!!

Sincerely, / Arthur

P.S. Congratulations on becoming president [of the Poetry Club]! Who has my job?

MS: Stanford

¹Maurine Smith had died on March 8 at the age of twenty-three. She had been a member of the Poetry Club; YW would edit *The Keen Edge,* a selection of her poems. Also see Janet Lewis, "The Poems of Maurine Smith," *Chicago Review* 37 (winter 1990). This essay is the only substantial criticism on Smith's poetry.

TO HELEN HOYT

March 23, 1919 / P.O. Box 306 / Riverside, Calif.

Dear Miss Hoyt:

Will you please add the enclosed revision to the other two I sent you? I think that the line omitted in this version rather muddies up the image without adding much when it is left in.

Ezra's translations almost moved me to break forth with a triumphal chant of some sort—something beginning, say, "See, he returns," etc. The last one, especially, gave me about as big a thrill as I have gotten in some time. It is really a comfort—for one of my opinions and predilections at least—to feel that Ezra has not yet collapsed. Of course I noticed that his name was missing from the back of *Poetry,* but somehow I cannot work up any great amount of sympathy for your plight. I have a faint suspicion that *Poetry* will struggle along without him.

> But the poor little *Little Review!*
> What in the world will it do?

Which would almost move one to answer:

> *Little Review*
> Will go up the flue,
> Ta-tum-te-tum-te-tum!

It is unfortunate, I think, for M[argaret] A[nderson] and company, that intellect is not as contagious as are idiosyncrasies. And your aviator was all right, too—though a couple of his pieces rather reminded me of a poem on which Paul Jeans, Glenway Wescott and I once collaborated. We composed it by breaking up into rhythmic lines the Table of Classification for the Mastigophora, as set forth by Dr. Gary Calkins in his book *Protozoology.* O pote polysyllabic!

I have not read *The Great Hunger* yet—have read very little of anything in fact. My mind is coming to resemble certain cultures of pond life which I have at various times possessed—green and poisonous-looking, and full of little squirming things. I intend to do some reading shortly, however,—as soon as I get to Santa Fe again, and my mother and sister leave me. And the means of acquiring a number of books that I desire has suddenly been thrust into my hands. By some strange perversion of justice I won the Poetry Club's contest—which entails the acquisition of twenty-five dollars. The poem that won it is that "Dominus" thing—which I believe you saw. Indeed the ways of God are strange —though of course I have no kick coming; and I only won by the skin of my teeth.

Inasmuch as I realize that you and Miss Monroe are, to say the least, downtrodden working-women, my feelings will not be hurt if you do not answer all of my letters—in fact my conscience would be hurt if I thought that you thought you had to. And if I keep on doing things to my poems the way I have been lately you may hear from me very often. So do not feel constrained to answer this if you have anything else to do. I wish to apologize for anything I may have said in the past in regard to Williams's "Romance Moderne." I begin to see what it is about, and am really delighted with it. And I take a sort of unholy joy in some of the "Broken Windows"—especially "Complete Destruction."

We leave for Santa Fe April 10.

Sincerely, / A.Y. Winters

MS: Chicago

Helen Hoyt (1887–1972): American poet and editor. Although there is very little correspondence between the two, she remained sufficiently close to YW (and Janet Lewis) that their library contained a number of her books with presentation inscriptions.

TO HARRIET MONROE

April 2, 1919 / P.O. Box 306 / Riverside, Calif.

Dear Miss Monroe:

I am quite satisfied with your arrangement of my poems, but would very much prefer that the "Shimmering Veil" piece remain intact—that is in the revised form which I sent in a few weeks ago. My only regret is that you don't like my "Nocturne." I am ready to maintain against all opposition that it represents my principal claim on immortality. However, it will keep. From what you say about its punctuation, and one or two remarks I have heard you make, I rather imagine that your and my opinions on punctuation are fundamentally different. My contempt for that convention is profound and on the increase—fact of the matter is, I spend a good deal of time hatching up methods to violate it. If I can't do anything better, I may eventually withdraw myself into some such all-enveloping shell as M[ina] Loy's[1] and ignore it entirely. Would you publish me if I did? Between editors and critics, you know, I might conceivably be driven to forsake my sincere convictions. My system didn't work at the University, for instance—in freshman English (fifty per cent of grade for grammar, fifty for punctuation) I was almost demoted to English zero for not conforming to an entirely arbitrary system of punctuation. Of course I was forced to conform to regulations in the end, but the affair still rankles.

I leave for Santa Fe in a couple of weeks—and unless some unheralded event occurs I am likely to end my days there. Saw my physician the other day—he has been out here for a short visit—and he advised me to stay at Santa Fe until my temperature has been normal for three months. Up to date my temperature has been doing exactly the same things that it was doing when I left home, and gives little promise of doing anything else. However, I can think of worse places to stay than Santa Fe. Riverside is one. From my brief period of observation, I should say that Santa Fe is the most civilized city west of Chicago. Which is, of course, in its favor.

I am about to take a plunge into Sundermann and am vigorously praying that he will be better than any German prose I have heretofore read. My imagination conjures up a sort of aesthetic Hades. *Aber,* as Ezra has remarked, *per aspera ad astra!*

Sincerely, / A.Y. Winters

MS: *Chicago*

[1]Mina Loy (c. 1883–1966): American Modernist poet. YW's admiration for what he considered her best work was lifelong. He owned *Lunar Baedecker* (Dijon: Contact, 1923), mentioned her favorably in print early (and reviewed *Lunar Baedecker*), wrote about her in *Forms of Discovery,* and included two of her poems in *Quest for Reality.*

TO MAURICE LESEMANN

May 16, 1919 / St. Vincent's Sanitorium / Santa Fe, N.M.

Dear Maurice:

I have just finished reading *Pavannes & Divisions* & would suggest that you read it with the utmost care & attention. As bad-tasting medicine, if you like, but read it. It is a great book. The essays on the troubadours, the Elizabethan

Classicists, Arnold Dolmetsch, etc. are great stuff. Likewise "Jodindranath Mahwohr's Occupation." And there are other things. I would suggest further that you drop Aiken like a hot coal & put Hueffer away temporarily. Then you should read H.D.'s "Sea Garden," everything of [Richard] Aldington, C. L. Skinner, T. Hardy, Wallace Stevens, W. C. Williams, & E.P. that you can get hold of—not, as you have done in the past, with the intention of finding their weaknesses, but with the sole & express purpose of discovering those multitudinous beauties that have made all the respectable critics of this period fall for them. Read them with the "Retrospect" section of *Pavannes & Divisions* in mind. A little of J. Joyce's prose would do you a world of good. Also H. James & G. Meredith. Lawrence is not, perhaps, so desirable for your particular malady, but if you have not read *Sons & Lovers* would suggest that you read it—if only that you may reach an intelligent appreciation of his verse. I have just finished *Look! We Have Come Through* & wish to state that I consider you batty. There are in the book, perhaps two or three very badly written poems (a new departure for Lawrence). There are others that would be of no value outside the sequence. But the book as a whole is magnificent & contains three or four poems that can stand alone (perhaps more) & that are head & shoulders above anything else that has been done in this our contemporary era. I refer chiefly to "The Sea" & "Martyr à la mode"—& a few lesser pieces. Another thing—in a great deal of your verse you talk about "dreams." As Miss Fitzgerald gently pointed out to me about a year ago, "dreams" are a sign of the adolescent poet, by which ye shall know him. I know that Carl talks about them, but it's one of the things he does that he shouldn't do.

As regards standard English literature, I would suggest that you read such of the following as you have not read, & then re-read the rest: *Beowulf*, "The Seafarer," Chaucer, John Donne, Golding (if you can get him—see *P. & D.*), a little Dryden ("St. Cecilia's Day"), a little Shelley, Coleridge, Browning, a little Swinburne, Henley & Poe. Compare the "hard" tradition as here shown with the "soft" tradition of Spenser, Marlowe, Keats, etc. The latter in Spenser is largely decoration; in Marlowe (the "hardest" of the lot) it is, I grant you, great; in Keats, not quite so great; in Tennyson & Morris it borders on imbecility; & burbles out into spluttering blat in W[illiam] Watson. I deliberately leave Whitman & Shakespeare unclassified—they rather merge the two, & are different anyhow. Compare Donne's "Valediction Forbidding Mourning" or "The Seafarer," or, say, Browning's "Serenade at the Villa" with anything in Keats. That does not mean that I do not admire Keats—I do intensely, but there is no denying that he was not a master of style. Read a great deal of Chaucer.

Which will be enough advice, abuse, etc. for the present. It is really for the good of your soul, you know. And I might almost add that it hurts me more than it does you.

I am enclosing some recent verse—three things that I sent Glenway & that he may have shown you & a couple of experiments in futurism. Please show them to Marjorie [Barrows] when you have come to decisions upon them. In case you may not be sufficiently educated in Italian futurists, etc. I offer a little explanation for the second of the two experiments. The five vertical lines are to be read simultaneously—or at least to be read & then considered simultaneously, thus merging the five images as one would merge five musical notes into a chord. The final line (horizontal) should be read alone. It serves as a conclusion. The vertical lines should not be *considered* individually. Certain of them, if so taken, would, I admit, be utterly ludicrous—not to mention Arsenic-ish, but combined I think they produce a rather artistic effect. The final line is, of course, a quotation; but I think that I am justified in using it—at least as justified as was Aldington in using a quotation in concluding his "Lesbia." The first of the two poems needs, I think, no explanation. I shall be interested to learn what you think of them.

If Glenway is still around when you get this, please tell him that my opinion of his "After" poem has advanced considerably, but that I still abhor the title.

Sincerely, / Arthur

MS: *Stanford*

TO MAURICE LESEMANN

July 2, 1919 / St. Vincent's San. / Santa Fe, N.M.

Dear Maurice:

Glenway tells me that you were rather hurt at the tone of some of my recent letters, & that you thought I was taunting you with your occasional lapses into the sentimental. If my letters gave that impression I humbly apologize. They were not so intended. My admiration for what seems to me your best work is so considerable, that when I saw you apparently slipping into an attitude & general method which I heart & soul dislike, one which seems to me an inartistic attitude apart from personal predilections & aversions, I just up & howled —considerably more vehemently, I now perceive, than the circumstances demanded—in an attempt to turn you aside before you would have a chance to become sot in your ways. If I had thought that there was nothing else in your work but the sentimental, I should never have bothered to write the letters. It was the intrusion of the sentimental among your other qualities that aroused my combined ire, fear, etc. My letters are very apt to be horrible examples of the exaggeration, lack of restraint, & so on that I object to in other people's poetry. They should not be taken at their face value. Inasmuch as you apparently did take them at their face value, I hereby offer my most profound apologies for their distorted features.

I repeat my congratulations on your winning the McLaughlin prize.

Please accept my apologies & write when you get a chance.

Sincerely, / Arthur

MS: Stanford

TO HARRIET MONROE

July 21, 1919 /St. Vincent's San. / Santa Fe, N.M.

Dear Miss Monroe:

The group title "Monodies" which you suggest is all right so far as I am concerned. I really don't care much what you call them & only gave them the other title because it was the first that occurred to me.

Regarding "ecology," it is a very profound science, being the study of habits & habitats—i.e., the relation of animals & plants to their environments. I know more about it than any other branch of biology, save, perhaps, Protozoology.

They have at last found bugs in my right lung, though not very many. I am told that I may be able to attend school out here this winter & return to civilization some time before attaining senility. I may, however, try out a new cure in Oregon. One fellow who was here & was worse off than I am writes back that he has been pronounced cured. He went up there about May 1. It is an intravenous injection affair that is supposed to kill the bugs. Very rapid.

Have had one poem in *Others,* three in *Youth,* & one accepted by *L.R.*

I have really become a model patient, though I never expected to, & spend 24 hours per day in bed, eating & sleeping & reading Boswell's Johnson.

Sincerely, / A.Y. Winters

MS: Chicago

July 28, 1919 / St. Vincent's San. / Santa Fe, N.M.

Dear Maurice:

You might have expected some sympathy from me for your malaria if you had not gone down the Drainage Canal, but really . . .

Another thing. Next time you write, please, if it is not too much trouble, sling your letter together in a slightly more orderly fashion. It may be a mere personal prejudice, but I do dislike chasing the sentences of a letter around the corners of half a dozen sheets of paper when they jump so many sheets.

I have not seen Aldington's book. I do think, however, that his stuff in July *Poetry* was mediocre. Not to speak of D.H.L. I'm strong for the [Hilda] Conkling kid.

Have you seen June *L.R.*? Starts a new novel by Dorothy Richardson, which is nearly as brilliant in its manner as Joyce, though doesn't seem, as yet, at least, to have Joyce's stuff. You should really take *L.R.* regularly. Seems to me to be about the best paper in the country today. Also has diverting piece of prose by [Emanuel] Carnevali[1] & picture of Carnevali by Sophia.

From the few "common men" I have talked to & heard from, who were in the fighting, I should say that the "common man" was not very much "inspired" by the war. Have you read [Henri Barbusse's] *Under Fire*[2] or [Siegfried]Sassoon? If not, please do so. Toward the end of *Under Fire* there is a passage where half a dozen French & German soldiers, having been washed out of their trenches, are wallowing helplessly in about five feet of mud. They are discussing civilian writers, propagandists etc. As I remember it—after a year—it goes something like this. "'Let them call it anything they want—(here a string of adjectives I cannot remember)—but beautiful! Bosh!' And he spat & sank back in his spittle."

What is the war you refer to, in which you will need Glenway's support?

I was examined a while back, & they found TB in my right lung—a not very large or active spot. My fever continues with variations, & I probably have three or four more months in bed ahead of me—have been in bed for about six weeks now. My folks want me to come home for a couple of months—advice of Chicago doctor who has seen me once in six months—but I am not much impressed by said doctor's knowledge of TB & am much impressed by men out here, so they will, mostly likely, only get me home over my dead body, so to speak. They say I may be able to attend school out here this winter, but do not know when I'll be able to go home. Probably a couple of years. If I do attend school out here, shall drop everything but language work—go on with French, German, & Latin, &, if possible, take up Greek or Italian, or maybe both. Semester system. I may try out a new cure in Oregon, which if it works, would cure me in about six months. Then again I may not.

I have sent most of "Rhapsodies" with group preceding, of which Glenway & Marjorie have copies, to *Poetry* with suggestion that they be substituted for other group, but have not yet heard from her. Glenway has [a] couple of pieces of prose I should like you to see if you go up there. Or you might get him to send them. Both very short. I am writing a slightly longer piece now. Please let me know which of my things you decide to use for anthology. Of course I would much rather you would use some of late things if you are not going to print it in a hurry. And then H.M. may not take them anyway. Incidentally, please strike out 3 & 4 stanzas of "Service for All the Dead." Glenway's suggestion. Great improvement.

I have been reading *Don Quixote,* which is great, & Boswell's Johnson, which is diverting. I am confined at present to San. library, which is scant, & books I order from Chicago, which are slow in coming. Have five on way now, but God knows when they will get here. One ordered ten weeks ago. Have never had courage to attempt *The Ring and the Book,* though I have Browning here. Have not as yet fulfilled my promise regarding Conrad. But then have had reasons. I have been reading a great deal of Hawthorne. If you have not read him, do. James is only man in his class. Perhaps Joyce. Read *The House of the Seven Gables, The Scarlet Letter, The Blithedale Romance,* & some of short pieces —"The Minister's Black Veil," "Ethan Brand," etc.

Imitators of Joyce are becoming almost as common as poets of *Others* melting-pot type. Damned bore. I started to do it, but have decided to be original, & think I have worked out beginnings of a prose style with possibilities. But we shall see. Most contemporary fictionists build style on James, i.e. get effect of "inner psychology" by certain hazy presentation of psychological & emotional data. Consciously hazy. James did it & yet remained definite. It was a thin haze with sun shining through it. See "Pandora" for short example. Joyce remains clear. His imitators are muzzy. Even Dorothy Richardson, who has nothing of Joyce, might be clearer. [Wyndham] Lewis has done without the haze. Hawthorne did without it. I shall try to do likewise.

The immortal Hartley is back in town, but I have not seen him. He had an atrocious piece of prose in last *L.R.* Tries to be satirical & is jocose. He should stick to his painting.

I am much impressed, of late, with Carnevali.

Sincerely, / Arthur

MS: Stanford

[1]Emanuel Carnevali (1897–1940?): Italian poet. Although a minor figure, Carnevali enjoyed a brief vogue when, in Chicago, he was taken up by Harriet Monroe.

[2]Henri Barbusse (1873–1935): French novelist whose *Le Feu; journal d'une escouade* (*Under Fire: The Journal of a Squad*) remains one of the important World War I novels.

TO MAURICE LESEMANN

Aug. 23, 1919 / St. Vincent's San. / Santa Fe, N.M.

Dear Maurice:

Your fatherly "you will wake up etc." irritates me beyond my powers to describe it to you. As to Yeats, I have admired him for some time now,—having reread him after a space of about two years. When I read him first my critical sense was distinctly embryonic & unpracticed. As to Conrad—*Victory* at least —there is nothing to wake up to. It is a good novel. It is head & shoulders above Wells, Bennett & Co. But it is not a great novel. Lawrence is a great writer. Joyce & Lewis are very much greater. Lewis has the most dynamic personality in literature today, & Joyce is undoubtedly the most sensitive writer of prose. Hawthorne & James are the only fictionists in English that are comparable to the latter two. As to Joyce's style, it is an impressionistic style which eliminates entirely extraneous matter & unnecessary verbiage, & is carried much further in *Ulysses*. When you have read *Ulysses,* you will doubtless perceive wherein it departs from his predecessors'.

As to my two prose pieces the "Delirium" thing is not worth a damn. I still cherish some slight affection for the other, however, & think you are quite wrong about verse rhythms therein, though you may be right about monotony. Your objection to "material" as such is high-schoolish. . . . I am damned sick of the cosmic sob in literature—of all sorts—& also of the sloppy gestures of the metaphysical tragedians. (See touching death of Lena in *Victory*, etc. etc.) That is why Lewis is a blessing & Joyce is a blessing & Lawrence is not a blessing though a great writer & Conrad a bore though a good writer & why James is capable of a more poignant tragedy (see Charlotte in *Golden Bowl*) than Hardy & why *A Pair of Blue Eyes* with ironic tragedy is greater than *Tess* though not so well constructed & why "Prufrock" or "La Figlia etc. Piange" is worth most of Hueffer & why H.D.'s "Priapus" or a few other of her things are worth most of Sandburg (cosmic gesture, here, not sob, with no more emotion behind it than in gesture-less H.D., & with all due respect to C.S.) etc. ad infinitum.

I envy you your proximity to a decent library. . . . I hope to perfect an arrangement, however, whereby I can draw books from Public Library here by means of a messenger boy. I imagine I can find enough to keep me going for six months anyhow. I have to read Russians & French—in translation—& must also go on with James. . . . *Please* don't tell me about reading French in the original. I lie & gnash my teeth & send up my temperature. I am helpless without it, *helpless*, HELPLESS. It is HELL & nothing short of it. And on top of this, recent examination shows my condition to be practically stationary, so that there is no telling when I can get back to school. Think I shall make desperate effort to go on with French alone, but have damn little energy. I have been fooling with German, but do not need it in anything like [the] manner I need French. I apparently have low resistance to this damn disease & may never get rid of it. N.M., Ariz. & Colo. for rest of brief life-time. Glory be to the Father. . . . But if I had French it would be endurable. Do you know of any case in which these dictaphone language courses have worked? Also do you know addresses? I shall send home for Latin texts & go on with that. I may be able to read Catullus & Ovid anyway. I used to be pretty fair at it. For God's sake look upon me & take warning. *Don't* take canoe trips down or go swimming in drainage canal, *don't* make habit of working fool head off five days in week & plunging into icy waters of Desplaines in early March on other two days, *don't* study physics 3 S. . . .

Regarding "Prelude" in *L.R.* it was first poem in group of several, & only one of group published. Why group title was published I know not. . . . They have done it before, however. . . . Don't know anything about *Others* ms. you speak of . . . please send details . . . such of my poems as they possess would be grounds for my assassination if published.

My parents leave for here Sept. first & will be gone about two weeks. House will probably be closed, while they are away, & my sister at my aunt's. Don't know my aunt's address but will get if & send it to you, so you can get key of house there if you should go for magazines while folks away. If you should go to my aunt's, better go after school hours or on Sat. or Sun. when my sister is there, as my aunt might mistake you for gentleman housebreaker. . . .

"A Chicagoan Chants Hatred of His City" & "Vivian" are great poems & among very best you have done & are essentially serious & should be taken seriously by you & not as vaudeville. 4th line of 3rd stanza of former approaches journalistic humor & might be improved upon, however. I received exquisite titillations from both. The other two are punk—a melange of Wordsworth, Aiken & others. Don't be philosophical. You can't do it gracefully. I can imagine you as a great poet, but somehow as a great fictionist the image eludes me. Quite likely I am wrong, however, as I know only your verse.

I enclose a couple of sing-songs—the second of absolutely no value. In a few days I shall send piece of prose, which I wish you would read, form & record an opinion of & then send to Glenway, as I should like criticism from both of you in fairly short time, if possible.

I am disgusted with practically all verse I ever wrote including the "Rhapsodies."

Why do you waste time on Paul Fort when there are so many first class men to read—Jammes, Régnier, Romains, Vildrac, et al.? See Pound on Fort—*P. & D.*: ". . . the ill-starred Paul Fort . . . wallowed in metrical journalism . . ." & ". . . popular fads & crazes like Maeterlinck, Claudel & Paul Fort . . ."

Probably the chief difference in our attitude toward fiction is that you believe primarily in the big sweep & I primarily in perfection of detail. . . . This is not idiosyncrasy or parallel of my career as a creative poet, but firm conviction that more piercing emotional effects can be produced in that manner . . . again see James . . . My opinion of Conrad is not based on this predilection, however. I think he fails in his own attempt. . . .

Sincerely, / Arthur

Read [Sherwood] Anderson's *Winesburg*—genuine stuff. Not up to Joyce or Lewis or perhaps Lawrence & a bit rough & frightfully uneven, but absolutely authentic & solid. He has this country-small town life & what-not as no one else has gotten it in prose or verse. Smell of the prairie. Hartley says smell of new-turned loam. Great stuff. Also smell of fresh-mown hay.

MS: Stanford

TO MAURICE LESEMANN

Nov. 18, 1919 / Sunmount / Santa Fe

Dear Maurice:

Letter received. Also letter from my father & mine [from Glenway?] saying that Glenway is coming out here, for which I am, of course, doubly glad. When I wrote my father I was in doubt as to his financial situation (it fluctuates) but his letter would seem to indicate that all is well & Glenway may forget his worries. New office in N.Y. apparently a success, etc., etc. My principal regret is that I did not rescue G. sooner, but perhaps a rest will fix him up anyway & my father says he will send him to U of C. when he returns.

I am astounded at what you say about my not answering your ten pages & poems. I answered within an hour after reading them & mailed letter addressed to 4949 Indiana Ave., but perhaps you are not receiving mail there. But it should have been forwarded.

What you say about your work gives me the greatest pleasure because I disagree with you profoundly & am moved to hope—it's a faint hope—that my opinion of my own work is due to the same causes. That is doubtful, however, as you have a much more personal style than I, & so forth, even if you misuse it sometimes. The poems.

"Tramps" (second version): not great poetry but quite delightful.

"To Himself in Autumn": Whole effect very good, a few lines great, & none that I object to. Great tune.

"Appointment": great poem of a genre that is diametrically opposed to what I approve of & am striving for. It moves me, however, & I am forced to admire it. Excellent prelude for your first book.

"The Withered Ones": Very fine. Am not sure that I understand last two lines.

"The Crying Cranes": Trite in theme. Well written. Should go into the scrap-heap.

These poems [are] harder than anything else you have sent me, & for that reason I like them better. You will be a great poet. Sometimes I am inclined to believe that you are one now. I bow to you, monsieur. Anyone who doesn't like your work is an ass. Of all the new "young crowd" I think you are quite by yourself. But you are still a hell of a critic. Which is my only consolation, as I have to feel superior about something.

My piece of prose has temporarily stopped, but is nearly finished & I will complete it within a month surely. It will not be a novel by a damn sight. I feel a necessity to write verse at present & am trying to devise a means whereby I can put into verse things which I had always considered impossible to verse. I think I am beginning to see my way. Probably by means of rhyme & possibly also by means of a long tense free verse rhythm. But I cannot yet manage the latter altogether. I want to handle poetically certain impressions & intuitions which I have been trying to put into fiction, as I find that I am much more at home in verse than in prose. But . . .

I have been wondering of late whether you & I & Glenway could not—in, say, four or five or six months or more or less—publish together a cheap paper-covered volume in a small edition. I have five or six poems for which I cherish some slight affection & may acquire a few more, & Glenway has as many or more that are worth something, & you have probably a few more than either of us. It is merely a speculation, of course, but offers some advantage. By banding together we could probably fill a small volume with fairly decent verse, & could get before the critics & maybe get some worthwhile suggestions—J[ohn] Rodker, for instance, is nice to young poets—before any one of us could fill a volume. You, of course, may be able to fill a volume by yourself before a great deal of time passes, as you seem to have a curious genius for long poems of considerable merit, & the scheme may not appeal to you. It may not anyhow. And it may not appeal to me three months from now. But it is worth turning over in our minds, I think. I am impressed with the necessity of poets publishing in paper covers: I have become the possessor of *Prufrock* for only fifty cents, whereas I have to pay a dollar fifty for a book by Pound or Sandburg. One could afford everything in contemporary verse if paper covers prevailed. Incidentally, I have ordered Eliot's new book & can ship it to you by & by if you like. And also *Prufrock*. Which reminds me to inquire whether Glenway gave you my *Tarr* & *Winesburg*, & if he did, if you are through with them; & if you are, if no one else is using them. If they are in use, or if you have not yet gotten around to them you may keep them as long as you like, but please don't lay them aside & forget them, as I have promised them to people here when you are through with them.

I want to write about California farmers . . .

And also about respectable north-siders . . .

It will be a great deal of fun.

But I want most of all to write curious poems. A certain tone value & rhythm—of structure, not of line—has been haunting me for some time. It is different from my desire for prose impressions. I cannot materialize it. . . .

I hereby offer you a curse-in-general. Damn.

Arthur

MS: Stanford

Dec. 27, 1919 / Sunmount San. / Santa Fe, N.M.

Dear Maurice:

*   *   *

I spent the day before Christmas writing damn jingles for a celebration hereabouts, Christmas eating too much candy, and yesterday recovering. Glenway played Santa Claus. He also saw three Indian dances, and swears that he will spend the greater part of his remaining years in these regions. And thereby hangs a tale. Santo Domingo is a Cochiti pueblo and is the most untamed pueblo in these parts and has to be suppressed quite regularly by mounted police and troops. Of late certain Domingo braves have been rustling cattle, and the night before Christmas one was caught with the goods, and now reposes in Santa Fe. On Christmas Day the mounted police went to search the houses at Domingo for hides, and appeared in the middle of a war dance which was being repeated for the twentieth or so time just after Glenway had left to see the Eagle Dance at San Felipe. They shot at an Indian who skipped for the distant desert with a hide across his shoulders, the dance broke up amid whoopings, and the Indians got out their guns, but were finally calmed down sufficiently to call a council and talk the matter over. It was a stormy council however, held in the store at Domingo town. Glenway, returning from Felipe, had to pass again through Domingo. All the white men in the vicinity were found with chalky faces, departing with all their belongings. But Glenway and his party, driven by Tom the Taxi man whom nothing daunts, as he once spent a year and a half in the state pen for killing his brother-in-law (or maybe it was his mother-in-law, the point seems to be in doubt), stopped at the store to see the pow-wow. Whereupon Glenway marched up to the counter, bought a handful of cigars and passed them around to the chiefs, who were immediately put into a good humor, as were the government men by looking at Glenway, and war was averted. This is the truth and nothing but the truth, and absolutely unpolished. Incidentally, four of Glenway's Borregos were working with the Indians and are now in the coop.

*   *   *

Arthur

MS: Stanford

January 28, 1919 [1920]¹ / Sunmount San. / Santa Fe

Dear Miss Monroe:

I sent in from here the other day a cowboy ballad by one Phil Le Noir, an illiterate person who has been all through the southwest and down into Old Mexico for the last seven or eight years. Mrs. Henderson says it is a damn sight better than Piper and wishes it to be stated that she approves of it. I think it is a damn sight better than anything in the whole far western number or the next one which I have seen in proof. It is far from a masterpiece as you will note, and is far far behind Jack Thorpe or Badger Clark but it has a nice movement here and there—first three stanzas for instance—and a few nice lines and is not wearyingly long and is very well done. The far western number bored me from start to finish. There are some superb things being done by actual punchers down here. Why can't you get hold of them? Glenway swears that some recent things he has seen by Jack Thorpe are among the most strangely original things he has found in contemporary poetry. Badger Clark is one of our best second rate poets—much better than [Vachel] Lindsay, I think. People are too apt to look upon the cowboy poets as merely amusing phenomena, whereas they are really of huge importance. They are your true Anglo-Saxon-American folk-poets and are likely to have as big an influence in shaping any American tradition that may grow up as either the Indians or the Negroes. I will grant that, for the most part, however, they are not as sensitive as the Indians are in their shorter pieces—"The Butterfly's Song," "The Sky," "The Magpie," etc. This despite the fact that I am not profoundly interested in an American tradition. I simply pass it on to you who are. I am interested, however, in the quality of certain cowboy poems, and a bit more so in the almost supreme beauty of certain Indian "images."

Thus "The Butterfly's Song":

> In the coming heat
>> of the day
>> I stood there.

People may say it is not "big," but it is as big as its form—i.e. the specific density is very high—and the thing is wonderfully sensitive. It eats a hole into one's brain and stays there. And there are finer ones. One of the things I felt about Jessie Dismorr's work and tried and probably failed to say in my unfortunate outburst in *L.R.* ["Concerning Jessie Dismorr"] to which Mr. Rodker took an almost as unfortunate exception (violence due, perhaps, to my psychology of composition?) was that her specific density is so very low—by the time she has got through talking about an emotion or thought, the emotion has all leaked out at the corners. One has guessed what it is all about after the tenth or eleventh word, and after the fiftieth or hundredth or so, one is quite asleep. . . . Turbyfill[2] occasionally writes a line which gets much nearer to the root of things than Miss Dismorr: "I am the surprised young man, light walker on night lawns." He almost never holds up through a poem—never, perhaps—but he may some day.

I have decided that professional criticism is the worst thing that can befall a young poet, and so have decided to choke my aborted critical career. In the future my criticism will be confined to correspondence and conversation. I still think H.D.'s poem an abomination. Worse than Aldington's love poems, if that is possible. Why Williams should like it is beyond me. Sandburg's poems in your new number struck me as being rather sad. Very dull echoes of himself. He ought to know that the sea is allowed to do things that poets are not. The rest of the number is worse. If you will pardon my frankness, I will say that I fear *Poetry* is sliding rather too rapidly, and will soon be, as the saying is, among the dogs. So far this fiscal year, and in the two preceding it, the only things I can recollect as having been at all achieved or at all important—from my standpoint —are the two groups by Stevens, Pound's fourth Propertius poem, a couple of poems by Williams, and a couple by Mrs. Henderson. There are also a few stray lines that seem alive—notably by Syrian and Carnevali and perhaps Morris Bishop. Maybe some others I don't now remember. The sad part, however, is that you will print things that are absolutely dull and without excuse and abominably done, such as Helen Birch, for instance, or practically all of Simpson, and reject things, however slight they may seem, which are polished and sophisticated to the last degree, and, as far as they go, at least, absolutely valid, expressions of a genuine emotion. I am thinking now of Glenway Wescott. And he is not even slight, as compared to most of your stuff, has a very personal technique, etc., etc. I am not trying to defend him as a poet. You may even say he is damnable. All I will try to argue is that he is less damnable than ninety-five percent of the stuff you print. Quite incidentally, Glenway is doing the finest prose now being done in this country. He makes Anderson look like a carpenter and [Joseph] Hergesheimer like a paper-hanger. Even Djuna Barnes, I think, is not so good. If it is not likely to break me, I may print a very small volume of poems privately ere long. I have about fourteen or fifteen poems of varying lengths lying around for which I have some affection. My veterinary work is temporarily, at least, at an end. I continue to get well slowly.

Very truly yours, / A.Y. Winters

MS: *Chicago*

[1]Obviously, YW forgot the New Year; someone in the *Poetry* office penciled in the correct year.
[2]Mark Turbyfill (b. 1896): American poet, dancer, and dance critic.

TO HARRIET MONROE

February 7, 1920 / Sunmount Sanitorium /
Santa Fe, New Mexico

Dear Miss Monroe:

I enclose three poems that are to some extent at least new stunts for me and that are probably not entirely achieved. Whether or not they are worth anything I know not.

In my carping letter of the twenty-eighth I overlooked such scalps to your credit as Yeats and Noguchi,[1] and such slighter persons as Jun Fujita and Haniel Long. And Sarah Unna. God bless her for a beautiful poem. I suppose a magazine justifies its existence if it prints one great poem a year—if so you continue to justify your existence and quite a bit beside. The slump in minor verse in the last two or three volumes—for I still think there has been one—may well be due to the perishing of so many of the gang you rounded up a few years back and the failure of a new crop. Bodenheim, Aldington, H.D., [Orrick] Johns,— where are the poets of yesteryear? Lindsay and [Edgar Lee] Masters in the last stages of decomposition, Sandburg decrepit (or such are appearances at present) and Ezra middle-aged. Sandburg and Ezra are the ones I love the most, and I would gladly give an eye or two eyes or more to see more poems like "Mammy Hums" and "Fish" and the "Shadow" forthcoming. They, at least, have been great poets—and I hope they still are, but . . . Stevens and Eliot seem to be holding their ends up and Williams is only getting started, and Mrs. Henderson continues to produce fine poetry. Those four seem to me about the best we have right now. Stevens seems to me a veritable Titan. I have always admired him, but until recently when I saw Glenway's typed edition of his collected works, I never knew just how huge he was. Yeats is the only contemporary who moves me as terribly or as often. "Sunday Morning," "Le Monocle de mon

Oncle," "Peter Quince," the French Solider poems, "The Wind Shifts," the Blackbird poems, "The Weeping Burgher," "Colloquy with a Polish Aunt," they are beautiful beyond almost anything.

Glenway had intended to bring out Maurine Smith's poems in a private edition, but that has fallen through, and now he is going to send them to a regular publisher as soon as he can get the material for a biographical note. Meanwhile we will probably send you a new and larger and more representative group of her things. Had we known you were going to print the other group at so early a date we should have left it with you, but we expected to have them in book form very shortly after we withdrew them. If you should accept any of them we should appreciate if you would let us know when you intend to print them as soon as you do know, so that we can make definite arrangements with a publisher.

Glenway may send you some of his more recent things before long. Some of them I do not like as well as he does, but others I like very much. They are very curious in spots.

As to the puncher poets: Jack Thorpe is a discovery of Mrs. Henderson's, so you will probably see some of his work as soon as he does enough that she approves of. She is completely batty about him, and I thought she might have mentioned him to you. He is an old-timer and knows all the dead and reformed bad men, and probably a few yet in action. From what I hear of him he may well have been one himself. Mrs. Henderson read a few of his things to Glenway and he recited snatches to me, which is all I know of him. As to other puncher poets, I don't see their work until it gets into print, and am not yet able to scout around and round it up before it is printed. If Le Noir does anything more that I like I'll send it in. Piper's "Whoa, Zebe, Whoa," was nothing but a rather flaccid combination of half-a-dozen themes and refrains to be found in [Alan] Lomax's first anthology. The rest of his work did not excite me any more than that one piece.

A.Y. Winters

P.S. Why don't you pack up your office & move to Santa Fe this summer? Mrs. Henderson says you have never seen it, & it is really quite the most beautiful place that I know about. Perfectly good office could be hired—in a 'dobe—for two or three dollars a month. The Jemez & Sangre de Cristo mountains are much nicer to look at than Rush St. Bridge.

MS: Chicago

[1]Yone Noguchi (1875–1947): Japanese poet and critic who wrote in Japanese and English. He helped create interest in Japanese writers.

Nov. 16, 1920 / Sunmount / Santa Fe

Dear Glenway:

I forwarded a letter to you last night, apparently from your cousin or aunt.

Your order of poems seems first rate, though I do not, apparently, recollect "I in My Pitiful Flesh." Is it one of the "Serenades" or is it new?

I do not think I wish to change *The Immobile Wind.*

I am glad you have spoken with Sandburg. Please recollect that he is the third instance of my beating you to a similar conclusion by many moons. I am out for scalps in this matter. I don't think you can flaunt any scalps before me, nor do I recollect missing my guess on any occasion.

I think I shall send Harriet six or eight of my six-syllable poems, and make her print them. They are by all odds the best poems I have written—they make the others look like mud-pies. In the future I shall write nothing longer.

I informed the young lady who has moved in next to Miss Staples that LeNoir had some six or eight notches on his gun according to rumor, and she, having been told many other tales that she had subsequently found to be false, asked for information and learned that I was stringing her. Whereupon I wandered in and reestablished the tale, even to the point of receiving many apologies; and the following night I burst into her cottage with hair and hands flying, demanding what she had told LeNoir, that I had never used a six-gun in my life, etc., and left her nearly in hysterics. LeNoir appeared shortly, and the more he denied all knowledge of the matter the more she pled with him not to do anything. After several days of it she began running a temp, and it was called off. She now lives in the belief that "Chief Nagel" and his sons will give a war dance on Thanksgiving Day. Wealthy, retired Osages from Oklahoma. Hum . . . Mrs. Stevens told her that I am really married, but that there was a lot of scandal about it, and it is going to be annulled. Such is my life at present.

Miss [Lura] Conkey has returned.

Arthur

MS: Yale

Glenway Wescott (1901–1987): American poet and novelist. YW's father paid his way to Santa Fe (see letter of November 18, 1919) both for his health and to give YW companionship. Their correspondence commences when Wescott leaves New Mexico.

TO GLENWAY WESCOTT

Nov. 27, 1920 / Sunmount / Santa Fe, N.M

Dear Glenway:

Your book came this noon, and is very beautiful. I am more proud than I can tell you to have it dedicated to me. You need write nothing more, I think, to be a fine and ineradicable portion of literature.... "The Bitterns" and "After-Image" are as beautiful, finished and of as fine a grain as anything in Herrick, and five or six others are behind them by only an infinitely small shade. There is nothing, I believe, that should be omitted. The omitted "and," next to last line of "The Bitterns," is a great improvement. It imparts a most exquisite rhythmic shiver. This and other rhythmic subtleties, such as fourth line of "After-Image," are surpassed by nothing in Herrick or even Rimbaud. You are, my dear, as I may or may not have noted previously, a great poet. Seeing the poems in print makes me more sure of it than ever—certain of the poems that I was not quite sure about before fall into place very beautifully in the sequence.... Please tell me what is said of the book by any persons of importance to whom you may send it.

Fredrik [Nyquist]'s cover is very fine, it is agreed by all. I also liked most exceedingly the sketches he sent me for a cover for my book.

And Monroe [Wheeler][1] is a most superior printer.

I am glad you cut the stanza from "Clear Joan." With that stanza cut, I think it very nearly as fine as anything you have written. Anent the two recent poems. "Chansonnette, of a Lion"—the movement is not quite rapid enough to hold the poem together, it would seem. If the poem could move as swiftly and sinuously as a lion it might be very beautiful—but it doesn't. "The Hunter"— my principal and perhaps only important objection is to "hungry" in the last line. I insist that hungry in any of its manifestations is a loose word—if used where a loose word is wanted or at least where a loose word makes slight difference it may be all right, but it doesn't belong in this image, which is very beautiful otherwise. There are other words that mean the same thing (the meaning is correct) but that have a smoother surface. Please look them up. In the second line "peaked" seems a bit unpleasant though I may be wrong. There ought to be a more exciting adjective for this state. And in the sixth line "silvery" seems a trifle facile, though again I do not insist. Change "hungry" and it will be very beautiful.

As to Miss Andelson's[2] poems: "Autumn Rain" seems facile. "Out of an

Early Snow" shows signs of intelligence and may presage poetic ability—or it may not. Both poems are clean and well set down—very well set down. But do not be overwhelmed by the mention of Moses. It does not, you know, indicate genius when done by a Jew. But please send me anything more that she does that may look interesting—if you can.

Marjorie [Barrows] is a good scout, though surpassingly grotesque.

Elizabeth [Madox Robert]'s poems look better than ever in print. She, too, is literature—the quality of tempered steel.

I have not yet seen *Poetry.*

My love to you, / Arthur

P.S. Please look up the meaning of "nonce."

MS: Yale

[1]Monroe Wheeler (1899–1988) was Glenway Wescott's partner and, at this time, a publisher. He published YW's *The Immobile Wind* and his edition of Maurine Smith's *The Keen Edge,* as well as books by Janet Lewis, Marianne Moore, Glenway Wescott, and William Carlos Williams. Subsequently, he became director of exhibitions and publications at the Museum of Modern Art.

[2]Pearl Andelson (Sherry) (1899–1996): American poet and former member of the Poetry Club.

TO HARRIET MONROE

December 3, 1920 / Sunmount / Santa Fe, N.M.

Dear Miss Monroe:

I am sorry you don't like my six-syllable poems. —However, they remain better than Sandburg.

I suppose you have seen Glenway's book ere now. If you review it I hope you will treat it kindly, as I think him a great poet—"After-Image" and "The Bitterns" and "Subtle Rhythms," and also things in the long poem—are several leagues ahead of all save a scant half dozen or so of our contemporaries.

I hope to have a book out ere so very long. If you should review that by any chance I hope you will spare me the humiliation of Mrs. Seiffert or the heroic Miss Strobel.

In six months or so I shall probably print twenty or twenty-five six-syllable poems in a booklet, and shall by then be well on my way toward the upper ether. My next book will be in four syllables, the next in two, and then I shall vanish. If you would only catch hold, I might be able to take you along, but with your feet stuck so everlastingly in the prairie mud, it will require some effort from you. And then with Miss Strobel fastened around your neck . . .

I trust you will have a fortunate effect on the Poetry Club, as Glenway is suffering loudly over it. Don't spare them.

I am reading *L'Education Sentimentale,* which is marvelous. Pellerin did not admit that there were beautiful women (he preferred tigers); etc. Translation from memory, so perhaps inaccurate. It is like the old days in Chicago (three years ago) when I took the little *Others* seriously—meaning Miss Strobel. . . .

I am feeling very well, and my hopes of getting out of this hole are rising.

With best wishes, / Winters

MS: Chicago

TO GLENWAY WESCOTT

December 18, 1920 / Sunmount / Santa Fe, New Mex.

Dear Glenway:

Your two letters received. As for the new poems: "My old bane" is a phrase used by Stevens, I believe in one of the "Pecksniffiana," and savors of him somewhat too much. "That tumbling" applied to "cloud" is too much late Yeats. See "The Hawk." It is harmless enough in each case, but it is well to avoid the mannerisms of people whose mannerisms are so very strong. Both these can be easily fixed. Stevens' almost colloquial use of the bizarre word, and Yeats' almost bizarre use of the colloquial word . . . Otherwise the poem is very fine. "The Night that is still to be silent" is too much Stevens. I think it comes in principally in the last line and a half of the poem ("The spirit wakes in the night-wind, is naked") and possibly in the second stanza, though I am not sure if or where. If that line and a half were fixed, possibly the other would not be noticeable. "Uncuckolded" irritates me—possibly because of the sound, possibly without reason. Otherwise I should greatly dislike losing any of the second stanza, which is superb in sound and image. First stanza all to the good. You are acquiring a tremendous tightness of late, but look out for tricks of speech— your own and one or two other persons'.

It is well to be a Narcissus—your difficulty, I think, is that you are too self-conscious and not sufficiently indifferent a Narcissus. You do not lose yourself sufficiently in your contemplation of yourself. There is always lurking in the back of your mind—and sometimes not so far back—an image of the trees of the forest standing about admiring the pattern you are making with your image, and when you occasionally look up and discover that they have fled, you are properly aghast. Very few of them will be properly impressed by your pattern, ever—even of those you might sometime most wish to be. But why bother. Also, do not come out of your shell too much for your audiences. You have still to learn—I mean *learn*, not state with a sophisticated gesture—that people in general, and all except an infinitely minute number in particular, are filthy vulgar asses, and really don't give a damn for you or your poetry or anything else except hot meals and soft beds and someone to sleep with. You have a trusting soul. You will have a longer and happier life if you train it. I know the north shore infinitely better than you are likely to in several years.

I popped into the dining room the other day for a few minutes before meal time, and found Alice Corbin standing by the stove. Before I could say anything, she had swooped down on me like the wolf on the fold, and was shaking my hand and asking me how I was and how Faith [YW's sister] was and how glad she was and how much she liked my poems—which is ungrammatical, but probably she was too. She has been rather morbid of late—especially worrying about what the younger generation would think of her book, so I dropped in on her for a minute this morning to set her mind at rest on that score simply out of humanity—probably praising the book more than it deserved. I don't think I shall carry it any further, however. She says she greatly likes your book with reservations here and there, and intends to answer your letter as soon as she gets time, which information she wished me to impart to you. 'Tis imparted.

As to her book—I think "On the Acequia Madre" and "Listening" are of a very high order, like "Los Conquistadores" pretty well, and "Candle-Light" and one or two of the "Sand Paintings" perhaps a little better. I like the translations —especially "Madre Maria" and "Coyotito"—and a few other lines and passages. For the rest I think the book is pretty shallow and facile, and often very sloppy. However with the few fine poems in this book added to some of the earlier poems, there is a distinctly considerable achievement, and I am not carping.

Aunt Phoebe is a decent soul albeit old and gray and full of sleep.

Mr. Stevens is here, and up to date I like him greatly.

Is [Lew] Sarett as stupid as everyone supposes? Sandburg gives me a more and more acute bellyache.

Two poems are appended.

Arthur

MS: Yale

TO MONROE WHEELER

Jan. 20, 1920 [i.e. 1921][1] / Sunmount / Santa Fe, N.M.

Dear Monroe:

I send the proofs herewith. I am not acquainted with printers jargon and hieroglyphs—at least not very well—and as I was not utterly sure of the intentions of some of your marks on the proof I reinforced them—perhaps unnecessarily. About the only things I found that you didn't indicate with some sort of a scratch, were a couple of places where stanzas were run together. These I indicated with a line to the place where the break ought to have been, at the end of which line was attached the phrase "Single space." I trust that will be intelligible to printers. If not, I suppose you can translate.

Your check and note received today.

I wrote Glenway a note last night saying that I wished you and him to be absolute arbiters in the matter of the cover design. Which stands. But perhaps I gave the idea that I demand a Chinese masterpiece or nothing. I don't demand that. Only please don't let it go through with any green-and-yellow effect or too much flop around the edges. I would rather have nothing than something not reasonably restrained and finished. I do not want to give the idea that I want Fredrik to make something to order—I am quite aware that every artist has certain inalienable rights. But that applies to the poet also. I have the right to reject. There should be no trouble about it if it is necessary, I think. I will abide by whatever you decide upon—even green-and-yellow if they seem to you a reasonable green and yellow, and seem to turn the trick. Your and Glenway's notions of such things are pretty much in accordance with mine, I think.

Hardin Masters is now a patient here. I haven't seen much of him. He seems more or less of a bore up to date—uncooked and pompous. One has a sense of his sense of the authority that he believes to be back of him. He may prove better after further observation, however. Though I doubt if he and I have any great spiritual affinity.

My third Ronsard ["Oh, why sleep, my soul, benumbed, with hidden face?"] sonnet needs a bit of revision in the last six lines.

Arthur

MS: Yale

[1]Brackets and date added, probably in Monroe Wheeler's hand.

TO MONROE WHEELER

Jan. 29, 1921 / Sunmount / Santa Fe, N.M.

Dear Monroe:

The cover design has just come. I do not want it. The clouds are like a feather-bed or a bunch of bed pillows, and the only well-drawn lines in the thing are the ones he did with a ruler. Do not show this to Fredrik. Simply tell him that I reject it and will write him why. It is one awful mess—to my eyes at least. I could make a better design myself, or could take this design & do better with it. I think you had better have no design, but simply a plain cover with the titles and my name in fine type of whatever size and sort you think best—you know more about such things than I do. The grey-brown stuff that you send seems excellent, or anything else that you think might be better under the circumstances—something restrained.

My poems are not great poems, but they are fastidious and intelligent, and should not be put behind a cover by a sprawling amateur.

I will return the cover, etc., when I can scare up a large enough envelope.

I have finished the [Cunningham-]Grahame[1] book, and am very greatly enthusiastic over a large portion of it. There is much that one cares to reread, and I am very glad to have it. Where he is finished there is a turn and surface that is finer than any contemporary stuff of the length that I know except *Dubliners*. I wrote Glenway what I thought were the places in which he fell down.

How does Glenway seem to you now as regards health? And also, what is Fredrik's attitude and activity now where Glenway is concerned—exactly? Fredrik's letters are mostly very unintelligent, often illiterate, and possessed of a very youthful and unpleasant pretentiousness. I do not like him. I did not like a certain sly smile that he had when he was here, but liked the little I saw of him otherwise. His letters corroborate that smile. *Le paysan matois*. Glenway seems fated. Fredrik's last letter said that from what he knew of us, you and Faith and I would "think him a cad after the ensuing melee." Please give me some details.

Arthur

MS: Yale

[1]R. B. Cunningham-Grahame (1852–1936): Scots politician, traveler, and short story writer.

TO GLENWAY WESCOTT

Feb. 27, 1921 / Sunmount / Santa Fe, N.M.

Dear Glenway:

Your note with "The Chaste Lovers" just received. It is one of your very best poems, almost your best, I think. It is the final word in the elimination of your glamorous gesture, and would seem to be the perfection of the manner attempted or begun in the witch poem. I suggest two cuts, however: The third line in the last stanza, which is obvious and not very interestingly stated, and which is implicit in the crows anyway. It interferes with the otherwise beautiful and startling statement of what I take to be your main concern at this point. The funereal is implicit in most of the poem even aside from the crows. Also, the stanza beginning "Crawling beneath / The unoccupied sky" is all cliché, I think, and is implicit in the last two lines of the preceding stanza and the last two of the following, which are very beautiful and are greatly improved by being unaided. The omission of this stanza also speeds up the movement of the poem at this point, which is very desirable. May I make these two cuts in my copy?

Thank you greatly for such labor as my book has cost you. It is a beautiful book.

Do you want Ezra's *Umbra?*—it is reprints from all his books save *Lustra*. There were only a couple of poems I had not seen and they were bad—very bad—and probably in *Quia Pauper Amavi* anyhow.

I sent Monroe a poem the other day, called "At Evening," which I consider the best poem I have written and which pleases me greatly—a thing which only three or four other of my poems do, and those six-syllables. Do you like it?

Your new poem has a most insidiously intriguing beauty. To make a satire (a very gross word and with unpleasant connotations) as fine-grained and beautiful as this is a great achievement. It is as great as Hardy. The exquisite pomposity of movement reduced to such cosmically minute dimensions—but I trail off into inarticulate involvements and had better stop ere I become ridiculous. First twelve lines very beautiful.

I have almost finished a copy with carbon of Elizabeth's poems for you and Monroe, which I had intended to do some time ago, but have been incapable of doing for a month or more past. I hope you have not got bored with waiting and acquired a copy. Will send tomorrow or the next day. When will her book appear?

Arthur

MS: Yale

TO GLENWAY WESCOTT

Mar. 2, 1921 / Sunmount / Santa Fe, N.M.

Dear Glenway:

Thanks for the information about V.B. I will send Lawrence. I apologize for my theory concerning your attitude toward Faith, but I still think Faith's attitude toward you is one of very dazzled attempted imitation. Her letters, though a mosaic of stereotyped phrases and opinions, nonetheless show a very definite attempt to achieve something like your more expansive style. Your surface glitter and mannerisms are very impressive to the young, as you are doubtless aware by this time. The type of person who takes this surface for some previously undiscovered universal truth, and who thinks to perceive that truth by assuming the surface, is exactly the person, who, however much temporary pleasure he may give you (and there is no denying that he usually does) never pierces beneath that surface and finds out what *you* really are or what you are about. So that when this person wakes up to the fact that the surface is the crassest sort of a fake where he himself is concerned, he naturally supposes that you are the crassest sort of a fake, he never having perceived anything in your being but this same surface. The result is Fredrik, etc. Occasionally, as with Frau Zimmerman, your victim is removed before precipitating anything unpleasant, but this is the exception. And though you doubtless have not encouraged this attitude in Faith, you do encourage it in other people very often, you know, and enjoy it a great deal. I do not condemn the practice as such, if you think the cost is worth the pleasure; and you doubtless consider the cost, if not part of the pleasure at least part of the profit. I merely try to explain my suspicions concerning Faith. This is one of the reasons why I think you are, despite all your protestations to the contrary, temperamentally naive. I do not object to your being so in the least, but merely amuse myself with analyses of this sort and deductions therefrom. It is, so far as I can see, an excellent way to be.

As to Fredrik, my "defense of your right to live" was merely an attempt to make him see a little light, made in the belief that he was going to stay in Chicago longer than he did. I hoped to assist you in some degree, if possible, and took no pleasure in it as jousting at all. My evangelical tendencies of former days have, I can promise you, been not only conquered but annihilated by my intellect, and are the merest pinch of ashes. I think, considering Fredrik's labor, such as it was, upon my cover, it would be courteous to send him a copy of the book as I asked to be done in a former letter, but unless something very extraordinary occurs I have written him my last letter. Had I not been afraid of in some way precipitating an unpleasant scene for you, I should have ended relations in my usual simple fashion some time ago, by expressing my unadorned feelings and letting my opinions go to hell. But inasmuch as I have used up so much good taste in the matter already, it would be as well, I think, to send him the book and do it up right for once, for I doubt if I shall ever accomplish anything like it again.

Patton has been writing a few poems of recent months that seem to me rather fine in a very tiny and fragile way. Whatever their weaknesses, they are not slush, and he seems very much aware of his own limitations, and writes surprisingly well. He gets everything out of his perception that there is in it and is willing to let it stand alone. This one, which I quote from memory, is probably the best:

> The Day-Moon
>
> The changing moon's a toy balloon
> Blown up by winds each day;
> And when they've found it's white and round
> It slowly shrinks away.

Having, apparently, topped Jessie [Dismorr], he is much pleasanter and healthier this year than previously, and, strange to relate, no longer admires Austin Dobson. He is experimenting in free verse of late, and wrote a rather nice one therein the other day—almost as nice as the one above.

I found this by Agnes Lee, the other day, and think it one of the few minor poems of our time that have any class or intelligence whatever:

> The Sweeper
>
> Frail, wistful guardian of the broom,
> The dwelling's drudge and stay,
> Whom destiny gave a single task—
> To keep the dust away!
>
> Sweep off the floor and polish the chair;
> It will not always last.
> Some day, for all your arms can do,
> The dust will hold you fast.[1]

Arthur

MS: Yale

[1]This poem remained a YW favorite and was included in *Quest for Reality: An Anthology of Short Poems in English,* selected by Yvor Winters and Kenneth Field (Chicago: Swal-

low Press, 1969). Agnes Lee Freer (1868–1939): American poet. She was a Chicago friend of YW, mentioned periodically in these letters. YW wrote the poem "A Dedication in Postscript / *for my poems of 1940 / Written to Agnes Lee shortly before her death*" for Lee. Not entirely happy with it, YW thought of excluding it from his *Collected Poems* on aesthetic grounds but decided to retain it for its tribute to Lee.

TO GLENWAY WESCOTT

Mar. 10, 1921 / Sunmount / Santa Fe, N.M.

Dear Glenway:

Are you still all right financially? I take it that you are, but if you are not, there are several sources of income upon which you can draw, exclusive of me. There is no reason at present for your risking your health to make a living or in any attempt to do without one.

Mrs. Stevens had a letter from some person at the U. of Wis. the other day, to whom she had written of you, and I guess you are on their list for a lecture next year.

Would refer you to any sanitary report, regarding the relative value of decent light or lighting and polished maple floors. I beg of you to move.

I am glad you like the book. I find many flaws in it myself, and have a hard time looking at anything else. I like the goat song ["Song for a Small Boy Who Herds Goats"] fairly well, though, and possibly a couple of others. By all means have Elizabeth send a copy to Maurice. I will send payment to Monroe.

Am I permitted to make the cuts that I suggested in "The Chaste Lovers"?

I send you a few translations from Gautier. One should not judge Gautier by them, as he is really a serious and profound genius, and at his best an impeccable artist. I translated these things because they amused me and seemed easily translatable and involved a couple of technical problems that interested me. Also send two poems from a sort of testament which I wrote the other day, having nothing better to do and little energy to do it with. There was also a self-epitaph, which is less interesting, and which is a shameless stunt, though fairly well-done, and not a cry from the bottom of my soul as these two are and as this sort of thing should be. And a couple of other poems.

The other morning Patton, Mr. Galt, and I went out over the mesa to poison Coacher, who had been biting children and killing sheep, and probably doing other things as well. Patton and Mr. Galt waited up on a hillside while I took the dog down into a gully and fed him about a dozen grains of pulverized potassium cyanide wrapped up in a piece of meat. Five grains, according to Patton's poison manual, will kill a man in less than five minutes, and will send him into a faint almost before he gets his hand away from his mouth; so I expected some fast results. But Coacher gulped it—a little suspiciously—and walked back up to the rest of the party, and was only restrained from going off hunting with the greatest of difficulty. We sat upon our "beam-ends," as Mr. Galt happily expressed it, on the hillside in the sun, for an hour and ten minutes while Coacher took several naps and caught two or three fleas, and while we discussed oriental philosophies, and then Mr. Galt up and shot the beast. The nuances of the ridiculous which the scene contained would evade any pen, I think, save that of James.

I have just read "The Two Magics," and don't much care for either tale. *The Turn of the Screw,* a tour-de-force, pure and simple, and fearfully naive at the finish—reads like Flaubert's *Temptation of Saint Anthony.* When Saint Anthony thinks upon the voluptuous Queen of Sheba, the arms of the shadow of the cross swing forward and become the shadow of the horns of the devil; and when he cries out to his God they swing back again. Which is all right in Saint Anthony, though that work, for other reasons, doesn't amount to much. "Covering-End" long-drawn-out-twaddle with a crass finish. Neither tale has, for me, the real Jamesian thrill.

Masters fils is a shade better than I thought him at first, but not profound.

Arthur

MS: Yale

TO MONROE WHEELER

Mar. 30, 1921 / Sunmount / Santa Fe, N.M.

Dear Monroe:

Thanks for the books. I had forgot I had ordered so many, but I can use them so it is all right, and I trust you know whether I paid for them. I will send on the book to E. Fitzgerald.

April fifth or a little before will be, I believe, about the time limit set for the book to pay for itself. If you will tell me then about how much remains to be paid, including incidental expenses such as wrapping, stamps, advertising, etc., I will send it to you. And again thank you greatly for it—it is a beautiful job.

If you go to London this summer, I will not go to Chicago until you return

—or maybe I shall go before you go. Or maybe not at all—God knows. Do you have any idea of how long you will stay?

What you say of Fredrik is about what I had thought, but his motives, as indicated, even stated, in his letters were much more intricately stupid than you say, possibly more so than you know.

Have you seen any of Glenway's novel yet? If so, how does it go, and when will it be completed?

Mitchell Dawson and his wife are here and I like them both greatly—like them better the more I see of them. We went to Santo Domingo and San Felipe on Easter Monday for the spring corn dances. I have never seen anything so beautiful as San Felipe and shall probably live there. The pale colors of the land across the river—weeping willows and earth, the pale blue cockle-shell San Dia fifteen miles or so away, the black mesa behind, the heavy pink of peach-trees laid in jagged spots. Among other events I was introduced—timidly—to W. P. Henderson by his wife, an occurrence which was greatly enjoyed, I understand, by certain onlookers.

Sandburg did his stunt here, and gave me one of the most curious and subtle shocks of my existence. Two and a half years have changed either him or me a vast amount. I have never seen a man so lost in his pose, so gently and yet so irretrievably overcome, so subtly wooden. His reading was rotten—chautauqua stuff for the country-folk, learned, I am told, from Sarett. He cornered me for a ten or fifteen minute talk which I shall never be able to reproduce with any justice. I don't know just what he expected of me in this encounter, but probably not very much—maybe an occasional terrified gasp of adulation. He eyed me sometimes in pauses much as a hen eyes a hole from which a worm ought to crawl at any moment, but the worm didn't crawl, so he went on again. I spoke occasionally, however,—naively threw in the most commonplace politenesses, and my voice against his cosmic bass was the merest of quick, piping tenors. I was uncomprehending, which was sad, because some people would have understood him perfectly. . . . At each response he blinked and gulped a little, like a turtle, and started over. As I expected, I had to give him a copy of my book to be polite, and he asked me to inscribe it, which I did in this fashion:

To Carl Sandburg
    "—you sleep in the house of our song"
Yvor Winters
Santa Fe.

It will be taken comfortably, I think, and will save my reputation in case of necessity. Of course he did write "Pool" and "Mammy Hums," which are beautiful poems, but I could almost weep to think that he did.

I am trying to save my soul with a free verse technique, as my rhyme won't work any more and my six-syllable form won't hold everything, though it seems fair enough for a great deal. I sent Glenway a poem the other day, which doesn't seem quite successful, and enclose one herewith which I like better. Do you like it?

Arthur

MS: Yale

TO GLENWAY WESCOTT

April 1, 1921 / Sunmount / Santa Fe, N.M.

Dear Glenway:

The Dawsons were up last night for supper, and left this morning for Frijoles, from where they intend to take in the Española Valley. I like them greatly, and think them very intelligent despite the fact that they like *Smoke and Steel*.

They and I and Mrs. Stevens and others went to Santo Domingo and San Felipe on Easter Monday for the spring corn dances. San Felipe is more beautiful than anything else I have ever seen and I shall doubtless live there.

I wrote Monroe of Sandburg, so will not repeat to you. He is a disgusting fake. I don't see how we ever fell. He is much worse than I thought he would be.

I discover that the Dawsons like your poems greatly, and when they read mine they liked them also. At the start I did not think they would, though I wasn't so surprised later that they did. They are not at all Othersy, and I don't quite see their connection with Saphier or with M. Strobel, unless it is one of simple amusement, which it seems to be.

I am getting devilishly discouraged with this damned TB. I can't notice any gain in strength through the winter, have been given no more exercise, and Dr. Mera grows more and more vague about when I am going to be able to do anything. I don't care a cent's worth about kicking in be it a year from now or ten years from now if I could only live as, or even where, I wish, in the meantime. It is the silliness of the waiting that gets on my nerves. However, if they can only get around to diagnosing me a chronic, I suppose I can accept my father's offer to give me a permanent income, import a Chinaman from the coast, and settle down at Felipe or elsewhere till living becomes too much of a bore. I think the life would agree with me—temperamentally at least. I could even adopt opium. . . . I should at least be free from the constant irritation of the shoddy conventionality of minds behind beautiful faces and mannerisms, above beautiful bodies. Katherine Stinson, whom I thought I liked fairly well, was actually embarrassed when I read her "The little fox he murmured" in the most approved fashion, though she tried to conceal it, and she liked Sandburg's elocution (Alice Corbin says he learned it from Sarett), and thought it "simple and direct and sincere," and, I gathered, manly. Ho, hum . . . I like Chinese cooks and Indians and Phoebe Stevens (who does the Dance of the Wild He Goats all over the assembly room whenever the victrola starts) and Tom Galt, who paints like a whirlwind and writes poems like the rather extraordinary child that he is and curses his sisters and thumbs his nose at the world and does anything else that he damn well likes.

> I fled from wisdom that perceives
> The underlying virtues of
> The twisted veins of blighted leaves
> As I had fled away from love.
>
> I saw myself, who fled the dull,
> As in a dream fled out of hell
> A man, his hand grown in a skull
> Laughing like a rising bell.

Which is a poem that never got finished—result of a conversation with Miss Conkey and Mrs. Stevens on "The Two Magics" and of a dream in which I was a spectator and which was more terrible than anything I have ever read, dreamed or experienced. I have tried to write it, but cannot.

I am hovering upon the disconnected, and so shall cease. I send a new poem.

> *Mon Dieu, à quoi donc rêvent-elles?*
> *À des Rolands, à des dentelles?*
>
> . . . .
>
> *Jamais! Jamais!*
> *Si tu savais!*[1]

Arthur

P.S. The damned spiders are waking up for the summer again.

MS: Yale

[1]This is apparently the new poem, thus in English: "My God, what can they be dreaming about? / About Rolands, about laces? // Never! Never! / If you only knew!" (translated
by Daniel Lewis Winters).

TO GLENWAY WESCOTT

April 8, 1921 / Sunmount / Santa Fe, N.M.

Dear Glenway:

As to French prose, would advise you to try E. de Goncourt's *La Fille Elisa,*
which has, I believe, sufficient verve of its sort. The first half or so is largely a
bit dull in itself but has tremendous cumulative effect later, and the whole
book is short. It is devastating. Flaubert in *L'Education* is superb—suave, working on the surface with consummate finish and precision, and so cold that
when he turns his screws one comes near to dying on the spot. He is as great as
James there, though utterly different from James at every other point—his disciples in English are Conrad and Joyce. He is greater than Conrad, though
maybe not up to *Ulysses* in so far as I know it. Stendahl, in *Le Rouge et le Noir,*
of which I have so far read one volume, is almost as great in a less finished and
somewhat wilder fashion. As to the poets I spoke of I still insist that they have
certain technical (aside from other) achievements which are of very great value
and which are not duplicated, to my knowledge, anywhere in English. My
technical analysis, which is temporarily laid aside as too great a task for my
present energies, covers them. I doubt if you have more than the vaguest sort
of an idea of what they are. Gautier's "Les Affres de la Mort" is, I think, one
of the greatest poems ever written—there may be others, but I haven't gone
through him carefully enough to know. One has to take Laforgue or leave
him—I like him here and there. I don't think you can get around Corbière.

Don't bother about my condition—you have enough difficulties of your
own to think about. I shall either get well or not get well, and it matters very
little either way. In either event I shall not continue this life more than six or
eight months longer at the outside. Dr. Mera is going to examine my nose—
shall try to get him to do it in the next couple of days—and as the nose specialists in Chicago found that it needed fixing I suppose that he'll do likewise. He
says I am strong enough to stand the operation. So I am likely—if it is agreeable to my family, and I see no reason why it should not be—to be pulling out
for Chicago around the end of the month or early in May. But this is in no wise
certain, and I may not come at all.

Faith's vacation is from April ninth to twentieth, according to my father's last letter. I do not think my letter will prevent her seeing you.

I think I misjudged Hardin Masters. He seems a very nice boy, very much worn out with the physical and nervous strain of trying to prevent his parents' divorce. He broke down working in a brokerage office by day and somewhere else by night to support his mother, whom his father had left without support in order to force her to divorce him and try for alimony. Artistically, he has certain perceptions but very little taste—he has read little or nothing, and is soft and babyish about writing. If he would learn to write he might be a poet. He very seldom imitates his father, is very little concerned with mid- or any other Americanism, and has written one very decent poem and a few half-poems and a number of fine lines. All mixed up with the most hopeless shoddiness. Nice in his way, however, though not very interesting.

Hope Butler, niece of Jack and Charles, goes home to Boston or Philadelphia or someplace very soon. A very likeable, polished, educated and traveled young lady, who came west a few months ago for the first time in her life and saw her two western uncles for the first time in her life. It is, I think, a pleasant subject for meditation. Her uncles are bloated with pride of her—Jack vast and gentle and shifty-eyed about it, and Charles spry and intimate like the old gamecock that he is.

I enclose a new poem. I will send you any of the French novels I mention if you want them. I will get you a Rimbaud. Also, if you will give me your room address I will send on a consignment of your books and have the museum pack and send your teapot, which Miss Meadors gave me a while back.

I encountered Alfonso [Roybal; Awa-Tsireh] in the museum the other day, and he said he would bring some pictures out tomorrow.

Arthur

MS: Yale

TO MARIANNE MOORE

June 6th, 1921 / 633 Forest Ave / Wilmette, Ills.

Dear Miss Moore:

Thank you greatly for writing me and even more greatly for liking my poems. I had about decided that no one would like them, and even though— most of the time, at least—I have ceased to like them myself, there is considerable comfort in having them liked by some one whom I very much admire.

I sent them to you because you seem to me one of the greatest and finest-grained of the not too-large body of contemporary poets that count for something. I have known your work—aside from a few scattered things, anyway —for less than two years and have admired it for probably not more than a year and a half, but my admiration has been intense and I have my youth to excuse me for the rest. I believe that I used, at one time, to make rather stupid and unpleasant remarks about it, but that was long ago, and one has, I think, some sort of right to be forgiven for certain by-products of an incomplete growth. At least, I hope so. You see I am only twenty, and of a rather dogmatic nature.

Such poems as "To an Intra-Mural Rat" and certain other early ones in the *Egoist*, "Pedantic Literalist" and more recent ones in *Others* anthologies, which I do not have in Wilmette and the names of which I cannot remember seem to me to leave little room for discussion. Maybe I am wrong, but right now I don't think so. Rodker's and Ezra's talk about there being no "emotion" in your work is the merest twaddle. You have it packed in so tight they can't swim and are forced to skim on the surface. Though one has a right to expect a little more than that from Ezra.

It would be a kindly act on your part, I think, to publish a book—I know many people who want your poems, and want them badly, and it is very difficult to gather them up from magazines, especially if one lives in the desert as I do. Why won't you? I hope you don't have Mr. Stevens' unwashed aversion to book-publication. It *is* untidy, you know. People who leave poems littered around in the magazines are so very much like people who leave papers around in the parks. But that, I suppose, is their own affair. . . .

But thank you again for your kindness and please pardon any seeming officiousness on my part. It comes of being a little bit Irish and, much to my sorrow, cannot be helped. If you are at all interested in Mexican or pueblo art —some of which is of a very high order, in case you don't know it—or if I can be of any service to you in any other way in my country I trust you will let me know. I have been a lunger for some two and a half years, but am just about out of it now and am able to scout around a bit and find out about things.

Very truly yours, / Yvor Winters
Permanent address: / Sunmount, / Santa Fe, / New Mex.

MS: Rosenbach

Marianne Moore (1887–1972): American poet, critic, and, from 1925 to 1929, editor of *The Dial.*

July 24, 1921 / Sunmount / Santa Fe, N.M.

Dear Miss Monroe:

I enclose revised versions of "The Fragile Season" and "Old Spring." Please put "The Fragile Season" at the end of the group.

In rejecting "Apocalyptic Harvest" you reject the best poem I have ever written, and a very good poem indeed. But as you will, as you will . . .

I think a title for this group would have to be a very general title indeed, and as my time is limited and much occupied at present, I think it would be wise, to avoid vacuities and sentimentalities, to merely call the group "Poems."

It is difficult to prove a poet's greatness, but if you can find the time—perhaps on the train—to study carefully for three-quarters of an hour Miss Moore's "A Graveyard" in the July *Dial*, and after that spend a couple of hours more on "Black Earth," "Pedantic Literalist," "A Talisman," "Reinforcements," "Radical," and a few others in the Egoist book, you may get a glimmering of what I see in her. With the exception of Mr. Stevens, she is about the only person since Rimbaud who has had any very profound or intricate knowledge and command of sound, and I am not sure but what I think her about the best poet in this country except for Mr. Stevens.

And as far as that goes, I think Mina Loy a genius, though I don't know any of her work that is as perfect as Miss Moore's best. I mention her simply because it is customary, for some obscure reason, to always speak of her and Miss Moore together.

A.C.H. seems at least as well as when I last wrote you and maybe a little better, but I don't see much of her. Too precarious. I never know when I may be giving her three degrees of temperature.

If you will let me know when you return from the east, I will make you some candy and send it you.

Sincerely, / Winters

P.S. I am shocking the village with a black beaver sombrero, cerise bandanna, & silver earrings.

MS: Chicago

TO MONROE WHEELER

Aug. 1, 1921 / Sunmount / Santa Fe, N.M.

Dear Monroe:

Your letter came this noon, as did also the books from Mark [Turbyfill]. I am glad you are improving so fast. I myself was examined this afternoon and am informed that my lungs are, to all intents and purposes, cleared up, though I probably have a little glandular trouble left. Shall be X-rayed for that later. Don't think there can be much of it, as my temp is mostly very quiet. I am to be allowed to try riding Villa, and if nothing happens—and nothing will, as I lope and trot and run Hoke all the time—I shall continue to ride him.

I shall go east for the dog shows in September. For this fall, at least, Peg should sweep everything before her. I fear, however, that by next year her color will have changed, and while color is not of the first importance, it will reduce her chances a bit. So I am going to win everything I can while the winning is good, and then sell her pups on her reputation.

Shall I bash Mark's jaw for you? It would give me pleasure.

I like about eight or nine poems in his book—some better than others—and think the rest execrable. They are not exactly "trimmed with fire," however, and the first one in that section is the most profoundly ridiculous thing I have ever read. But some are decent enough, so I suppose one shouldn't quibble.

I am proud of Glenway. I hope I shall do as well when I get my 'dobe. The 'dobe I had picked out, I found upon close examination, is a stone tool house with iron-barred windows. But I have found another up the canyon, with quince trees and a small field, and uninhabited. The place and the view are beautiful beyond belief.

I have little time for work and many kinds of work to do. Have written eight or nine thousand words of my story and hope to finish it soon. It ought to sell—very clever plot, and cleverly silly line work, with a sufficient amount of action.

I have reduced Maurine's poems to two groups of ten poems each. Don't know if I can find a publisher for so small a book. If I cannot, would you do it when you get over? I would bear the expense. Or if you could instruct me about printers and printing I might do it here. I don't think there is any use in keeping the poems I have discarded. They are mostly sentimental or childish, all unsuccessful, and are in no wise justified by the occasional fine lines that a few of them contain. The good things are too good and the book as I have it, too lean and stark a thing, for dilutation.

Janet will almost certainly come to Santa Fe for the winter and spring. I have got her a job in the high school, if she can pass examinations sufficiently high to beat possible competitors. Don't think there will be much competition, however, as it involves Latin. I can get her other jobs if that fails.

I received a bundle of Maurine's letters from Wilmette the other day.

I send you more poems, and a later version of "Old Spring." Marianne Moore's Egoist book is very great, but contains many mistakes. Ezra's new "Cantos" superb . . . He must be writing a very great poem of whatever sort.

Like Williams, "I am tired but happy." I am strong as six, however, and keep going stronger all the time.

My love to you both, / Arthur

MS: Yale

TO GLENWAY WESCOTT

August 20, 1921 / Sunmount / Santa Fe, N.M.

Dear Glenway:

Your letter came tonight and Monroe's last night. I write briefly, for I am goddamned tired.

I am getting off various correspondence concerned with dog shows and putting the last touches on the dogs, and getting more and more impressed with the magnitude of the job I am undertaking. Though perhaps it won't be so bad when I get at it.

Monroe asked me if I should not be able to see you between shows somewhere before you sail. I fear I shall not, much as I should like to. My only interval will be between Louisville and Chicago—my fourth and fifth shows. It will be a matter of about ten days, and I shall have been on the road ten or twelve days by that time. I shall probably be exhausted—I am that before I start out—and the dogs will probably be tired and in need of conditioning for the Chicago show. I had better light out for Chicago and lay up for a week at home. If I went east I could stay for only a day or two, would preclude any chance of a rest on the trip, and would probably have my dogs in bad shape for Chicago.

Damn all labor.

I traded Hoke today for a big lanky rapid-travelling three-year-old that was the property of Mrs. Max Eastman—which Mrs. M. E. I don't know. The colt is only about half broken and balks a little at times and rears, and the lady was afraid of him. But he is worth two of Hoke, and I think will be easier to sell. He tried rearing with me today, but I brought him down in short order and believe I can easily break him. He is not at all mean. If I don't sell him he will be a good horse for Janet this winter. I don't think I can sell him now—but I am almost bound to try. Shall farm him out somewhere immediately till Janet comes.

I am going to ride every other day for a while and try to rest up. I was so limp coming home on the colt today that I couldn't grip him at all and sat dangling in the saddle, expecting to fall off almost anywhere along the road. . . .

I like "Drifting Deer" better than anything I have written for a long time. Maybe I am wrong.

I dislike Plato, except for the occasional phrases or sentences that seem to me very beautiful. The quotation is one of them.[1]

Jadedly I yearn for a raison d'être or the energy d'être or the courage not to. "Life swift as the dart of a bird."

There is no tragedy in that. But Li Po was simply making a beautiful gesture from a lie. It isn't. It is life all muddled up in damnfoolishness. Airedales and wobbly knees and uncertainty.

Hell.

I wish I could hibernate.

Arthur

MS: Yale

[1]This quotation was one of two epigraphs to "Drifting Deer": "Socrates . . . Now the thing which moves another and is by another moved, as it may cease to be moved, may cease also to live; it is only that which moves itself, inasmuch as it never quits itself, that never ceases moving. . . ."

TO GLENWAY WESCOTT

Dec. 9, 1921 / Madrid, N.M.

Dear Glenway:

*   *   *

I live in a small room, of a frightful blue color, and grimy with coal, but covered in patches by brown burlap against which I have hung a few pictures—two Santos, and two Alfonsos. Some Japanese silk of marvelous texture and pattern, lent me by Katherine Stinson, hangs against my wall. And there are my books, and my gay yellow cups from which I drink coffee alone every Saturday. I live alone in this camp and seem to need no friends—have come to be happy enough. The Meras invite me to come to Sunmount whenever I wish—and I was there for Thanksgiving, shall be there for a week at Christmas. Then there will be three months in camp to my spring vacation. Next year I am promised a Mexican village, probably in the Española Valley, and if I get what I want, shall more than likely stay there indefinitely. I have no wish to travel, no wish for anything but a reasonable amount of leisure and some quiet. And a clean house and beautiful country. Although this country is as beautiful as anything in itself. But pure desert. No people except those supported by the coal. The Sangre de Cristos, thirty miles away, are low and clear and hard in the winter air, and the red foothills at their base, tiny, compressed, and round. The desert from here to there is white and dead.

I feared at first that this work would sap my strength, but I have no more fear of that now. I think I am quite equal to it, if I don't rush matters.

My chief friends in this country at present are Miss Conkey, Katharine Stinson, and John Meem. The last a young man raised in the wilderness of Brazil—his father is a missionary—who has been at various times a soldier, an engineer, and a banker. Now about twenty-six, and since he has been at Sunmount, has suddenly come to life intellectually and aesthetically, and is rapidly becoming a very fine if not even a great artist in ink drawing. A precise and exquisite soul, and puritanical, and completely fine, I think. I have seen a good deal of him in the last eight months. You would certainly like him.

*　　*　　*

I return to my coal and my pale country.

My love to you, / Arthur

MS: Yale

TO HARRIET MONROE

Dec. 10, 1921 / Madrid, N.M.

Dear Miss Monroe:

Enclosed is my review of Robinson. I am sorry to have taken so long a time on it, but the exigencies of school-teaching, as well as the size and importance of the book, rather slowed me up. I will try to do Mark and A. Wickham inside of a week. May do the former tomorrow.

It is possible that you will not think this review worth printing, and if so, I shall not object. But if you do consider it worth printing, I trust you will print it as I have written it, and will make no changes without my permission. I shall not quibble about minutiae of style so long as I am allowed to judge whether or not they alter my meaning. I am aware that I have expressed several opinions in this review that are at variance with your own, but you have a chance to express your own opinions every month, and if you are to have a live magazine, I trust that you see the necessity of allowing such persons as you consider sufficiently intelligent to contribute to express their own opinions as they see fit. Otherwise the whole thing becomes a farce. Also it is scarcely fair to a reviewer to misrepresent him publicly.

I like Carnevali's funeral poem very well, although it was a conceit rather than an image and a little bit on the prettily playful side—like Kreymborg. He still seems sloppy most of the time.

I am reading Hopkins with great admiration.

Sincerely, / Winters

MS: Chicago

TO MAURICE LESEMANN

Jan. 7, 1922 / Madrid, N.M.

Dear Mr. Lesemann:

As we have been able to get neither a football, nor a basketball ground, up to date, and as it seems desirable to have some sort of interschool athletic contests, I wonder if you could find among your boys a few boxers who could compete with a few of the Madrid boys. I have organized in a rough way a sort of boxing team here, and have found a fair amount of promising material, and the boys are all interested in it.

I would suggest, as general rules to govern interschool bouts, that the boxers be within three pounds of the same weight on the day of the bout, and in the clothes in which the bout is fought, and that they be within two years of the same age; that the rounds, instead of being of the regulation three-minute length with an interval of one minute, be two minutes long, with an interval of two minutes; and that no bout be over three rounds. I have found that short rounds and bouts are about all that the half-trained boy can stand. In the ring, I think the usual Queensbury rules should stand. If you have any suggestions to make in the matter of rules, I should be glad to have them, and merely offer these tentatively.

If you have no gloves, I think Mrs. Warren would be glad to get you some. She got us two sets within two weeks from the time I asked for them.

My team, as it stands at present, is of the following ages and weights:

      110½ pounds, 14 years

      95 pounds, 12 years

      94 pounds, 16 years

      85 pounds, 11 years

      77 pounds, 13 years

      73½ pounds, 12 years

      73 pounds, 11 years

The boys weighed in on the company store scales without coats or hats, but otherwise fully dressed. If you have good boxers of other weights or ages, I might be able to find some one to compete with them, but my maximum weights and ages are on this list.

Hoping that I shall hear from you in this matter, I am

Very truly yours, / A.Y. Winters

MS: Stanford

TO MAURICE LESEMANN

Jan. 21, 1922 / Madrid, N.M.

Dear Lesemann:

Your letter came several days ago. All that you say about interschool boxing is doubtless true, although as we have equipment for nothing else, I had hoped to do something with that. However, since writing you, we have rigged up a sort of makeshift volleyball court, on rolling and slanting ground, and with a very battered net, and are doing our best to get some action out of this court and a basketball. If Mrs. Warren will send us a volleyball, we should like to play you at that—sometime, say, before the end of February. The company has long promised a basketball ground, but has done nothing, and we have no place where we could even pretend to play it. And in the spring, of course, we shall be very glad to play baseball with you.

Sincerely, / A.Y. Winters

MS: Stanford

Jan. 21, 1922 / Madrid, N.M.

Dear Glenway:

Another Saturday. Strangely enough I become more interested in teaching[1] and think I shall stay with it and forget the coffee-house, which would be more work and more precarious, and would necessitate living in Santa Fe, which I do not greatly want to do. I seem to function infinitely better in solitude, than under other circumstances, and if my solitude were properly located, I should be very well off. Also, given a school permanently, I could make a very pleasant thing of it. If Mrs. Warren keeps her promise and sends me north next year and out of the penumbra of Albuquerque, I suspect that I am her man for good. . . .

The war cry of the sideline at the school boxing bouts seems to be largely a matter of, "Hit him under the jaw, Martinez—whenever you git a chanct." It is most often delivered to Marion Cunningham, my "fistic marvel," by his little brother Romero, who drifts about with enthusiastic indifference and whoops whenever his brother gets hit.

As yet I have not entirely got used to myself engrossed in books on elementary education, but suppose I shall by and by.

I enclose a couple of second-rate poems.

My sense of the reality of Elizabeth is rapidly melting, for some curious reason, and even her poems do not stir me as they once did, though I still recognize their fineness. She has enveloped herself in a mist of prettiness for protective or other reasons, and has become damn near useless. And then, sometimes, as in her last letter, there is a flash of genius that leaves me breathless and with my hair on end. I don't know what is the matter. Maybe she needs to write prose— maybe I need to leave the coal camp. Certainly the physical actuality and horror of the camp must affect me, at least temporarily. But at present, anyway, her *intentions* seem to me largely false and sentimental, and her achievements accidental. But you know her better than I do, and have probably reached conclusions on these matters long since. Janet seems to me an infinitely sounder and finer artist. I am not sure but what she has carried our principles of specific density, etc., much farther than you or I. All of which, however, is speculative rather than dogmatic. As nearly as I can make out, Pearl is undergoing so many of the same stages of damnfoolishness that I underwent, that I await her outcome with interest.

I received a very gentlemanly note from Seldes. I suppose I owe him an apology, but have no great inclination to offer it.

My lot, I suspect, is one of celibacy and (relative) silence. And at the moment I am well enough pleased.

Arthur

MS: Yale

¹About the school itself, YW wrote Wescott: "This school is much the same sort as the Eagle Rock school of my childhood. Sex. A twelve-year-old in my room already shattered, twitching—gone. Others going. In a community where whoredom is so public and so profitable, as well as the only alternative to getting drunk when off duty, it is not remarkable. One cannot combat it by talking. Talk doesn't register. If we had decent school equipment —inside as well as out—we might have a chance. I brought two decent books to school— *Andersen's Fairy Tales* and *Aesop's Fables*—and they fight for them with all the violence and dishonesty of gutter puppies. They haven't a chance. One simply stops to remember that one is a philosopher. Your pale Christ is a winter breath, the dream of a virgin or a Saint Francis. Give me Paul. And a basketball court, and a library, and an assistant athletic instructor" (January 24, 1922).

TO GLENWAY WESCOTT

Feb. 4, 1922 / Madrid, N.M.

Dear Glenway:

Another Saturday P.M. I have received a couple of coverless copies of my new book [*The Magpie's Shadow*], & it seems a very decent job. One—the first —had four pages missing due to a slip in binding, & as I took the error more seriously than it apparently ought to have been taken, the book has been held up a little & I have not yet had the covered copies. But I should have them in a day or two. I will send you a copy, & send one to Monroe when you return. One copy is doubtless all you will care to carry around, if you will want that.

We have had a clairvoyant lady among us. She lived in the front room of our house & corralled her mule & two horses in our chicken-yard. She called herself Madame Petite & talked like an Arkansas mid-wife. She has a dry farm somewhere up in the hills, & every so often makes the rounds of the camps & villages. She made a tremendous haul here.

H.M. informs me that Brownell is answering my review in the March number. I am invited to reply in the April, which I may do, though I have not yet seen the proof. I left one or two unfortunate openings & as Brownell is or was some sort of a fellow in philosophy somewhere or other, I rather fear the worst. But perhaps I can come out with a nearly whole skin if I try hard. At least I hope he has good manners. I can forgive a beating if it is politely administered.

Time passes with unprecedented rapidity here, as I slide more & more into the routine. I don't think I would go back to Sunmount, now, if I were given the opportunity, though there are many other places I would go to.

Please, my dear, meet all the celebrities, as it is the only way to become one yourself. Remember that I am alone in the foothills, with only the desert & Cerrillos between me & the world, & I am trusting you to tide me over on your fame. Fame is worth at least two hundred dollars a year, & God knows I need it.

I hope to get to work, soon, at a miracle tale for children, which should be good if blasphemous—

My love to you both, / Arthur

MS: Yale

TO GLENWAY WESCOTT

Santa Fe, N.M. / June 2, 1922

Dear Glenway:

I like "Les Funérailles," "The Penitent," and "Black River" very much— "Primavera" very little.

If Monroe is publishing nothing else now, would he want to, and could he afford to publish Maurine? I have reduced her poems to eighteen, from which I think it unwise to cut, and which I think about the only ones of any consequence. I have written a short foreword—about three very short paragraphs—not more than a page.[1] This could be omitted or altered at your own discretion, or you could write one if you wished. No large house would bother with so small a book. Frank Shay is the only possibility, and if you wish I will send the book to him first. What do you say? I was reimpressed with the poems lately, especially some of the later ones—"Ceremony," "The Keen Edge," and "This Is Loneliness" are flawless and inimitable. We can do nothing better. They should be published soon now.

I dare say you are right about "Windless Wisdom." I have chucked "Of a Day," and shall probably chuck "Evening Confidant." As to reinstating the various soft poems of your predilection, I have my doubts.

I take Maurice's job at Cerrillos next year—high school English, ancient history, and athletics. I shall probably get a hundred and thirty. Good job, and I like the place well enough. I seem to have displayed some ability in handling hard boiled boys and I guess I shall have trouble in getting out of the mine country. But I like it well enough, with a 'dobe to live in. This damn town has gone to seed, and I wouldn't live here on a bet. John leaves in about six weeks, and Miss Conkey will not stay on forever. No one else here who is at all essential. I shall go where there is a bit more ferment and less bad painting. The villages are pressed flowers that I have almost forgotten.

Arthur

MS: Yale

[1] It is clear from this letter that YW not only wrote the foreword to this volume, *The Keen Edge,* but was in fact its editor.

TO HARRIET MONROE

[ca. April, 1922?][1]

Dear Miss Monroe:

I am enclosing another poem to be considered along with my "Poems in Autumn" group and may send yet another in the course of time and again may not.

I hear that you have lost a couple of guarantors on account of Carnevali. I am sorry, but pity them more than I do you.

> May hell wipe out divinities
> And a-cerebral infinities
> And other asininities,
> Praise hell, praise hell, praise hell.

Which is the beginning of a chant to my Deity which I hope to complete some time ante mortem.

I hope you do not curse me a great deal for my haphazard way of sending in poems. Please don't mail me a bomb, anyway.

The two men in the cottage behind mine have been trapping for coyotes (I envy them their naive faith) and have caught numerous magpies, one towhee, one golden eagle, which is now caged up behind their cottage, where it is impossible to let him loose without getting caught in the act. I have written them a letter purporting to come from the state game warden, however, and hope to scare them into letting him go.

If one were to write of pale lavender clouds in a pale green sky, people would say one was drunk or imitating Conrad Aiken, and yet I have seen this here. Curses be.

I have been acting as veterinary to an Airedale with distemper, and have been assistant nurse at the setting of a couple of magpies' legs, and hope to trim the tails of the pups which the aforementioned Airedale is expected to have in the course of time, so life is not so bad here after all.

A.Y. Winters

MS: Chicago

[1]This letter is undated by Winters. The date given above is written on the letter in an unknown hand, obviously at a later date. If the year is correct, it seems unlikely that the month is. The reference to the cottage seems more likely a reference to Sunmount. After teaching at Madrid and before moving to Cerrillos, YW spent time back at Sunmount (see previous letter).

TO HARRIET MONROE

Cerrillos, N.M. / October 12, 1922

Dear Miss Monroe:

I am mailing in another envelope a group of poems which you may use if you wish. Please do not make any alterations in order, punctuation etc., without consulting me. I am enclosing a return envelope with this note.

Have you reached any decision upon my *Notes*, as yet?

My job here is much better than the one I had last year—all high school work, and two or three rather amusing pupils. This is where the damn Teuton was last year, as I daresay you know.

Janet is at Sunmount, where I saw her just after her arrival, about a month ago. She is tutoring there. Have heard that Glenway is in New York. Monroe in Bremen—has just brought out a small booklet of Maurine Smith's poems [*The Keen Edge*], which you will doubtless receive soon, if you have not already. He is planning other publications for the immediate future.

Remember me to Miss Strobel.

A.Y.W.

MS: Chicago

Cerrillos, N.M. / Nov. 15, 1922

Dear Glenway:

What you say of yourself, I have known for several years. The position you have taken has seemed to me for a long time, if not inevitable, the only alternative to dissipating yourself utterly.

If the *Tyro* you speak of is the one containing Wadsworth's "Port & Portland," I once owned it, but allowed Burlin to get away with it. Those two things, in reproduction at least seemed extraordinarily fine. I like some [Wyndham] Lewis I have seen, but he appears too full of semi-assimilated influences—primitive Italian, certain Japanese, etc. You have doubtless seen more of these men than I, however, & are fitter to judge.

Uriol [Garcia] is not yet writing for publication—he has too much trouble with English. But I am certain he will. He is an extraordinary personality.

I am glad you like the translations.[1] John [Meem] reads & speaks a little Spanish, but has never studied it, & makes no claim to be a scholar in it. I am uncertain about the original [Olavo] Bilac. I would send you my Heine, but my Corona is crippled. It is not so good as the Ronsard.

At the moment, I see no further development in the direction of the "Virgin." I am doing Madrid—gradually—in small bits of prose that are rather cleaner.

Have not seen *Waste Land*.

I become more of a provincial, I suspect, but do not greatly care. I like Cerrillos better than anything else I have found.

Arthur

MS: Yale

[1]This reference to the appearance of *Diadems and Fagots* places it third among Winters's early books. Previously, it was thought to be his second. The book consists of two sonnets and two fragments from the Brazilian Parnassian Olavo Bilac translated by John Gaw Meem, subsequently a distinguished New Mexico architect, and the last sonnets, four in number, from Pierre de Ronsard translated by YW.

TO HARRIET MONROE

Cerrillos, N.M. / Nov. 15, 1922

Dear Miss Monroe:

I have recently heard rumors—which appeared to emanate from Chicago—to the effect that I have broken with Glenway. As your position in Chicago is rather a central one, you could easily contradict these rumors, & I would thank you for doing so wherever you meet them. I have not broken with Glenway, have never contemplated doing so, & shall not do so. He is the only intelligent individual I have ever had the pleasure of knowing & the most unfailingly interesting in all his aspects. His & my intellectual & aesthetic lives have been & are so closely connected that any break between us is utterly impossible. Next to Glenway I know of no one so generally interesting & sound, or of whom I am so fond, as Monroe Wheeler. It would make no difference whatever if all of the suppositions & suspicions of the various perambulating Sadistic curiosities of Chicago & Santa Fe were correct. (Incidentally I know exactly what percentage of them is correct & what incorrect.) I do not give two damns for all moral codes or any respecter of moral codes. I am interested in intellectual processes & artistic results, & find Glenway an intellectual master (I can think of no other at the moment) & one of the few great artists extant. I share—morally, sympathetically—in everything he has done up to date, & whoever damns him, damns me, & for the same reasons. I thumb my nose at Chicago, individually & collectively, excepting only Mrs. [Agnes Lee] Freer, Mr. [Henry] Fuller, Dr. [E. H.] Lewis [YW's future father-in-law] & [Mitchell] Dawson—&, as always, yourself.

Yours— / Winters

P.S. I trust you have almost reached a decision on my *Notes.*

MS: Chicago

TO PEARL ANDELSON (SHERRY)

Cerrillos, N.M. / Dec. 1, 1922

Dear Pearl:

I have just returned from a teachers convention at Albuquerque, which was pretty damn bad. A basketball game just terminated also. I saw Janet in Santa Fe a few days ago, and she showed me the two pieces of prose you had sent her, which I liked a very great deal. Structure very hard and concise, writing excellent, and they stay in the mind. They are the best things of anyone's that I have seen in some time. In last *Poetry,* I like "Dialogue" down as far as the end of the hound's speech, but think it should terminate there. The thought appears to be complete there, and the poem certainly is, and after that it weakens markedly, the finish being very weak. Can't you cut it off there for your book? It would be an excellent poem.

"Chapter" iv is no good. The others are sharp, accurate epigrams, first two best. "Out of a Weariness" ditto. "Thin Refuge" not so good—perception a bit obvious at end. "A Trivial Day" as good as Mark's more decorative things but that is not quite good enough. It attempts to escape the obvious by such words as "frail," "wanly," "subtle." These are worn too thin even to carry so slight a weight. If used at all, they must be carried. If these were left out, and also the first stanza, the poem might possibly be reduced to something very slight, but nevertheless very accurate and lovely. "Sea-Girl" bad. Sea-girls in general are bad.

I think I shall like your book, and trust I shall be informed when it is out. I hope you are including the Moses poem of a couple of years back, as I like it greatly.

Do you see the *Broom?* It is running some very amusing, though not altogether sound because not altogether comprehensive stuff on this our mechanical age.

Great excitement in my end of Cerrillos the other day. As I was eating lunch with my Mexicans, a little girl came in very much excited. "*Un hombre está muerto. Un viejo—americano.*" "*¿Dónde?*" "*Esta casa—aquí.*" And I, being the only male person about went over to see the dead man. He was lying on the floor of a vile-smelling room, very dirty and half covered by a dirty union suit and dirtier blankets. He was white and gave no signs of life. I lifted the blankets a bit, and, forgetting that he was an American addressed him in Mexican, on the chance of his answering. He gave no sign, but in a moment commenced to curse at me in very thick but quite recognizable Americano. He was simply paralyzed with white mule. I dare say he has recovered by now. He is a very old man.

Do you know if H.M. intends to print the technical notes I sent her some eight months ago? I have never had an answer from them.

Arthur

MS: Stanford

TO MARIANNE MOORE

Cerrillos, N.M. / Dec. 4, 1922

Dear Miss Moore:

All four of the books you mention having sent have arrived, and I thank you greatly for them. I shall endeavor to get them back in time. Thank you for the two magazines, as well.

I am glad you like *The Keen Edge.* I agree with you that the two last poems are easily the best of the lot. The cover is abominable, and I don't see how Wheeler ever permitted it to go on.

When I have returned the books that I now have, I may ask you for some of the others you so kindly offer. Some of those you mention I possess, but some I do not, and should like to borrow. The James I asked you for, I wanted primarily for school work, and so I chose the simplest things possible. It is worse than useless to attempt anything difficult. Is Cummings' *Enormous Room* worth anything? I simply despise the man *tout entier*—his perceptions are so hopelessly cliché and his method so hopelessly flat, unsubtle, and obviously tricky.

I dislike *Waste Land* on the whole, despite its excellent scattered passages. It does not seem nearly so good as "Gerontion." Echoes of his former self, and echoes of others. Also it does not hold together—perceptually or rhythmically.

My review of *Sour Grapes* is in *Poetry* for July 1922 (Vol. XX, No. IV). Other reviews (and a reply to one of them) are in *Poetry* for February and March 1922 (Vol. XIX, Nos. V and VI). If these are not where you can get hold of them easily, I shall be glad to send them to you. I mentioned the Williams review simply by way of apology in case you should see it. The others are not unduly excellent. I was simply in need of money at the time, and even stooped to reviewing for H.M. (You must not gather from this that I in any way humble myself before or agree with Brownell—I consider him an ass and not worth answering.)

I have taken to pencil drawings—landscapes—lately, and am, curiously enough, rather pleased with my results. Shall very soon return to wood carving, a little of which I did a few years ago. I have been doing a little prose, also, but can't get very far with it—for one thing the medium always fails to hold my interest.

"Mysticism of Money" et al. in *Broom* unsound because not comprehensive, but interesting. Machinery as sculpture appears to be over-estimated, but some of the ads quoted are interesting.

Sincerely, / Yvor Winters

MS: Rosenbach

Cerrillos, N.M. / Dec. 13, 1922

Dear Glenway:

I will send you my notes as soon as I have done a little repairing that they require. I hope this will be fairly soon. H.M. has had them for about eight months without comment. I should not object to taking them from her. I have not seen Burke's[1] paper.

Ulysses, as I believe I have assured you for some years, is one of the greatest —perhaps the greatest—achievement of our time. *Waste Land* echoes himself —diluted Eliot, diluted symbolism excellently managed for short stretches (the lowest of the dead), and a few good hard spots—the lovely woman, the dog paraphrase, etc. Meter bad in that it breaks—weakly, because it cannot go on— continually. Very little fusion of sound and content. Stretches of verbosity as weak as Carnevali's, and lacking his conviction. By all odds the worst thing Eliot has done, and not a tenth as good as "Gerontion."

My parents stopped off at Lamy on their way to the coast, where they will stay indefinitely. An uneventful visit. My father appears to be in very bad shape. Faith, as you possibly know, is at Ann Arbor, and will be in New York—with the Brosnahans—for Christmas.

I enclose a copy of a paper received from my second best genius today— José Lucero.[2] It is not the first he has turned in. He is fifteen, and in second year high school. Uriol's work is less lyrical, more balanced and hesitant, and much more intricate.[3] I discover that Uriol is only fourteen, though he has the appearance and brain of a boy—and a genius—of nineteen. I have never seen a more beautiful manner—or more beautiful manners.

And poems of my own. Do you like the piece of prose I sent Monroe?

Arthur

MS: Yale

[1]Kenneth Burke (1897–1970): American critic and poet.

[2]In a notebook containing her own poems, as well as those of Glenway Wescott, YW, and others, Janet Lewis has preserved Lucero's "How Frightful the Way Home!" There is no way of knowing if it is the composition mentioned in this letter, but it provides a sense of the young man's writing. It is brief: "Oh! but it was a frightful trip when we were coming from Dolores at midnight. No object of light could be seen but the stars above in the heavens, and the trees that seemed to be ghosts that were coming after us. And what could be more frightful than the wind whistling through the pinetree branches, and each one of us shivering with cold. We would run for a while until we were tired. Once in a while one of us would tumble, because the stones were invisible. // But we were lucky that we were not lost, for as the dawn of day was coming, we found that we were in Mr. Sam's ranch. We

went to wash our faces at the spring, the water was cold. After having rested we proceeded on our journey until we got home."

[3]In the same notebook is the following untitled prose poem by Uriol Garcia: "Once as my father tells me, when the moon was bright and clear in a thick forest near golden mines, by the Dolores Mountains, a fox used to come out at midnight, crying. She cried like a woman. All the people were frightened, and didn't dare to go out at night and hunt for the woman."

T O   M O N R O E   W H E E L E R

Cerrillos, N.M. / Feb. 24, 1923

Dear Monroe:

Thanks for the Williams. "Hot House Plant" comes very damn near to being the last word—the nearest thing to absolute abstraction, poetry about nothing, what you will, that I have ever encountered. That he should have covered so minute a territory with such completeness and passion, and with such a tune, is enough to make one shut up shop. The one which he likes best, I like a great deal also, and I like "The Rose," despite the more or less cliché calculus, which (the copper and steel roses and the steel line) could be easily removed from the poem to its very great advantage. The remainder I like, but more mildly. I believe Janet agrees with me very largely, concerning them.

"The Crystal Sun" is not all it might be, but I'll let it live for the present. I think I could convince you of its flaws, if I set out to. A poem which I recently sent Glenway, "José's Country," is about the first decent poem I have written in two and a half years—since "The Stone Mountains." "The Watchers" is discarded, along with most of the others I have sent recently.

Williams' prose in *Broom* is very beautiful. Likewise parts of Burke's, although the whole is seriously marred by a certain Wyndham Lewis swash, which he attempts to use as a sort of filler when he can't write honest to God stuff. He ought to have kept the story around home longer.

I think I can write very good prose if I take my time to do it, despite the fact that I hate the occupation more than almost any I know. Prose gives me no satisfaction whatever when I have done with it, for one thing. But I shall doubtless write a novel sometime in the next ten years. Elspeth's [Elizabeth Madox Roberts] prose is magnificent, although it is everything that mine will not be. What I really wish to do more than almost anything is carve in wood, but I have not time for it, although I have a decent set of small chisels.

I am going to make a desperate effort to get out of teaching next year. Not that I have any further dislike for it, but that the wages are damn small and, at present, damn uncertain. I shall try to get a newspaper job or else get into a bank. Much as I dislike the thought.

Arthur

MS: Yale

TO GLENWAY WESCOTT

Cerrillos, N.M. / April 30, 1923

Dear Glenway:

You seem to have curiously and completely melted from our ken, and I am trusting that Monroe knows your whereabouts.

A villainous sandstorm has descended upon Cerrillos, and sweeps through the budding tamarisks with a silken whistling. It stings the face like hornets. The biggest store in town burned down the other night. Behind the cinders, in the mule corral, are weeping willows, faint green, and a white mist of plum trees; and on the hills are peachtrees. The river is a thin red trickle this side of them. The feud between the Mexicans and the Italians is on again; and the dances drip blood. A prostitute was stoned at a dance by a Mexican recently, until she could hardly walk—was hit in the back and head—and an Italian fought him. The Italians complain bitterly of the Mexican fashion of mob fighting, but mostly have the best of it. And Uriol, with nonchalant gray eyes, and the head and throat of a chrysanthemum, paints like a young Cézanne. He is one of the greatest geniuses now living, and inside of three years will prove it.

Janet will leave Santa Fe for Neebish about the tenth of June, I think; and I shall be leaving for Boulder somewhere around the same time. I shall go in for Romance languages, I suspect. The new superintendent promises to get me a job in one of the normals upon my return. I may try for something in Old Mexico or South America.

I daresay you have heard of the death of the elder Galt girl, Madeleine. I saw the Galts the other day. Mr. Galt has returned to Chicago, but will be back in the summer, and the others are staying on.

I enclose various poems, dull enough. Heubsch wants me to write more fairy tales and send them back to him, so I have a good six-months' work cut out for me. But there may be money in it. Fred Kabotie ran in the county track meet the other day, for Santa Fe High School, taking second mile and half-mile to an Indian school Hopi named Yeppa. News is scarce. Do you still cast a shadow?

Arthur

MS: Yale

TO KENNETH BURKE

Santa Fe, New Mexico / June 5, 1923

Mr. Kenneth Burke, / *The Dial*,
152 W. 13th St., / New York City.
My dear Mr. Burke:

At last I can understand how you must have felt when I compared you to a "small river boat getting ahead of the water." It is scandalous indeed. As I have at hand no copy of Dr. Williams's "Hot House Plant," and as we are both too busy to go into a detailed study of the four other poets you mention, I shall confine myself entirely to a defense of those poems of my own which you so outrageously fail to appreciate at their just and rather considerable value. I enclose them,[1] not that you may reconsider them for publication (for after what has occurred I shall certainly submit them at once to some rival paper that is entirely outside your jurisdiction) but simply that you may refer to them for your own clarification. This is a greater kindness than is customary with me.

The last act I should even contemplate would be the removal of a single grain from—let alone the breaking down of—anything a quarter so sacred as my own categories; but yours—"pictures should be painted, melodies sung, and ideas written"—appear to bear about the same relation to your usually so acute observations as does the art of the average veterinarian to that of Dr. Carroll: as bond, they weigh upon me more lightly than morning cobwebs.

If you had stopped for a moment's more thought, instead of proceeding in the hasty and somewhat metaphorical fashion in which both of us have too frequently indulged, you would have recognized that, whereas the painter invents relationships between form and form, and the musician between sound and sound; the poet invents relationships between form and sound, or between idea and sound, or between all three. Had you read my *Notes on the Mechanics of the Poetic Image* more carefully, you would doubtless have recollected without stopping. That document is, with perhaps the single exception of [Ernest F.] Fenollosa's *Chinese Written Character [and the Art of Poetry]*, the most fundamental and comprehensive piece of critical writing since the *Poetics* of Aristotle; and a careful study of it might save many a good man considerable embarrassment. In a sequel to these notes, I have demonstrated that the prosateur is a sort of abortive and unhappy hybrid, but I cannot go into that at present.

In the last analysis the poet deals, presumably, with states of mind. States of mind are the results of, and can be expressed only in terms of, sensory impressions or ideas. One has nothing else. Can you define your "literary pores"? The relationship between "form" and sound is the image; between "idea" and sound the anti-image. As all ideas go back, in their origin, to sensory impressions, the image may be the more direct way, but I offer no argument for it as opposed to the anti-image. I simply claim my right to it. My taste is catholic. Moreover, as Pound has demonstrated in a note to Fenollosa's remarkable essay, the poetic image is capable of actual motion ("José's Country"), which the picture is not; in [word missing] of kaleidoscopic progression from image to image, thus achieving a more complex and subtle mood than that of which the picture is capable. Moreover, in a picture, the form is presented, not by its similarity at any point to another form, but entirely by its method of juxtaposition to another form; whereas, the reverse may be true in a poem, and a relationship of the entire form combination to the sound is involved. This makes it possible for the poem to present panorama entirely devoid of the painter's "significant form," but in itself and in its sweep beautiful and impressive; to present a landscape composed of minute and beautiful details, uncorrelated as regards the painter's forms. This is the difference between pictorial and literary landscape; although one landscape may be treated in both ways with diverse if equally great success. You should waste no time and spare no effort in apprehending this.

The fallacy, of course, of Verlaine, was that he attempted to subordinate sense to sound, believing verbal sound to have more or less the same properties as musical sound, which it has not in any comparable degree. That is, verbal sound, as I have shown elsewhere, possesses rhythm and tone. Musical sound possesses both of these, in a much less hampered manner, and scale besides, so that, as a pure medium, verbal sound can scarcely compete with it. Moreover, the very nature of words involves both idea and sound in a poem, and if one be subordinated to the other, that one becomes so much excess baggage, and the other suffers from lack of its natural support, so that the poem is doubly weakened. If you can demonstrate that we have reversed Verlaine's process, subordinating sound to the pictorial, you may have something to talk about; but that you cannot do—not while I am alive to guard the bridge.

In closing, may I ask why you have attacked us for that of which we are in no sense innovators—of which even the imagists (at whom you might better have cast your somewhat blunt dart) did not even claim to be innovators? You are undoubtedly a man of remarkable mentality, but I feel that you are, at times, misguided; and unless you mend your ways, and that at an early date, I shall, with the greatest of ease and the greatest of friendliness, scour you from the earth. Meanwhile, I trust that you will profit by this letter and return my two poems at an early date. You may keep "The Precincts of February."

Sincerely yours, / Yvor Winters

MS: PSU

¹The poems in question are "José's Country," "The Solitude of Glass," and, presumably, "The Precincts of February."

TO HARRIET MONROE

Nov. 1, 1923 / 1415 12th St. / Boulder, Colo.

Dear Miss Monroe:

If you have not already asked someone else to review Miss Andelson's book, I should like to make one more effort. Your understudy did not state her objections to my first attempt, but I suspect she turned it down because I mentioned a few names, so I'll be more careful this time, the more willingly as I have lost the original review. Editorial etiquette is the most profound & devious of all the subjects into which I have ever dipped.

I have been irritated at various times by your policy of having no policy, but the chances are I am overly irritable, & the harsh experiences that appear to accrue with the years have led me to believe that no policy is better than the wrong policy. I am one of several who are glad to see you once more on the job. And I envy you your vacation.

I do think it a pity, however, that you continue to let an ignorant girl like Marion Strobel maltreat works of genius in your pages. I do not so much object to a reviewer's disliking a great poem ("The Rose") as to his using a book review as an excuse to work off a personal irritation & to show off a sort of sloppy & contemptibly contemptuous familiarity. The poems are impersonal enough, & are so in good faith. They deserve to be considered by some one who can at least comprehend & respect the attitude of the author.

Also, I cannot make out whether Muna Lee¹ holds me or Ronsard responsible for the pleached alleys. If they exist, I am quite willing to shoulder the blame, but I don't think they do in either case. As to Meem's love for Bilac's work, he has only the most profound distaste for it—even for the poems he translated. He did them to amuse himself one night when he had a cold, & showed them to me months afterward. As I was fairly certain he would never do anything of the sort again, & as I admired them profoundly as they stood in English, I suggested the pamphlet. Meem is a genius in three or four separate ways, but spends his time trying to disguise, &, if possible, eliminate, the fact; & tortures himself, because, when nearly thirty, he is not making ten thousand a year. . . . This, not because I object to M.L.'s statement, which is excellent in its place, but simply for your private enlightenment should you be tempted to study Portuguese. It only goes to prove that a gentleman can make a poem out of anything. . . . This is the corner-stone of my aesthetic.

Sincerely, / Yvor Winters

MS: Chicago

[1]Muna Lee (1895?–1965): American poet and translator. YW is responding to her review of *Diadems and Fagots*, "Bilac and Ronsard," *Poetry* 23 (November 1923): 113–14. Of YW's Ronsard, she wrote, in part: "Translations reveal strange accordances: if he [YW] had translated the elegy by its one perfect line, which is after all Ronsard's surest claim on immortality, it would have seemed more fitting—one can imagine Mr. Winters' writing an elegy so, exquisitely and completely. But the sonnets one should hardly have expected so stern a technician to attempt. It is true that here Ronsard is himself rather than the courtier; but his meaning nevertheless slips down a pleached alley of verbiage as always" (113–14). About Meem's Bilac, Lee wrote: "It is . . . refreshing to come upon some translations . . . which grew out of a real love for a poet's work" (113).

TO HARRIET MONROE

Jan. 11, 1923 [1924][1] / 1415 12th St. / Boulder, Colo.

Dear Miss Monroe:

The group is O.K. I am indifferent as to the order. Better simply call them *poems*. [Witter] Bynner[2] has commenced exploiting New Mexico & I have moved—into a region where, I believe, no one can follow me. The next poems I publish will have no mark upon them of any sort whatsoever. I am playing safe.

Elizabeth Roberts is at the Riggs sanitorium at Stockbridge, Mass. I believe I can get her through their course of treatment there safely—they keep no one, I am told, over three months. They seem to think they can help her, & judging from her letters, they apparently are. I should like, if possible, to be able to turn two or three hundred dollars over to her at the end of her stay there, so that she might stay on in N.Y. for a while. Her parents are, as far as I can judge, out of sympathy with her, & refuse to recognize that she is ill, & Kentucky preys upon her anyway. She is forced into a very unhealthy isolation there. This is, of course, between us. The sanitorium is making special rates, which helps, but I don't know just how much I'll have at the end. I am giving a series of lectures in Denver shortly, which may contribute something. Anyway, for the present, she seems to be improving.

At the moment I am puzzled by your refusal of "José's Country" in the face of your acceptance of some of the others. It appears to me about the best poem I have written—& to Mrs. Freer & Miss Moore, likewise. *The Dial* & *Broom* have both turned it down, taking inferior poems instead. Curious.

Sorry about the envelopes, but I can't keep track of two kinds at once & prefer the small ones for general purposes.

I exhibit my Airedale in Denver in February. Don't know how I'll come out, but Mr. Galt & I won with her mother, who is not nearly so good, at Chicago & Milwaukee. She'll be in poor shape, however.

Sincerely, / A.Y.W.

MS: Chicago

[1]The date added in brackets by an unknown hand in the *Poetry* office.

[2]Witter Bynner (1881–1968): American poet and man of letters. The only Bynner book that was of any interest to YW (it was the only Bynner book in his library, in fact, present in multiple copies) was Bynner's edition of *The Sonnets of Frederick Goddard Tuckerman* (New York: Knopf, 1931).

TO GLENWAY WESCOTT

July 6, 1924 / 1415 12th St. / Boulder, Colorado

Dear Glenway—

After figuring the thing out from various angles, I have decided that, for various reasons, I had better cease to write you while I am here and receiving money from my father.[1] Not to ease my conscience particularly, for in this matter I have none to speak of, but because of possibilities and liabilities that make it seem—perhaps—politic, and more still, humane. My father's health is precarious; his intelligence is not great; and for the time being it seems best to conform to his code, which will give me a certain strength of position in case of a clash with him, rather than to mine, which he could not possibly visualize as a position at all. It will simplify matters for more persons than myself and my parents, and seems desirable. I can give further explanation of my decision in a year or so. Also of my coming here at all, which may seem strange to you.

There is no great reason why we should not have news of each other. I will have Lura Conkey forward letters to you, and ask her and Janet, perhaps, to forward your letters to me. You see the whole thing reduces itself to a rather quibbling technicality, but I think it wise to observe it nonetheless.

And meanwhile be sure of my love for you and loyalty to you. And if there is any reason for direct immediate communication with me, don't hesitate to break the ban. And remember that in all matters within human power I am eternally at your service. This thing need not last for more than a year and a half at the outside.

Will you please send this letter back to Monroe, as he, too, is included in all of the above. You will be informed if at any time I change my address, and I will see that poems are sent you when I have any. At present I have none.

"Men Like Kites" and "Easter Motion" are beautiful poems. I was doubtful about them at first, but am no longer so. Why do you not try to publish a volume? You could have a marvelous one.

In the *Dial* version of the "Horse," I was doubtful about one alteration from the original version—the change from the "mist of pebbles" etc. to the other. The revision, of course, possesses a harder sound, and so is possibly more in keeping with the revised poem; and the image is lovely. But so is the other image lovely—at times I think it almost lovelier.

My neo-Mexican tales advance apace. They are perhaps more than anything else like Kreymborg reduced to prose and to art—that is, intelligent writing. The most illusive of mockery in brief, slight forms. Not profound, but more or less amusing, and may possibly sell. I don't think on the whole I need be ashamed of them, nor yet tremendously proud.

My criticism also comes on slowly. I shall have a fairly impressive book of it in due time. Perhaps another year. Then I shall do no more of it.

Boulder is in a lovely place, although a stupid enough village in itself. Great red mountains jutting up on the edge of it—sawtoothing into green pale distance, the valley, at twilight.

Be sure of my love for you. And for M.

Arthur

MS: Yale

¹The homosexuality of Wescott and Monroe Wheeler had come to the attention of Winters's parents and precipitated an explosion. The complicated elements of the situation are present in this letter and others. The situation was exacerbated because of YW's sister Faith's admiration for Wescott. Earlier rumors (also present in these letters) had attempted to link Winters himself to homosexuality.

TO MARIANNE MOORE

Nov. 4, 1924 / 556 University Ave. / Boulder, Colo.

Dear Miss Moore:

My edition of Emily Dickinson is published by Little Brown, and my Hardy is the American Macmillan edition of several years ago, and not quite so complete as the latest edition of the same company. Should you care to see them, I should be glad to send you both of them, as I shall have time this year to read almost nothing in the way of poetry save late nineteenth century Frenchmen. I have, however, been reading a little Crashaw, during the past few days, and find him very beautiful. My knowledge of him had been extremely fragmentary. This sort of thing:

Be it enacted then
By the fair laws of the firm pointed pen,
God's services no longer shall put on
A sluttishness for pure religion:
No longer shall our Churches' frighted stones
Lie scattered like the burnt and martyred bones
Of dead Devotion; nor faint marbles weep
In their sad ruins; nor Religion keep
A melancholy mansion in those cold
Urns.

I am delighted that the Dial Press is printing you. It must be rather a relief to feel that you are going to be printed properly after having been printed so very improperly. I hope you are including some of the poems that didn't get into the London edition. The poems that Miss Monroe printed in her revised anthology, it seems to me, should go in, especially "A Graveyard" and "Sun!," which are magnificent. "To an Intra-Mural Rat" has always seemed to me excellent in every way, and distinctly to be prized, even though somewhat slighter and simpler than your later work. And there were poems in the early *Others* anthologies, not reprinted in your book, that I regretted bitterly, although I don't possess them and don't remember the titles. And you should also include "Marriage." And there are probably others that I have overlooked. I hope you are doing it properly. . . .

I have not seen H.D.'s *Heliodora,* and should greatly like to. Curiously enough, I have recently encountered a member of the department of English Literature here who is a first cousin of H.D. and spent much of his early life with or near her. He knew, slightly, Dr. Williams and Mr. Pound in the days before the great exodus. . . . His name is Wolle.

I am extremely glad to hear of your mother's improvement.

I have asked Dr. [J. S.] Watson to hold the pictures till you and Glenway and Monroe can see them in case he can do nothing about them.[1]

Sincerely, / Yvor Winters

MS: Rosenbach

[1] In 1920, Watson and Scofield Thayer bought out *The Dial.* I believe the pictures mentioned are reproductions by one or more of the Native American artists YW championed (and some of whose works he owned).

TO HARRIET MONROE

December 1, 1924 / 556 University Ave. / Boulder, Colo.

Dear Miss Monroe:

Sorry I got in my bid for H.D. too late. *Heliodora* is a great book, and I should like the chance to say so. As to Miss Moore, Mr. Eliot recently stated very baldly in the *Dial* that she was, for him, one of the five most exciting poets writing in any modern language at the present time so far as his knowledge extended. You see, I have a distinguished precedent for my high opinion of her. You have already stated your opinion, so that it might be fair to give some one else a chance. I have, in the past few years, conducted investigations into the nature of poetic method farther than anyone else, past or present, has ever done, and Miss Moore, structurally, is more intricate and more interesting than anyone else, past or present, has ever been, so that chances are that I could teach your readers more about poetic method, with her an as example, than Mrs. Seiffert and Miss Strobel together. I refuse, however, to do this if I am, in the end, merely to put into good English the opinions of Mrs. Seiffert or Miss Strobel, great as this service would be, and although I should be doing this service for you for whom my good will is infinite, and despite your present crippled condition. I should like to review the book, but that is up to you.

I am, however, and in spite of the above, awfully sorry to hear of your being laid up.

Janet improves gradually, and is developing into a remarkable sculptor in soap, though her lack of strength prevents her trying a more inspiring medium.

I may some day send you some translations from the Spanish and Latin, and, possibly, from the French, though as everyone reads French, or nearly everyone, I daresay there isn't much use in these last. I have done the opening of Ovid's "Phaeton," which makes an excellent unit, and Virgil's first eclogue, which is a perfect Noh play (I copped Pound's long free verse line for this last, as the nearest thing available to the Latin hexameter), and have also done a few early Spanish ballads. Wish I had the courage to try the hind end of the fourth *Georgic,* as it is the greatest piece of Latin verse I have ever read and magnificent beyond description, or seems so to me.

I hope you recover in a reasonably short time. Your injury is of a nature about as undesirable as possible, and you surely have my sympathy.

Sincerely, / Arthur Winters

P.S. As regards the above translations, my Latin is excellent. The Ovid is free, but I know where.

MS: Chicago

TO HARRIET MONROE

Dec. 22 [1923?][1]

Dear Miss Monroe:

Thanks for finding so much money, which will be of great assistance. Will you please send it to me at 1415 12th St., Boulder, Colo. I am collecting what I can, & paying the bills. Miss Roberts has sufficient for her personal expenses at present. It was difficult in the first place to get her to accept help at all, & I fear that odd sums drifting in might at this juncture rather upset things. It seemed necessary that someone act as business manager, so to speak. Mrs. T. W. Stevens was doing it, but has had something of a collapse & it has once more fallen to me. Miss Roberts herself is in so unstable a nervous & physical condition that we thought it best that she simply go & be taken care of, without, for the present, too great a knowledge of the complications involved in raising the money.

Again many thanks. And a Merry Christmas to the office.

A.Y. Winters

MS: *Chicago*

¹The manuscript is marked "1924?" in an unknown hand. However, given the subject matter of the letter and the address mentioned in it, the date of composition is more plausibly 1922 or 1923.

TO MARIANNE MOORE

January 18, 1925

Dear Miss Moore:

In stirring up some book wrapping of late, I came upon a piece of cardboard mysteriously bound &, in cutting it open, found *Hymen*. Please receive again my thanks for sending these books, as I admire H.D. beyond saying.

The two poems I sent you recently were pretty bad, & I think you had better burn them. "The North" was a most unusual abomination.

I expect to have a copy of your new book [*Observations*] here in a day or two. Miss Monroe has given me permission to review it on the condition that I don't praise you dogmatically & unreservedly. I would, in all humility, leave it to fall into better hands, except that I am certain that it would fall into one of three pairs than which none, I believe with thorough modesty, can be worse— those of Mrs. Seiffert, Miss Strobel, or Miss Swett. I suspect that this will be the last time that my name will ever appear in *Poetry*, as, despite my affection for Miss Monroe, I find her paper increasingly distasteful. Mr. Pound, however hampered he may have been, did manage to keep it above the level of a village literary & sewing circle.

If you have been able to read this far, I hope you will accept my congratulations on the *Dial* award. I should transmit them on my Corona but that a baby is sleeping in the next room, &, having been initiated into the habits of babies over the recent holidays, which I spent with my mother, sister, & young nephew—8 months old—I am a changed man. However, to return to the prize, I am more than glad that it fell to you, as the intensity, perfections, & originality of your work, &, what is more astounding yet, the mass of uniformly achieved work & the almost complete absence of anything not achieved, impresses me more every time I think of it or look at it.

The asinine controversy between Mssrs. [Waldo] Frank & [Malcolm]

Cowley[1] in Mr. Seamen's young paper has moved me to wonder if Mr. Lindsay is not to be regarded as a possible forerunner of at least one phase of the American Dada in question. It would be amusing to suggest it if one had time & a sufficiently strong urge. His "Samson" certainly has more outline, more firmness line for line, & more grandeur of imagery than any jazz so far achieved by these young men. Not that my admiration for the poem is tremendous, or that I would defend Mr. Frank, whose original article seemed to me to be pure twaddle, or very nearly pure.

I feel more & more acutely that, inasmuch as you are going in for animals, you have devoted remarkably little attention to the porcupine, who, I am sure, would reward you richly should you study him.

Jerry, however, is specializing in police dogs at present with much greater success than when he tried porcupines. On the hill above us there is quite a herd of them that he keeps very nicely herded. I find that one Airedale of 45 pounds in weight can usually account for three or four police dogs of sixty or seventy pounds each. I dislike the brutes intensely.

I hope that your mother is well.

Sincerely, / Yvor Winters

MS: Rosenbach

[1]Malcolm Cowley (1898–1989): American poet and critic.

TO MARIANNE MOORE

Feb. 3, 1925 / 556 University Ave. / Boulder, Colo.

Dear Miss Moore:

The copy of your book came nearly a week ago, and I am very slow in acknowledging it. It was extremely kind of you to send it, and I thank you greatly. I believe that there is nothing in it that does not give me a very genuine pleasure of one degree or another, and the poems that excite me most excite me as much as any poetry I have ever read—and more than almost any. I think those that seem to me to have a slight advantage over the others are "Fear Is Hope," "My Apish Cousins," "A Grave," "Those Various Scalpels," and "New York," but the three long poems and a dozen or more of the others move me almost as much. It is an astoundingly intense and compact achievement.

I have sent a review of the book to Miss Monroe, but am not at all sure that she will print it.

I have decided to send you the corrected version of one of the poems I sent you some weeks ago, as I should like the thing to die as respectably as possible. I don't much like it, however, and am aware that the other was extremely bad. I fear I shall never have the courage to send you anything again, as I seem to be rapidly gaining momentum in my career from bad to worse, and it is rather an imposition.

We have entered upon a very luxurious premature spring.

I hope that your mother is well.

Sincerely, / Yvor Winters

MS: Rosenbach

TO MARGERY SWETT

556 University Ave. / Boulder, Colo. / May 8, 1925

Dear Miss Swett:

Thanks for the letter. When I was teaching school in Madrid, New Mexico, about four years ago, I encountered this person on the Lamy platform one Sunday evening as I was heading back to Madrid from Santa Fe. He and I were the only individuals in sight and exchanged a few casual words, on the basis of which, and my streamline spectacles—then more or less a novelty—he suspected me of being a correspondent for *Liberator*. He was at that time, and I dare say still is, a wandering scout and speaker for the underground communist movement, and was making his way about as a peddler of faucet filters which he bought in the Woolworth stores of the larger towns for ten cents apiece and sold in the villages for fifty. His real name I don't know—he is wanted by the police in most of the towns of Arizona, New Mexico, and Colorado—and changes his alias every few months. He is a short, fat, and very common-looking Russian Jew, who, despite his letters and his appearance, talks very amusingly —or at least tells very amusing details about the private lives of various radical leaders and the way they clean up on their poor constituents and admirers. He spent one evening with me in Madrid, and then went on to Albuquerque, where he was arrested because of the complaints that poured into the water company's offices about the cyclopes and stentors (he knew their names, which helped) that he was catching in the filters. While he was in jail, some papers in his pocket almost gave away his identity, but he got away and rode an engine to Trinidad, from which town he sent me a very hysterical account of his adventures. The next letter I had from him was from the southern end of Mexico about a year later, and this is the third, which you send. For some reason he conceived a great admiration for my work, but this letter leaves me a little in doubt as to whether or not he retains it. His other great literary passion is—or was—Anatole France, one of whose books he once sent me as an expression of his admiration. I trust this clears up the mystery, though it may not do as much for my reputation. He is not, in any event, one of my intimates.

Sincerely, / Yvor Winters

MS: Chicago

Margery Swett: business manager of *Poetry*. She has written on the letter the following comments, which clarify the occasion of the letter: "An amusing letter. About a very strange letter I opened by mistake & sent on to Winters."

TO MARIANNE MOORE

July 14, 1925 / 556 University Ave. / Boulder, Colo.

Dear Miss Moore,

I wish to congratulate you on your beginning [as editor of *Dial*], though I have not yet read all the number. Mr. Cowley's sonnet seems to me remarkably fine, in its rhetorical but very genuine force & in its hard resiliency of cadence.

What you said of Glenway is only too true. I fear his erudition will always be a rather limited affair, as he will never pause long enough in his adventures to consider its limitations. As to the rest, I don't know. In New Mexico, he, & later I, had a red pony that, temperamentally, was very much like him. It was as affectionate as a puppy when unsaddled, but, under the saddle, & especially when fresh, was given to performing single & unexpected half-bucks in the most savage & irritating manner. It had a mouth of iron, & whenever it crossed a bridge was so impressed by its own resonance & magnification in the void beneath, that no mortal hand could hold it for the next half-hour. . . .

But I continue to think some of his poems extraordinarily fine notwithstanding.

Next year I shall teach French & Spanish at the University of Idaho—at least according to present plans. After that, I don't know.

My magnificent critical system—if one can call it a system—is complete & is serving as a master's thesis for the time being. It is a rather ponderous affair, however, & I shall probably let it rest in the obscurity that gathers about all such theses in a very short time.

Strangely enough, I find that my formerly great opinion of Wallace Stevens has dwindled in an appalling fashion in the last year. I have not ceased to admire him, but he used to seem to me Shakespeare's only rival. . . . I don't know just what has occurred.

My poems in *This Quarter* were rather feeble. I had forgot that I had sent "Quod Tegit Omnia" till I saw it in print, & was sadly vexed thereby.

I suppose that I ought in all decency to begin to make up my mind to quit, or at least to quit publishing, but the game amuses me, & it is about my only contact with civilization. And perhaps if I keep on working & the Good Lord continues to crucify me with western villages, I may someday write a decent poem.

Incidentally I at last feel that you are justified in your opinion of [Robert] McAlmon.[1] His prose impressed me as tremendously as prose can. I wonder if his verse has advanced as far.

Carnevali continues to be rather commonplace, I think. His best phrases ring like pebbles chucked at a bright tin roof by a very irritated man; but he never gets beyond purely personal irritation.

As to prose fiction, it seems to me that all one has to do to damn it eternally is to read in fairly rapid succession the first & last paragraphs of about twenty stories of any sort, & then follow it by a similar sequence of paragraphs from the middle. That probably sounds like one of Carnevali's reactions, but I really find the standardization of even the best prose abominably irritating.

I hope I am not quite as much a barbarian as I doubtless seem, but I admit that the chances are against me.

I hope that your mother & yourself are well.

Sincerely, / Yvor Winters

MS: Rosenbach

[1]Robert McAlmon (1896–1956): American writer and publisher, practically the archetype of the expatriate writer. He cofounded, with W. C. Williams, the little magazine *Contact* before moving to Paris. There, he founded his own publishing company, Contact Editions, which published among others Hemingway, M. Loy, Stein, and W. C. Williams.

Jan. 12, 1926 / 904 West A St. / Moscow, Idaho

Dear Miss Moore:

The January *Dial* has just arrived and I have read the various matters by and with reference to Cummings. In the light of what you said in your letter regarding your review, I do not know just how much I ought to feel insulted. However, I don't. Your review I like very much, as I like practically all of your reviews. But I distrust it, as I distrust practically all of your reviews. You gather bright bits here and there (as you have done from guide-books, dictionaries, and heaven only knows what), and carry them off, as a crow picks over an ash-heap and leaves the ashes behind. Do not misinterpret me—I am not, this time, trying to compare Mr. Cummings to the ash-heap. I merely compare you to the crow. You out-do the crow in that you are a high-grade interior decorator, whereas he is a mere collector. After you get your bric-a-brac embedded in three or four pages of crackling prose it is lovely. But you have the air of believing, at least, that your finished product and the ash-heap are one and the same—whereas to the innocent bystander there is an appalling difference. When you say definitely that you like or dislike something I give considerable importance to your opinion. But I give it more importance when you say it informally than when the statement fellows three pages of scene-shifting. This is possibly unjust, but it rankles in my breast.

So much for yourself. As for Mr. Cummings, my opinion of his first book remains unchanged—I find it charming in spots, exciting nowhere, and messy on the whole. I have not seen the others, but shall read them shortly—not in any attempt to bolster up my prejudices nor out of any desire to atone for them; nor yet because—primarily—of your review and the prize. But because the first poem in the new group is the first poem of his for which I have ever felt any genuine enthusiasm, and because I am aware that some poets do and some do not publish excessively and only the Lord in Heaven can be blamed for it—and if Mr. Cummings has written one such poem he may have written another. I agree with you that the infinitude of passages like that of the angels sharpening their little beaks on air are charming, but most of them seem to me to have an extremely thin emotional content, and when a poem, with no noticeable outline and of considerable length, is composed entirely of such, I find it over-tenuous. Occasionally, as in his recent upward glance at the new moon, he makes the cosmos quiver like quicksilver. For that I admire him—and if he could write half a dozen poems like that from beginning to end, my admiration would be boundless. Maybe he has—I have read only one of his books.

So much for Mr. Cummings. As to his admirers—his public admirers—in general they have bored and repelled me by several tricks that are all too common with the average hit-or-miss critic. Mr. [Scofield] Thayer, in his recent note, in order to make his man appear a giant selects a straw-man as his opponent. I don't know the quotation that he uses for comparison, but it must come from Bodenheim. Rodin beside Lorado Taft would seem a Phidias. If he is interested in comparisons of epithets, their rapidity and impact, he might start off with the Canto beginning "Palace in smoky light," Mr. Eliot's "Gerontion," and Dr. Williams' poem about the crowd at the baseball game. In which case he would have to make a better selection from Cummings—which even I am willing to admit he could easily do. I was prevented reading Verlaine for three years by the quotations I had seen in anthologies and essays. When I read the *Romances sans paroles* I could have wept. I have, if you like, my own stupidity to thank for it, but such is the case. Your selections are enticing, but, as I have already said, I suspect you on the basis of one or two past performances. I shall, however, read him myself very shortly, so that is that.

I suspect that my backings and turnings in connection with Cummings and others seem to you ridiculous, and what is worse, I suspect that they actually are ridiculous. I do not deny occasional pangs of jealousy—but I suspect that few other persons could make such a denial without blushing. I occasionally even say or write things under their influence. But I beg of you not to think that I fail to recognize them for what they are or for what they are worth. It would be easier to love all of one's neighbors in Paris or New York. Here one lives on dirt, and one wants to crowd the other fellow a little to make up for it. When the try for a nudge is over, I can make what I believe to be an honest estimate of the other fellow so far as my powers allow, and admire him for what he seems to me worth, and without any qualms. One maintains a grain of decency in spite of Idaho.

The genuine stupidity consists in talking about such things, and that is what I shall stop.

Sincerely, / Winters

MS: Rosenbach

TO KENNETH BURKE

August 26, 1926 / Sunmount / Santa Fe, New Mexico

Dear Mr. Burke,

I have taken the liberty of having sent to you a novel that seems to me very great—*The Time of Man,* by Elizabeth Madox Roberts. I wonder if, provided you like it, you would write a review in its behalf somewhere. The author is a chronic invalid—TB, anemia, & some undiagnosed & incurable nervous disease, from which she has suffered from childhood, & which causes intense physical suffering—& cannot survive, I fear, so very many more years. The length of time that she manages to survive plus her general happiness & literary efficiency depend to a considerable extent on the success of the novel, & it seems to me that it deserves a fair success as successes of good books go. It might at least add a little to what her relatives can do for her—which is very little—& give her a measure of independence. I am not begging for intellectual charity—if you don't like the book don't bother about it. But if you do think the author worth saving, I think you are probably one of the four or five persons who could do the most to save her—by a public word or two.

I hope I don't seem unduly officious.

Sincerely, / Yvor Winters

MS: PSU

TO ALLEN TATE

November 6, 1926 / 904 West A St. / Moscow, Idaho

Dear Tate:

Thanks for your note regarding Hart Crane: I received a note from him in the same mail as your own. My image of the Indies in general in a hurricane is more or less similar to one that remains to me from my childhood of a Pacific coaster on which my father once made a trip and of which he told me shortly thereafter. Going around Cape Flattery he had to shin up the smoke-stack—more or less—to keep from being washed overboard. The cabin, I gathered, was a sort of aquarium, or pickling vat.

I have just made arrangements to publish a book—sometime or other—with Four Seas. But I have a couple of extra mss. lying around and will send you one, so that you may choose what you like—if you like anything. The first group in the mss.—the New Mexico pieces—I like very little, and I may be wrong in including them in the book. I don't know. But there were one or two of them that I hadn't quite the heart to throw away, and so I made up a group of the best dozen I could pick and let them go. Most of them had been previously printed anyway. It is on the remainder of the book that I really pin what hopes I have. . . . If you use any of my poems, however, please be sure to take your copies from the ms. and not from any printed versions, as one or two of those that have been printed were sadly butchered by the printers, and there have been revisions in others. Similarly, if you should want to use anything that you have seen in any magazine and do not find in the ms., please let me know, so that I may send you the corrected version, if there is one. I am delighted, of course, to think that you like my work well enough to wish to include it. If you are making an American anthology, however, I hope you don't share Crane's aversion for Williams, who is, I think, a supremely great poet and the best we have had since Emily Dickinson.

I have seen two books by [Archibald] MacLeish—*The Pot of Earth* and *The Happy Marriage*—which I don't at all like, and a few pieces in magazines that I have liked very much, especially some things called "Signature for Tempo," which I found really magnificent. Until very recently I labored under the delusion that he was an Englishman. I believe it was the fault of some stray remark in the *Dial*. Of your own work, I have seen absolutely nothing, though I have seen and heard it spoken of with a good deal of admiration. I trust you will make yourself reasonably visible in your anthology, as, at this distance, and with a limited income, it really is beastly difficult to keep up with the sporadic and, considering their short lives, rather costly outlaw papers that most of us seem to be condemned to. Best of wishes for your anthology.

Sincerely, / Yvor Winters

MS: Princeton, Allen Tate Papers

TO ALLEN TATE

November 18, 1926 / 904 West A Street / Moscow, Idaho

Dear Tate:

I am interested in your critical problem as I am at the moment working on a very similar [one] in French—not that I prefer either that literature or that language to our own but because the publication of anything so utterly and unreadably mathematical as my critical system—a primitive version of a part of which, a small part, appeared in English in Secession—seems impossible, and because two Frenchmen—Franck Schoell and René Lalou—having seen it were pleased with it and thought they could find me a publisher in Paris. Or rather, this thought was Schoell's. So last summer I put the completed essay into French and am now finishing up the anthology (Leconte de Lisle to Radiguet) to illustrate it. Later I shall apply the mathematics historically to English, French, and American "modernism." Probably in French also, however, as I am going over in a year or so to take my doctor's degree.

I think you are wrong about Williams, purely and simply. I am not moved by any youthful admiration for technical gymnastics and what not in my liking for him—he moves me more profoundly than any other living poet save Hardy, and as do only a handful of poets dead: Hopkins, Arnold, Emily Dickinson, Browning, [Tristan] Corbière, and sometimes Baudelaire and Rimbaud. These are men who presented a blank wall to their contemporaries—even their contemporaries of genius (Rimbaud and Corbière never heard of each other though their only books were published in the same year, a thing which is indubitably fortunate, however)—largely because their contemporaries (like themselves) considered themselves sufficiently intelligent to recognize a genius without labor. When absolutely new perceptions appeared, absolutely bare of recognizable literary connections, they were not perceptible to the genius who refused to work for them—very frequently, at least. Browning, of course, was and is popular, but for his bad poems and qualities, which are abundant. As to my admiring Williams, I do not lay it to superior intelligence but to my having spent five years in a definite effort to undermine him theoretically and to my having demonstrated to my own satisfaction at least that it can't be done. It was for that purpose mainly that I worked out my mechanics of poetry. He is the hardest come by of any poet in my gallery, and, I suspect, will be the last I shall ever give up. The prose of *In the American Grain* I admire more than that of any contemporary—only Joyce and Elizabeth Roberts seem to me comparable to him, and I think I like him better. This may sound exaggerated to you, but, believe me, I am not exaggerating, but expressing profound convictions resulting from the very profound excitement that his work awakens in me. It is an excitement that goes to the bottom of my consciousness. The popularity of a man like Cummings, who does little but dilute and sweeten things that his immediate predecessors have done better, in the face of the neglect in which a man like Williams is left, all but sickens me.

I have ordered Crane's book [*White Buildings*] and told H.M. that I meant to review it for her. She probably won't print my review, however, as she believes that I inhabit some utterly mythical fourth dimension (she has never recovered from *The Magpie's Shadow*), and I have insulted her right and left recently, anyway—largely on the subject of Crane.

I should be interested to know your quite honest opinion of the stuff I sent you, and should, of course, be delighted to have you review me, though I fear you may find a fearful disparity between my rather meager muse and my passion for prophets. The book, they tell me, will be out around February 1. I shall probably stop a few days in New York next spring, summer, or fall, and should be awfully glad to see you. I'll let you know when I am going through, and we may be able to arrange it.

Sincerely, / Yvor Winters

MS: Princeton, Allen Tate Papers

¹This French manuscript was never published and seems to have disappeared. A manuscript anthology of French poems, much lengthier than the one meant to accompany the critical work, is in the possession of the Winters family.

TO HARRIET MONROE

904 West A St. / Moscow, Idaho / Nov. 27, 1926

Dear Miss Monroe:

Thanks for your good wishes, which I shall communicate to Janet, at Sunmount.

I'll send you the review when—and if—I ever get the books. I have almost lost hope.

I am not "left wing" however, but a humble and sincere classicist and am at the moment finishing up an opus in French on modern classicism. Not because I regret being an American, but because of the deplorable impossibility of publishing decent criticism in this journalistic land. The essay of which you long ago scorned to print a part aroused nevertheless the enthusiasm of Lalou, who is a great critic, and of another Frenchman, Franck Schoell, and the latter has promised to find me a Parisian publisher for it. This is not for publication.

Shall have a book out with Four Seas around Feb. 1. Title: *The Bare Hills*. If you should review it, and wish to review it unfavorably, my only prayer is that you do *not* give it to Marion Strobel or Mrs. Seiffert or M. Swett. Aside from that you are perfectly welcome to do your damnedest. I don't believe you'll care much for it, though it is in no wise obscure.

I trust you have checked *The Time of Man* up on your list of my "I told you sos."

Crane is writing a long poem that, among other things, will do more or less what Mark [Turbyfill] tried to do. The other things, however, are numerous and profound. I have seen a couple of sections of it, and I am sending you the advance information that it is one of the supremely great poems of our time. Remember *The Time of Man*.

You do not mention Williams's *In the American Grain* among the works in prose that you admire—and yet it is, if there is such a book, a greater book than *The Time of Man*. It and *Spring and All* alone would suffice to place W. as the greatest master since Hardy.

Best wishes, / Yvor Winters

MS: Chicago

TO FRANCIS VIELÉ-GRIFFIN

Nov. 29, 1926 / 904 West A St. /
Moscow, Idaho

M. Francis Vielé-Griffin, / Paris, / France.
Dear Sir:

I have been unpardonably remiss about thanking you for your very kind permission to use my translation of your poem. I have been hindered by a multitude of complications: uncertainty of the planned book of translations, work on an anthology of modern French poets, which M. Franck Schoell believes that he can place for me with a Parisian publisher, my own marriage, etc. The book of translations, unfortunately, has fallen through, owing to the ill-health of Agnes Lee's husband, Dr. Otto Freer of Chicago, for which, I fear, there is no cure, and which has prevented her revising and organizing her share of the book. My wife (Janet Lewis, who did the sonnet by Valéry) and I, however, will try to get some such book together in the next year or two, and shall wish, of course, to include your extraordinarily beautiful poem.

As to the anthology in French, which will be a small affair, as I am using it really to illustrate a long critical essay, expounding certain theories of modernism of my own, I should like to include at least the following poems by yourself, if you have no objections: *"La Source," "Pour le 2 novembre," "Thrénode pour Mallarmé," "Aussi bien je me dirais joyeux," "Demain est au vingt ans fiers."* It would be a very great favor if you would let me use them.

I took the liberty a little while ago of sending you a novel called *The Time of Man,* by one of my closest friends, Elizabeth Madox Roberts. It deals with a part of this country that I imagine must be—or have been—fairly familiar to you, and so I thought it might interest you. Personally my admiration for the book is boundless.

And unless you object very promptly I shall allow myself one more luxury of the same sort—that of sending you a book of verse of my own which the Four Seas Company of Boston will publish along in February, along with a couple of small pamphlets that I published five or six years ago, in the hopes that one of the three may contain something to please you. The earliest is very "French," having been written before I could read French, at the age of about 19. The second was influenced mainly by Frances Densmore's translations from the Chippewa and by the paintings of the Tewa Indian Awa-tsireh, and the new one, I suspect, is simply American.

Meanwhile I remain with the greatest admiration for your work

Very sincerely yours, /
Arthur Yvor Winters

MS: Princeton, Vielé-Griffin Papers

Francis Vielé-Griffin (1864–1937): early French symbolist poet.

TO ALLEN TATE

Jan. 10, 1927 / 904 West A St. / Moscow, Idaho

Dear Tate:

Thanks for your letter, which is very interesting, and your appreciation, which is very cheering. I disagree with your preferences in the ms., as with Crane's, and my future procedure will probably be along the lines you least like. The poems you like best were more or less accidental and strike me as a shade inflated, empty. Good sound, good swashing rhetoric—and a few perceptions. If such matters at all interest you, here is my chronology, as nearly as I can remember it.

Born October, 1900.

First poem in *The Immobile Wind* (title poem) September 1919.

Last poem in same book, "Alone," January, 1921.

The Magpie's Shadow written between about Nov. 1920 and June 1921, published early in 1922.

First poem in "Upper River Country," "The Fragile Season," written about October 1921.

Last in same group, "The Upper Meadows," summer of 1924.

The Bare Hills

Winter of 1923–4: "Digue dondaine," "The Muezzin" (first draft only—finished early in 1926), "Song" ("Now the precise"), "The Streets," "The Rows of Cold Trees," "Man Regards Eternity."

Spring of 1925 and late winter 1924: "Genesis," "The Vigil" (first draft), "Alba for Hecate," "The Cold," parts of "Nocturne" (finished autumn 1926), "Quod Tegit Omnia," "March Dusk," "Midnight Wind," "The Bare Hills," "Prayer Beside a Lamp."

Winter 1925–6 and early spring 1926: "Exodus," "Moonrise," "The Lamplight," "Flesh of Flowers," "Under Rain," "Complaint," "Song" (final version—this goes back to beginnings at least two years earlier), "April," "Full Moon," ("Love Song" and "Sleep" were written just after the publication of *The Magpie's Shadow*), "The Cold Room," "The Barnyard," "The Grosbeaks."

Autumn 1926: "The Dead: Mazda Wake," final version of "Nocturne."

"Eternity" was written in the late autumn of 1921, and "The Passing Night" in the winter of 1924–5.

This is purely for your private consumption, but you see how far your favorites come from being any sort of chronological culmination. For me, the best poems in the lot are "The Barnyard," "The Grosbeaks," and "The Dead," and for them I would willingly toss the rest away. My belief is that it is possible to touch certain obvious physical facts of existence in such a way as to invoke— or evoke—or expose—as by one single electric shock an entire existence or phase of existence. Emily Dickinson does this for me in such a poem as "The last night that she lived," Hardy in "The Darkling Thrush," Williams in the first poem in *Spring and All*, or, in *Sour Grapes*, "To Waken an Old Lady." This is what I am endeavoring to do. It is more exciting to me than whole libraries of Pounds, Eliots, or even Rimbauds. Perhaps I am all wrong.

If there is any perfection in the poems it is, I fear, the product of labor rather than dexterity. It is only recently—in the stuff I sent [Paul] Rosenfeld [*American Caravan*]—that I have felt myself to move neatly and freely. The rest is an infinitely slow and painful accretion—I cannot begin to tell you how painful—sheer agony. You seem to place me about where I place H.D.—though I think I like her less than you claim to like me. She has all the mannerisms of extreme concision and intense passion, and, most of the time, is verbose and cold. My intentions, at any rate, are about as diverse from hers as possible.

The stuff sent to Rosenfeld is in an entirely different mood—you are welcome to any of it you like, but please let me know what you choose, if anything, as I am still revising it. I have made one or two changes also in the ms. of the book. I did not mean for you to return either ms. or booklets. I have other copies and don't want them.

Wescott's verse is probably a little soft around the edges and none too hard in the middle, but I think he is due to write some very great fiction—probably in his as yet unpublished second novel. I hope you aren't prejudiced by his person, in case you have met him—his mannerisms, obvious nervous aberrations, and Byronic hair and voice drive most people crazy and did me till I got to know him. He is about as remote from myself—by nature a simple farmer and dog-handler, and, were it not for one or two defective organs, pugilist—as any one can be, but I think he is fundamentally sound.

I will write the *Dial* for *White Buildings* if you like, but then who the hell will do it for *Poetry*? This is damn serious. I haven't got my copy yet, but it ought to be along soon. I am meditating magnificent phrases, and really think I'll do a fair review of it. Would MacLeish do it for *Poetry*? I'll write the *Dial* tonight and cinch both of them, and then relinquish either one you like to your candidate, if you'll provide a candidate. I think Miss Moore will let me have it.

This letter does not require an answer except in regard to the review.

Best wishes, / Yvor Winters

MS: Princeton, Allen Tate Papers

TO ALLEN TATE

Jan. 11, 1927 / 904 West A St. / Moscow, Idaho

Dear Tate:

Just got *White Buildings* and have read it through a few times. It is about as great as they come. Your essay is a magnificent piece of criticism, and will leave little to the reviewer, I fear. However, I shall try to give a little practical advice to beginners, etc. . . . and may succeed in making myself useful.

The essay clarifies your letter, but I disagree with you in spots: that is, what you say about Crane is correct, but I still refuse to admit that my method (I am not talking about my poems—they don't reach Crane) is [not] inherently as sound as Crane's and capable of as much. The imagist poem *was* a complete world: the best poems of Hardy or Williams lay *the* complete world naked at a stroke. That is, the ideal poem of my type succeeds in implying—quite clearly and definitely—as much as your ideal poem succeeds in stating, and is likely to have the advantage of greater speed. The second rate poem of my type becomes a good hard little toy, whereas the second rate one of your type is awfully likely to be no bigger and a damn sight less tangible. This is not criticism, of course, but an attempt to throw sand in your typewriter. . . .

Crane must have read my simple western ditties with a certain amount of bewilderment. At the moment I regard myself as the logical successor to Sara Teasdale.

I wish I knew in what mysterious places you publish your criticism. This essay is about the finest criticism of a poet by a contemporary that I have seen.

Best wishes, / Yvor Winters

MS: Princeton, Allen Tate Papers

TO ROBERT LIDDELL LOWE

Jan 11, 1927 / 904 West A St. / Moscow, Idaho

Dear Mr. Lowe:

Thank you for your very pleasant letter and for your admiration of my work. The postage stamp was quite unnecessary. Writing my admirers will never seriously affect my income. Here is a more or less tabloid statement of the information you wish:

Born in Chicago, October 17, 1900. Went to California with my parents and younger sister about three and a half years later, and until I was about 12 years old lived in the foothills north of Los Angeles, in a place called Eagle Rock, now a part of the city. At the age of 12 we moved to Seattle, where we stayed for about a year and a half, my family then returning to Chicago, and I staying on with my grandmother for a year in Eagle Rock. I then returned to Chicago, or, strictly speaking, Evanston, went through the Evanston and Senn High Schools in three years and entered the University of Chicago in the fall of 1917. There I was a member of The Poetry Club of the University of Chicago, then in its second year, of which were also members at that time or soon after, Elizabeth Madox

Roberts (author of *The Time of Man*, a recently published novel), Glenway Wescott (author of *The Apple of the Eye*, a novel, as well as of two small books of verse), Pearl Andelson (author of *Fringe*, a small but very fine book of verse, published by Will Ransom, Chicago), Maurine Smith, dead at the age of 23, but the author of a few lovely poems, published by Monroe Wheeler in a book called *The Keen Edge*, Maurice Lesemann, and my wife, Janet Lewis. I entered the University as a major in zoölogy, my chief interests having been since about the age of 14, metaphysics and the more experimental phases of modern morphology and protozoölogy. After four quarters I discovered that I had contracted tuberculosis, and went to Santa Fe, New Mexico, where I spent three years in bed. During the first of those three years, between about September, 1919, and January, 1921, I wrote my first book of verse, *The Immobile Wind*, which was published by Monroe Wheeler, and in the next six months or so wrote my second, *The Magpie's Shadow*, published the following year by The Musterbookhouse of Chicago. During my stay in New Mexico, I learned French and Spanish, and, after two years teaching grades and high school in Madrid and Los Cerrillos, coal towns about thirty miles south of Santa Fe, I entered the University of Colorado, in the summer of 1923 as a major in Romance Languages. I took my A.M. there in the summer of 1925, and have been instructor in Romance Languages since at the University of Idaho—where, unfortunately, my poems are little known and less admired. I shall be publishing with the Four Seas Company in the next month or so a book of poems called *The Bare Hills*, and shall contribute next September a group of some twenty odd poems to *The American Caravan*, a new yearbook of American literature, edited by Alfred Kreymborg, Van Wyck Brooks, Lewis Mumford, and Paul Rosenfeld. My favorite poets in English are: Shakespeare, Donne, Vaughan, Blake, Arnold, Browning, Gerard Hopkins, Hardy, Emily Dickinson, William Carlos Williams, Marianne Moore, Mina Loy, and Hart Crane. In French: Villon, du Bellay, Racine, Baudelaire, Mallarmé, Rimbaud, Verlaine, Corbière, and Valéry. And of course Turoldus. In Spanish: Quevedo and Góngora. My marriage occurred last summer. Which is about all that I can think of. My literary associations of the last few years probably haven't penetrated the colleges yet: the group of younger men publishing in *Secession, 1924, This Quarter*, etc. If you are interested in such matters, however, that is where the main current of life is at the moment, I think. *The Dial* has crystallized and dear old H.M. would if she knew how, but I fear she will never do anything that definite.

Inasmuch as you like my early poems—which I admit I don't any more— I shall give myself the pleasure of sending you copies of my two first books, which you probably haven't seen, and which I believe are rather hard to get by now. Please pardon the queer bias in alignment of this letter. My Corona seems to have run amuck.

Best wishes, / Yvor Winters

MS: *Tulsa*

Robert Liddell Lowe (1908–1988): American poet, scholar, and educator.

TO ALLEN TATE

Jan. 21, 1927 / 904 West A St. / Moscow, Idaho

Dear Tate:

Thanks enormously for the poems. I shall read them as soon as my blood pressure sinks to normal: its recent rise is due to a brush with a customs inspector in Montana, who has a package addressed to me containing what he describes as "pictures of nude women." I am appealing to our Congressman, a decent, enlightened soul, to get the Treasury department to boot his behind. Meanwhile I am exposing all of my profane vocabulary before the president of this university and the head of our department, in councils regarding the best way to proceed. I suspect that the trouble is due to a book of Eluard's, containing illustrations by—I think—Picabia, but am not sure. He won't tell me.

I shall tell you exactly what I think of the poems.

In my notes in *Secession* ["The Testament of a Stone, Being Notes on the Mechanics of the Poetic Image"], I was using Eliot to illustrate a mechanical fact of composition, not criticizing Eliot. The form in *Secession* has been revised and altered—added to. It is now—in its French version—a very complete system of poetic mechanics, with full illustrations and analyses, both of the line and the poem, and provides certain instruments of criticism that I believe might be valuable. I shall probably never have time to make much use of them, as I am too swamped in the pursuit of Romance and English philology, and God knows what else, in order to make a living, that I put what time I have left on my poems. And I am probably not a critic, anyway—those notes are the notes, primarily, of a poetic technician, and my reviews are merely reviews, and not remarkable, except in so far as my judgments may be intelligent. If the judgments *are* intelligent, the reviews, God knows, are remarkable.

I have sent a review of Crane to Miss Moore, with instructions to return it if anyone else wants to review the book—and praise it. If she takes the review, and MacLeish can't do it for *Poetry*, I'll try to get Pearl Andelson to do it for

H.M. P.A. is no great critic, but is quick on her mental legs as a spider, would like the book enormously, and would do a decent review. She likes anything she can't understand, and for that reason used to consider me to be the greatest poet in America—because of *The Immobile Wind*—and has never forgiven me for changing my tactics.

I think you flatter yourself in regard to the effect of your insults on H.M. I insult her regularly every couple of months, and have never made her turn a hair. And whatever my rank as a poet, no one living or dead can equal my invective. Not even Pound, whom she survived for several years likewise.

I'll write MacLeish.

I have corresponded off and on with Miss Moore for five or six years, and she has been very kind to me in a number of ways. And I admire her poems. But I can't fathom her. Perhaps you saw my review of Mina Loy—whom I consider a magnificent poet in spite of you. Well, M.M. returned it when I sent it in, demanding that I do not quote the lines about the buttocks. I refused and kept it, and she sent for it and took it anyhow. Dorothy Dudley is doing some sort of an article for the *Dial* on Brancusi, and mentioned that B. thought the world would be better off without religion. M.M. asked that that be left out likewise. And for three or four letters she almost died in her efforts to get me to alter the remarks about God and Jesus in "The Streets"—gave me every conceivable reason save her real one: that she was shocked. I thought her review of Cummings a year ago a great review, but rotten criticism. I don't like C.'s verse, but that had nothing to do with it. Her other reviews have been unspeakable and she is strangling the magazine. This would all be normal enough if she weren't a great poet—and, what is stranger still, the greatest satirical poet I have ever read.

Without having as yet read your poems, let me borrow your terminology —which I wish I had invented, as it is more ingenious than chess—to say that for me a poem is an architectural structure (theme) built of bricks or other units (perceptions), and that the closer the bricks are fitted together, the longer the structure is likely to stand. Pardon the metaphor. I admit that I use them and that I shouldn't. I think it is possible to indicate—very clearly—the general, by stating only the concrete, and that it tends toward greater speed and density to do so. This is what I tried to do in "The Barnyard" and "The Grosbeaks." But this argument is ridiculous and could go on for ever.

Thanks again for the ms. which I shall read to the best of my ability.

Sincerely, / Yvor Winters

MS: Princeton, Allen Tate Papers

Jan. 24, 1927 / 904 West A St. / Moscow, Idaho

Dear Lowe:

I am glad you like the books, but they are not as good as you say, and if I were you I wouldn't trust them too far. A few of the things in them I still like up to a certain point, but not enormously. I think my new book will have a few fair poems in it. It seems to me that the dynamite of the "modern movement," or most of it is to be found in the following books of verse: W. C. Williams's *Spring and All* (Contact Press, Paris), *Sour Grapes* (Four Seas), and *Al que quiere!* (same); Marianne Moore's *Observations* (Dial Press); Mina Loy's *Lunar Baedecker* (Contact Press); Hart Crane's *White Buildings* (Boni and Liveright); Wallace Stevens's *Harmonium* (Knopf); Archibald MacLeish's *Streets in the Moon* (Houghton Mifflin); Ezra Pound's *Personae* (B. and L.); and T. S. Eliot's *Collected Poems.* If you don't know where to get these things or where to get in touch with the "underground" magazines, write The Walden Book Shop, Plymouth Court, Chicago. *The American Caravan* will not be an anthology, but a sort of glorified magazine, and in all likelihood the best thing we have ever had.

I don't like the three poems you enclose, but that is not astonishing, nor does it prove anything. You treat rather commonplace themes without having really felt them. By that I don't mean that you didn't work up a certain amount of emotion in doing the writing, or before it—you probably did. But that is easy to do. To really penetrate a theme, discover its entrails, is damned hard work. It is largely a matter—given a good perceptual intelligence—of learning to separate the significant from the insignificant. And that is a matter of education—which you have to acquire by yourself. And which you might in part acquire by laboring over some of the above-mentioned writers. The Fletchers, Lowells etc., seem to me to lack a genuinely intense vision, and this sense of discrimination. I should be glad to see anything you might like to send me at any time, but give you fair warning that I am hard as the very devil to please.

[George] Dillon is no genius. He's a nice kid who has learned the knack of a sweet manner and is apparently satisfied to go on with it indefinitely. He'll join the troop of Bynners, Teasedales [*sic*], etc., in a few years. Except that he *does* write better than B., who is usually simply funny. Crane is the greatest thing on the horizon right now. He is doing a long poem called *The Bridge,* of which he has sent me three sections of an appalling profundity and beauty. Dillon with his bird-song stuff, and H.M.—who translates the bird-song into a sort of barnyard cackle—don't get him, but neither have they ever got anyone else of the first order. They run to Saretts and Sandburgs. Let them run.

However, enough gratuitous preaching.

I once took a course in the history of the epic with Wolle, and like him very well—can't say as much for Glick. Dr. Irene McKeehan is the finest scholar in that department and a woman whom I admire a great deal from every standpoint.

My portrait has never "appeared." [Ernest] Walsh meant to print a picture of me in *This Quarter*, but Walsh is dead—and his death is more of a tragedy than will be realized for several years. I enclose a snap of myself, taken several years ago, but still a good likeness.

You are lucky to be in so pleasant a school as Baylor. Most of them are calamities.

Best wishes, / Yvor Winters

MS: Tulsa

TO ALLEN TATE

Jan. 30, 1927 / 904 West A St. / Moscow, Idaho

Dear Tate:

I enclose some notes that I made in reading your poems. Looking over them, I seem to find in them something resembling an extraordinary amount of self-satisfaction—which I don't feel and didn't intend, so please discount it. I am not inclined as yet in regard to any of these reactions to recant—except in so far as my admiration for "Causerie II" has increased a good deal. It is a magnificent thing. My desire for the book, however, is thereby only intensified. As for the other poems, it seems to me that they are the product of very great ability and a certain amount of laziness. I suspect that you hold yourself to a less strict discipline here than in your critical essays. What that discipline could do for you seems to me to be made sufficiently evident by your criticism and by "Causerie II." I don't believe this is due to a difference in our theories. I don't really object to your method of procedure at all—I have offered objections mainly in self-defense. I simply insist that every detail of a poem—whether sensual or abstract—be absolutely firm and be made to count in a definite fashion. Some of the most haunting lines I know—in Racine, for example—are pure abstractions, pure rhetoric even. If these notes move you to curse me, go right ahead. I've done as much to others and shan't mind in the least. I am going to keep the poems for a week or two longer if you don't object.

The Apple of the Eye as a whole is a very weak—not to say bad—novel, but I think it contains here and there some noteworthy prose. W[escott] was only about 23 years old when he finished it, which is pretty young for a novelist. The chunk of his new novel in the *Dial* for March 1926 impressed me a good deal, despite the traces of his old stained-glassiness. He *has* this tendency—a tendency toward bill-board organizations of the dramatic and picturesque; and his future will depend to a certain extent on his controlling it. It is cognate with a similar tendency in his private life, that is really the root of most of his literary difficulties. He sees himself—or used to—as an heroic and dramatic figure, even in the most trivial situations; yearns for a perpetual swirl of company— preferably old and adoring ladies, whose praise he consumes avidly, and with much greater pleasure, I fear, than he would yours or mine. The old and adoring ladies are never lacking, and they make it altogether too easy for him to ignore any sort of adverse opinion—the one thing that would be most valuable to him for some time to come. And, in matters literary, he has a terrific inferiority complex that moves him to translate adverse or different literary tendencies into terms of personal hostility. So that his intellectual insulation is almost too great for his health. But he is at this writing a little short of 26 years old, and I have not seen him for about 5 years and have heard next to nothing from him in 2 or 3, so that I am really sitting more or less on the fence in regard to him till his new novel comes out. He may have reformed since I last saw him, though from all reports I fear he hasn't. But he does have intelligence of a high order, and if he could separate it from all his nervous nonsense—which he may some time do—the result would be momentous.

If you are interested in finding a really great novelist, read *The Time of Man* by Elizabeth Madox Roberts. It is a story of Kentucky white trash, and I think supremely great. She also was of the same gang as myself at the U. of Chicago some years ago, but is some ten years older than the rest of us. I have here now a part of the ms. of her new novel—to be called *Green Pastures*—that is likely to be much greater. It deals with a high social level—that of the land owners— and so gives her more psychological leeway. This one, I am sure, would be enormously to your liking even if the first weren't. It is really devastating. If there is any writer living with an Elizabethan vision, I believe that she is that writer. Personally, she is the reverse of Wescott—a nervous and physical wreck since childhood, suffering horribly, hating most people and distrusting the rest, more solitary than anyone I have ever known, putting everything she has into her work. A voice that is scarcely audible ten feet away.

I shall be interested to know what you think of the stuff I sent Rosenfeld when you see it. If you haven't seen it up to date, please don't accept any invitation to look at it for about three weeks at the very soonest. After that, I shall probably be through with it.

Best wishes, / Winters

"Ignis Fatuus": Pardon the forthcoming metaphor. Trees, I am told, are "petrified" and so made immortal by their being placed, due to some accident of nature, in such a position that water, bearing and depositing certain minerals, can trickle through them. Gradually every cell in the tree is replaced by a mineral deposit. That is how I write most of my poems, and that is how I suspect you ought to write yours. This poem is an admirable outline for something better, but is too damn soft in its details. Except for a couple: "rat-pillaged meadows," and the last two and a half lines. Midnight, for instance, does *not* sniff the tracks of dusk, and dusk leaves no tracks. The image is facile, empty. The juxtaposition of the words is too simple and obvious to awaken any of Crane's overtones. The way of breaking "I fell [/] Companionless" is admirable. The last two lines of the first stanza contain the germ of something, but I don't think you drive it home. My favorite sport when I have no poems to write is to make translations. The art of translating consists mainly, I believe, in spotting the most dynamic phrases in a poem; discovering what elements of meaning, word-order, and placing of words and syllables in regard to accents and line-ends make those phrases dynamic; and then translating those elements in some sort of equivalent form and situation and writing the poem in around them— in a style as nearly like that of prose as possible. I don't know whether you have ever attempted much of this sort of analysis or not—that is, as a poet, trying to put it into practice; but I'd almost bet you haven't.

"Obituary": I think this one does much better. In stanza 1, line 4, however, "contests" is absolutely vague, poetically meaningless. Line 4 of the next stanza seems irrelevant. Or if you want something irrelevant, its irrelevancy is not sufficiently driven home. The first three lines of this stanza are very beautiful. These, the last line, and the fifth line from the end ("Time," etc.) I like the best. The rest seems good up to a certain point, but you don't give it, somehow, the final twist of the screw. Your style is somewhere, I think, a shade loose—you fail to fill every corner of the line, the stanza, the poem, with significance. And in your use of the rhymed pentameter line, you tend to monotony and heaviness by using a line loose in itself that nevertheless fails to "overflow." I think a short poem should tend to metric precisions—either in free verse or rhymed or blank—with very precise violations when violations seem necessary. That is one thing that I like in Crane's blank verse. A loose movement requires a large scheme to contain it.

"Spring Poem": Same remarks as before. I like very much the last two lines of each of the third and fourth stanzas, and all of these stanzas up to a certain point. Also the second line of the second stanza and the "false dawn's pith of light." Not the "Vergilian gloom of hair," however, nor most of the first two stanzas. The beggars I come near to liking least of all.

"Idiot": I think it foolish to do psychological studies of Idiots unless one has been one. I judge from this poem that you haven't. Neither Blake nor anyone else have ever succeeded at it. Wherever you try to get into your hero's mind you are facile and false. The poem has three lines that I like a great deal, and that need have no connection with an idiot: the first three of stanza three. The fourth line is awful. Here, if ever, is a place for some sort of generalization, and you fall flat with an utterly empty visual image, which spoils the in itself very beautiful preceding half line ("magnolias drench the ground") and reduces the entire stanza to the level of the insignificantly visual. Until that line appears the stanza is a rising movement, just ready to culminate in some significant emotion—and then you prick the bubble. I don't demand an "explanation" of the preceding emotional values in the fourth line: any abstract—or concrete—statement, valuable in itself, that would serve as a culmination, would turn the trick. Lines react upon each other, just as chemicals do, when placed side by side. Or as colors do.

"Sonnet to Beauty": I like the line and a third about Christ, but find the rest bad. "The unhappy error we bewail" sounds like a professor's translation. I'll bet you wrote this in half an hour or less and never revised it.

"Elegy": Too long and vague. I don't like it at all.

"Causerie I": First 18 lines need cutting or intensification. You offer too many small details with the air of believing that they mean something, when it seems to me that they don't. The pheasant, grasshopper, etc. All true, but not stated with any great penetration. From there on you get under way, and I like it a good deal. I don't believe that the Latin contributes an enormous lot.

"Causerie II": Very fine, and the meter entirely to my liking. This sort of thing, to reach its greatest possibilities, should go on to cover the whole scene, form a book—like Whitman's *Song of Myself*, perhaps. If you could manage any such work in this manner it would be tremendous. The danger in this type of thing, I think, lies in this: your Elizabethan masters used this type of writing as a part of a large structure. A play or novel succeeds—if it succeeds—by piling up small ripples on a large wave (excuse me)—fine minor details on a large theme. The great lyric ("Dover Beach" or "The Seafarer") succeeds by condensing a large theme into a few very potent terms. The novelist (Joyce, for instance), or the dramatist (perhaps less necessarily, as the condensation of poetic drama is greater than that of the novel) when he attempts the lyric, too often simply gives us some more—but unattached—minor details. If you cut some of the greatest Elizabethan dramatic passages out of their context and forget their context, there are few that will stand comparison with the greatest lyric poets. For this reason. You have therefore—I think—to look out that you don't write excerpts from non-existent works. You don't reach here the high spots of "Gerontion," but you cover more ground. If you could cover the *whole* ground, of which such poems as these "Causeries" indicate the existence, you would be a very great poet. Or so I think. And you might reach some very high spots—one way or another—in the process.

MS: Princeton, Allen Tate Papers

TO ALLEN TATE

Jan. 31, 1927 / 904 West A St. / Moscow, Idaho

Dear Tate:

Your letter came just after mine left. My review of Crane is rotten—this is not modesty but fact—and I have been on the verge of withdrawing it and rewriting it for H.M., as it is about her speed. Temporary exhaustion is my excuse in this case. I have been working like hell for a couple of months and substituting coffee for sleep, and now have got to the point where the coffee doesn't suffice.

My additional metaphors may explain one another or they may move you to profanity. I agree that the poem must be about something—the more definite the better. In this respect, however, I think that "The Barnyard"—to go back to a much-booted example, which can stand a little more booting if you like—is "about" a great deal more than "A Prayer Beside a Lamp," and states it much more precisely. A poem, for me, is condensation into more compact and consequently intense terms of the facts or suspicions of one's existence. The facts or suspicions in a given poem should be related to or form a part of a more general fact or suspicion: this last is your theme. Or I think it is. The perceptions of your terminology and the bricks of my metaphor are simply the minor details. I think they all should contribute or if they can't contribute get out. If so many have to be thrown out that the main structure collapses, I think the main structure should be kept around in secrecy till the gaps can be properly filled. I believe that a poem should have just as organic a rhythm (not of the line but of the whole) as a picture: it should be a main movement involving minor variations. I don't think the subject matter of a poem has a damn thing to do with its value, so long as there *is* subject matter that has been thoroughly perceived by the poet. This perception cannot take place unless the material is an integral part of the poet's milieu and unless he is adapted to perceiving that particular kind of thing. The life of a farmer is just as definite, just as unmetaphysical, and very nearly as numbing and terrible today as it was in the time of Langland. It is still valid material *if one sees it*. My milieu is relatively unmetaphysical. I am and have been for years forced into daily and intimate contact with the most purely animal phases of humanity. In New York, you have escapes, intellectual people here and there when you want them. Here I have none. No skyscrapers, no rush—these things are all vague memories of a few years in Chicago and Los Angeles. Hills and men gripped on to them like death or digging into them—these are the immediate realities here. One meets physics but little metaphysics. These backwoods universities—in one of which I am teaching—are entirely beside the point: like a Turkish scimitar on top of the dome of a village courthouse. I think that this material is just as good as anybody's—regardless of my powers to handle it or lack of them. If you will suggest some material that is incapable of producing great poetry, I shall be glad to suggest a poem or two that you'll have a hard time explaining away.

I'm skeptical as hell of your ability to tell what you mean by "purely aesthetic." The contemporary French pursuit of purity is twaddle. [Albert] Thibaudet, I believe it is, defines in a recent *NRF* the French Dada movement as a "pure" movement, because it has produced nothing but manifestoes. An attempt to escape from subject matter is as silly as an attempt to limit it. The thing that counts is the ability to smelt it—the more matter and the more complete the smelting process the better. The aesthetics of a poem consist in *what is done* rather than in *what something is done to*. The existence of the material is a constant that one takes for granted. Note that I say that it is the *existence* and not the *material* that is constant. The material changes with times or milieux. But one can judge that it has changed for a certain poet only if he gives aesthetic evidence. One cannot say that aesthetic activity on his part is necessarily limited until he recognizes certain changes that are evident to you or in your part of the world.

This I think is one of the two main points on which I quarrel with you. The other, of course, is one of method. I don't object to yours, but I think you have some undeveloped nerve center somewhere that prevents your reacting to mine—or, if you like, Williams's. To say that "Garden Abstract" is a perfect example of imagism is like saying that Conrad Aiken is a perfect example of your ideal poet. Crane's genius lay somewhere else, and "Garden Abstract" is the shell of a poem—as H.D. is a shell of a poet. If that is the best you can say for imagism—I use the term roughly—you haven't discovered it yet. As I think your opinion of Williams proves.

I enclose a couple of poems from my new group that you might like. If you do, however, don't consider that it proves that I have deserted my guns. If you don't, you may consider it as evidence that I haven't.

And don't tell me that modern scientific developments etc. have altered the farmer's outlook on life. It would sound too much like Sir Philip Sidney descanting on rural joys.

As ever, / Winters

MS: Princeton, Allen Tate Papers

TO ALLEN TATE

Feb. 7, 1927 / 904 West A St. / Moscow, Idaho

Dear Tate,

Pardon my diverse transports of a few days ago. I am now quite calm once more. You see I am really very busy and very tired, and am trying to get together my scattered rags of knowledge in order to start work next year on a doctorate. I would rather be a bootlegger.

I revised the review and sent it to H.M.—I believe she'll take it, though she may want it shortened a little. She will be printing in a month or so a couple of my translations. If you want to tickle my vanity at little expense, you may praise them, especially the version of the Spanish ballad, "Fontefrida." I have a large bunch of translations—from the French, Spanish, Portuguese, German, and

Latin, but am afraid to publish them, on account of the awful disparity between them and my own work. They are really good ones—especially my versions of du Bellay, Mallarmé, Verlaine, and Baudelaire.

But what I write this for is to say this: if you really believe that any profundity may be wrenched from what I still consider a rather foolish argument, I think the thing will have to proceed in more concrete terms. I therefore offer you these two fields on which to battle:

1. First poem in Williams's *Spring and All.* Theme: beginning of life, contained primarily in the main symbol of the trees, and secondarily in the subordinate and introductory symbol of the weeds etc.

2. Hardy's "Darkling Thrush." Theme: withdrawal of life, contained in the combined symbols of landscape, man, and aged thrush.

These two poems for me are surpassed by almost nothing that I know and are equaled by not over thirty or forty poems in English. The condensation of each, the amazing cross-rhythms of the first, the stony weight of each phrase in the second, are, to my mind, beyond praise. They contain, for me, a crystallization of a much greater vision than that, say, of a *Paradise Lost.* Milton is a marvelous mummy—these things are alive. These poems are both almost pure imagism. If you want to attack them, and prove some one of your favorites superior to them, go ahead. Leaving, of course, Shakespeare's plays outside the question—his genius is so great, that it is scarcely fair to use him as an example of a method. "Dover Beach," I think, is an equally great example of your method —but no greater.

I think that our generation needs above all to discover the Victorians. The Elizabethan age was an age of drama, and the drama is dead—replaced by the novel, Eliot to the contrary notwithstanding. The Elizabethan lyric was a subordinate form—used by brilliant but fragmentary and capricious geniuses like Donne or by one-sided geniuses like Vaughan. A standardized method and masses of standardized material made possible a mountain of fine minor work. This sort of thing amounts almost to folk art—like our contemporary bathtubs and auto bodies, the sort of civilization poor old [Ananda K.] Coomaraswamy yearns for. All interesting and charming, but minor. The English romantics broke into individual channels, had charm and some but not enough genius. They were original, but could not master a sufficient amount of living material. The great Victorians: Browning, Arnold, Hopkins, Emily, had brains along with their genius. I believe they had more genius among them than all the French symbolists. Their outlook was more complete, was not hampered by literary prejudice. They were aware of and in some degree reacted to the thought of their day: which is made most clear and unforgettable in their *images*. Hardy belongs with them, and aside from Emily is probably the greatest of the lot. I doubt if there is any supremely great lyric poetry in English between them and "The Seafarer." There is certainly none so complete and fully-rounded.

Go ahead and do your damnedest—if you are not tired of it.

Sincerely, / Winters

MS: Princeton, Allen Tate Papers

TO ALLEN TATE

Feb. 9, 1927 / 904 West A St. / Moscow, Idaho

Dear Tate:

Thanks for your very complete and organized answer to my random ejaculations. I agree with everything you say, I think, but still you did not really touch our starting point—the possibilities of the imagistic method. If you have any energy left, I should like, as a matter of curiosity, to see you demolish or prove non-imagistic either or both of the two poems I suggested. The argument *is* proving of interest to myself, I find, but I fear my own contributions have been rather desultory.

I did not, however, say that all of your poems seemed unachieved— "Causerie II" seems quite the reverse, and very beautiful indeed. Your explanation of what I claimed to be your faults, and that of your method of procedure are both quite sound—much sounder than mine. I have no objections to your objective attitude—I am fully aware of the limitations of the subjective one, but am unfortunately bound to it. I lived for two years in the worst sink of sin in the southwest—a pair of coal camps south of Santa Fe—and had to get all my scandal from a painter who came down and stayed for only five or six months. He scoured into everything—and being a painter, had no great use for anything that he found out. You should have been there—you'd have found an external system that would have astounded you.

I have just finished rereading *Paradise Lost*. It *is* a symposium of the intelligence of the age, but I really wonder if there is as much great poetry in it, in number of actual lines, as there is in "Lycidas." Or if the poetry is as great. The first four or five books have great beauty, and the last two, but in between— where most of the symposium is to be found—I got pretty damned bored. The Victorians interest me because of their reaction to a new wave of thought—

and a greater one—but they give, mostly, crystals rather than skeletons. But again I am running in circles. . . . Anyway, they excite me more than Milton, despite his occasional Greek-tragedy grandeur. And despite my having inherited through some unknown route, his evil disposition.

For which I must apologize. It is partly due to isolation, partly to too much strong coffee, and partly to my mother and her ancestors, all of them a little queer and more than a little murderous. I started out in this world with the physique of a Dutch pirate, and at the age of 14 was studying to be a pugilist, with great success till I over-did it and messed up my heart. I then took to metaphysics and psychic experiments (my mother, strange as it may seem, *has* foretold about 20 or so deaths) till I wrecked my nerves, and then took up protozoölogy, making of my bedroom a horribly stinking laboratory, till I wrecked my lungs. This at the age of 18 or so. I have since recovered from all of these calamities, but remain irascible. My two Airedales and my furniture, I fear, get the brunt of it, but some of it—too much, I am aware—leaks into my correspondence. I shall really try to reform.

My wrath at Miss Moore has largely passed by this time, though I find her smugly cautious and slightly dishonest manner, both in rejection-notes and in her reviews, a source of sufficient irritation. I *do* think, though, that someone ought to protest against her editorial policy, and if you think sufficient people would join in, I'll gladly start it.

Don't take too seriously my rather irritated enumeration of Wescott's vices. I am pretty sure the next book—which will probably be out in a couple of months—will justify him. He and I landed in the same freshman English class at the U. of Chicago, in 1917, and our names placed us side by side. We sat there and hated each other for nine months, and at the end of the year were on opposite sides of a political dissension in the U. of C. Poetry Club and were not speaking. A little later I found myself in bed in Santa Fe with TB and he came out to recover from a nervous breakdown, and circumstances forced us to become acquainted. His openness to ridicule and my natural tendencies to ridicule have caused painful situations between us at one time or another: he has always objected to my vile manners and I to his. But despite his queer ways I am sure he has brains, and I think he will be an artist when he grows up a little more.

Wescott *has* a genius for epithet—he may amuse you if you meet him, now that he is back. He and Miss Moore, very affectionate at first, ended by being thorns in each other's sides. I received from them simultaneous letters, hers remarking that he, despite his qualities, was no St. Francis; his, sent from Olympus, letting drop something about "Marianne, that precious Leyden jar." Which is fair for a metaphor.

And now a second apology: for the length and number of my recent communications. I shall reform on that score likewise.

And thanks again for the poems, which I'll return very shortly. I *do* think you a fine poet, regardless of my quibbling.

Best wishes, / Yvor Winters

MS: Princeton, Allen Tate Papers

TO ALLEN TATE

Feb. 15, 1927 / 904 West A St. / Moscow, Idaho

Dear Tate:

Here at last are your poems, with my very sincere thanks. I'll back up a little about the "Sonnet to Beauty," but not far; "Elegy" contains beautiful lines for which I gave you no credit (the brute curiosity of an angel's stare, etc., to the end of the stanza), but in general I stay where I was. "Obituary" I like better and better—right now I think it a damn good poem. "Spring Poem" I like better and better where I liked it first, but no better elsewhere; "Idiot," the same. To "Causerie I" I withdraw my objections, except for the Latin—I don't like linguistic or rhythmic shifts on general principles—may be wrong; "Causerie II" gets better with every reading. Very few people now going, I think, have done anything to equal these two last. This work is worth a damn sight more than my own rather pinched putterings and I should have been more respectful while booting it around.

I saw your article in the *New Republic* and must credit you with one more first class essay. I agree with you most of the way, but still hold to the notes I sent you the other night before having seen the essay: as regards two or three reservations which you will probably find foolish. The notes, of course, are intended purely and simply as a contribution to our private controversy, and they don't touch the question of imagism, which I think—unlike yourself—is quite aside from the question discussed in the notes or your essay.

As to Miss Moore: don't let her rejection of the review bother you for the review was rotten—I tried to play her own game and was too tired to do it well. I have revised it with considerable advantage, though it is still superficial—but there isn't space or a chance for anything else in *Poetry,* and it may save the book from some fool who won't like it. My irritation at Miss Moore is more profound and far-reaching. When Burke was stealing Thayer's ideas, he must have cleaned him out.

I am glad you are on the side of the True Religion as regards Brooks. He gives me the colic, and I said so in my rather half-baked French masterpiece that may some time find a publisher. I didn't dare mention it when you spoke of Cowley's article on this subject, as my contempt for the psychological critics is so sulfurous that—had you survived it—you would have come all the way to Idaho to kill me. That is, if you had been one. I feel the same way also about certain popularizers of science: it is no job for a full-grown man.

Last night I wrote a cosmological poem for your especial benefit. If it survives a few weeks' wear I'll send you a copy.

Sincerely, / Winters

P.S. Feb. 19. Having composed the above, I decided that I wanted to keep a copy of "Causerie II" (which I will give up if or whenever you desire) but was prevented from making one by various untoward matters. The thing by this time exerts a very great fascination over me. Then arrives your letter of the 14th, which forces me into a long postscript.

I don't know what you mean precisely by metaphysical. I don't like the etymology of the word, considering the present state of physics: the only cosmology which would interest me would be an equation or series of equations coming from a [Robert] Millikan. The end toward which physics seems to be unquestionably directed, provides already, it seems to me, the basis for any one of several very definite attitudes toward the universe. Mechanistic theories don't seem to me poetically numbing: quite the contrary. Hence my lack of concern over this problem, and my greater concern over method and form. I have never attempted to concern myself with my own cosmological suspicions till the last year or so, and up to date have done next to nothing with them, but give me five years more, and I'll show you something.

I have searched out a number of your articles in the *New Republic* and the *Nation,* and shall go after more presently. You are by all odds the most competent critic on the scene that I know (I haven't read [I. A.] Richards, but shall at once), and your critical style is nothing short of a miracle of condensation and precision.

But:

1. Your remark about the [John] Webster line is nonsense. Science will never *change* the fundamental phenomena of existence as we experience them emo-

tionally and sensually, though it is likely to go on redefining them forever. The individual always will die: he is not composed of the brute matter that is reorganized, but of a certain relationship that that matter temporarily assumes. The relationship dies. The only doctrine that could conceivably invalidate the Webster line was that universally current when it was written: the belief in the immortality of the soul.

2. You run the risk of wanting or seeming to want poetry to infringe on the rights of the text book: one has to keep desperately in mind that the material of poetry is contemporary human emotion. Your pseudo-statements are nothing but metaphors, syntheses, and will be legitimate to the end of time so long as they possess symbolic density.

3. My first real intellectual training was received in the State Microscopical Society of Illinois, of which I am still technically a member. "Metaphysics" especially right now means too damned often a half-absorbed pseudo-scientific jargon tied, untied, retied, and Q.E.D.ed. A few years ago it was psychoanalysis and now it is physics in the hands of mystics (i.e., people too lazy to work in a laboratory). I answer the Why quite simply, as did my spoiled little Mexican friends of some years back: *Porque me gusta. Je fus mystique et ne le suis plus.* Waldo Frank writes pages of mystical nonsense justifying Spain—a country purely and simply dead and uninteresting because of its vices of intellectual laziness, self-satisfaction, and hollow pomposity. It always was third-rate and always will be. A mystic makes the obvious and cheap mysterious.

4. And last—and at last—if you agree, to use your own words, with all I say about the excellence of the Hardy poem, you automatically surrender on the question of imagism, as I said a good deal.

I am not very erudite linguistically: I know French, and French literature from its beginnings, pretty well, Spanish, and its literature to the end of the 17th century fairly well, and, thanks to a couple of devilishly stiff courses in Romance philology can read Italian, Portuguese, and what not with reasonable ease, though I haven't read much of them. My Latin and German are only so-so. I imagine that your own erudition is considerably greater than my own: it is surely better organized. I have no Greek, but mean to acquire it. I'll send you a few translations some time. Should like to see yours.

Your remarks regarding [Gorham B.] Munson agree with my own conclusions. I should be interested, however, in anything you might add on the subject —or any other.

I suspect that by this time we know fairly well where we stand in relation to each other, and that if the matter were sifted down to essentials we should be in agreement most of the time. I should be interested, however, to have you name a few major poets. Here are some of mine (aside from those recently named): Shakespeare, Marlowe, Milton, Molière, Racine, Baudelaire, Corbière, Rimbaud, Valéry. My Victorians would rank among the highest of these.

I gather that the word "lyric" in your vocabulary is a form of insult. In my own it is very general, and applies to you, Crane, or "Religio Laici." The advantage of the purely personal (lyric?) God of Hopkins over the epic God (latitude, longitude, and distance from the moon known and noted) of Dante or Milton, is that he is easily and immediately translatable into any philosophical terms that the reader pleases.

P.P.S. Can you still draw a line of distinction between my objections to "abstractions" (your word is unjust) & Miss Moore's?

P.P.P.S. I trust you are enough of a scientist to be aware of the exceedingly erudite & subtle & cosmological image of the crystals in my poem "The Deep."

MS: Princeton, Allen Tate Papers

TO HARRIET MONROE

March 15, 1927 / 904 West A St. / Moscow, Idaho

Dear Miss Monroe:

If it is not too late I wonder if you would correct a couple of small slips in my review of Crane: 3rd paragraph, 3rd line read "and occasionally to attempt"; same paragraph, last sentence, read "His faults, however, are the least interesting phase of his work"—i.e., *phase* should be singular.

Thanks for your recent checks, and for your generosity in printing the praises of poets you don't like.

In this latter connection (it may be in this latter connection, I mean—I don't know) Allen Tate mentions in a recent letter that he has sent you a poem called, in my ms. copy of it, "Causerie II," which I think a very beautiful thing. In case you find it obscure, may I offer this explanation of it, which should not be publicly quoted, nor yet quoted to Tate, as it may be all wrong. I do know, however, in a general way, what Tate is driving at, and though I disagree with some of his favorite critical theories, I think him one of the finest poets now writing—agreeing with Mr. Ford. But to the poem.

Tate's position is roughly and crudely this: The Cosmos, up to the modern scientific movement, was explained in qualitative terms, which provided a logical order of thought available to poets and artists in general. The scientific movement demolished this Cosmology, substituting a quantitative Cosmology, composed of abstractions rather than things. Tate believes this metaphysically unsound (as do I—I once argued with you briefly about this years ago), but sees no alternative system unless it be something employing art as a point of departure (see [Ramon] Fernandez in the March *Dial*), art being the only material available of an absolute qualitative value. That is, it is either this or a return to primitivism (imagism) and a concentration on isolated facts of experience rather than upon experience schematically organized, which he believes leads to secondary work. I gather that I, in this scheme, am a modern primitive (!), and it is along in here somewhere that his (and Crane's) aesthetic and mine begin to part ways, but that is beside the point. It is obvious at any rate that as things stand a poet of the Dantesque or Miltonic variety is out of the question: this doesn't worry me at all, but it worries Tate a great deal, which is, after all, his own business. Thus, his personal and poetic problem, as he sees it, is a search for a scheme—and a theme (see his introduction to Crane)—and a search for a means of unifying his universe and intellectual life: i.e., of substituting for the quantitative Cosmos of science a qualitative Cosmos that will not exclude qualitative perception (art) and which qualitative perception will not exclude. This is roughly also the position of Whitehead (if you want a scientist), of Fernandez and the more advanced French thinkers, and of Richards.

Now as to the poem (again).

1. It opens ("What are the springs of sleep," etc.) with a lament for the "complete" heroes of the past.

2. ("I've done no rape," etc.) The anguish of the incomplete individual, with a "vision" but no "theme" (see introduction to Crane).

3. ("Where is your house") The surroundings of the individual already postulated, that is, the degenerate qualitative aspects of a quantitative culture.

4. ("For miracles are faint"). Collapse of the old myths that sustained the "heroes." Backwoods visionaries, clinging to a dead doctrine.

5. ("Year after year"). The old myths bore us up, have now vanished in a "precipitate flood of silence," and left us a "drenched wreck off an imponderable shore." Man in himself is not mysterious, but rather his desire for the absolute, "the rigid heavings of my tribal air."

6. Return to "the essential wreckage" of the abstract or qualitative age, and the invocation of the "heroes."

Whether you agree with Tate's notions or not, the poem seems to me a thing of amazing beauty, and aside from Crane, I don't think any of the younger writers have really equaled it. It has, like MacLeish, certain superficial resemblances to Eliot, or rather to his masters, but it has more range and more organization and more actual *mind* at work in it than Eliot was ever guilty of. With this outline to clarify its general drift, take it through phrase by phrase and see if you don't agree with me as to its beauty. I don't see how you can fail to. It seems to me—and to Tate—his best work. You have Ford's opinion of Tate in general. Why not risk it, even though you may be a little suspicious? It is, in my own opinion, one of the small number of contemporary poems that no serious magazine can afford not to have printed. . . .

Best wishes, / Yvor Winters

MS: Chicago

TO ALLEN TATE

March 19, 1927 / 904 West A St. / Moscow, Idaho

Dear Tate:

Here goes for a final survey of our differences.

1. You say, "Can you see, smell, taste, or feel force?" The first three, no; but did you ever meditate on the electric chair? But this is a side issue, and you probably can insert some metaphysical wedge between Force and the electric shock. Only it doesn't seem to me worth the trouble.

2. My rather nebulous deification of Force does not displace individual phenomena for me. I can be aware of circulating blood and functioning entrails at the same time that I am aware of the presence of a human being as such. This is because I do not believe in the possibility or desirability of any absolute system of metaphysics or ethics beyond the beauty of art and the desirability of being an artist, whereas you are a misplaced theologian. Damn me for an opportunist. But get thee to a nunnery.

3. You refuse or neglect to touch what is for me the final proof of the whole situation: the relation or lack of relation between the Cosmologies of Chaucer and Dryden and "The Miller's Tale" or "MacFlecknoe." Also there is *The Bridge*, which, in the seven or eight sections that Crane has sent me, demolishes you. There *is* in it an element of decadence, a tendency to worn phrases and movements here and there of which I can't wholly approve, but they are twigs in a spring torrent. The thing *is* on a grand scale (there is nothing greater in English poetry than the lizard passage and certain others in the same section), and

on the whole is new, tremendous. As far as I can visualize the complete poem from what I have here, I can't see any earthly reason why it shouldn't be just as great as Marlowe.

4. You find in *The Time of Man* a lack of "universality." I found in it so much that it paralyzed me for weeks after reading it. Granting that I am right, you did one of two things: you explained away your blindness by a convenient theory, or, what is more likely, you blinded yourself with an a priori metaphysical concept into which you could not fit the book. If my purely aesthetic reaction was accurate, it merely proves the inadequacy of your concept. If yours was accurate, it doesn't of necessity prove the contrary. In this connection, it seems to me that your attitude toward art is perilously close to the scientist's attitude toward nature, according to your own definition of his attitude: you are setting up abstractions by which to measure absolute phenomena, that, in any final analysis, are not classifiable. This, as you suggest, is all right so long as one doesn't take the abstractions too seriously. But I think you do. Some day somebody is going to come along too ignorant to know that it is impossible to be a great poet any more, and he'll surprise you awfully. Your prediction that this is impossible is the rashest thing I have ever seen on paper. Personally, I think the prediction already obsolete, but this is due simply to a difference in degree of admiration for certain specific writers. I should not be so bold as to say that my reactions are more exact than yours—except hypothetically.

5. I continue to believe that "universality" is nothing but intensity of vision. Blake's grain of sand. If you look at it hard enough, and are the right person, the grain becomes incandescent, all you have ever known or felt focuses in it. That is a great poem, whatever its length. It may or may not be metaphysical or have anything to do with metaphysics. See Emily D.'s "The last night that she lived," or "The long sight of a frog." Also Hardy's "In Time of 'The Breaking of Nations.'"

6. Your explanation of my distrust of Milton is ingenious but unjust. The real reason for my distrust of Milton is quite simple: in all of *Paradise Lost,* I found, in my recent perusal, exactly two lines and a half that excited me in any way comparable to the exaltation that I feel in reading any one of twenty-five or more lyrics by Hardy or Emily. And those lines, blessed Heaven, were in the 11th book. . . . I do not deny the presence of a lot of other admirable poetry in *Paradise Lost.*

7. If I wanted to answer you in a similar fashion, I could accuse you of setting up a metaphysical barricade as a defense reaction: against your own inability to see your way through to a poem—by yourself—of the sort that

you most admire. And here my argument comes to its crux. You have argued yourself—poetically—into a corner, to wit: you have your choice of what you refer to vaguely as a "primitive" position (my position—the grain of sand), which you don't think worth the trouble; of an openly decadent adoption of an obsolete metaphysic, of which, on the whole, you are probably too intelligent to be capable; or of writing poems about the impossibility of writing great poetry, which, in a way, you have done. This last is likewise openly decadent, as it involves of necessity a more or less borrowed style. It may be beautiful—in your case I think you have achieved a good deal of beauty with it—but your recently-predicted Elizabethan revival can be nothing but abortive, because it is not the outgrowth of any natural tradition. The pins have been knocked out from under our tradition, social and metaphysical. The old methods of metric and phrase grew out of the old systems. The first signs of something new are to be found among the Symbolists and the better Victorians. I have no fear of the primitive point of view, *poetically*, because I agree with Blake—and myself. I shall continue to stand by Williams and the Navajos, admire the modern Elizabethans—and demur. My party at least starts out with a clean house, and in five or ten or fifteen years we may be able to do something besides short lyrics: if we don't it doesn't really matter, because short lyrics are just as good as anything else if they are good enough. Crane, as an Elizabethan, is a delusion: the Elizabethanness vanishes as soon as you focus on it. I have not read Miss Gottschalk [Laura Riding] except in quotations, but am moved to suspect that her failure to organize her material successfully is due primarily to its not being her material, but that of Donne and Webster, she groping toward it across two and a half centuries, like a medium toward a stammering ghost. It is possible to make poems as clean and hard and as free of metaphysics as an arrowhead . . . as the Indian made the arrowhead . . . because one knows one's medium, one's intentions, and one's material, and because one is convinced that the result is necessary to life.

8. And last. It is futile to go one with this. My own critical theories culminate in imagism (which you confuse with something quite different, Parnassianism) as the point of highest poetic intensity, because it is the only poetic form that unites in a small space all of the possibilities of the poetic medium. If you saw my complete notes, you might not awfully object to most of them. But where we differ I am afraid there is no earthly help for it. *Je suis comme l'hippopotame.* I would apologize for this if I didn't think you were, too.

I am forwarding your letter and a carbon of mine to [John Crowe] Ransom[1] at your suggestion. Thanks for the introduction—and the compliments.

My book, so far as I know, is not even on the press, but I have written for information.

Best wishes, / Yvor Winters

MS: *Princeton, Allen Tate Papers*

[1]John Crowe Ransom (1888–1974): American poet, critic, and educator. He originated the term "New Criticism" with his book of the same title (1941).

TO HARRIET MONROE

June 28, 1927 / 343 Delgado St. / Santa Fe, N.M.

Dear Miss Monroe:

I have meant for some weeks to answer your note in regard to Tate's poem, but examinations, packing etc. have prevented. I am sorry my explanation added to your suspicions as to the validity of the poem: to be horribly honest, I didn't think the poem needed an explanation nearly as much as you did. You should have taken into consideration that I, who do not know Tate and have exchanged only a few letters with him, was able to explain it. However, you now have the poem in the third number of *transition,* and can meditate upon it at your leisure. I hope that you will. It is not only an exceedingly distinguished piece of writing but is one of the two or three most important landmarks so far created, of a new philosophical and literary movement that involves most of the best minds of Europe and this country at the moment, and that is very likely to sweep most of your benighted middle-westerners and the hysterico-sentimental ethical attitudes that they and prohibition have created into the drainage canal within about ten years time or perhaps less.

I write you thus out of pure affection: you are about three movements behind the times, and the present movement is really important. You ought to catch up. Your refusal to take risks is ridiculous. As your magazine now stands nothing could hurt it, and variety would at least be a change, and might, even without your realizing it, result in something more.

As a gage of my disinterested altruism, I might add that I myself have sworn to contribute no more verse to *Poetry* until you shall have written me requesting a group of twenty-five translations by way of general atonement. This would have nothing to do with any new movement, but would act as a sort of disinfectant, and improve the paper. I don't expect you to do it, however, so don't be annoyed.

I shall be in Santa Fe all summer, and next year shall go to Stanford to work on a doctorate. I am contemplating a thesis (subject already approved by that home of classicism and western culture) which will establish beyond all cavil the dynasty of Emerson, Dickinson, Williams and Crane, and simply eliminate yourself unless you get into line quick. Remember Ford's editorial on nasty poets. It pleases me to think that I may have helped to suggest your suggesting the subject. If so, I have done my bit for culture.

Janet is much better and will go to California with me.

Best wishes from both of us, /
Yvor Winters

MS: Chicago

TO HARRIET MOODY

Sept. 30, 1927 / RFD1, Box 267A / Palo Alto, Calif.

Dear Mrs. Moody:

Having had such good fortune once before when I presumed to ask you to help out a painter, I have decided to try once again. This time the painter is a Hopi Indian, Otis Polelonema, & I enclose photographs of three of his pictures, a snake dance, & two single figures. I will send you more in a few days.

Polelonema seems to me the greatest of the southwestern Indians who are painting, & very great indeed. He is one of the youngest, &, of the four or five best, perhaps the least known, though he is not without reputation. I sent the two single figures enclosed to *transition,* in Paris, & they accepted by cable. They should be published within a month or two, which will help a little.

P. writes me that he has been having trouble with his eyes, needs a doctor, is not paid enough by the dealer in Santa Fe, & needs more money, which he can get only by a better market. His people suspect him of betraying religious secrets in his pictures & try to make him stop painting, but so far without success. Most of the other Indian painters have met this difficulty by moving to Santa Fe, & their work suffers—they take to booze & commerce. This P. will not do. He stays at home & works under difficulties. I think he is the real article. I have arranged exhibitions here, am pretty sure I can fix one in San Francisco, possibly in L.A. & New York. Don't know. Could you show a few of his things, do you suppose, or could you suggest anyone who might? I should be tremendously grateful for any help or suggestions you might give.

Did you know that Vernon Hunter has been seriously ill for months? A whole series of operations for every conceivable reason. His address is Texico, New Mexico.

Janet at last seems to be getting well rather rapidly.

Best wishes to you, /
Arthur Yvor Winters

MS: Chicago

Harriet Moody (1857–1932): widow of the poet William Vaughan Moody, and a figure of some prominence in the art and literary circles in Chicago.

TO ALLEN TATE

Box 267A, RFD1 / Palo Alto, California / Feb. 18, 1928

Dear Tate:

Just got a copy of *Fugitives*,[1] probably through your intervention, for which I thank you. Have written H.M. that I mean to review it for her, though you may not thank me for the review. It is great to have your poems together, but I confess that most of the other contents strike me as a bit weak. I do not like the first two of your group, nor the "Idiot" piece, though you seem to have improved lines here and there. "Mr. Pope" and "Death of Little Boys" are among the finest things that have happened. Also "Obituary," though some of its lines seem to me still to travel a bit light. If you live long enough to write fifteen or twenty pieces as good, you will rank very high in this century. "Causerie II" I still like a good deal, though the shorter pieces get farther and farther ahead of it in my affections. The "Confederate Ode" is curious. It is composed of some of your very finest writing with a few lines that suggest fearfully the pre-Websterian Eliot (the two "he knows it all" lines, for instance); and, at the end, the lines about the grave are pure Webster (not as in Eliot). The difficulty with this is that you are too damn clumsy to do good pastiche, and the things stick out a mile. I wish to God Eliot had never been born. Why, in God's name, don't the lot of you imitate Jonson or Marlowe or somebody first rate, instead of Webster? And why don't your friends *really* imitate Webster if they must, instead of giving Eliot's broken down version of him? It is really tragic. You yourself have vastly more integrity and dignity of spirit than Eliot—your best poems are tragic rather than whimpering. As a nihilist (so far as his poems represent any personal contribution at all, they represent a nihilistic refusal to live), tragedy, the facing of which alone can lend life dignity, becomes impossible to Eliot—as he admits when he tells how the world will end. Unless one will accept the ultimate tragedy, one can do either what Crane is doing—try to escape through some incredible mysticism, or cringe with Eliot. You are a better man than Eliot and you damn well deserve to be kicked for letting him impose on you. What this generation needs is to be fished by somebody's boathook out of the marsh of Eliot and steeped in the good bitter stoicism of Hardy and Emily Dickinson. They are dynamic stoics, who accept tragedy, and grow to the last gasp. So do you, when you are writing the way God meant you to write.

I am aware of the beauty of Eliot's criticism. In the Dryden booklet, he gave the finest definition that has ever been given of the genius of the metaphysical poets. But that doesn't prove that their way of being great is the only way, or that Emily, though unlike them in superficial tricks of style, does not have fundamentally the same type of genius on a larger scale. Wait till I get my dissertation finished up a year and a half hence.

Now then, as to the rest. So far as I have made out up to the present writing, the only other writers in the book who suggest any very valuable possibilities are Ransom and Laura Riding. And, as a matter of fact, they both seem to me so slight, so involved in elaborate and clumsy tricks and so devoid of any genuine thought, feeling, or intention, that I can't take them very seriously. L.R. gives herself away entirely in her book on Modernist Poetry (with Graves) —uninformed, made to sell, uncritical, and absolutely stupid and pretentious from beginning to end.

At your suggestion a year or so ago I wrote Ransom, and he apparently scorned to answer my rather hit-or-miss communication. I mention this because you may know of it and think that I was sufficiently irritated thereby to let it color my view of his poems. I wasn't. Though I think it rather foolish to be so damned elegant—especially when one's poetic style isn't.

If, however, this estimate of the book strikes you as unjust, please protest at once, and you may convert me before I finish the review. Though I doubt it.

Best wishes, / Winters

MS: Princeton, Allen Tate Papers

[1]*Fugitives: An Anthology of Verse,* edited by Donald Davidson (New York: Harcourt, Brace, 1928) includes poems by Tate; the eleven poets represented in the anthology had published their work in the journal *The Fugitive* (1922–25) in Nashville, Tennessee.

Box 267A, RFD1 / Palo Alto, California / April 21, 1928

Dear Mr. Pound:

I memorized your address, or tried to, while looking at a letter you had written to a dazed little French professor here anent an article on Amy L[owell], a flea-picking affair. If this letter doesn't reach you, it means I got something wrong.

I resent your manners in outbursts of that sort like hell. Because I can't indulge in similar outbursts, for fear of losing my livelihood, when God almighty gave me a worse temper than yours. I believe yours is mainly rhetoric. But God be with you. I taught Racine and Molière for two years at the University of Idaho.

I enclose some poems for your magazine. I read Old and modern French, Spanish, Italian, Portuguese, & Provençal; modern German, Old English, and Latin, though there are no swipes in these poems to prove it.

When [Morley] Callaghan[1] gets around to giving me more definite information concerning your whereabouts, I shall probably send you a copy of my recent book. I have sent you two books up to date. The first you did not acknowledge, of the second you wrote me a postcard. Unless you write me a letter in acknowledgement of this—and I don't care a damn fundamentally whether you like it or not—it will be the last.

Faithfully, / Yvor Winters

P.S. I note that a young Guggenheim recipient from the U. of Wash. (Seattle) is being sent over to study you. Congratulations.

MS: Yale

[1]Morley Callaghan (1903–1990): Canadian fiction writer and man of letters. YW admired some of Callaghan's early work, especially the short stories. He corresponded for a time with Callaghan and received a brief mention in *That Summer in Paris* (1963), Callaghan's memoir of his days in Paris in 1929 with his friends Hemingway and Fitzgerald.

TO JOHN CROWE RANSOM

RFD1, Box 267A / Palo Alto, Calif. / May 14, 1928

Dear Mr. Ransom:

Tate sends me your letter with his to me, which he seems to be sending to you. The easiest way out of this seems to be to send a carbon of a letter to you to Tate, *tout en gardant* one for myself in case you misquote me. This is a bit complicated, but let's go forward.

Both you and Tate show some irritation at my having published such a review in *Poetry*. This, of course, is quite ridiculous. *Poetry* is very bad, but so is every other magazine now running. I fail to see that the *Dial*, for instance, is much better. As to the audience it reaches, I can only point out to you that it seems to have reached yourselves, as well as Crane. That is pretty good considering the present state of civilization. I confess I don't see much grounds for choice among contemporary "audiences." As to its being out of scale, that is obvious. But barring Tate, yourself, and possibly Warren, I was able to find nothing in it awfully dissimilar from the stuff by the young ladies hanging out their babies' clothes, etc. I confess that I touched a good deal more territory than I covered, but an anthology is a mean thing to review unless one simply chooses to be polite and say nothing—like your other reviewers. I am covering the territory a bit more in my doctoral dissertation here at Stanford, which will be finished up some time inside the next year and a half. I can't cover it in a letter.

You may know Hardy better than I, but if so you know him very well, and I am glad someone does. I am not awfully impressed by his capitalized abstractions—you accuse me, it seems to me, of something a bit childish. For the sake of at least a degree of clarity, I cite the following titles, things that seem to me especially great: "Song of Hope" (118), "A Broken Appointment" (124), "A Spot" (127), "The Darkling Thrush" (137), "In Tenebris I" (153), "I Have Lived with Shades" (169), "Shut out that Moon" (201), "I Say I'll Seek Her" (207), "My Spirit Will Not Haunt the Mound" (299), "The Voice" (325), "The Musical Box" (453), "The Wind's Prophesy" (464), "During Wind and Rain" (465), "Who's in the Next Room" (473), "The Shadow on the Stone" (498), "In Time of 'The Breaking of Nations'" (511), "Afterwards" (521).

The question of meter is again too complicated for this letter, but if you are interested, I will send you some specimens of scansion some time in the next year or so. Specimens of "free" verse, that is.[1] My own, Williams's, Miss Moore's, perhaps Pound's. I believe that, allowing for irregularities (as in much blank verse) most of the good free verse—and there is quite a bit of it—is based on a line of primary and secondary stresses, the first being normally of a fixed number and the second and unstressed syllables varying. Sometimes the line is deformed for various reasons, but can usually be straightened out if one has a counting-complex. At any rate I will fight for what pleases me, not for what can be measured by a footrule, and I believe that the above-named poets write verse whether it can be measured or not. I can, incidentally, scan most of my own verse of the last five years on this principle, having done it.

You and Tate seem to share with most of the contributors to the philological journals the belief that Amy L. really had something to do with Imagism. I am astounded to have to point out this error to anyone having played a part in the contemporary poetic field. She merely grabbed the name and stuck it on the billboards over her own pictures. As to the other imagists, I believe that H.D. did a couple of excellent things as far as they go, and Pound quite a few. Some of the *Cantos* strike me as at least better than Swinburne. They are not supreme poetry, but they are damn good writing and will stick around a while. It would do you good to read Williams, Tate to the contrary notwithstanding. I will take him up in my dissertation. There is no use arguing about him here. It is a fact, however, that very few people are ever clearheaded enough or unprejudiced enough to recognize a profoundly great and original man. Cf. the history of the reputations of Blake and Rimbaud. You confess that you know nothing even yet of Hopkins and Corbière, who died in the eighties. I think that both you and Tate are blunt in your perceptions. If Tate wants to scuttle my ship, I shall watch him in all friendliness, but so far he hasn't seen the ship—which will be ready in a year and a half. I am, I believe, the only person living who has taken the trouble to analyze and synthesize the formal innovations of the last century or so, relating them to formal methods of the past and to philosophical movements. This is infinitely illuminating on a multitude of points that neither you nor Tate nor any living editor has yet suspected.

As to the meters of Milton and Shakespeare I think each one a masterly instrument for its particular purpose. Shakespeare's purpose was infinitely more complicated, subtle, and profound, and his meter follows his purpose as Milton's could not have done. Shakespeare's meter, however, would not have been the ideal instrument for a long narrative. Any one of the eight or ten great tragedies towers above Milton into another universe. And above all else. Racine, perhaps, gets closest.

As to the meters of the anthology, they are correct enough, mechanically, I guess—I didn't count them—but they simply have no life. The reason being, of course, that the perceptions and central impulses (if they exist) have none.

All of this leaves us where we began and worse. If you are really concerned about my fallacies, I should be glad to send you my book if it ever gets published or the ms. when finished or in progress. It is the only possible way to clarify my position, which by now is hopelessly complex. I shall begin knocking the thing into shape around Christmas. I value your intelligence, as I do Tate's, and some of your poems up to a certain point. Tate's a bit more—one or two, quite a bit more. I suspect both of you, as I have said, of being insensitive as critics and of building up ramifications of a more or less logical nature to support yourselves. Like the little clam. Tate's mainly metaphysical, yours (to judge from this letter) mainly documentary. I don't deny the value of either discipline; on the contrary I endeavor to acquire what little I can of both. But there are many great masters of both who have never discovered poetry. This, of course, approaches insult, but is not so meant. Every man, you will, I am sure, admit—especially every man who writes poetry—has a right to be an egoist.

This is about as far as I can go short of the dissertation, so I close with my best wishes. I should be very glad to hear from you should you care to write. Shall be here for a year and a half at least.

Best wishes, / Yvor Winters

MS: Princeton, Allen Tate Papers

[1]The interested reader should consult "The Influence of Meter on Poetic Convention," *Primitivism and Decadence* (New York: Arrow Editions, 1937). The third section is titled "The Scansion of Free Verse."

TO EZRA POUND

June 12, 1928 / RFD1, Box 267A / Palo Alto, Calif.

Dear Mr. Pound:

Thanks for your notes. After my usual brief consideration of such matters, I decided to write you a letter. But at the outset, I want to say that I still like you, that your notes did not in any manner irritate me, and that I am feeling fine. I am in the midst of a vacation, have at last got some sleep, and have the best bunch of puppies on hand that I have ever bred. I inform you of all this because I mean to curse you out. As you have spent all your life giving unsolicited advice to the young, I am sure you won't mind if the tables are turned. Your advice was very useful to me when I was about 17 or 18, and now I have got to the point where I might be useful to you. Well, allons! Vamos!

In the first place, nobody said you were a journalist but myself and I qualified it with an adjective. It is the horrible truth, so far as your prose and editing goes. Invariably and inescapably. It is something in your soul. My dear man, Homer, poor old Homer, blind as he was, doubtless saw just as much imbecility in the world as you and I, but, not being troubled by any Romantic, Celtic, or Dowsonish notions of a Golden Age, and having something really serious on his mind, he didn't pay much attention to it all. It is all right to "revolt" at 18, or, if one come from Idaho, at 25, but at 45! Or whatever the horrible number is—fill it in correctly. There is something quaint about your perpetual capering, it is scented with lavender and mothballs. You are like the village spinster, who, in spite of everything, is still hoping for a husband.

You labor under at least one awful delusion in regard to your native land: i.e., that the young poets all regard you still as a combination of cher maître and Grand Turk. We are all of us indebted to you in just about the fashion Eliot suggested. We are all (I think) glad you got the Dial prize, which you deserved. We all hope that the Guggenheim youth will run hell out of you and get what he wants—it is so thoroughly amusing to contemplate. We all (I think) admire you, line by line at least, as a stylist—we are not plain fools. But your general mentality strikes most of us as awfully fuzzy. In general, the scholarship of the younger men is much better than that of your middlewestern contemporaries and rather better than your own. The illiterate of my generation have trailed after you to Europe. Your poetic gift is a sort of cross between Swinburne and Gautier—the former's ear, the latter's eye (without his wit), and just about enough brains to make some interesting use of those secondary gifts.

It is for these reasons and perhaps for others—I don't remember—that I assured you I didn't care enormously whether you liked my work or not. As you don't like it, and my attitude toward you is what I have suggested, we ought to be able to exchange these few compliments in perfect friendliness. I would be willing to bet fifty bucks, however, that fifty years hence my name will be in better repute than yours. Not, however and once again, that I care enormously or am likely to at that time. Joyce is fabled to have told Yeats at some time or other that it was a pity the latter was born too early to be influenced by him. I feel almost the same way about you. Not that I think myself a Joyce, exactly, but I could have done you more good than Joyce. Things being irretrievably as they are, however, I wish you the best of luck. For the love of mud don't bother to answer this—we'll never get anywhere, and I can't take your dialectic any more seriously than you can take mine.

Sincerely, / Winters

P.S. I have always wanted to thank you for tooting when you did for [Henri] Gaudier-Brzeska.[1] Without you, I should not have known him, and I think him one of the three or four colossi of this century. And without you, I should probably have gone for a long time without Corbière.

P.P.S. One more piece of advice. You ought, in all decency, to abandon your synthetic epistolary dialect or use a typewriter. If I was insulted in any of your recent communications, consider yourself insulted in return—you would have been had I been able to read it. But I don't quite think I was, so don't want to take any definite steps in the matter.

MS: Yale

[1]Henri Gaudier-Brzeska (1891–1915): French sculptor. Henri Gaudier (who added the last name of his partner, Sophie Brzeska) was a founding member of the London Group and an exponent of Vorticism. During World War I he enlisted in the French Army and was killed at Neuville St. Vaast.

TO HARRIET MONROE

July 31, 1928 / RFD1, Palo Alto / California

Dear Miss Monroe:

Hart Crane sends me your note regarding his "Moment Fugue." Not begging help, but in disgust. Out of admiration for Crane, however, and pure affection for yourself, I am volunteering to parse the thing for you. Please return this copy of the poem to me whether you use it or not—it is my own copy and I want it. Envelope enclosed. I suspect Crane needs the money and you certainly need a good poem. I have been considered competent to teach freshman composition at this august institution, which, I would bet a dollar none of your staff could do, so perhaps you will feel some confidence in my ability to dissect a sentence even though you don't always follow me. Here goes:

First stanza. Subject: the syphilitic (adj. used as noun)

selling—pres. part. mod. subj.

violets and daisies—objects of pres. part. *selling*

calmly—adverb mod. pres. part. *selling*

by the subway newsstand—adverbial prep. phrase mod. pres. part. *selling*

Verb: knows

how—subord. conjunction introducing adverbial clause.

hyacinths—object of *offers*

2nd St.   This April morning—subject of *offers* and of adverbial clause introd. by *how* hurriedly—adv. mod. *offers*

In bunches sorted freshly—adv. phrase mod. *offers*

2nd main verb (with subject *syph.*)

bestows

on every purchaser—adv. phrase mod. 2nd main verb.

(of heaven perhaps)—adj. phrase mod. *purchaser,* or more precisely an objective genitive, though to understand this fine point you are supposed to know Latin (call in Prof. Hale).

3rd stanza Object of 2nd main verb: His eyes. This object is a pivot word, functioning also as the subject of the next verb, *fall.*

like crutches hurtled against glass—adj. phrase mod. *eyes,* or adv. phrase mod. *fall.* Take your choice, though strictly speaking the former is correct.

mute and sudden—adj. mod. *eyes.*

(dealing change for lilies)—part. phrase mod. *eyes,* or, if the metaphor is too much for you, let it mod. *syph.* in 1st line.

last line—adv. phrase mod. *fall*—contains an adj. clause, perhaps evident.

The poem, so far as I can see, offers two syntactic difficulties that would not trouble you had you not decided early in your editorial career that all the poetry of the past was ipso facto affected and ridiculous and hence not to be read. There is one poetic inversion, the prose order of which would be: "How this April morning offers hyacinths" etc. See any of the English classics for precedent. Or simply see any of the English classics for a few elementary notions of style in general. There is also one pivot word, *eyes.* This is not common in English but has been sanctioned by some 3 or 4 centuries or perhaps more of Japanese classical tradition, not to mention some 3 or 4 years of Mr. Crane, Dr. Williams, and myself. This ought to make it fairly respectable.

Might I suggest on my own hook that if you do not want your contributors to send you work already published abroad, a practice that is sanctioned by every other magazine I know, you ought to publish a statement to that effect on your cover every month instead of talking like a juvenile court judge or an irritated auntie to one of the three or four major poets of our century.

Yours for the advancement of reason,

as ever, / Yvor Winters

MS: Chicago

August 20, 1928 / RFD1 / Palo Alto, Calif.

Dear Tate:

Many thanks for the book [*Mr. Pope and Other Poems*]. It came this afternoon, and I have spent most of the time since consulting lawyers about ways and means to get an ex-landlady down, so have not yet read all of it, nor has my mind been in the most receptive possible mood. I'll read it all carefully in the next few days and write a review of it, which I'll try to publish somewhere, and of which I'll send you a copy for your amusement. The book is awfully impressive. The last six lines of "Light" are as tremendous as the best of Emily Dickinson, and the poem stands as a whole. I still like as much as ever the things I have said I liked in the past, and still dislike a few things. I don't know whether you are a major poet or not, but you certainly come close to it, closer than anyone in our generation save Crane. In all likelihood you are, as you will outlive most of the romantics, and who the hell is going to prove you are not? My objections, in a general way, are to a certain stylistic and rhythmic clumsiness of which I have complained before, which occasionally (as in "Mr. Pope") does not occur, or, as in "Death of Little Boys," occurs only for a few instants, but which seems to me to predominate in, for example, "Prayer to the Mountain Woman." The theme is somehow huddled and cluttered, not stripped clean, and the same is true of the rhythm from line to line. Or so I feel. I know I am neat and superficial myself, but rhythms etc. are as definitely instruments of thinking and perception as meaning-content, and you can't slight them and get away with it. And why the devil is "Obituary," say, less "imagistic" than my own poems on kindred themes? "Strength out of Sweetness" or "Mazda Wake"? Either you or I continue in a daze on this point, and I am pretty sure it is you. But when I have done complaining, the book is tremendous, and it is a great luxury to have it.

I have almost finished a fifty-page essay that will form the core of my dissertation and my complete declaration of faith. This one is quite serious and I think pretty well worked out. I wish you had the time to look it over, but I fear you haven't.

[R. P.] Warren spent the night with us not long ago. I think he was a little bit dazed by our menage, but he was very likable. I hope there were no fleas in the bed we gave him. There are almost everywhere else on the place. This climate is hell.

Incidentally, I wish you had never put that jaguar (the fleas remind me of him—our kitten has them) in the "Confederate Ode." I can't make any connection with him, and he would never for an instant think of leaping at his image in a pool. Get yourself a pussycat and give her a chance to jump into the dishpan, and see what happens. Even our own, who thinks she is an Airedale, would never consider it. . . .

The first quarterly edition of *transition* makes me sick. Damn French enquêtes and French opinions about America! American commerce and publicity methods are confined at any rate to soap and canned fish, and certainly strike me as preferable to the French variety that preys on poetry. I think I'll withdraw all my mss. from them and let them mold at home. Yourself and Crane seem to be the only members of our generation who remain un-gallicised in such matters. For God's sake hold out, for the honor of provincial America. Even Burke and Cowley, alas, have slipped.

Best wishes, / Winters

MS: Princeton, Allen Tate Papers

TO PEARL ANDELSON SHERRY

Sept. 1, 1928 / RFD1, Box 286 / Palo Alto, Calif.

Dear Pearl:

Your letter to Janet with the pictures came today, and I am writing you before Janet because I have once more some clever ideas to expound. We enjoyed the pictures, and shall try tomorrow to take some of ourselves, the house, goats, dogs, and cat.

Here are the ideas. I have a fairly respectable (as to size) book of verse, and another of translations. You must have a good bunch of verse. Daly might have another. Perhaps we could locate another somewhere. The owners of these books might band together and incorporate as a publishing company, bringing out these books in fairly rapid succession, and running half a dozen carefully placed ads. We could officially take over Janet's book [*The Wheel in Midsummer*]and run it in our advertising list, to swell numbers. We could publish fairly cheaply through Mangan, Janet's printer, who is a fine printer, very reasonable as to prices, and willing to act as a sort of business manager. Each individual would bear the printing and advertising cost of his own book. If there were any profits they could be divided in some fashion between the author and the firm —the firm's share going to pay for additional advertising. It might conceivably be possible to get to the point where we could publish outsiders at our own expense, as a regular house, but that is probably a pretty wild dream.

This would be of advantage only to persons who are not popular enough, nor likely to be popular enough, to command a regular publisher. I don't know whether you have tried any of them or not. I have tried a few, and see little likelihood of my getting anywhere with them. People who live in N.Y., like Crane and Tate, get their books through, via personal connections and devious political routes that don't exist for us. We should have no right to ask any such persons to join us, nor do I think you ought to risk it without giving the regular firms a fair trial. Mitchell Dawson might join us—he is a slight poet, but capable and nothing to be ashamed of. The [Jessica] North-Dillon crowd have no need of us, and I would not accept their company as a financial favor (which it would be) because I think we ought to remain strictly respectable in a literary way. This sort of thing would not interest Maurice, and he should have little or no trouble publishing his work regularly; but if he could not publish his work and were interested, I at least shouldn't mind taking him in.

Janet's book, an edition of 250, cost about $70. Cheaper paper and cover would be possible, of course. I imagine mine would cost around $150 or $175. Yours probably less. A little should be added for advertising. I think we could be pretty sure of at least three or four decent reviews per volume, and possibly more. The books should be priced a shade high. Janet's is selling for $.75. A similar book we should put on the market at about $1.25. My book perhaps $2.00 (about 35 short poems). The copyrights of some of these things may be worth having ten or fifteen years hence.

We could name ourself after some early and admirable American writer, with no philosophical or other controversial connections. I would suggest *The Philip Freneau Company*. Emerson has connotations to all of which all of us might not subscribe, and his philosophy is a dead issue but still remembered— though he is a fine poet. Emily Dickinson's name is probably too tied up by recent copyrights. A novelist wouldn't do for us. Freneau is distinguished, American, remote, and modest.

We should not publish anything till we have at least three or four books ready to shoot through in fairly rapid order. I would be willing to be the first victim, if necessary, and try it out. If I flopped, no one need follow, and I would be the only loser. But I am pretty sure we could sell at least 100 copies of my finished *Fire Sequence*[1] inside of four or five weeks; and I have an idea we could do about as well for you and possibly Daly and Dawson. If we got started properly we might at least break even, have our books well printed, and hold the copyrights in our own hands until later. The advantages, if you think the matter over, are partly mercenary and partly not. What do you think?

Janet is writing prose that I think quite exciting.

Incidentally, I don't think I ever thanked you for the piece in the *Forge*—which we liked a great deal.

There is a person here by the name of Howard Baker,[2] who will have a couple of rather ordinary things in the 2nd *Caravan*, but who has written some lovely verse and will do much better. Really quite a person. 23 years old, and starting work next year on his doctorate.

Best to yourself and family, / Arthur

P.S. How does one make oneself into a company? Do you know? Ask Ed.

J[anet Lewis Winters].

MS: Stanford

[1]This title refers to a book-length work, not the sequence of the same title subsequently published. Subsequent letters discuss the dismantling of the book, in effect. It was rethought, reorganized, and published as *The Proof* (1930).

[2]Howard Baker (1905–1990): American poet, novelist, critic, educator, and rancher; member of the *Gyroscope* group and, with YW and Janet Lewis, one of the magazine's editors; poems included in *Twelve Poets of the Pacific*.

TO ALLEN TATE

Sept. 4, 1928 / RFD1, Box 286 / Palo Alto, Calif.

Dear Tate:

My political star flickers upward again in spite of everything. Simon and Schuster write inviting me to call on them or submit ms. or both, and Mr. [Robert Morss] Lovett asks me to review poetry for the *New Republic,* beginning with your book. I am convinced there is nothing like trampling on editors. Even Jessica North whines out a capitulation after I had insulted her so thoroughly I trembled for fear I might have done her physical injury. As to Jolas[1] and his crew, I have been disgusted with them for months, but wasn't quite irritated to the point of writing until their last number appeared. I exterminate them in passing in my new essay.

Your essay on Emily is without any doubt the most brilliant piece of criticism of our time that has come my way, and I thank the Lord you applied it to Emily. You have all of the brilliance and precision of Eliot's best criticism, plus a much more definite and valuable fundamental point of view. Your critical position emerges more plainly and completely here than elsewhere; and, again, let me reiterate that I am heading in precisely the same direction, but from a slightly different angle. I think my new essay will contribute to strengthen the values you set up, by relating method—considered in a very fundamental sense —to attitude; and a definition and evaluation of possible methods is damned necessary now that Eliot is trying to rejuvenate a dead syntax and Jolas preaching Salvation through somnambulism. I only wish I could write prose as you do. The devil is in my prose: I know it but I can't help it. I labor over it like a rock-breaker, and it comes out sounding like a cross between Gorham Munson and Waldo Frank.

I had thought [Edmund] Wilson would do your book for the *N.R.* and meant to try something else, but as long as they invite me I guess I had better accept. W. is the only person, probably, who would be allowed to praise you in the *Dial* if he wants to do it. I'll do the review at once and send you a copy. It's a glorious book.

If my mother ever gets up here from Pasadena with her high priced camera, I'll send you a picture of the classiest Airedale on the coast, now four months and one week old. His name is Covarrubias, and his sister is La Cucaracha. But you are probably not a good enough Mexican to appreciate the conjunction of titles.

Until then farewell, / Winters

MS: Princeton, Allen Tate Papers

[1]Eugene Jolas (1894–1952) and his wife Maria (née Mcdonald, 1893–1987) were the American founders, with Elliot Paul, of the literary quarterly *transition*.

TO ALLEN TATE

Sept. 15, 1928 / RFD1, Box 286 / Palo Alto, Calif.

Dear Tate:

This will probably be the last letter with which I shall afflict you until you return from Europe. I don't know just what Crane did to irritate you, but I am really sorry for it. As a poet he has all the limitations I set forth in my review of you, but he *is* a great poet, and that implies a rather formidable amount of intelligence, even if said intelligence is a bit disorderly. I can imagine he might be irritating enough, personally, except that he is one of the very few persons at whom one should never allow oneself to be irritated. He admires you tremendously, and I should think you might be rather good for his muse.

Your book gets better with every rereading. So far as I am concerned personally, it is greater poetry than Crane; but it is less spectacular, has less objectively demonstrable glitter; and it will take a long time, and a lifetime of poetry, to make its quality soak in. Similarly Baudelaire is greater than Rimbaud, but less showy. Took me a long time to see it.

I hope you have sense enough to get a university job when you come back. In a small town. Crane thought I was handicapped as a poet for not knowing N.Y., but I doubt it. The emotional reaction to the traffic, the roar (I knew it in Chicago), is really a reaction to something more fundamental. The traffic seems in some part an expression of it, and so diverts the attention in that degree from the real emotional problem. The synthesis attempted in my *Fire Sequence* is a damn sight more complex than that of *The Bridge*. In so far as the poetry falls short of *The Bridge*, I have to blame, I believe, only my native talents.

But the real thing is this: if you live on in N.Y. doing hack work and odd journalism you will die at forty-five or fifty of angina pectoris or TB. For a complete statement of your intelligence you need to live to be 80. With a slow job in a slow town, and a few carrots to keep your muscles in shape, you can do it. If there is any sense in attempting poetry—which is for you at least as much as for me a personal discipline, a mode of definition and growth—it is only reasonable to desire to make it complete. Look at Hardy and Emily. They are better than Baudelaire but just a shade, and in part for that reason.

Winters

MS: Princeton, Allen Tate Papers

TO ALLEN TATE

Christmas Night, 1928 / RFD1, Box 286 / Palo Alto, California

Dear Tate:

I answered your valedictory letter almost immediately upon receiving it and then destroyed the answer. It was written in one of my more nervously vocable moods. I seem to owe you some sort of an apology for whatever it was I said about you and Crane. My reason for picking at his poems is the same as yours, and I don't question yours. But the fact remains that your personal irritation was evident. Also, he told me a year ago that you were peeved at him, and he seemed genuinely sorry about it. And it struck me as too bad that the two most intelligent men in New York shouldn't have sense enough not to squabble. Though of course I know nothing about the whole affair. Anyway, a recent letter from Crane says he is sailing for England—he must at this writing be there or nearly there—so you may run into him. He is looking for a quiet island off—I believe—the west coast of England. Or maybe it was Iceland.

Your recent reviewing has struck me as especially fine. The *Caravan* essay was probably more important than anything you have done save the one on Emily Dickinson. And the reviews of Moore and Van Doren were brilliant, especially the former. And my feeling for your poems does not diminish.

I have been reading *The Tower*—the first Yeats I have had since *The Wild Swans*. It is the first Yeats I have read that has seemed to me in any sense major, though I have admired him a good deal. It is superbly written, though his sublimated sentimentality and charlatanry are still present. The third stanza of the "Byzantium" piece might have been written by a true admirer of Aquinas. The fourth, alas, could not have been. He is continually being magnificent (as in "The Gift of Harun al Rashid") over symbols that are slightly tangential; so that some minute but important connection is never made. He allows himself to be satisfied with mystification in an apparent search for a metaphysic. Or else he escapes me.

St. Thomas tortures me with an inescapable logic that I cannot accept. Euclidean arrows stinging the heart—but shot in the void. Terrifying. A few moments in Thomas Hardy seem to me still to be more wise.

The Hamlet of A. MacLeish displays some admirable writing, but is hopelessly unsound. A deal of exhibitionism, hysteria, cosmic petulance, based, as nearly as I can discover, on the laxative theory of art and on personal irritation at his self-advertising contemporaries. Or that plus his native bog. The book made me impatient. Also, he seems to have swallowed Jessie Weston, chapel perilous, Bleheris, bait, hook, and sinker. These modern metaphysical skeptics make me laugh.

I am anxious to see Van Doren's new book. Williams's new novel [*A Voyage to Pagany*] is so bad it is funny. The man is a mess in his cerebrum, but his emotions are healthy, and he has superb moments, even though you haven't discovered them. Wescott's *Goodbye Wisconsin,* in spite of an unspeakable foreword, is at least adult in its attitude and fairly well written. It is the best work he has done, and I feel at least a little cheered about him. It is certainly better than Hemingway, Anderson, and so on. Elspeth Roberts's new book is negligible.

My wife has a story in the December *Bookman* should you chance to see it. She has nearly finished a book of them.

I enclose a new sonnet, along with copies of several old ones to which it is related. The order of sonnets should be I and II (as here), the two in the *Caravan*, the one to Emily, and this new one. These, followed by "The Deep," form the last (and fifth) section of the *Fire Sequence*. The first section ("Shadow") is the coal camp stuff; the second ("Sun"), the "Orange Tree," "Polelonema," "Song of the Trees," "See L.A. First," "Bison," etc.; the third ("Earth"), is the "Idaho," "November," "Strength out of Sweetness," material, ending with a piece called "Simplex Munditiis," which will appear soon in the *Dial*, and which is closely related to this new sonnet in its statement—in simpler terms—of my attempt at an ethical resolution; the fourth section deals with the phantasmagoria, "Snow Ghost," "The Longe Nightes," "Bitter Moon," "The Vigil," and so on; the fifth section ("The End") attempts a definition and final resolution and depersonalization. Bad summary: but the thing is finally ready for a publisher— which it will hardly find. It is at least more mature than *The Bare Hills*, which was pretty brash.

I am hypnotized by the cadences in Crashaw: cadences like the definitions of Aquinas.

Regards to Warren if you see him.

Best wishes, / Winters

MS: Princeton, Allen Tate Papers

TO HENRY RAMSEY

Jan. 12, 1929 / RFD1, Box 286 / Palo Alto, Calif.

Dear Mr. Ramsey:

If it would not inconvenience you, I wonder if I could persuade you to drop in for tea with us Sunday (tomorrow) afternoon, around four o'clock? Your recent comp on Trinidad Head, though a trifle undisciplined in spots, could only, I am pretty certain, have been written by some one who cares to write and who has really astonishing ability. I have small interest in English 2a as a literary assemblage, and have a great preference for encountering intelligent people under less cluttered circumstances. I myself have been mixed up in the so-called advance guard movements of the last ten years; my wife writes verse and prose (in the last *Bookman* she has a story called "Sunday Dinner," that might barely amuse you) and draws a little, and we were both enormously impressed by your performance. Sunday afternoon we shall have out here Howard Baker, a graduate student and assistant in the department, who has written some very fine verse and published a little, and another of my students, Miss Ruth Lockett,[1] who writes exceedingly well likewise. I have a feeling that people who care to write and who write well are good for each other. When I was a student at the University of Chicago we had a Poetry Club, some of whose members, in addition to my wife and myself, were Elizabeth Madox Roberts, Glenway Wescott, Pearl A. Sherry, Maurice Lesemann, and one or two others of some ability but of small fame. I think it was pretty good for everyone concerned.

Anyway, drop around Sunday if you can, and if it is impossible, we'll try to get you out some other time. Our address is 607 Oregon. To reach us drive out University to Cowper, right to Oregon (the first unpaved cross street), left to the drive (or rather pair of ruts) going in just beyond the first house on the left side of Oregon. We live in a small red shack (once a chicken house) under an oak tree, with four dogs, three goats, and a cat. Outside is what was once a carrot patch.

Sincerely, / Arthur Yvor Winters

MS: *Stanford*

Henry Ramsey (1910–1989): career diplomat; student of YW and member of the *Gyroscope* group; poems included in *Twelve Poets of the Pacific*.

[1]Rowena Ruth Lockett: American poet and short story writer. Lockett was a former student of YW; she published regularly in *The Gyroscope*, on whose masthead she was listed as an advisor. She became the first wife of Henry Ramsey and, as nearly as I have been able to discover, disappeared from public view about the time she disappeared from these letters.

TO PEARL ANDELSON SHERRY

May 21, 1929 / RFD1, Box 286 / Palo Alto, Calif.

Dear Pearl:

Your letter to Janet is charming but nonsensical. We deny in the manifesto [to *The Gyroscope*] nothing that we practice and very little that you practice. You seem to be some sort of mysticised—or mystified—pantheist, and that I mildly deplore. Otherwise we agree in the main with your actual practices. You suffer in general, however, from the blight that has enervated practically all of American letters this side of Robinson: sheer ignorance of everything even approaching the nature of abstract thought and a rather placid and complacent attitude toward your own ignorance. That manifesto is a summary of the commonplaces of the modern humanistic movement, which is merely a revival of the humanism of the past. Modern humanism holds the critical and philosophical field in an absolutely impregnable fashion. You had better get acquainted with it. I suggest Irving Babbitt's *Rousseau and Romanticism,* René Lalou's *Défense de l'homme,* Ramon Fernandez' *Messages* (in English), the works of Albert Thibaudet on Mallarmé and Valéry, Whitehead's *Science and the Modern World,* and the essays of Allen Tate, in back numbers of the *Bookman,* the *Nation,* and the *New Republic.* Also my essay which will appear in the third *Caravan.*

One is born a genius, perhaps, but one is not born perfect or even intelligent. For a genius to make himself intelligent would seem to be the most difficult of tasks, or at any rate the rarest of accomplishments. You are lisping ideas originally perpetrated and popularized by the poetic morons of the early nineteenth century; you accept them as self-evident fact, not knowing where or when they arose or what a fine structure they displaced; you are an absolutely innocent and unthinking victim of the contemporary orthodoxy, which is one of ignorance and self-indulgence. Poets born into an age with a sound orthodoxy may become major poets without thinking; in this age they cannot, as the contemporary orthodoxy absolutely precludes the possibility of full human development. The manifesto is a brief summary of the commonest forms the contemporary orthodoxy takes, and the terminology is mainly that of Babbitt, who is known to the corners of the earth.

We most decidedly want your poems, if you care to let us have them; but for heavens' sake do read occasionally from some other source than the editorials of *Forge* and *Poetry.* If you do you will probably be a major poet presently; as it is you are just one of eight or ten clear-eyed and innocent geniuses who wander about hoping they'll not stub their toes on an idea that may annoy them. Pardon my irritation, but it is justified.

Yours, / Arthur

MS: Stanford

Sept. 16, 1929 / RFD1, Box 286 / Palo Alto, Calif.

Dear Miss Porter:

Thanks infinitely for the superb piece of prose ["Theft"]. It got here while I was running off our third issue, and I have succeeded in squeezing it in. The issue will be ready to mail in a couple of weeks. I'll send the ms. back to you in a few days, in case you have any use for it. Mrs. Tate said you had things around that she thought were unsaleable: if this is so, we should like to beg another for our fourth issue. But we hesitate to ask for anything that you have any chance of publishing more advantageously. Your generosity in sending this one piece is very great—the more so, as it seems to me at the moment one of the most extraordinary pieces of short fiction that I have seen in a long time.

Pardon my bad manners.[1] But you will have to admit that it is something or other to tell a man that a credo based on a ten years study of his favorite poets is in complete disaccord with those poets, without so much as giving him a reason. If you don't like my adjectives, pick another. As a matter of fact, I don't think we have anything very serious to quarrel about—unless you start wondering how various people might misinterpret that rather broad summary (Cowley objected to our using the word "classical" because some people might confuse it with "pseudo-classical"!); and if you feel tempted in that direction, you should stop and think how many people there are and what most of them are like. A controversy through the mail on a subject that is at once broad and intricate is very difficult: hence my preferring to wait till you have seen the four pages in the third *Gyroscope*[2] and the fifty odd in the third *Caravan*.[3] After that, if you still disagree with me, our disagreement can be at least definite and subject to lucid discussion. I would send you a ms. except that I haven't one that is not full of errors, and the thing is very nearly out, or should be.

The Camilo of your story reminds me curiously of a young Puerto Rican friend of mine, a fellow-instructor in French and Spanish at the University of Idaho a few years ago. The only thing that I ever knew to overcome his aristocratic indolence was the way I kept—or didn't keep—my clothes. He actually pressed my trousers for me on one occasion.

You said in your last letter that you might care to undertake some such venture as *The Gyroscope* presently. Next year I shall be too busy to go on with the thing, unless we double the price and get enough subscriptions to hire a printer. We are not sure that we shall attempt that either, for a variety of reasons. But we thought we might lend you our mimeograph machine or our name or both if you wanted them, and salvage as many subscribers as possible. And yet I am dubious about this, too; for the time and the sheer physical labor involved in getting the thing out are such that I am dubious about your ever going through with it. One can hire the work done, of course; it costs less than a printer, but more than doing it oneself. If you do that you should charge at least a dollar and a half to get out of it whole.

If you wish, you may choose another recipient for that third subscription, and we'll take over the responsibility for Louise Bogan's.[4] But when you gave me no clue of any sort, you really can't blame me for picking some one you didn't want picked. The inter-animadversions of women who write really worry me more than I can say. One never knows where one is. Louise is terrible, so is Elizabeth Roberts, so is Alice Corbin. Louise once invited me and Alice Corbin —who don't love each other much, personally—to the same tea-party. But drinking tea at Alice's elbow struck me as incomparably less precarious than drinking it in the same room with Louise and Alice. . . . That atmosphere was so tense you could see it bend when somebody reached for the sugar. I don't mind explosions, but I hate a tense atmosphere. Alice's relations with me were those of a perfect gentleman—we had fought so hard that all New Mexico knew of it, and so could meet at a tea-party in perfect peace and relaxation. But with another woman it was different. I don't pretend to pass judgment upon this, be it noted; but I merely remark upon it in passing to explain my innocence and my good intentions.

Anyhow, thanks again for the story, which ought to establish our rights to all claims we make in the first two issues.

Sincerely, / Yvor Winters

P.S. Your check has not come back to us, so I guess it reached your bank.

MS: UM

Katherine Anne Porter (1890–1980): American short story writer and novelist.

[1] The main subject of this paragraph is the "Statement of Purpose" for *The Gyroscope*, YW's mimeographed little magazine. In no. 1, YW stated that the journal would attempt "to fix in literary terms some approximation of a classical state of mind." There followed a long catalog of "forms of spiritual extroversion" that *The Gyroscope* would oppose. Also relevant is the "Further Explanation" in the second number. Unfortunately, only the first of these documents is reprinted in *Uncollected Essays and Reviews*. The second is too lengthy to reproduce here and must be consulted in the original.

[2] "Notes on Contemporary Criticism." Reprinted in *Uncollected Essays and Reviews*.

[3] "The Extension and Reintegration of the Human Spirit through the Poetry Mainly French and American since Poe and Baudelaire." Also reprinted in *Uncollected Essays and Reviews*.

[4] Louise Bogan (1897–1970): American poet and critic; for many years poetry reviewer for the *New Yorker*.

TO MALCOLM COWLEY

Sept. 21, 1929 / RFD1, Box 286 / Palo Alto, Calif.

Dear Cowley:

I hope you got the copy of the 2nd *Gyroscope*, which I sent you perhaps a week ago. The issue is now exhausted, & the next will be mailed in about a week.

I have thrown over the arrangement of my book as you saw it. *The Fire Sequence* has been reduced to its original & proper dimensions—i.e. those that it had in the first *Caravan*, with the addition of six or eight poems that the *Caravan* rejected at that time. This is the first section of the book. The third is composed of the sonnets & other recent pieces, & in between is a mixed group of everything else. I really don't think the arrangement matters much, except that the elaborate one you saw was too little justified. The book in any case is a collection of lyrics. The first & third groups form rather loose sequences.

Best wishes, / Yvor Winters

MS: Newberry

TO LOUISE BOGAN

Oct. 16, 1929 / RFD1, Box 286 / Palo Alto, Calif.

Dear Louise:

Thanks for your letter. You are probably justified in complaining of my reference to Hardy, not because of his sex (there is Emily), but because of his age. However, some of his earlier pieces have much the same quality ("Song of Hope," "A Spot"), though the statement is not quite so dense. I am glad if the review pleased you in any measure; I have rather feared that it might seem a bit pretentious. I have not yet received a printed copy of it. I myself am an outstanding example of the fallacies inherent in our educational system, but if I live long enough I hope to pick up a good many of the loose ends. Tate is almost the only one of our generation I know who picked up a really systematic education at the proper time. I envy him his philosophical training, but not his lack of languages. I can eventually acquire the former, but he'll never make up for the latter. However, such is life.

We have not yet received a copy of the *Caravan*, though it is out. We'll be glad to lend you our copy when we get it. Last year I bought the damned thing, and then two months later received a specially bound copy from Macaulay. So this year I am waiting. I have not received Wilson's book, either, though I have a long-standing order in. It will doubtless be along presently.

I have been reading the lyrics of Rochester and of Dorset for the first time in years, and have seldom had such dazzling entertainment. The criticism of Sam Johnson is just about as good. He was a very great man.

I feel a good deal of resentment at Janet's writing you about what goes on in our kitchen, for she knows next to nothing of that subject, is taking upon herself a good deal of unmerited glory, and is very likely to mislead you.

Best wishes to both of you, / Arthur

How do you like our two discoveries in the 3rd *Gyroscope*?
Janet has an early story in the Oct. *Bookman*.

MS: Amherst

TO HENRY RAMSEY

Nov. 19, 1929 / RFD1, Box 286 / Palo Alto, Calif.

Dear Henry:

＊　＊　＊

As to coining words in general, I should advise you to do it with extreme caution, and if possible to refrain from it entirely until you are at least as old and learned as Joyce, by which time I hope you may be wiser than Joyce. English has the richest vocabulary to be found in the modern world; it is a vocabulary that has been cultivated by the most astounding succession of geniuses in the history of literature. Most of these geniuses have added a few words, but only a few; they have not invented two or three to each sonnet. They have enriched the existing words by the way they have used them. If you really know English, you will find small need to add to it; too often the creation of a word is merely a sign of ignorance or laziness. And if you can pick the old word that is right, you have a word that is familiar and will fall unobtrusively into place, and that in addition has a certain amount of history and circumambient feeling; a large part of Hardy's genius lies in his masterly understanding of the history (I mean the artistic and human history, not the philological) of every word he touches. When you create a word, the reader is startled by its newness and too often repelled by its skeleton-like nakedness. The prose stylists of the 17th century, Browne and the rest, who shoveled words into the language, at least had the advantage of being first rate Latinists; and most of their innovations died out anyway.

I have been reading Dr. Johnson's *Lives of the Poets* and miscellaneous criticisms of late, and am tremendously impressed by the value of his criticism. He attends especially to the style of the writers criticized, criticizes them in minute detail, and with infallible judgment. There is nothing else of the sort quite as valuable in English. You had better read him. Also, when you find time, read Dryden's translation of the *Aeneid* and the songs from his plays.

*   *   *

Yours, / Arthur Winters

MS: Stanford

TO ALLEN TATE

Nov. 20, 1929 / RFD1, Box 286 / Palo Alto, Calif.

Dear Tate:

[W. S.] Knickerbocker wrote me a while ago that he thought my long essay in the *Caravan* began where your "Poetry and the Absolute" left off; this morning I wandered around and read your essay, which, for reasons unknown, I had never before examined, and I rather imagine he is right. That is, I agree with your essay at every essential point as far as it goes, but I think it stops short at the near edge of completion. You leave the artistic experience, that is, every individual artistic experience, in a kind of insulated aesthetic vacuum; I have endeavored to indicate the experiential connection, in the life of the individual, from poem to poem, and from aesthetic experience to non-aesthetic experience. Remember, I do not in any sense confuse these two last; I accept your distinction between them in every detail; but I deny that the latter is not in any way influenced by the former. If it is not, one is continually driven by the storms of experience to, ostrich-like, poke his head into the nearest little poem-nirvana; one is not up to his ears in aestheticism, but up to his neck in reverse order. There is no escape from making a choice between these two positions, and there is no other choice to make once you eliminate the rather innocent approach of Babbitt. Perhaps the clearest statement that I have made of my choice is in my reply to your reply, but it seems to me that I have made myself perfectly clear elsewhere.

Now then, I am aware that the alternative of aestheticism will be rejected by you; if you thereupon refuse to accept my choice at the same time your position amounts simply to your refusing, through sullenness or stupidity, to formulate any position at all. My own position in this regard is not any doctrinaire solution of the evils of the universe, but a definition of an attitude and a psychological phenomenon. I arrive at this position not deductively, but inductively, from an observation of experience. The irritating thing about this argument is not that I think you *ought* to agree with me, but that I am reasonably certain that you *do* agree with me. Our formulations have been arrived at from different starting points and through a different set of terms; but I cannot see any real point of difference so far as our basic conclusions are concerned —you have simply not got around to extending your terminology to one or two final points to which I have extended mine, and you choose to quarrel with me mainly because I have not extended your set of terms to cover the remaining phenomena instead of extending my own. This is ridiculous.

I do not wish to insinuate that I have done a better job than you for I have not. Your work has been better ordered, better documented, and more complete. I have taken for granted and left half-defined a number of notions that you have seen the necessity of treating systematically. All I wish to point out is that we are fundamentally in accord; that most of our differences are either on minor points or in matters of taste.

For example, you make what seems to me a ridiculous issue of my use of the phrase a "belief in existence." I should never be so rash as to attempt to defend logically in public an absolute belief in existence, especially in a universe containing yourself; you are, apparently, like those oriental demons into whose power one falls as soon as one believes in them. But there are certain ignobly pragmatic, yet nevertheless very interesting, aspects of the question that one might pause over. For instance, a "belief" as you say is not a syllogistic formula, but a complete affirmation on the part of something more than the reasoning powers. Some beliefs are hard to affirm and require rational support; others can scarcely be destroyed even by the most complete rational attack. If I disbelieve in existence, I of absolute necessity disbelieve in the loss of it, or death, to exactly the same degree. I don't know just what this means in terms of human experience, but it is nevertheless inescapable. The fear of death is thus in some measure eliminated; and the fear of death would seem to be one of the chief threats to man's moral equilibrium. If then you grant—as you have granted— my statement that the least pleasant of the hypotheses available is the one that one must accustom oneself to, as a basis for sound moral judgment, a belief in existence is justified on purely practical grounds. It can neither be justified nor discredited logically, but experientially, morally, it is necessary. Your remarks about the way I shall commit suicide are bad poetry and bad manners.

You commit yourself to another ridiculous statement when you say in your last letter that my poems "The Barnyard" and "The Empty Hills" are as different as day from night. As a matter of fact, they are different versions of the same poem. The basic theme, the spiritual sterility of the human protagonists, is the same in each; the scene in one is Moscow, winter and poverty—in the other, Pasadena, summer, and wealth; you have the dog for the humming bird and free verse for traditional; and as a conclusion to each the protagonists wobble into an oblivion that is described in terms of the landscape. There is just as much doctrine behind the early poem as the later one; the difficulty is that your own literary history makes you rather unsusceptible to certain types of meter and perhaps unduly susceptible to a smooth traditional meter and a certain amount of literary hocus-pocus. "The Barnyard" is a damned good poem, and I wish to goodness I could do another that might please me as much. I am fully aware that it is out of fashion and that the next Supreme Genius will be recognized by his embodiment of most of the vices of the later Yeats, but that doesn't matter to God or Sam Johnson.

These last two paragraphs, however, deal with matters of small moment. What I meant to say was that I think it ridiculous that we should fight so much and that all that is needed for a cessation of hostilities is a more philosophic caution on your part, and the subjection of your statements to a colder and more exacting scrutiny. I am not on Babbitt's side of the fence, and I dislike being forced to fight with persons with whom I am on the whole in agreement.

It appears that O'Brien[1] will use my wife's story "The Swamp" in his 1930 collection. It is a bad anthology, but, I imagine, good business.

Yours, / Winters

MS: Princeton, Allen Tate Papers

[1] E. J. O'Brien: founding editor (1915–41) of the annual collection *The Best American Short Stories.*

TO HOWARD BAKER

Nov. 27, 1929 / RFD1, Box 286 / Palo Alto, Calif.

Dear Howard:

What you say about Crane is rather surprising, the more so as I thought myself a fairly good guesser in such matters, but it really hasn't anything to do with my remarks on his poetry. I never claimed for him more than certain specific virtues, and those he has. Crane, as a poet and a man, is a magnificent fragment. Certain ranges of experience that he touches in his poems are wholly false, apparently for lack of contact; personally, he is, within those ranges, of about the same degree of delicacy as the average thug. But where he is good, he has power and control, and Eliot, though he is doubtless a virtuous and civilized man, has neither. Crane's vices, especially if you are correct, are socially the more spectacular, but I wonder if they are any more insidious or dangerous. I believe it is good Catholic morality that the worst sin is spiritual passivity, for it lays one open to the reception of the devil. I don't think I have ever claimed that Crane was "philosophically integrated"; as a matter of fact he is nearly as illiterate as Covy, and I thought I intimated something of the sort in my review of Tate. As to Louise, her education is very little better, and again I have made specific qualifications when praising her. When I get around to doing Crane in an essay I shall dissect him completely enough—don't worry. I have been cataloguing his weaknesses for the last four years. I have already said all I have to say of Louise. (On the basis of my acquaintance with her I should call her a sort of neurasthenic egoist—her "venom" is a more or less accidental by-product. I don't wish to exculpate her on the basis of any such shift in terms, but she has personal virtues as well as weaknesses. We know her fairly well.)

The only poets in America since Robinson who have my unreserved admiration are, if I must declare myself, Tate, yourself, and Janet. I may be prejudiced in favor of the last two, and Tate would probably claim that I am, but I am reasonably confident that I am right. I have, God knows, no reason to be prejudiced in favor of Tate; he has nothing but his genius and basic integrity to recommend him; I have never had any contact with a more stubborn, deliberately perverse, and generally irritating individual, in my somewhat hectic career. He probably has certain graces when encountered in person, but he will never inspire much purely sentimental attachment among his remote correspondents. Probably I don't either. Anyway, all I am trying to do is vindicate my opinion that he is a great poet. So were Ben Jonson and Landor, both of whom I should have in all likelihood valued personally above all of their contemporaries and with both of whom I should almost certainly have fought.

As to Williams, I know nothing about his morals, but I am as aware as Tate that he is an unconscionable ass. He has done more good, and better, writing, however, than anyone of his generation, and, I believe, than Crane. His writing, *when good,* is rounded and healthy and vigorous. I suspect that he is finished, however, as all of the definitely anti-intellectual geniuses seem to write themselves out very quickly, and he has been treading water for at least five years.

It seems to me that in what I have written of these persons I have taken due precautions in guarding my statements, if the whole of what I have written is read instead of the high spots. Tate, in his private battles with me, usually reads one set of high spots before one attack and another before the next. And it is, of course, only fair to remember that I have not yet dropped the subject. My essays on both Crane and Williams will be about eighty percent destructive; so will be my essay on Yeats. There is no denying, however, that all three of these men loom very high, as poets, as compared to most of their contemporaries, and particularly as compared to Eliot. My essay on Tate will be almost pure eulogy.

As to my claim that poetry is a "moral discipline" in the light of these facts, it is perfectly sound if you stop and speculate on the complexity of human nature. Crane is specifically and profoundly moral in certain respects and situations; he is as definitely the reverse in others. His limited range of moral soundness (and within that range he has "disciplined" himself) can be seen in "Repose of Rivers" and "Voyages II." His unsoundness can be seen in any of his love-poems, and the mixture and inter-crossing of the two in nearly anything else. Do not get the idea that Tate has, and that my possibly dogmatic prose may give, that I am a blind bigot; I do not mean that the composition of one good poem indicates a fundamentally sweet moral nature, and that three in a row make one a candidate for canonization. I simply mean that the poetic medium has certain definite possibilities as a means of studying and extending the spirit and of fixing for future reference what one has found or achieved. Very few poets realize those possibilities in more than a very limited and almost paltry fashion. Most contemporary poets have mastered poetically—and morally—only a small range of experience; most of them are ridden by half-baked theories that prevent their getting any farther. But a limited mastery is better than none, and indicates the possibility of further mastery. The fact that a man has remained a thug in certain regions, and so remains socially impossible, does not mean that he is not profoundly admirable in other respects even though one may find it more convenient to admire him wholly on paper. In a man of Crane's vitality, both vice and virtue are likely to appear in vigorous or violent forms. I deplore the vice as much as anyone, but after all one can arrange not to be bothered by it; and the virtue will wear longer and in all likelihood accomplish more in the cause of the angels in the course of the ages than the purely negative and discreet virtues of a good many souls who are charming socially.

What all of this amounts to is, briefly, that the contemplation of human nature in general makes me, if I look at it steadily, sick unto death; but out of the dungheap of human history and histories I have at one time or another succeeded in extracting certain moments and even longer fragments that I have found extremely salutary, and I am very much interested in studying their composition.

As ever, / Arthur

P.S. The short pieces in Callaghan's *A Native Argosy* are witty, humane, varied, and admirably written. Look them over before you classify him permanently. I like them much better than any Hemingway I have seen; and they are *not* like Hemingway. His novel is, and is not so good.

MS: Stanford

Harry Lewis Winters, Yvor Winters's
father

Yvor Winters, about two years old

Faith Evangeline Ahnefeldt
Winters, Yvor Winters's
mother

Faith Winters, Yvor
Winters's sister

Yvor Winters, about six
years old

Yvor Winters, about fifteen
years old

Harry Lewis Winters and Hokusai ("Hoke"); Yvor Winters and Villa outside Yvor Winters's cabin at Sunmount Sanitorium, Santa Fe, 1919

Puppy show at Sunmount

Yvor Winters and Janet Lewis at Sunmount, 1924

Glenway Wescott, New Mexico

Monroe Wheeler, New Mexico

Maurice Lesemann,
Cerrillos, New Mexico,
1920s. *Courtesy of
Frederick Lesemann.*

Yvor Winters in his Sunmount cabin, 1921 or 1922. The painting over the stack of books, by Tonita Peña (Quah-Ah), is reproduced below.

Hopi painter Otis Polelonema; photo
inscribed "To Yvor Winters from Art Otis
Polelonema," 1924

Painting by Otis Polelonema

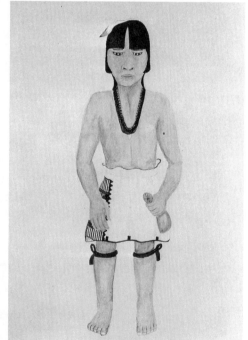

Yvor Winters with his baseball team, Cerrillos, 1922

Informal wedding photograph, Sunmount, Santa Fe, June 22, 1926. *From left:* John Gaw Meem, Yvor Winters, Janet Lewis Winters, Cecil Clark Wolman, Loulou Hunt (Louise de Vilmorin)

Yvor Winters, Moscow, Idaho

To Yvor Winters
with the highest esteem of
Allen Tate

August 14, 1928

Preliminary page of Allen Tate's *Mr. Pope and Other Poems*. Yvor Winters and
Janet Lewis frequently pasted into books pictures of the authors.

Janet Lewis, Oregon Avenue, Palo Alto, 1929, with
Coocoo (head foremost) and Covy

Portrait of Hart Crane by
Janet Lewis, 1929

To Emily Dickinson

You who desired so much—in vain to ask—
Yet fed your hunger like an endless Task,
Dared dignify the labor, bless the quest,—
Achieved that stillness ultimately best,

Being, of all, least sought for,—Emily, hear!
O sweet, dead silencer, most suddenly clear
When singing that Eternity possessed
And plundered momently in every breast;

—Truly no flower yet withers in your hand.
The harmony you shed and understand
Needs more than wit to gather, love to bind.
Some reconcilement of remotest mind

Leaves Ormus rubyless, and Ophir chill.
Else tears heap all within one clay-cold hill.

Hart Crane

Holograph copy of Hart Crane's "To Emily Dickinson." Along with the collage Crane made for, and inscribed to, Yvor Winters, this hung in Winters's study until he died.

Mrs. Dodds, Dorothy and Howard
Baker, Ford Madox Ford's daughter,
and Ford, Paris

Yvor Winters in front of the goat
shed, Oregon Avenue, Palo Alto, 1931

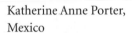

Katherine Anne Porter,
Mexico

Caroline Gordon (Mrs. Allen Tate), her daughter
Nancy, and Robert Penn Warren's sister

Pearl Andelson Sherry and her son, Leonard, 1930s

Achilles "Tex" Holt, Palo Alto

J. V. Cunningham, Palo Alto, 1931–32

Noted on verso in Yvor Winters's hand: "Coocoo (La Cucaracha) now lost."

Janet Lewis Winters and Yvor Winters with their daughter, Joanna, in the front yard, Los Altos

Yvor Winters and his son, Daniel, in the front yard, Los Altos, 1940

Yvor Winters and Champion Buckthorn Sal, 1946

Yvor Winters and Champion Buckthorn Black Jack, 1948. *Photo credit G. E. Dean.*

Yvor Winters receiving his lifetime membership in the NAACP, 1957

Yvor Winters in his Stanford University office. *Photo courtesy of the News and Publications Service, Stanford University.*

Yvor Winters in his
Morris chair, Los Altos,
1962

Yvor and Janet Lewis Winters in their front yard, Los Altos, 1962. *Photos this page courtesy of the News and Publications Service, Stanford University.*

1930-1939

Jan. 3, 1930 / RFD1, Box 286 / Palo Alto, Calif.

Dear Howard:

I enclose three new poems. I hope the amount of repetition to be found in them is not too great, but if you think it is, kindly say so, as I have been pondering the question. I sometimes find it hard to shake off a certain theme till it has cropped out (nearly always unexpectedly) two or three times.

I have apologized to Tate for any reflections I may have made upon his honesty, as they were wholly unintentional; I have retracted nothing else I have written him, for the other remarks *were* intentional, and, I imagine, justified— they were in any event no worse than a good many things he has written to me. As to the element of irritation in my note in reply to his note, I should scarcely deny it; but why he should object to the expression of irritation that he had so deliberately sought to arouse is beyond me. The verbose and inane attempts at wit in the thing made me angry, and the whole affair struck me as bad. He complained that I made him appear an ass in the *Caravan* essay (though I still think he deserved it and one of his last letters proves that he hasn't profited by what I said) in an unjustified fashion; so I thought I would give him a chance to revise or retract this time. But it is hard to attack a man in a way that will be wholly satisfactory to him. If he romances in public about what I "believe," believe me I shall reply to him. As to a "belief in existence," I am unable to envisage any notion of ethics that does not start from it as a hypothesis at the very least. Ethics is the science of conducting existence; insofar as one concerns oneself with ethics one believes in existence, for the time being at any rate. In one's moments of skepticism about existence one is equally skeptical about the value of ethics. Tate complains in one letter that I ought to doubt his existence and ought not to doubt his honesty. Practically all epistemological problems lead to contradiction and confusion, and may very well lead one to despair of the absolute logical justification of such a belief. But the ethical problems are nonetheless pressing for all that.

All of this does not mean that my opinion of Tate has altered. He is the best critic now writing in English and is a great poet. But I can scarcely regret the loss of so irritating a correspondent.

"The Swamp" antedates the earliest of the other stories by several years— years in which Janet wrote no prose whatever. That fact probably accounts for the slight stiffness that one discerns in it. I confess that I should hate to see the best of the later ones altered—the two in the *Gyroscope*, "Sunday Dinner," "The River," "The House," and "Nell," especially.

I gave your name to a new magazine, *The Miscellany*, and you may have heard from them by this time. I wish you would, as a special favor, try anything you have on them, *Pagany*, and *The Hound and Horn* (except for the four things I am using in the next *Gyroscope*) in order that we may see whether there is any point in getting out a printed bi-yearly next year. We shall all of us do the same thing. Try *This Quarter* likewise. I'll leave the matter up in the air in the fourth *Gyroscope*.

Have you seen Frost's latest volume, *West-Running Brook*? It is far the best collection he has put out and is very little short of great poetry. It is beautiful from absolutely any angle.

I shall have a long review of [Robinson] Jeffers in *Poetry* presently. It is the best review I have ever written; if you have no way of seeing it, let me know and I'll send you a copy.

Yours, / Arthur

MS: Stanford

TO LINCOLN KIRSTEIN

Jan. 10, 1930

Dear Mr. Kirstein:

I'll do the work on V[ielé]-G[riffin] if it isn't too metaphorical for my feeble powers. The academic mind rather swamps me sometimes, though. I think from the reviews I have read of Taupin that I should like to do him; I suspect he is all wet, and I am tired of seeing Stevens and others referred to as parasites on French symbolism.

I am going to send you sometime soon a review of a book of verse by Agnes Lee, just published. You probably don't like her, perhaps don't even know her; but I am convinced that she is a vastly better poet than V.-G. You have only to return the review if you don't want it.

Incidentally, the legend that V.-G. is really "American" is very amusing. I had two short notes from him several years ago anent a translation I made of his poem for Mallarmé. The first was English throughout, but of the most curiously strained and unidiomatic variety I ever saw, and the second broke down into French halfway through.

Sincerely, / Yvor Winters

To be perfectly honest with you, I think [Robert] Fitzgerald's review of my book is silly. He refers to disassociated imagery, a term which by no stretch of the imagination has any meaning; and, without giving its source, speaks of Mallarmé's metaphor of the poetic "word" as if it were some modern theory that I have filched from my betters and not merely a figurative expression descriptive of Campion or whom you will. Poor old M. wasn't trying to start much of anything; he was merely trying to break back past Hugo to Racine. Refer the young man to Lalou. And I have no desire, I confess in all Christian humility, to please an admirer of Jeffers very profoundly. And, finally, no young man should be allowed to talk publicly about his inherited taste—it sounds like Molière's *Précieuses:* People of quality are born knowing everything. What little taste I possess myself, I confess I have had to sweat for.

MS: Yale

Lincoln Kirstein (1907–1996): American poet, dance company founder and executive, and writer. Although best known as cofounder of the American Ballet (1934) and general director of the New York City Ballet, he is most important in YW's correspondence as cofounder and editor of *The Hound and Horn* (1927–34), one of the foremost literary magazines not only of its time but in the history of American literature.

TO HOWARD BAKER

Jan. 14, 1930

Dear Howard:

What you said about Janet's prose has moved me to meditate on contemporary prose in general and to offer the following theory. It would seem more or less true that the psychological novel has tended more and more from its inception to the present to emphasize the content of the character's mind. That is, your modern fictionist tends to cover his narrative ground by means of trivial scraps of conversation, observation of the rain on the sidewalk, the color of a roof, etc., anything that runs through his character's head. Fielding would have considered this beneath his dignity: he would have summarized in two or three highly stylized and very carefully calculated paragraphs the content of two or three dozen pages from most modern fiction. He would have got over the ground just as thoroughly, and he would have done it more effectively because of the greater condensation, the greater degree of artistic transmutation (the material goes through Fielding and comes out art, instead of remaining raw material precisely seen through meticulously colorless prose), and he would have got over more material as a result of being able to move faster. The difficulty with this last advantage is that he might run out of material: the first third of *Joseph Andrews* is superb, but the remainder is limp repetition. But it is invariably true that the finer and more desirable the method the harder it is to handle.

The best modern fictionists have done one of two things: they have written autobiographically (Proust and Joyce) or they have frankly taken the reader into their confidence, discussed the character's problems and their own machinery in the text itself, and have done it at length (James, Hardy, etc.). The modern ideal of objectivity is lost either way, but something much more complex and much more valuable arises in its place. The more complex situation is harder for the artist to dominate, but, once dominated, it is greater art. In short fiction it is easier for the artist to inject himself into his material without frankly announcing himself (*Dubliners,* Callaghan's "Girl with Ambition" and "A Cocky Young Man," [Janet Lewis's] "Proserpina").

Now then, the art of really vigorous prose, prose that is capable of plunging into a nest of such difficulties, mastering them, and dragging them on in its wake, is rather rare today.

Read Fielding, Melville, or *The Golden Bowl,* and then try some of our cleanest modern objective stuff that tries to conceal the fact that it is art, a form of major poetry. The comparison is pathetic. In the opening chapters of *Joseph Andrews* the "machinery" is as obvious as it is in a power house, and it is just about as magnificent. The attempt to conceal your machinery by letting weeds grow up between the wheels is, I think, fatal. The important thing is to make it work. There is no need for art to be ashamed of itself in any form—and most of the art that can be disentangled in modern fiction *is* ashamed of itself. The impulse is confused and the result is weakness. Unless something is going on in the prose as prose, as well as in the narrative as narrative, you have a very incomplete and an ultimately unsatisfactory form of art.

The pups are entered at San Francisco for Jan. 25–6. Dan Shuttleworth tells me the Flashlight people have a young dog that is a knockout, so Covy will probably lose on his eye and his gradually widening skull. Coo, however, is about as near perfection as they usually come, and I am expecting her to do something.

I enclose a perfect Petrarchan sonnet.

Yours, / Arthur

MS: Stanford

Jan. 19, 1930

Dear Howard:

The two new poems are both fine and at the top of your achievement. I had about decided to use nothing more of yours in the next *Gyroscope,* in addition to the four I had, but these would add so much to your group and help so much to round out the final issue that I am tempted. If no one else has them, please let me know at once, and these will be the last I'll seize unless we go ahead with our printed bi-yearly. I have been busy, and have been slow in getting this last issue out, but it should be ready in four or five weeks.

[Robert] Shafer's measured and Aristotelian pronouncements in the last *Bookman* are a bit sickening, but I don't know but what Tate really deserves some of it. Knickerbocker's essay in the last *Sewanee Review* is one of the best that the mess has called forth. My own attitude to the situation, I think, could be summed up quite simply: [Norman] Foerster writes so badly that he is vulgar and deserves almost no consideration. Neither he nor any other of his contemporaries has added anything to what Babbitt has said and they have rehashed Babbitt badly. There is therefore no need to talk of them. Babbitt has a number of weak spots but he is much better than Tate makes him out to be. His position is much like Arnold's, save that, since he is not a great poet, he has a tendency to be a bigot and a preacher. His use of Aristotle is not what Tate says it is; it is skeptical, gentlemanly, and measured, and, so far as I can see, perfectly sound. His morals are practical, and they are the best morals available, whatever their limitations. He does not know how to get the arts into his system (Arnold did) nor out either—that is the worst of him. But one can take care of that for oneself. Beyond a certain point these questions are a source of nothing but mathematics and bad manners.

Arthur

Pagany is pretty fair, thanks mainly to us, I think.

MS: Stanford

Jan. 20, 1930 / RFD1, Box 286 / Palo Alto, Calif.

Dear Mr. Kirstein:

Here are the reviews. Please append the [Léonie] Adams review as number three. I hope they are satisfactory.

Crane has just sent me a complete and corrected ms. of *The Bridge,* as it is to issue from Paris next month, and has asked The Black Sun Press to send me a review copy. I think he would like me to review it somewhere, and I should like to. I wonder if you would care to let me do it. He has sent me most of it as he has composed it during the past three or four years, so I am pretty familiar with it, am not in my first daze at all. It is tremendously powerful in spots, but curiously misguided and turgid a large part of the time. A very strange book.

Sincerely, / Yvor Winters

MS: Yale

Feb. 1, 1930

Dear Mr. Kirstein:

As to Crane's book, I am only too glad to step aside for Tate. I had imagined he would be doing it for [Edmund] Wilson [in the *New Republic*].

As to Ransom and MacLeish, I had always regarded them as belonging more to my generation than to Aiken's.[1] Stick them in if you like. I am not gone on either, but they are both good in a sense and probably at least as good as H.D. Not as good as Mina Loy, however, in my opinion. Their inclusion may make my chronology look wild, but I have already exasperated both of them at one time or another, so never mind the chronology.

Crane's book contains some of the greatest romantic poetry I have ever read and some of the worst. The book as a whole seems a failure. The best of his work strikes me as sufficiently clear in intention.

In today's mail I sent you a letter withdrawing my poems; now comes your acceptance. Keep them if you like. I wanted to do something definite about the next *Gyroscope* mainly, and I really didn't think you would care for them. Of all the poets in America who are reputed in a vague way to be good, I am probably the least admired if the prospective admirer is pinned down to specific poems.

Sincerely, / Yvor Winters

[1]Lincoln Kirstein had written YW about his review of Conrad Aiken, expressing surprise that YW had mentioned Mina Loy but not Ransom and MacLeish as among the best poets of Aiken's generation.

TO HOWARD BAKER

Feb. 2, 1930

Dear Howard:

*   *   *

Covy went first in his three classes at S.F., and first Winners. He was beaten by the winning bitch, Champion Flashlight Western Girl, and she was beaten by Ch. Flashlight Blaze for best of breed. Western Girl is better than Blaze and usually beats him (she was best of breed here, if you remember), but I don't like either one of them. Coo was robbed, being placed second to a bitch called Weyburn Model (reputed to be one of the three best bitches on the coast) and beating a Flashlight bitch, Marqueta. My dogs were beaten, I believe, because of three things: an "all around judge" who didn't know too much, their light eyes (which are easy for an all around judge to notice) and the record of the Flashlight dogs (likewise easy for an all around judge to notice). Weyburn Model was brought in stripped to the skin (she grows a soft coat), had a high skull, a badly deformed shoulder, and a backline that was none too straight. My dogs were in full coat (they have about the best coats on the coast); they had the flattest skulls on the bench, the shortest backs, the straightest backs, the heaviest bone, and the heaviest jaw. Not to mention the most style and fire. It made me sick. A number of breeders who felt them over were of the opinion that Cove has the heaviest muzzle and bone in the west, regardless of size. And when I got through working him over, he did *not* look coarse, as I had feared. His skull is no wider than that of Blaze, who has never chewed a bone and who has no foreface under his whisker. But such is art.

*   *   *

Crane sent me the ms. of *The Bridge* recently. The additions of the last two years are very weak.

Sincerely, / Arthur

TO LINCOLN KIRSTEIN

Yvor Winters / Route 1, Box 363 / Palo Alto, California / Feb. 3, 1930

Dear Mr. Kirstein:

I am sorry you sent my note to Mr. Fitzgerald, as it was very bad-tempered, & the matter was of no consequence. I transferred, for a time, to the review, a bad mood in which I found myself chiefly because of an epic row with a fond papa whose son I flunked last quarter.

As to Mr. Fitzgerald's elucidations, I confess myself unable to grasp a shred of significance in his analogy of poetry & chemistry; & so far as Mallarmé is concerned, I think he is confusing two distinct issues.

I am pretty dubious, also, about the company in which he thinks I belong. I have undergone, as a poet, two distinct types of influences, & have undergone them almost simultaneously: one, composed mainly of Hardy, E. Dickinson, & Baudelaire, affecting my attitude toward experience very profoundly & my style scarcely at all; & another, composed of Williams, Stevens, [T.] Sturge Moore, & Bridges, which has in various ways formed my style, diverse as these men may seem. There are other influences, but they are slight. I am about as remote from Crane, Mallarmé, & Rimbaud, as I am from Chaucer—in fact, more remote.

Yours, / Yvor Winters

MS: Yale

TO HARRIET MONROE

Feb. 10, 1930

Dear Miss Monroe:

I have a complete ms. of Crane's book here. I will do a review of it some time soon and let you see it. If you don't want it I'll send it to some one else. Crane has major faults; they are more evident in this book than in the last. But he also has major virtues, and they ought to be insisted upon in a world composed mainly of cheap journalists and scandal-mongers. I do not believe him the "whole show"; he is not as good a poet as Tate, nor, I suspect, as good a poet as Howard Baker is likely to appear within a year or so. But regardless of all that ails him, he is incomparably better than such impostors as Jeffers and such weaklings as MacLeish.

Janet is working on a rather ambitious piece of prose [*The Invasion*] that seems likely to absorb her for a good many months. It ought to be very remarkable. Her prose and verse both seem to me very extraordinary, but as I dislike anything that may look like family log-rolling, I endeavor to keep my opinion to myself. She is also an unusually capable draughtsman and sculptor.

I was sorry to hear of Wallace Stevens's difficulties. He seems to have sunk more or less from the scene in recent years, and it seems a great pity, for there are very few poets comparable to him.

Sincerely, / Yvor Winters

MS: *Chicago*

TO HENRY RAMSEY

Feb. 23, 1930

Dear Henry:

Your note came just after the completion of the *Gyroscope* and we mailed your copies promptly. You should now have them.

Pagany in general seemed cheap and unsatisfactory. The essay on O'Neill which you admired—and regarding which I agree with you—was written by the younger brother of Harvey Fergusson, the best-seller. We saw more or less of Francis Fergusson the last summer we were in Santa Fe. He hails from Albuquerque and his family still live there. Ruth [Lockett] is doing very little; she tried a couple of short stories recently, but her plots went beyond her experience, and the results were not very convincing.

Your attitude toward publication is sentimental and dangerous. The publication of one's work in the first place is an exchange of courtesy to persons who are publishing theirs. In a country the size of this, publication is the only means of intellectual contact. Also, it enables one to make more or less personal contacts—via correspondence and what not—of value. I am certain for myself that Tate and Crane, in print and in private, have been very valuable to me. Also, the unwillingness to expose oneself to honest criticism can spring only from fear or from a morbid lack of humility, both of which feelings are natural but undesirable; one should endeavor to eliminate them. Criticism is irritating but valuable. A critic may even be specifically wrong yet theoretically right: Paul Elmer More, for instance, damns all modern literature with one irritated and uncomprehending gesture; he is academic and insensitive. The tragedy of it is, that most modern writers could learn a great deal from him if they did not find his irritation so irritating. Through meeting his moral deficiency with its equivalent, they merely hamper themselves. I hold no brief for appearing in such an affair as *Pagany*—which has two more of my poems and one of Janet's stories, but to which we shall send nothing more. But it is only decent, it seems to me, to at least submit work a few times to such eminently serious ventures as *The Miscellany* and *The Hound and Horn.*

Again, the above is not to be taken as an attempt to evade, on my part, an admission of normal human vanity. Fame is flattering, although one should not take it too seriously. It seems to me a bit unhealthy to refuse, like Jeffers, to admit one's vanity at the same time that one issues one fat volume a year. Incidentally, did you see my review of Jeffers in the Feb. *Poetry?* It is the best review I have written.

The short story plot looks very good, though not so short. You ought to struggle with some prose of some sort. [Achilles] Holt[1] blossomed forth at the last moment with a grand story. He is really quite a person. You had better get back here next year and get acquainted with him.

Also, as a final piece of moral advice, let me warn you against letting yourself be too tortured by the presence and unpleasantness of your immediate intellectual and moral inferiors, such as Kirby and Cathcart, whether you meet them in person or suspect their presence among your readers. I have wasted a great deal of energy that way myself, and regret it. They are always present and they are frequently profoundly unpleasant or try to be; in pure self-defense one has to toughen one's skin and forget them. Greet them cheerfully when you meet them—which is easy—and forget them the rest of the time—which isn't so easy. If they contribute to your feeling about publication, your allowing them to do so is weak again. If everyone shared your fear, culture would be at a standstill and life would be very dull. It may amuse you to learn that Dr. [Margery] Bailey tried twice to get Holt into the English Club and failed; they elected Ruth for some reason, and, I imagine, wonder why. The thought of her among them really amuses me no end.

Yours, / Arthur Winters

MS: Stanford

[1]Achilles "Tex" Holt (1911–1993): poet and fiction writer; student of YW; work published in *Twelve Poets of the Pacific.* YW thought highly of Holt, to whom he dedicated "To a Young Writer" and "The Anniversary." By way of a pun, YW's poem "Chiron" deals with

YW and Holt as teacher and student. YW paid tribute to Holt's scholarship in a note to "Herman Melville and the Problems of Moral Navigation": "In my remarks on the symbolism of *Moby Dick*, I am indebted for a good many details to an unpublished thesis by Achilles Holt, done at Stanford University. Mr. Holt examines the subject very minutely, and I have used only a small part of his material; his thesis ought to be published" (*In Defense of Reason*, 200). Holt's writing career ended early with the onset of severe mental illness.

TO LINCOLN KIRSTEIN

March 4, 1930

Dear Mr. Kirstein:

A few days after I had sent you my essay, and after I had sent it to Tate, as a kind of final word in a long and grueling private fight we have been carrying on for several years, I received a note from Tate regarding the volume you mention. I was already revising the thing, and then added a couple of sections to fit it more exactly to the volume.[1] I disapprove, almost bitterly, of group pronouncements of this kind, but the way in which Babbitt and [Paul Elmer] More—who must be the most curiously innocent and unsuspecting pair of men alive—allow themselves to be exploited by cheap academic journalists and careerists like Foerster and Shafer and Chase and Elliot, even to the prejudice of our struggling but on the whole fairly decent literature, makes me at moments almost venomous. Neither Babbitt nor More knows enough about literature to rattle in a peanut, but they both know enough about a multitude of other things to be very useful in their way. Foerster doesn't even know how to write syntactic English. For these reasons I should like to join Tate and Cowley in their present venture.

I am reviewing Crane for *Poetry*. The book disappoints me. The most powerful things in it are "The River" and "The Dance," and both are unsound structurally, mere conglomerations of superb fragments. In "The Dance," I am not at all sure that the finest passages ("O like the lizard," etc., for instance) ultimately mean much of anything. "Cutty Sark" is perfect but slight. Perhaps the best piece is "Southern Cross." Nothing in the volume equals, for me, two pieces from his former volume, "Repose of Rivers" and "Voyages II." Another crushing blow I have recently received is Elizabeth Roberts' novel, *The Great Meadow*, which left me in a sweat of exasperation. She has been one of my best friends for ten years, and my admiration for her first two books is very great. But she seems to have got into the first two everything she knows and is now diluting it. Such are the fruits of sentimentalism.

Sincerely, / Yvor Winters

MS: Yale

[1]"Poetry, Morality, and Criticism," in *The Critique of Humanism: A Symposium,* ed. C. Hartley Grattan (New York: Brewer and Warren, 1930).

TO MALCOLM COWLEY

April 10, 1930 / RFD1, Box 286 / Palo Alto, Calif.

Dear Cowley:

Your excellent essay in the *New Republic* reminds me of a certain wonder of my own, about which you might possibly set my mind at rest.

A couple of weeks ago I had a note from Mrs. Tate [Caroline Gordon] from some point remote in the south, and I gathered that her husband was with her. Only a short time previous I had mailed to Tate my completed essay for Grattan's volume; I wonder if it ever got to anyone. Later I sent Grattan some corrections for it, but couldn't find his letter, so had to look up an old Payson and Clarke address which may or may not be good now. That letter was never answered. I wonder if the essay or the corrections ever arrived. If they did not, and the book has proceeded without them, I should like to find out so as to publish elsewhere the first part of my essay, the only part that much interests me.

Further, I wonder mildly from my state of innocence, whether it is necessary to write about the city landscape in order to give order to the emotions of the city dweller. Whatever there may be in the "modern mind" that is peculiar seems to me to be bound up with something more important than the traffic. The confusion of the traffic might become a symbol of the deeper confusion; Tate did this with the subway. But simply writing about the subway (as Crane has done) will not give order to the confusion. Crane's "Repose of Rivers," on the other hand, should be as valid within its limits as Tate's sonnet, for the city-dweller; so should Valéry's mathematical vision of the sea ("*Masse de calme, et visible réserve,*" etc.). When Williams praised [George] Antheil for giving order to the traffic he was bughouse. It is impossible for the artist to do anything at all for the traffic; neither can the traffic do anything to him except weary him physically. But he may utilize the traffic as a symbol for something deeper, or he may utilize something else. The traffic cannot confuse or sicken him spiritually unless he is already confused or sick, and in this case the cure may or may not come through the utilization of the traffic. The traffic, in other words, is a handy source of metaphor, like anything else. I have, of course, never seen New York, but I did have Chicago pretty well rubbed into me for several years.

Yours, / Winters

P.S. What did you think of Achilles Holt, in the last *Gyroscope?*

MS: Newberry

TO LINCOLN KIRSTEIN

May 9, 1930 / RFD1, Box 286 / Palo Alto, Calif.

Dear Mr. Kirstein:

Katherine Anne Porter has recently gone off to Old Mexico with a serious case of tuberculosis and $750 to her name, the money being an advance from Harcourt on a completed volume of short stories and an unfinished novel, of which the story you recently printed was a part. Having spent over three years in bed with the disease myself, and my wife having spent seven or eight, I am quite certain that any improvement in Miss Porter's health is impossible if she feels forced to finish a novel before $750 runs out. She should be in bed for the time being and should write relatively little.

Mrs. Allen Tate and I are planning a campaign to bring Harcourt around to doing something decent. Harpers, for instance, paid Wescott a couple of thousand a year for some two or three years till he got going. The plan is this: Someone in New York, probably Wilson or [Louis] Untermeyer, of some kind of official standing, will write Harcourt personally, explaining Miss Porter's situation, pointing out the fine quality of her work and its probable salability, and pointing out that a small investment is very likely to be lost, whereas a larger one might be profitable. This person will then indicate a number of other persons of literary standing who share his opinion of Miss Porter, and who, he will inform H., will write him. At the proper signal, these persons will write, urging the same action. I wonder if you and Mr. Bandler,[1] individually or collectively, would be willing to be among these? If so, write Mrs. Tate (Clarksville, Tenn.) at once for exact instructions, as the campaign is ultimately in her hands.

We have invited Miss Porter to come up here with us if the plan fails, and occupy a shack on our lot near our shack, where we could look after her. The plan is better than nothing, but has disadvantages, the chief being that she will probably refuse, as she knows that my wife is an invalid. If nothing is done, however, she will certainly be dead within a year and a half. You might keep your eye open for a Maecenas at large, in case we can't do anything with Harcourt.

Sincerely, / Winters

MS: Yale

¹Bernard Bandler (b. 1904): one of the *Hound and Horn*'s editors; later a distinguished psychiatrist.

TO LINCOLN KIRSTEIN

May 17, 1930

Dear Kirstein:

A letter from Mrs. Tate has just arrived. If you care to help us in our drive on Harcourt, the final plan is this. The various assistants, of whom you will be one and Mr. Bandler, if he cares to, another, will merely write to H. and express their admiration of Miss Porter's talent and especially of her short stories, a volume of which H. is bringing out this fall. This letter should be written at once. As an editor, you could, if you cared, promise a favorable review. I am promising to review the book, and could do it either for you or the *New Freeman*, which is swamping me, for unknown reasons, with demands for reviewing. I sent them a poem ("Inscription for a Graveyard") just to be sociable, and they sent it back. [Granville] Hicks or [Newton] Arvin would probably like her, too. (Incidentally, if you could give me their addresses, I'd write them.)

After these letters have soaked in, some one, probably Untermeyer, will approach H. and strike him for a raise. U. has not been approached yet, but the Tates seem to think he will be willing to do it. Some one with influence in the publishing world is necessary, of course.

Incidentally, O'Brien is using Miss Porter's story from the third *Gyroscope*, and Mrs. Tate's from the same issue. He almost took Holt's, but not quite. Scribner's are reprinting Mrs. Tate from the fourth *Gyroscope* and seem to have taken her on permanently. O'Brien is using a story of my wife's from the *Bookman*. We are simply deluged with respectable approbation. I have not been so astonished by anything since that damned essay of mine appeared in the *Caravan*.

Sincerely, / Winters

MS: Yale

May 23, 1930 / RFD1, Box 286 / Palo Alto, Calif.

Dear Mr. Kirstein:

The plan for writing Harcourt is transparent, but will be made obvious almost immediately. As long as Harcourt will be the chief financial profiter by her postponed demise, I think he might very well bear some of the expense of the postponement. Publishers rather get my goat that way. One cannot get help from them when it is needed, and they step in and pick up the profits after it is given. Harper's and Heubsch both owe me a couple of rather good-sized checks, or rather they owe them to my father. If I thought they would ever pass them on to some prospective mealticket in distress, I'd call the debt settled, but I know they won't.

There are other reasons for rescuing Miss Porter. If the attack on Harcourt fails, it may be possible to get a Guggenheim Mexican scholarship for her. Tate has already applied. If she runs out of money before that starts, I think we can tide her over with no inconvenience. If the Guggenheim card plays, we can still manage the situation really very easily and with no particular expense, if she will come up and stay with us. If she won't do that, the situation is not so good. In any event, she has enough money to go on for several months, so there is no use in getting too frightened immediately. The only thing about the situation that I don't like right now is the inevitable nervous and as a result physical effect on a tuberculous patient, of an uncertain future and the need of working fast. That is damned bad. I had three years of the disease and I know. But we shall know two or three things definitely very soon, and some of the uncertainty may be dispelled. Thanks for your offer of money, but as things stand at the moment I almost certainly have no moral right to ask for it; that is, Miss Porter herself might well object. If the situation should prove desperate eventually, I'll let you know. I have an idea we can manage it, if her actual condition is not so bad that her way of life proves inadequate as treatment. If it does, she will simply have to join us and go to bed.

"Inscription" and "Communion" are both definitely to be in my book, if that affects your decision regarding them. I believe it is to be out early in the fall, but do not know the exact date.

Sincerely, / Yvor Winters

MS: Yale

June 29, 1930 / RFD1, Box 286 / Palo Alto, Calif.

Dear Mr. Kirstein:

It was very kind of you to send the MacLeish. I have read all of it, some of it several times, and am bound to admit that I still feel much as I did. I shall continue to read it, however, and may repent. It is indisputably good up to a certain point. Lines, for instance, like

> the struck foam
> Flames at the wind's heel on the far Pacific

are as good in their way as anything you can find. Pound, who is probably our chief master of that sort of thing, could hardly do better. But that sort of thing is a grace note, and if it is to achieve a maximum of power must have a very solid composition under it. MacLeish is morally weak; by that I mean simply that he is too lenient with himself, tends to wallow in his feelings and to get pleasure from doing it publicly—it is a kind of unhealthy luxury. I feel it all over the book, and all over the earlier ones. There is, as in the poetry of Aldington (which is not nearly as good), or in the poetry and prose of McAlmon and Carnevali, a great deal of personality which has no meaning in terms of art, that is, of unmastered prejudice of one kind or another that is irrelevant to the artistic issue. One can react to this sort of thing only on the personal level— one can like or dislike the man. I dislike Aldington from the bottom of my heart, feel rather sorry for Carnevali, feel rather impatient with McAlmon for remaining such an adolescent ass, and, as for MacLeish, should like to boot his behind to wake him up. The result of this self-indulgence is that he becomes uncritical of his actual details much of the time. The details preceding the line and a half above become real only if one pause over them and realize one's own experience of the thing described, the high plains of Wyoming, etc. Most of those things mean a great deal to me, but I don't feel that they are very often poetically realized. This hullabaloo about being an American rather wearies me, besides, regardless of the form it takes. Williams' novel, *A Voyage to Pagany,* is one of the most ludicrous things ever penned. He substitutes for the classical struggle of to sin or not to sin, the question of to stay in Europe or go back to New Joisey. It becomes a kind of musical comedy parody. One ought to take one's nationality as the Greeks took their liquor and their sex, without too much worry about it all. There are a great many fundamental facts that one has simply to get used to before one can begin to write seriously; one is America, one is our complex age, and one is the fact that life is tragic. Until one can begin to face these facts more or less indifferently, one will distort and sentimentalize nine-tenths of what one touches. In the light of these facts, or rather opinions, I believe that the best poets under forty years of age, using English, are Allen Tate, Hart Crane (once or twice and more or less accidentally—he is basically all wrong), Howard Baker, and my wife. The last two are unknown, and, if known, would probably be little admired. It may be personal prejudice that makes me believe in them. They seem to me to know a tremendous lot about the art of writing. What they do is basic and uninflated; they do what I should like to do. Of the four, Tate is probably the greatest; Baker, however, is very young—twenty-five or -six—and my wife writes only three or four poems in the course of an average year. It will be fifteen years before she has enough work finished to be generally visible.

Your article in your summer issue is very interesting, though I have not yet finished it, and my life passed almost wholly in villages on the high plains of Idaho, Colorado, and what not, does not make me a very acute critic in that particular field. I am similarly hampered as a critic of painting, but I have one advantage in that respect over your very dire correspondent, [A. Hyatt] Mayor —I am very familiar with the works of one very great American painter, Andrew Dasburg. One needs to see a great many of D.'s pictures, and look at them a long time, to realize their profundity. They are very small in acreage, very unassuming, very finished, and, once they penetrate, absolutely unforgettable. They become as much a part of one's spiritual furnishings as the poetry of Herrick. [Diego] Rivera occasionally equals him—as in the portrait of a Mexican baby, included in the recent volume of reproductions of his work, the original of which is owned in San Francisco, and is infinitely fine. In my imperfect experience, I have met no other living painter who equals him.

[Francis] Fergusson's review is correct to the minutest detail, and is the only good one of the subject I have ever seen. Knickerbocker asked me to review that Rhodes book,[1] but I gave up after half the first volume. The man's method is to set down an idea, or what passes for one, embellish it rhetorically and with metaphors so mixed that no man could follow them, for three pages, and then deposit the next idea and so on. I simply couldn't keep track of the chain of argument for the density of the foliage, and gave up in utter despair. My admiration for the mentality and moral quality of your reviewer is unlimited.

I should have added above that I greatly admire certain poems by your concitoyen, Grant Code.[2] Two or three that he gave *Gyroscope* seemed to me pure knockouts.

This letter is too long and too opinionated. You will observe that my prose has the defects that I attribute to the verse of MacLeish et al. I have ironed those defects out of my verse, but not out of my criticism; the reason is that I do not like to write criticism and do not take the occupation as seriously as I should—I seldom write save in exasperation. The inspiration of the first part of my essay in *The Critique of Humanism* was exasperation with Tate. But for this reason, Tate's review of Crane, contrary to your expressed opinion, is, I imagine, rather better than my own.

Best wishes, / Yvor Winters

MS: Yale

[1]S. Rhodes, *The Cult of Beauty in Charles Baudelaire,* reviewed in *Hound and Horn* by J. Robert Oppenheimer.

[2]Grant Hyde Code (1896?–1974): American man of letters. In the late 1920s and early 1930s, YW liked Code's poetry, publishing some of it in the *Gyroscope*. Code published two volumes of poetry in the early 1970s; most of his work, however, including novels and plays, remains unpublished.

TO GLENWAY WESCOTT

July 7, 1930 / RFD1, Box 286 / Palo Alto, Calif.

Dear Glenway:

Thanks for writing on behalf of Miss Porter. It appears that some wealthy soul in N.Y. is providing her with ninety a month (I think that is right) for the present, so, with the money from Harcourt, she ought to be able to proceed slowly enough if she will.

I have been going over Maurine's mss., and am convinced that there ought to be a popular edition of her poems, containing about forty pieces. I am going to write an essay on her shortly and try to peddle it; after which I shall revise the essay to serve as an introduction, and try to peddle the book, if no objections are forthcoming. What do you think? And can you give me the address of her sister? Her sister ought to contribute some sort of biographical note, and she ought also to be the legal owner of the book, recipient of profits, etc. Maurine was one of our best poets, I am more and more certain. I pulled one or two very bad boners in the way of exclusions, when I was making up the book we published; and there are many sound and excellent pieces in addition, not quite at her top level, that would serve as background—I don't mean the immature and sentimental pieces, of which there are myriads.

What did you think of Holt's story in the last *Gyroscope?* I was quite hit by it.

Best wishes,

Arthur

MS: Yale

TO LINCOLN KIRSTEIN

Sept. 2, 1930 / RFD1, Box 286 / Palo Alto, Calif.

Dear Mr. Kirstein:

Your theory of major and minor poetry is ingenious, but needs to be enlarged upon. There are one or two rocks, I suspect, on which you are in danger of foundering. For instance, most of your poets of opposition have been in opposition to what Babbitt calls the wisdom of the ages—that is, in Europe, to the common Christian standards of behavior. Now those standards in general are sound, and your rebel or heretic, out of the depths of his own naiveté, usually sets up some excessively simple scheme, which excludes from all consideration large and important ranges of experience. Such heretics are Blake, Lawrence, and Shelley. The question then arises, are they minor poets (if they *are* minor poets) because they are poets of opposition or because they are heretics? If because they are heretics, you have added nothing to Babbitt, who has added nothing to Arnold. If you are going to prove your original point you will have to concentrate on those poets who have been in opposition to a temporarily accepted heresy or state of decadence, and you will find very few such. Milton is one, and Baudelaire is another; though how far Baudelaire's gradual renunciation of and opposition to romantic dogma may be said to have invaded his poetry, it might be hard to say—it seems for the most part to have kept ahead of his poetry and provided a constantly broadening antecedent background. This obviously cannot be said of Milton, who wrestles with his soul and with Satan naked on the page. But Milton, though he is scarcely the "second-greatest English poet," is pretty damned great. Reread "Lycidas" and *P.L.*, Bk. 11.

Further, the dyad, major and minor (like the other, good and evil), is delusively simple. You really have not two classes, but a vast number of possible classes, and every damned one of them arbitrary. Leave out of the argument class one, containing Shakespeare, Dante, etc., and for the remaining classes stick to French and English literature, for my and for simplicity's sake. I should place in class two, Baudelaire, Racine, Hardy, Emily Dickinson, Donne, and

Jonson. Below this group, I should have a hard time classifying with accuracy. On what basis, for example, could one compare Chaucer and Valéry? Yet I should call both great.

And then those that fall just short of greatness do so for such curious reasons. Hopkins, for example, has two limitations, as I make it out: (1) His meter (like most of the best organized contemporary free verse, which scans on the same principle—Williams', H.D.'s, my own) lacks repose—that is the poem, and not the line, is the metric unit, to such an extent that the line hardly exists and the poem rushes through from one end to the other in a single roar. This is exciting, but it eliminates all save a certain kind of feeling and consequently tends to simplify feeling—Shakespeare's sonnets can be just as mad, but they can do more things at once. (2) His verse tends to deal a bit too exclusively with the emotion of a given situation (and here I am trying to keep life-emotion and aesthetic emotion apart) instead of with the situation in toto. Consequently, the poetry has not, somehow, quite the density of meaning that you will find in Hardy or Donne. I may not have made this clear, but I think it could be more clear with adequate space. Hopkins is nonetheless deeply moving; many of his poems tend to slip back toward the standard metric and consequently to greater complexity or at least greater potentiality, and some ("Patience is a hard thing," and a few others) have greater density than the general run. But in these two directions lie his weakness. Do they have anything to do with your theory? I really don't know. They do have something to do with each other.

Pound, much as I admire him, does not seem to me of the first order. His details are incomparable, but his direction wavers; he really lacks brains. So frail a creature as Adelaide Crapsey[1] comes nearer to greatness, for me, on a few occasions ("Anguish," "Roma Aeterna"). I should think Stevens would serve you more satisfactorily; he is really a pretty grand old guy.

But by now, I have probably got pretty far off the subject, so I had better stop.

Best wishes, / Yvor Winters

MS: Yale

[1]Adelaide Crapsey (1878–1914): American poet, probably best known as the inventor of the cinquain. YW admired her best work, discussing it in *Forms of Discovery*.

Box 286, Route 1 / Palo Alto, California / Sept. 11, 1930

Dear Henry:

To judge from your letter, it would be an excellent idea to get back to school. Let me assure you, from sad experience, that, however amusing it may be to wreck your health, there is damned little amusement in contemplating the wreckage from a cot in a hospital or a sanitorium. Crane has wrecked one of the greatest talents of our time through the almost systematic breaking down of his health, his reasoning power, and his sensitivity; your native gifts are probably as great. The primary advantage in being a great poet is not that you publish great poems and become famous, but that you develop yourself to the point where you can write great poems and so become intelligent. All the rest is amusing, but not important. To become more intelligent is to become more alive; you are, so far, about four-fifths blind and numb, but you have the ability to dissipate your darkness. Few people have that ability, and it is really worth having. Don't be a jackass. You don't "see life," acquire "experience," etc., by getting drunk; you merely deepen the darkness and ruin the digestion. A friend of mine, Vernon Hunter, who painted the wild watercolor in our parlor, had four or five yards of his tripe removed a year or so ago, in a series of operations that almost killed him. A few more gallons of bootleg *will* kill him, now, as he has no more organs to spare. He is not yet thirty.

I'll send you a copy of my new book in a few days, when I get another. Bunichi Kagawa is publishing a book of English verse this fall; and one of Japanese a little later. Holt has written three stories since the one we published, all superb, and is working on another. He is going to be a great novelist.

We are moving a little farther out of town in a few days, but shall be on the same mail route. If you come to town, you had better phone before trying to find us. We shall always be able to put you up for the night in the new place, which is eminently respectable.

Best wishes, / Arthur Winters

MS: Stanford

TO HOWARD BAKER

Box 286, Route 1 / Palo Alto, California / Sept. 19, 1930

Dear Howard:

We were very glad to hear of your marriage the other day, and send our best wishes to both of you.

I had the misfortune to lose your new address, and got it again from your mother only yesterday. In the interim, I sent you a copy of my new book [*The Proof*] addressed to you at 4 rue Princesse. I sent it only about ten or twelve days ago. If you do not receive it let me know at once and I'll send you another. The chief advantage of this new collection is that it costs next to nothing, and one can throw it around more or less recklessly. It is a cheap-looking little volume, and badly paged, but is neat and will pass muster.

Today or tomorrow I will get a money order for what I owe you and send it on at once—and will write you further.

We are moving next week to a place five or six blocks farther out. The house is not quite so amusing, but is more convenient, I suspect, and the premises are superb—about two and a half acres, with a dog run covering a good acre, good corral and out-buildings, orchard, flower garden, and God knows what. This neighborhood is getting too respectable for goats, and we had to travel. I wonder if all the American villages are as stuffy as this one. The amount of vulgar propriety in the place is enough to stifle you. Anyway we buy no more dog licenses, and I hope to heaven Covy scares some good citizen before we move. Pulga spends her mornings and evenings bleating her—and our—triumph to heaven. She is probably the handsomest and the noisiest goat in the county.

Our best to you and Dorothy, / Arthur

MS: Stanford

TO HARRIET MONROE

Box 286, Route 1 / Palo Alto, California / Sept. 23, 1930

Dear Miss Monroe:

I said the "Ode [to the Confederate Dead]" was the greatest poem of its generation and *one of the greatest* of the century. You really misquote me. As to the use of those two adjectives being forbidden in your magazine, you are, I am sure, mistaken. You once described the egregious Edna [Millay] as the greatest woman poet since Sappho, and to the tune of quite a few pages. How many centuries did it take you to arrive at that conclusion? You once headed a review of Hueffer, "A Major Poet." But perhaps the adjective was entirely military. I could recall dozens of such instances to you, and most of them just as lamentable. Believe me, I shall never be guilty of errors quite so gross. Furthermore, you rather leap at conclusions yourself, I think, when you haven't even read the poem of which I speak.

And why such breathless reverence for the word "great"? The periphrases which you would allow or recommend are really ludicrous formalities. The word is implicit in two or three other places in the review.

If, in consideration of these facts, and if, in consideration more especially of your own past record, you feel that you can, as a woman of honor and an editor of sense, delete that paragraph, by all means do so.

If you delete it, the opening sentence of the second paragraph may need a little alteration, to avoid its seeming abrupt. I leave this entirely to you.

The pamphlet is published. If you print the review, I will see that you get a copy. If you don't, I won't.

Yours, / Yvor Winters

MS: *Chicago*

TO LINCOLN KIRSTEIN

Box 286, Route 1 / Palo Alto, California / Sept. 26, 1930

Dear Mr. Kirstein:

I am not sure I follow all of your argument. You had better make an essay of it. Letters are too fragmentary. What I meant when I called Blake and Shelley heretics was simply that their attitudes, their ethical principles, even, seem to me to have been based on a very incomplete and a rather uncomprehending experience, and to exclude from consideration everything which their authors failed to perceive. Shelley's notion of the nobility of polygamy, for example, is a particularly asinine example of his blindness. The commandment, "Thou shalt not commit adultery," sums up so much more than the mere social contract. It stands for half of experience. It is conceivable that his relations with one of his ladies might have arrived at a normal end, and a new relation begun, but to expect two intelligent women to love him and each other at the same time indicates one of two things, or perhaps both: a colossal blindness to everything happening around him in the minds of others, or a colossal capacity for falsifying his own feelings to himself in order to gratify his momentary desires. A man so stupid simply can't write first rate poetry. Lawrence exaggerates the importance of sexual excitement because he is aware of so little else—that one phase of experience stands more or less nude in his literature, and so on.

Blake, though a better man than either of these, seems to me definitely comparable to them, and far inferior to Baudelaire—far inferior likewise to such men as Henry King or George Herbert.

This is a matter about which it is really impossible to argue. One's attitude toward it depends, I suppose, quite baldly on the nature and extent of one's private experience. But the orthodox Christian ethic is the product of many generations and takes into consideration almost every possible contingency; the amateur systems of post-Stuart literature—the systems that rose among the previously unvocal classes, after the intellectual tradition of the aristocracy had been attenuated to air during the period of the Restoration—strike me as in the main pretty naive. Not "philosophically," logically, but in the matter of actual sophistication. Keats, Arnold, and Hardy come near to being the only civilized poets of the 19th century. I should add Landor. And, in this country, Emerson and Emily, but Emerson only here and there and in spite of himself.

I venture to catalogue the major poets since Hardy: T. Sturge Moore and Yeats (by the skin of his teeth); Robinson; Wallace Stevens and W. C. Williams (a sound poet in spite of all his efforts to be a thorough ass); Tate and Howard Baker. Lawrence and Crane have written great poems, but are hardly great poets. What do you make of that?

I reviewed *Olive, Cypress and Palm* for the *New F.,* but they cut and altered the review so effectively, I had to withdraw it. Their literary section bores me—they seem to be concerned chiefly with the snappy and timely—so I asked them to send me no more books. As a matter of fact the entire magazine strikes me as pretty weak. It is opinionated and waspish, and concerned less with facts than with the ill-mannered reactions of Miss La Follette to the ill manners of her contemporaries. And I am interested in no ill manners save my own.

Yours, / Yvor Winters

I should add that I like the anthology very much.

MS: Yale

Box 249A, Route 1 / Palo Alto, California / Oct. 1, 1930

Dear Henry:

I went around to Culver yesterday to find out about student loan funds—a thing which you may have done previously, for all I know—and learned that they would loan nothing to a student who had been out a year till he had been back for at least a quarter, the theory being that he ought to have enough money to get him that far. I confess it seems reasonable to me.

It occurs to me that you might do this, if it is technically possible: If you can get hold of your scholarship all at once, you could get back for a quarter, and then possibly borrow some for another quarter. If you were here for a quarter, you could probably, by keeping your eyes open, pick up some job that would enable you to earn a little on the side.

Further, I think you are foolish not to ask your father for a loan. I don't know what he said to you that so angered you, but it is hardly likely that he said any more than you deserved. You have behaved like a thorough-going fool, and the sooner you admit the fact to yourself and your family, the sooner you are likely to start acting sensibly. It is really not dignified, you know, to go on indefinitely like a modern version of Sir Fopling Flutter, of whom you may read in a play named after him, by Etherege. I do think, though, that if you ask your family for money, it ought to be in the form of a loan. You ought to begin to be just a little more responsible.

Or here is another way out. If you are, as I seem to remember your saying, earning forty dollars a week, there is no reason under heaven why you should not save half of it. By the beginning of the winter, you would have nearly enough to get through two quarters with the aid of your scholarship, or if you stayed out for a year, you would have more than enough for a year. This would probably be the bitterest pill of all, but, my dear boy, it would do you no end of good to swallow it. If you have so little character that you cannot save, that you are unable to prevent such ignorant, lazy, drunken and inconsequential fools as I take, from your description and his appearance, your friend Buck to be, from twisting you around their fingers and leading you around the gutters on a leash, the university would be perfectly justified in refusing you a loan indefinitely.

I know nothing about your salesman-friend in Vallejo (whose name I can't spell) except what you have said; but his getting you out of Eureka is much to his credit. If he is interested in getting you out of fool company, keeping you sober, and seeing that you earn a decent salary, I think you would be extremely wise to stay with him till you have saved enough to get back to school, unless, as I say, you can borrow something from your family.

Since this sermon has gone so far, it may as well go farther. You had absolutely no business to keep your Vallejo friend waiting for four or five days, as you said you did, without giving him fair warning. Anyone with sufficient patience and good nature to give you a good job after such an exhibition of irresponsibility and bad manners, must think a good deal of you. Your late arrival here the other evening, after you had said you would be in for supper, though it did not inconvenience us in any way (or greatly surprise us), caused Tex to decide that he would rather not go so far as to live with you for a year. And again, he was quite right—much as I like you (and he still likes you very well), I should hesitate to do it myself. Your irresponsibility throws too much responsibility and inconvenience on other people. It is bad manners, and, worse, it is, in the long run, immoral. You have no right to so much more freedom than other persons.

Now, then, if I could loan you anything at the present time, I think I should do it, in spite of the fact that you don't deserve it. But I can't. My salary is small and my expenses will be heavier than usual this year. I shall almost certainly spend more than my salary as it is. If you were ill or for any reason helpless, I would borrow money from my father, without any hesitation. But my father is dying of angina pectoris and is trying to straighten out his affairs in Chicago so as to get away and prolong his life for a few years if possible. As your troubles are due to your own nonsense, I cannot in decency bother him at this time, even for a small sum.

I hope this doesn't make you angry. Believe me, you deserve a cursing out. It is high time you began to act like an adult. You do not look as well as you did a year ago—to put it plainly, you look dissipated—and the dull company you have kept has dulled your wits a bit. You had better pull yourself together, work in the daytime, stay home at night, and spend a little money on good books instead of a lot on bad liquor.

I am giving some private work in English poetry this quarter, and if you do not come back to school, I will send you a carbon of the reading list. You had better follow it. You can get books at the S.F. library, in the second hand stores, and here, if you will come down for occasional week-ends. Or I can mail you stuff, but do come down. In spite of this letter, we are very fond of you.

Yours, / Arthur Winters

MS: Stanford

Box 249A, Route 1 / Palo Alto, California / Oct. 27, 1930

Dear Howard:

I'm glad you like the book. I guess the stuff is good as far as it goes, but it still strikes me as pretty airy. At the moment I am fascinated with heroic couplets. I enclose my first venture, which is a little clumsy here and there, especially in the matter of rhymes, but a fair start, I think. The examples which excite me most, I think, are in Dryden's Vergil and in the poems of Charles Churchill, especially the dedication to Warburton ("Health to great Gloster").

I have been reading Bridges and suspect he is a great poet. The best things are in the *Collected Poems* (Oxford) after the long sonnet sequence and before the quantitative experiments, and in *New Poems* (Oxford, 1926), especially "Low Barometer" and "The Old Mansion." I seem to recollect that Ford used to praise [C. M.] Doughty's poetry very highly. If you could get a list of titles and publishers from him, I should appreciate it. D. wrote an interminable epic [*The Dawn in Britain*], I believe, on English history, beginning with the mythical kings. I have an idea he must be impressive.

Bunichi has a very handsome book out [*The Hidden Flame*]. I'll send you a copy. It was privately printed at the Stanford press. Dr. Bailey and Ruth Mantz financed it. Achilles Holt is working steadily; he has finished three stories since the piece in *Gyroscope,* all at fully as high a level. He knows absolutely what he is doing; there are not more than two or three persons in America who have done any short things as good. He has extraordinary general intelligence. I am pretty sure he is a person of absolutely first rate ability.

Henry is back at school and living with Holt. He is wholly reformed for the present, studying furiously, revising his poems and writing new ones (he wants to publish a small book of them before his twenty-first birthday), and behaving like a model if still somewhat innocent youth. Holt is the best thing that ever happened to him. This year may even save his soul.

I haven't seen Callaghan's new novel; I have seen some very bad stories. He is young enough, though, so that he might go bad—especially in the long form —and still recover. He really did four or five of the best stories I know.

It will be five or six years before we get abroad. I had hoped to get to work on a book of criticism this quarter, but so far have done nothing but German, and little of that. I have been reading *Buddenbrooks*—it is the finest piece of modern fiction I have yet seen. I shall always be a third rate scholar, I fear. It is rather depressing.

We have a seven-weeks-old pup in the house for the moment. I bought him for some neighbors from Holbrook, the old guy in Los Gatos, that Miller gypped so badly. The pup is by the little dog he showed here that summer and out of the bitch. He is a nifty pup, and smart enough, but lacks a little of the genius that our pups had. He takes very readily to sleeping on beds, however.

Our best wishes to you and Dorothy, / Arthur

MS: Stanford

TO ALLEN TATE

December 29, 1930 / RFD 1, Box 363 / Palo Alto, Calif.

Dear Tate:

The "Ode to Fear" I like very much. It will probably take its place eventually among my eight or ten favorites. "Her Posture," I should like nearly as well were it not for the expression "expunger of the mortal streak of nature," which strikes me as clumsy and uninteresting. The thing actually said is unimportant —at least as you have said it—and the phrase strikes me as Gongoristic, to put it mildly. "The Oath" is good basically, and contains moments of great power, but the meter throughout seems to me incoherent and mussy, so that the poem is always starting over, and so that no given moment in the poem really has the rest of the poem behind it. I don't approve of irregular rhyming and irregular lines in general; and if you are going to use them there must be a very clear and smooth flow throughout the poem, as in "Dover Beach" or "Lycidas." Otherwise the poem looks too much like a lot of good notes. And I dislike very much the phrase "time sailing like a magic barque."

The line from my poem ["On a View of Pasadena from the Hills"] to which you object, I read as follows:

With *small* / round *tow'rs* / blunt-*peaked* / a*bove* / small *trees*

And that is perfectly regular. Towers is historically a diphthong, not a dissyllable. The Latin root is a monosyllable, and so is the modern French of it. The Old French and the English are diphthongal. Most diphthongs (our, bower, flower) if they end in a long consonant can be stretched out into a dissyllable occasionally if the meter demands it, but I seldom like the effect. I suspect that you pronounce the word tow-uh with a Deep Southern grunt in place of the r. But personally I pronounce it like an eighteenth century gentleman. I might insert a footnote saying that neo-Confederates may omit peaked. However, I'll put it up to as many competent persons as I can find to pass on it, and abide by their decision. The line is crowded all right, owing to the preponderance of long syllables and dentals in the second foot and third, but I did that deliberately, because the landscape was dry and hard, and I wanted to ease suddenly out of it in the next line. The preceding line is just about as hard. And you apparently don't object to *towers* being a monosyllable in the next line, which strikes me as inconsistent. Do I answer your objection or not? This matter must be settled soon, for the poem will appear in the Spring *H. and H.*

I have a copy of your Southern Symposium [*I'll Take My Stand: The South and the Agrarian Tradition*]. I don't like your own essay at all ["Remarks on the Southern Religion"]. It seems to me that you took a terrifically long way around to something not very difficult to get down, and the end is obscure to me. By violence do you mean a reopening of the Civil War, an Evangelical campaign, or an act of the will? I could believe any one of you, and all three seem to me wholly impracticable. I haven't read all of the book. Of the essays I have read, I like Frank Owsley's a good deal, though I am not historian enough to judge it. Ransom is good, but sounds a bit like Babbitt defending Ralph Borsodi. Fletcher is good but not as good as Babbitt on the same subject, and his ideas are identical with Babbitt's. Also he is a Goddamned slacker, for camping in a London accounting office or some such and shooting peas at American colleges. Why in hell doesn't he come back and help with the dirty work? As a matter of fact, why don't you? You will never be a decent farmer and you would be a first rate teacher. The colleges will be rotten just exactly as long as the best people are outside them. I don't deny that the secondary system should be overhauled, but a great deal can be done even in the present system by a few intelligent persons planted in the right places. To object to associating with the fools already on the job is childish. You refuse to put up with academic fools and as a result have to bite your tongue among journalists. I am free to swear at journalists, and believe me I do it. The academic fools I scarcely lay eyes on from one quarter's end to another. My own tastes are mildly agricultural, despite my background, but I have had a taste of professional agriculture and want no more of it. My uncle, Henry Ahnefeldt, died last year, an exhausted farmer; he started life as a brilliant classical scholar. A farmer has no time to be a scholar or a poet, regardless of how big a place he runs. And I'll bet a dollar that half you agrarians don't even raise your own milk. Anyway, the industrial mess is with us, and we'll hardly get rid of it. We'll simply have to learn to live in it and control it or else go under. And your view of the industrial peasant, like that of all New

Yorkers, is provincial. Most of the population of this country lives in small towns or near them. My next-door neighbor is an Irish peasant on three acres of land, with his own goats and garden, who works in a yeast factory in San Francisco thirty miles away. The peninsula here is covered with others like him. What have you better to offer him? Damned little. He has good hours, a dependable salary, vastly less work than a farmer, and most of the advantages of a farm.

Coward informs me that Howard's book will be out in February. I hope it is good; he has written me practically nothing about it save that he was disgusted with it.

It would be almost a pity to jump on the poor kid reviewing me for the *H. and H.* He is bad enough, God knows, but he is not as bad as most of the rest. He is ignorant and smug, but all reviewers have a right to ignorance, and reviewers for the *H. and H.*, I take it, to smugness. And he is almost certainly very young. The only thing that makes me a bit mad is his remark about his inherited taste. He sounds like Molière's *Précieuses*—People of quality are born knowing everything. I had to work hard for the little taste I possess, and if he thinks his is better, I am a bit inclined to wonder what he has to show for it.

Best wishes, / Winters

MS: Princeton, Allen Tate Papers

TO ALLEN TATE

Jan. 30, 1931 / R. 1, Box 363 / Palo Alto, Calif.

Dear Tate:

*   *   *

Eliot, my dear man, is something left over from your youth, a habit of feeling that you have never understood clearly enough to eradicate, like a nostalgia for Santa Claus. The lady-leopards-bones stuff is the most loosely thrown together bundle of stale imagery I ever saw perpetrated. If you can justify a poem's being trite, not in the introduction, but in every damned line, and with a kind of slip-slop balance of alternate wobbles in place of structure and precise movement, you can prove it a great poem, but not otherwise. It has all of Pound's structural weaknesses, in a much more obvious form, without his secondary virtues of detail. I am perfectly aware that Eliot is trying to do something more intelligent than Pound has the sense to attempt, but that doesn't mean that he is succeeding. If you think you got at my private objections to

Eliot in that review, you are miles from the truth; you didn't even touch them. My objections to his Christianity have nothing to do with my objections to his poetry; I am merely none too damned sure that he is a Christian.

Winters

MS: Princeton, Allen Tate Papers

TO LINCOLN KIRSTEIN

Feb. 1, 1931 / R. 1, Box 363 / Palo Alto, Calif.

Dear Mr. Kirstein:

I shall, of course, be glad to accept your invitation to act as a regional editor, though at the moment your extending the invitation strikes me as a trifle rash. The number of stories which you have printed since I have been reading you, of which I do not actively disapprove, I could count on the fingers of one hand, and the poems I could count on the other.

In your last issue, for example, you print, in Blackmur's essay, one of the chief masterpieces of contemporary criticism, a brilliant essay by H. B. Parkes, a brilliant review by Mr. Bandler, good reviews by Mssrs. [John] Wheelwright and [Dudley] Fitts, an amusing review by Miss Moore, and excellent chronicles. Along with these you print (excepting the moderately good poem by Stevens) the most inordinately bad prose and verse to be found on any news-stand, probably, within the last ninety days. The stuff is as dead as a salt mackerel and no more nourishing than saw-dust. Formally it is fifteen years out of date (if it is supposed to have any value as experiment) and actually (as regards absolute achievement) the methods are badly handled and get at nothing.

To print this junk you have passed up work by Howard Baker, who is one of the half dozen best poets now writing, Henry Ramsey, who is a damned fine poet, and Rowena Lockett, who belongs in the upper ten of contemporary writers of short fiction, and Achilles Holt, who is about as good. I am shortly to edit a series of pamphlets, containing work by these people and others, largely as a protest against your selections. But if I can be of any service to you with tastes like these, why it is with the greatest of pleasure that I place myself at your service.

Sincerely, / Yvor Winters

P.S. I want to make one reservation: the [Catherine] Hubbell story was good, though not exciting.

MS: Yale

TO HOWARD BAKER

March 6, 1931 / R. 1, Box 363 / Palo Alto, Calif.

Dear Howard:

Both sketches are fine, "The Freeze" being about as moving and flawless a piece of prose as I have ever read. If you can't sell them, let me try the *H. and H.* But try the better paying magazines first. I should think *The New Republic* would grab at "The Freeze."

I don't know what to do with my long story ["Brink of Darkness"]. It is too unwieldy as it stands. I could try to build a novel under it, a precarious proposition, or I could break it down into several shorter things, told in the first person. There is too much good prose in it to waste, but the prose is not functioning in the proper way. I still have an idea I could write prose if I could recover my sense of leisure. At present I am obsessed with the necessity of reestablishing my reputation at Stanford with a good dissertation. It is hell to write criticism. Literally, I mean: it makes one feel as if one had the mange.

Arthur.

I'll return the ms. in a day or so.

MS: Stanford

TO KATHERINE ANNE PORTER

Yvor Winters / Route 1, Box 363 / Palo Alto, California / July 11, 1931

Dear Miss Porter:

My father died June 21. I got there too late to see him, though I had visited him three weeks before. When I saw him he had become rather thin, and the more weight he lost the younger he looked. He was a very handsome man, with an extraordinary sweetness about him; three weeks before his death he looked younger than did I, and save for the fact that the blood had left the ends of his fingers, no one could have guessed from his appearance that he was ill. He knew he was dying at that time; he was very weak, and the spells of pain were very frequent and very terrible. He talked of his condition to no one save my sister. He spent his time fingering his favorite flowers, in a kind of sensuous dream, and struggling in a bewildered and pathetic fashion for some complete objectification of his feeling. His melancholy was appalling, but he concealed it with almost complete success from my mother. I have seen him walking about when he thought he was alone, his face drawn with despair, have seen him sit down at the radio, turn the thing on, listen to a cheap blast of music for a moment, turn it off with a horrible sick look, and walk off to try something else; and in half a minute, if he met anyone, his face would be entirely composed.

I suppose I have been unfair in my feelings toward my mother. She was fond enough of my father, and is crushed now. He, heaven knows, was naturally extravagant, and he deliberately misled her with great skill: that is, he immediately, and apparently wholeheartedly, wanted anything that he thought she wanted. She has a strange blind will to see only in one way; nothing can alter her; he might have altered her, but he chose to encourage her. I fear she is beginning to realize now what happened; heaven knows she has enough to regret. The house will be sold now at a great loss, for there is not enough income since the crash to keep it up; if the loss could have been taken two years ago, he might still be alive and fairly well. Or perhaps he might not. And he wanted the house himself, though toward the end it terrified him.

I enclose a snap of Tex Holt and one of Janet with the baby [Joanna]. Tex may have preceded the picture; if not, he will follow shortly.

I had to kill my second oldest dog, Bugs, the other day, on account of a bad bone infection.

The *H. and H.* has taken the first chapter of Janet's novel [*The Invasion*].

I fear you don't like Baker's novel [*Orange Valley*]; you need not fear to say so. I like it a great deal myself, though in many ways it seems clumsy. The prose is often inexpert, and the thing needs trimming. The conception of the character and action, however, of the latter part, especially, seems to me far more mature and valuable than anything to be found in any American novel of the last ten years or so. His next book will not be clumsy, I believe; he is an infinitely fine stylist in verse and should become one in prose. And he has what almost no contemporaries possess, a clear, precise, and profound mind, and absolute sanity of temper. He will develop a trifle more slowly than most people, but he will be a very great man. He and Holt seem to me the most promising people, chronologically, this side of Tate.

We await the appearance of your novel and of Mrs. Tate's with considerable impatience.

Yours, / Yvor Winters

MS: UM

Nov. 30, 1931 / R. 1, Box 363 / Palo Alto, Calif.

Dear Howard:

My last letter did not answer all of your letter, I believe. I should be only too glad to have you review my book. Kirstein may not let you do it, however, for any one of several reasons, no one of which he will confide in you. One of them is probably that he fears you will be prejudiced by friendship, etc. I did my damnedest to get *Orange Valley* from him, but found him as slippery as Proteus. Another reason is that he has to date no very high opinion of your abilities; he will probably prefer to give the book to another Harvard undergraduate, if there is another rash enough to undertake it. The *New Republic* did not review my last book at all, and probably will not review this one.

Harcourt saw a hundred pages of Janet's novel, which she had sent on to Mrs. [Dorothea] Brande of the *Bookman,* and wired her an offer of a five hundred dollar advance on it. She has accepted, and thinks she can finish by April.

I have received page proofs for my book, but don't know when it will be out. I'll send you a copy.

Coo has not come back.[1] I have tramped all over the marshes and have driven for miles through the adjacent byways, have advertised and offered sufficient reward to bring her back were she picked up. Covy has been spending most of his time and energy scouring the marshes, and came back the other night after an absence of thirty-six hours with a cold and a sprained hind leg, but nothing more. He is the most disconsolate dog I have ever seen.

I hope to take two examinations within the next few weeks, and my oral in January. Then perhaps I can get to Berkeley. When does Dr. Durham leave? I should like to see him before he goes if I can.

Our regards to Dorothy.

As ever, / Arthur

MS: Stanford

[1]This incident (described in two letters to Howard Baker) lies behind YW's "Elegy on a Young Airedale Bitch Lost Some Years Since in the Salt-Marsh."

TO HOWARD BAKER

Dec. 10, 1931 / R. 1, Box 363 / Palo Alto, Calif.

Dear Howard:

I have taken my minor examination, but haven't heard from it. The Masters' examination will be on the 14th. So on the 15th I think I could afford to relax. If you and Dorothy and John [Conley] would take supper with us, we should be very pleased—provided, that is, you do not mind beef and vegetable soup or lentils or some such thing for supper. We haven't very much energy at the moment—just recovering from bad colds.

Neiman's friend Cunningham[1] is here, living in the shed on the back of the place next to us and taking his suppers with us. He is Neiman's age, but more mature and intelligent. He is really a very fine poet.

Unless we hear from you to the contrary, we shall expect you.

Arthur

MS: Stanford

[1]J. V. (James Vincent) Cunningham (1911–1985): American poet, critic, scholar, and educator. YW thought Cunningham one of the finest twentieth-century poets. He published a separate pamphlet on Cunningham's work, revised for *Forms of Discovery,* and published his work in *Twelve Poets of the Pacific* and *Quest for Reality.* As the letters make clear, YW taught Cunningham much, but he was never YW's student in the usual meaning of that word. In fact, Cunningham discovered YW's work while on the road during the Depression and wrote him. YW subsequently helped Cunningham get into Stanford. He is one of the four or five writers most closely associated with YW in most minds.

TO HOWARD BAKER

Dec. 27, 1931 / R. 1, Box 363 / Palo Alto, Calif.

Dear Howard:

It seems to me that you got slightly side-tracked on two issues in the review, though I don't feel that my position in discussing them is necessarily more authoritative than yours. There is no reason why you should not hold to your opinion if you want to. I don't believe, however, that I have been very profoundly influenced by Protestantism. I had no real religious training as a child; my parents were both totally unreligious. I was never baptized, never attended church. As a small child, for a very short period, I attended Sunday School off and on for purely social reasons. I have naturally a dogmatic, more or less pedantic temper, have tended always to encase myself in some more or less violent moral code: always, that is, since I may be said to have begun to be conscious, at about the age of fourteen. But I ran through a good many codes before I arrived at my present one, most of them having been not only profoundly unchristian but anti-Christian. My present situation I arrived at, so far as I can judge, in a purely literary manner, by acquainting myself gradually with the tradition of free-thinking and through that with the Greeks, and so on. I have never even struck root in any social scene. I have never lived long enough in one place. In this sense I am perhaps more closely related to the American scene than Tate or even yourself: for the scene has no social character and I have no social roots. I am an almost wholly free agent.

The other matter concerns "The Critiad." I believe it is easy to over-estimate the stability of the standards of the past and to underestimate those of the present. At any rate my standards of criticism seem to me definite enough (they may be wrong—but some of the most definite systems of the past have been fearfully wrong) for Dryden or Pope. My social situation being what it is, there is very little to prevent my adopting the standards of Dryden, or at least adapting them. Secondly, in connection with this poem, I suspect you read into it more profundity than it contains. Mostly, it seems to me good horse-play, approaching doctrine, when it does so at all, mostly by round-about implication. [In the margin:] On rereading the review, I suspect this ¶ is unjustified.

Aside from these points (and a few careless phrases, which I have marked in the ms.) I like the review very much, though it is immodest to say so, for it praises me, I fear, beyond my deserts. In fact, I have no objection to your holding these two opinions that I disagree with, whether privately or publicly: I am simply dubious about them.

Cowley may object to the length of the review, but so far as I am concerned I should be more than pleased to see it printed.

The dress for the baby was very lovely, and the book will be useful and interesting. Many thanks to both of you.

Cunningham is curiously slow in his critical judgments, but is coming on. He admitted about a week ago that you had written great poetry, and last night even came around to Henry.

I am really dubious about the advisability of your publishing a book of verse till you have about forty poems; the quality of your verse is so quiet and the pieces are so short that I fear a small book would simply be overlooked. In a year or two you ought to have enough.

Our regards to you and Dorothy, / Arthur

MS: Stanford

Feb. 29, 1932 / R. 1, Box 363 / Palo Alto, Calif.

Dear Blackmur:

Thanks for your letter. Your comments on the poem are very interesting. I don't think I approve your revision of the couplet, chiefly, perhaps, because you spoil the connections with what precedes and follows. A poem is usually a series of compromises: the trick is to make not only the best individual compromises but the best possible series.

As to Eliot. He is a great critic, as I have always been willing to admit, and I don't really care much about his religion. But in his recent criticism, it has seemed to me that he has been going pretty vague, has been failing rather consistently, in so far as he has spoken of contemporary literature, to realize the literary implications of his theoretical position. He goes ahead awarding vague praise to things like the late Joyce, which, despite the expense of genius, is a waste of verbiage, and like St. Jean Perse. This stuff is anti-Christian, unclassical, and subversive to the state. It is sentiment running wild, running nowhere. And Eliot's poetry is like it. "Ash Wednesday" really strikes me as very feeble, and the stuff published since as worse. The damned seduction scene in *The Waste Land* that Tate praises so highly could have been written by anyone, given the idea and Eliot's early verse: the detail is loose and trite. Eliot's influence has apparently done you no harm, but it did untold harm to Tate for a while, and it sunk MacLeish. Everyone was weltering in it for a while. I don't really like any of his poetry, and his present critical position seems to me awfully ambiguous and wavering.

Your essay on Stevens is a masterpiece of its kind, especially when added to the Cummings piece. I don't agree with your estimate of Stevens entirely, but that has nothing to do with the execution of your essay. The "Comedian" seems to me frequently stiff and uninteresting and far inferior to a dozen or more shorter things. He seems to me definitely at his best when at his plainest, and the alliteration and other fantastic elements in his work seem to me too often the ghost of a Laforguian snicker: it seems to me the business of a poet to arrive at an attitude that he can offer without apology, and I find something definitely sloppy in poetry that establishes a slightly facile attitude only to laugh it down. There is much of this in Eliot's early work; there is little in Stevens. But there is enough in Stevens to make him seem a shade less serious to me than, say, Hardy or Bridges, men who knew how to push through to a conclusion of some kind.

Your poem in *Pagany* I disliked because it showed the influence of the peripheral Stevens, not the essential. I have a feeling that one should emulate in a poet only what he has in common with a few other poets, superficially different from him and from each other.

But I am very tired and am displaying small intelligence, probably. I shan't review Burke because I shan't have the time or energy. I don't like the direction he is taking.

My wife is just finishing a novel for Harcourt. I wish you luck with yours.

Sincerely, / Yvor Winters

MS: Princeton, R. P. Blackmur Papers

R. P. Blackmur (1904–1965): American poet and critic.

TO LINCOLN KIRSTEIN

March 23, 1932 / R. 1, Box 363 / Palo Alto, Calif.

Dear Mr. Kirstein:

I enclose a few more poems by Cunningham and by Miss Lockett. Miss Lockett's ms. contains one published poem and the things I sent you before, simply because I am too lazy to type out another ms.—this one I happened to have.

I asked a fellow named William Saroyan[1] to send you some stories, especially for a couple entitled "A Fist Fight for Armenia" and "A Composition for Ezra Pound." He is not as good as the people you have recently rejected, but he may interest you. He is one of the contemporary picaresque school—[Erskine] Caldwell, Sykes, etc.—with the advantage over most of them that he is not sentimental and does have a sense of style, though he is guilty of stylistic blunders. He can do very good farce, at the very least, and occasionally does something a little better. He is worth watching, whether you take these things or not. He is an Armenian, about 25 years old, with no education except what he has picked up himself, has peddled vegetables for a living, and done similar work.

Baker has done some very fine short prose recently, but it is probably a waste of time to send it to you. Let me reiterate, however, that in Baker you are rejecting a great man, just now coming to his full power, a master of both prose and verse, for a lot of clever drug-store boys who will be forgotten in two seasons.

There is a man in San Francisco named Clayton Stafford[2] who has done some very interesting verse and who is improving very rapidly, but who has not quite arrived. If he sends you anything, read it carefully.

I am taking the liberty of providing an acquaintance of mine, R. L. [Robert

Louis] Burgess, with a letter to you. He is driving east presently. I do not understand the man; perhaps you may. He is about forty years old, a newspaper man, and writer at large, now about half way through some sort of epic. The epic has its interesting moments, though it seems to me fundamentally bad. If you could give him any tips about where he could break into the free-lance game (at which he would be extremely competent) it would be a great favor. Don't let him talk you to death.

I am mailing you under separate cover a ghost-story of my own composition, about which I feel a good deal of curiosity but no certitude. It is not the sort of thing that I approve of in general, but I though it might be worth trying once.

Sincerely, / Yvor Winters

P.S. I'll get the reviews off in a week or ten days, including Tate.

MS: Yale

[1]William Saroyan (1908–1981): American novelist, short story writer, dramatist, and memoirist. YW knew Saroyan personally, and they corresponded briefly. During this period YW made various efforts on behalf of Saroyan's stories.

[2]Clayton Stafford (1903–1981): American poet and businessman; included in *Twelve Poets of the Pacific*. Stafford was a lifelong friend of YW.

TO ALLEN TATE

April 17, 1932 / R. 1, Box 363 / Palo Alto, Calif.

Dear Tate:

I have long meant to thank you for the book, but all of us here are working so damned hard we are next to sick most of the time. You already know what I think of the poems, so there is nothing much to say. A great deal of the stuff seems to me unpardonably clumsy; some of it—quite enough of it—seems to me very great, perhaps the greatest poetry of the century. I have done a review of it for Kirstein.

I took my oral preliminaries a while back, and am now working on a book of criticism, which I had thought once might serve as a dissertation, but which I suspect now will not be acceptable. Anyway, I shall have it finished and looking for a publisher in a few weeks. The scheme of it goes thus:

Chapter I. First section of essay in Grattan's book, slightly revised.

Chapter II. A definition of poetic convention and of certain types of it.

Chapter III. Long essay on the influence of meter on poetic conventions and themes.

Chapter IV. Short essay, on the mechanics of the image, salvaged and revised from the mess in *Secession* years ago.

Chapter V. *Caravan* essay, entirely rewritten, rendered coherent and comprehensible. Completed this far.

Chapter VI. Chapter on primitivism and decadence. Unwritten.

Chapter VII. Chapter on Bridges, yourself, and probably Howard. Mostly written.

I have been reading [Kenneth] Burke's *Counter-Statement*. It is a tremendously brilliant book, but basically a vicious one. It rests on several fundamental fallacies: that the artist can be provided with a morality on the basis of what society needs; that there is an arbitrary line beyond which the evaluation of technical method cannot profitably be carried; that sound feeling is by definition impossible (hence the need of protective irony); that art is non-moral. At its crucial points the book is as superficial as Cowley. For the rest, it is great stuff. Burke's imaginative prose is wrong from the ground up, chiefly as a result of his chaotic theories.

I enclose a bundle of more or less gnomic verses, some of which you have seen. One or two of them may not amount to much—"Before Disaster" and "Sonnet to the Moon" in particular—but on the whole I am really more satisfied with them than with anything else I have done.

My story, "Brink of Darkness," cut down to half the length in which you saw it and much clarified, I have sold to the *H. and H.*

Yours, / Yvor Winters

MS: Princeton, Allen Tate Papers

TO ALLEN TATE

May 1, 1932

Dear Tate:

I saw a small newspaper notice of Crane's death a few days ago. Do you know anything about it? My immediate guess was suicide—religious self-immolation. I may have been influenced by the fact that I had just completed my book of criticism, & all my analysis of his work pointed that way: quite hair-raising. And yet after [Harry] Crosby's death Crane wrote me that Crosby probably considered his death necessary to his further exploration of the universe. If it was suicide, he at least had the courage of his convictions, whatever cloudy notions they were based on, & definitely called the bluff of a hundred-odd years of hypocritical pantheistic mysticism. I suppose his best poetry was written & that he couldn't have lived long anyhow, living as he did, but it adds to the feeling of tragic waste that one has about him. He was a great poet, but he had the genius for a poet four times as great as he was.

Janet's book is postponed to Sept. I have sent my ms. to Harcourt. It is a bad time for criticism, though.

Burke's novel is as feeble a mess as Cowley's poetry. It is really contemptible. I wonder how I was so taken in by the opening chapters when they first appeared.

[Angel] Flores is publishing Howard's poems.

Winters

MS: Princeton, Allen Tate Papers

TO LINCOLN KIRSTEIN

May 4, 1932

Dear Mr. Kirstein:

I'll get a note off on Crane in a day or two, and something on Blunden and Miss Young.[1] Also a few revisions for my story.

I am rather dubious about the advisability of continuing formally as one of your editors.[2] I have sent you work that in several instances seems to me first rate, and you have rejected it in favor of work that seems to me beneath contempt. We have very little in common, I imagine, as far as tastes are concerned. I should not mind having my selections turned down, since, after all, you are paying for the magazine, but I am dubious about appearing publicly as responsible for the junk you select. Most of it seems not only bad as writing, but personally abominable. Our differences of taste might be summed up in our attitudes toward *Conquistador*. You find it a great heroic poem, and I find it a dirty little smear, one of the most abject and sickly messes I have ever labored through. I really am unwilling to stand publicly for your taste unless you are willing to put up with mine. If you were willing to allow me five pages an issue, with the privilege of taking it all at once for the year if I got a long story I really wanted, and the five pages to be filled by work I *select*, not work that I write, it would be another matter. As things stand, I am forced to submit wholly to the judgment of three gentlemen, who though wholly estimable have never done anything to make me willing to submit. As you probably know, I am not famous for my patience.

The above paragraph is not to be understood as a personal diatribe, but as a simple and honest statement. If I withdraw from your list of editors, I shall be only too glad to send you informally any interesting work that may come my way and to contribute my own work occasionally so long as you desire it.

Faithfully, / Yvor Winters

P.S. What do you know about Crane's death? I have seen only a small newspaper notice.

MS: *Yale*

[1]Edmund Blunden and Kathleen T. Young. YW added Young to his omnibus review but wrote nothing on Blunden.

[2]Lincoln Kirstein and Bernard Bandler convinced YW to remain the western editor.

TO GRACE HART CRANE

May 26, 1932 / RFD 1, Box 363 / Palo Alto, Calif.

Dear Mrs. Crane:

I have your letter of May 23rd. I have intended for several weeks to go through my papers to see what I might have of your son's, but both my wife and myself have been very busy and very tired, and I have not done it. I will try to do so, however, within the next week or ten days, and I will let you know what I find.

My present impression is that I have no unpublished poems. Your son was angry at my review of *The Bridge,* and our correspondence dropped at that time. The poems he had previously sent me have by this time (I think) all appeared in print. I trust that you are acquainted with the magazines containing most of the things not included in the two books: *transition* and *The Dial.* There is also a small piece in *Larus,* which I will copy out for you on the chance of your not having seen it.

I hope you will not take it amiss if I make a few general suggestions. Your son, when all the flaws in his work have been pointed out, was a great poet. One consequence of the fact is this: that his admirers will not soon forgive a poor piece of editing or of biography, the sort of thing, for example, that Emily

Dickinson's niece, Mrs. Bianchi, has done. I should advise against undue haste, therefore, as it is humanly impossible that you should act with the greatest possible clarity at this time. Further, I hope you will consult Allen Tate (address: Merry Mont, Trenton, Kentucky), as he is beyond a doubt the finest critic in America, and he is probably more familiar with your son's work than any other single person. The task of editing a poet, especially a poet so difficult as your son, is a very dangerous one for anyone save a specialist. People too close to him personally and not sufficiently familiar with his intellectual and literary background may do him a serious injustice and themselves a serious injury. Mr. Tate wrote me that Mrs. Cowley was designated by your son as an executor. Of this I know nothing. But, though she is doubtless an estimable person, I would strongly advise your obtaining an abler literary assistant if one can possibly be obtained.

The news of your son's death was a great shock to me. I met him only once, for a few days, when he spent a winter in California, but my correspondence with him extended over several years, and my admiration for his poetry, which goes back about ten years, has been very great. I shall cherish the few mementos I have of him.

I shall write you of my findings presently. If I can be of any other assistance to you, kindly inform me. Meanwhile, I hope you will believe in my sincere sympathy.

Faithfully yours, / Yvor Winters

MS: Columbia, Hart Crane Papers

Grace Hart Crane: mother of the American poet Hart Crane (1899–1932).

TO ALLEN TATE

June 21, 1932 / R. 1, Box 363 / Palo Alto, Calif.

Dear Tate:

I should have sent you a copy of the letter I wrote Mrs. Crane, but neglected to make one. I warned her of the dangers of publishing an inadequate book, and strongly advised her to consult you. I advised her against Mrs. Cowley. She has not answered me. I believe I shall do nothing till I hear from her and then refuse to cooperate unless I know with whom I am cooperating. I have no unpublished poems, and the task of rounding up the published things is a very small one. The job of copying and providing footnotes for Crane's letters to me is quite a big one, and one which I really haven't time for now. I could do it in a year or two and let the *Symposium* have them, if it seemed advisable.

Cowley gives me an earache every time I think of him.

I have been going over Crane's stuff, and think it can be reduced to three fine poems—"Voyages II," "Faustus and Helen II," "Repose of Rivers"—and a good many brilliant fragments. The poem to Emily Dickinson is very good, also, but not on so high a level, and "The Hurricane" is an evenly written thing but is basically diffused and descriptive, despite its brevity. That is, its images illustrate and expand the theme, like much of Hopkins: they are not the theme itself.

The material for Flores does not, as I told you, have to be new. "The Anabasis" is first rate. I think the E.D. essay one of your best, but it may be too long for him. You might ask him. The essays on "Regionalism and Sectionalism" and on "Poetry and the Absolute," would be two first-rate and shorter alternatives.

I am going to revise the central chapter of my critical opus, do a long introduction and some footnotes, submit it as a dissertation and for publication by the Stanford press (I believe it will be successful both places) and try to do a complete survey of Yeats this summer. I should like to do a book of about four long essays on separate contemporaries, to back up the book I am now completing. Thereafter, I shall do a study of Tudor lyrics from Wyatt to Raleigh, inclusive, but exclusive of Sidney and Spenser. It is badly needed, and I know my way around pretty well. Thereafter a study of the relationship of the Cavalier and Metaphysical poets to the minor Elizabethans: another neglected and curious subject.

Yours, / Winters

MS: Princeton, Allen Tate Papers

TO LINCOLN KIRSTEIN

August 6, 1932 / R. 1, Box 363 / Palo Alto, Calif.

Dear Mr. Kirstein:

I vote against all the enclosed mss. unreservedly and regardless of what else does or does not come in. It is better to get out a smaller issue, or an all-critical issue than to run stuff like this. To take the stuff up specifically:

[Walter] Lowenfels: "Mental Climate." A rehash of some kind of secondhand Bergsonism. Stylistically a bastard compromise between bad poetry and bad expository prose. [Julien] Benda on Bergson covers the subject thoroughly.

Lowenfels: "Bruno." Theme, a sentimental stereotype. Formal outline nil. Not a single distinguished phrase. This goes for everything by L. that I have seen so far.

[James] Laughlin: No theme, one or two fair descriptive phrases, nothing in the nature of poetic summary. No formal outline, undistinguished line-rhythm. Seems to be a nice kid, but don't publish him for that reason: ask him to tea and give him good advice. If this were handed me by a sophomore comp student, I might grade it B– –. Also, be on your guard against late Old Testament themes, now that T.S.E. is going in for them. E. is always easy to imitate: a kind of psychic impressionism, formless curiosity about queer feelings attendant on queer thoughts, and if poetic structure comes out hindmost, why the devil take it. Fergusson did it rather well, but the Joyce and Eliot epidemics are damned tiresome.

[Paul Eaton] Reeve: a very youthful attempt to combine Black and "*Bateau Ivre.*" Lines here and there suggest that the writer may learn to write, but so far he (or she) has not learned. Dead flat meter, utterly ludicrous and amateurish grandiloquence. No idea of where it all is going.

[Parker] Tyler: guessing black or white. No subject, hence no form or direction.

These people are all symptoms of the same thing: the decay of the rebellion of 1912. They think they are in an advance guard: they are really a rear guard. They cannot organize their material into precise statements within a precise form, because they do not know what they are writing about. They are myopic marksmen shooting at an atmospheric blur with a shotgun. Young writers doing this sort of thing should not be published in order to encourage them. They need to be discouraged and to have sound models put before them.

In the interests of controversy I shall send you under separate cover three poems by Baker, on which he is still working. These are not submitted for publication at present, for he is not sure that he is through with them. I shall enclose with them a detailed criticism of their faults and virtues. Even with their faults on them, they are superior to practically anything that is being written at present.

In the interests of controversy also, I suggest that you reread in the current *Poetry,* my wife's poem "The Clock," which you rejected a year or more ago because you did not like its rhythms. Do not write me and tell me you now like

it. Don't mention it at all. Study it. No one in my generation, and I do not except Tate or Crane, is capable of such firm and masterly rhythm. Set this down
to egoism, but keep on studying the poem. I would gladly sacrifice my reputation to civilize the *H. and H.* Incidentally, my wife has no poems for sale at
present.

I continue to recommend that you obtain poems from Grant Code,
T. Sturge Moore, Allen Tate, and Louise Bogan, all of them out of my territory.
Viola Meynell[1] is worth investigating.

Thanks for accepting Cunningham.

Incidentally, as a matter of policy, you ought to stop advertising contents
that your magazine does not contain. It really irritates a great many people,
and quite needlessly.

Sincerely, / Yvor Winters

MS: Yale

[1]Viola Meynell (1886–1956): British woman of letters; daughter of Wilfrid and Alice
Meynell. YW spoke of her poetry and essays.

TO LINCOLN KIRSTEIN

August 31, 1932 / R. 1, Box 363 / Palo Alto, Calif.

Dear Mr. Kirstein:

The enclosed mss. are innocent but dull. I am against them.

Your poems came the other day. I shall be glad to read them, and will write
you of them in a few days.

Holt will send you his Texas thing in a few days. He has been up here for
the past five days, and will get home within a week.

Soon after you asked me to act as regional editor, I asked William Saroyan
to send you some stuff. He had only one decent copy of his mss., which was
bound up in a cover like a magazine, and which he had been lending to a dozen
or so friends for amusement. He sent it to you and got it back with some sort
of smart crack from Flato about its being good enough for the circulation he
had, but not good enough for the *Hound and Horn.* The circulation he had was
small but fairly distinguished and it admired some of the work much more than
it can admire Flato's. In the future, when I ask some one to submit work, the
wise-cracks had better be sent to me and a rejection slip to my friends. Kindly

urge Flato to remember this: it is a matter of courtesy that would be natural even to the average newsboy. And kindly ask him to consider that his ass is kicked, with my compliments.

Two of the stories Saroyan sent you, I am going to return some time soon, for reconsideration, along with some of his more recent work. His best work, though it is not as good as Holt or Baker, is far above the level of most of the better known of the younger fictionists. He can really write prose. I would advise you all to read it carefully.

Yours, / Yvor Winters

MS: Yale

TO LINCOLN KIRSTEIN

Sept. 2, 1932 / R. 1, Box 363 / Palo Alto, Calif.

Dear Mr. Kirstein:

I have read the poems through. I have scratched up the ms. rather badly. After "You As My Blood," the unmarked poems are those which I found consistently dull, and I have marked passages I liked or have marked up generally poems that seemed worth further work. I take it the order is chronological. The earlier things are mostly a bad mess. The writing improves as you proceed.

"A Prelude" and "Notre Dame des Cadres" strike me as the best. They are the only things that really interest me as units. I should like to see them in the magazine. There are a few fine lines scattered through other poems, and some passable lines, all of which I have marked.

The surrealiste war sequence is done cleverly, but the trick is too easy.

In general, your themes are never sufficiently explicit and fail to account for your perceptions: the result is a good deal of repetition and incoherence. This is the vice of MacLeish and Miss Young. In general, however, their talents are more or less adjusted to the weakness, the degree of vagueness in the theme corresponding to the degree of vagueness in the image. Your best images are more precise, and hence point to the vagueness of your structure: it is as if, here and there, you had tried to suspend a stone in an aquarium. I like the stones, but not the intention of the effort. I should guess, then, that you would do better if you attempted a more reasonable structure: this, of course, is my critical advice to every one of late, but some people probably can't follow it. You will have to follow it, I think, if you are going to write coherently even as to feeling. Whatever talent you have is definitely at odds with your method. Miss Young's talent is adjusted to her method.

The two best poems are a little thin and tricky, and recall Eliot and Laforgue in ways that trouble me vaguely, but they have a great deal to be said for them. The experience back of "Notre Dame" (the Laforguian one) is, I think, immature and naive, but it is well defined. It is a kind of immaturity from which few persons have broken loose, but it is not inevitable. The best passages (the blank verse) in Blackmur's "Funeral for a Few Sticks" have a similar innocence: in B.'s poem, it takes the form of a sickly "disillusionment" over sexual experience, a turning away from something he had never taken the trouble to see and understand. I admire the writing—enormously—yet can't take it awfully seriously or read it with much pleasure.

If you were to set out to reform yourself along the lines I recommend, I suspect that the first steps would be rhetorical, rather than moral or philosophical. Just for instance, I shall list a few of the poems which illustrate most perfectly the qualities of style and construction I most admire:

George Herbert: "Church Monuments"

Lady Winchilsea: "The Tree," "The Change"

Charles Churchill: "Dedication to Warburton" ("Health to great Gloucester")

Barnabe Googe: "Dr. Bail," and epitaph on Grimald

Gascoigne: the poem on the spendthrift, in the series written on leaving the law courts

Howard Baker: "The Quiet Folk," "Travelogue"

Tate: "Ditty" (except the close of the first stanza)

Bridges: poems listed in review

Frost: "Acquainted with the Night"

I could list more, but this random collection will suffice. There is greater poetry than some of these things, but not more perfect poetry. The theme is definite, the procedure is economical, the feeling is exact, each detail contributes a definite and necessary part to the statement. In the school of poetry which you are emulating the theme (when it exists) is merely an excuse for spreading oneself over as much perceptual material as possible: the result is confusion and sentimentality.

Sincerely, / Yvor Winters

MS: Yale

Oct. 23, 1932 / R. 1, Box 363 / Palo Alto, Calif.

Dear Mr. Kirstein:

I shall have to keep Mr. Bandler's essay for a day or two longer, but will get it back as soon as possible.

The Macleod composition seems to me worthless. It seems to be one more attempt to render something of the mood of the latter part of the "Season in Hell," though there is little to base the guess on save the confusion, the cadence of a few sentences, the remarks about history, the mood to which he lays claim. The first paragraph is a good sample of the weakness that persists throughout. "Melodies and defeats" used in this vague sense are a dimly Rimbaldian stereotype. "Slovenliness of deceit" is more or more less similar, at least in its attempt to cover up a lack of precise perception, physical or intellectual, by a loose expression. "Soft colored walls" ditto. "Ponderous dark mountains" ditto. "Sharp" and "austere" are here used, ditto. "Cubistically": the attempt on the part of a writer to call in another art to his aid is always a confession of weakness, and this word has only the vaguest of connotations here, unless, at any rate, one is familiar with the fifth-rate paintings of the New Mexican art colonies. "Almost, but not" a further confession of inability to say precisely what he has in mind.

The theme, in so far as there is one, is confused, second-hand, and badly understood. All of the writing is as bad as the paragraph analyzed. Incidentally, I have never seen any Macleod that seemed to me any better.

The Reeve poem seems to me equally worthless. The theme, that of absolute bewilderment at the universe, symbolized by the entrance of the newborn, is an old one, and has always been dangerous. I object to the dangers, not to the oldness. It is suggested in Vaughan; it is the most considerable and evident aspect of Traherne's invariable theme of the beatitude of infancy; it is used by Blake ("Into the dangerous world I leapt"); and something like it appears in "*Bateau Ivre*"—the bewilderment is there, I mean, not the new-birth. The bewilderment of Rimbaud in general, however, is the bewilderment of a man who deliberately seeks a new birth, a shuffling off of all acquired meanings. The theme in general is unsound: theoretically, it means that everything is meaningless, and the only way in which anything can be even temporarily interesting is by virtue of its strangeness. Rimbaud, when limited by this theme, had sufficient genius to render his material surprising and at least temporarily interesting. So did Traherne. Blake and Vaughan spent most of their time on other subjects. The theme renders even a genius pretty bloodless, however, and Reeve is no genius. I cannot find a single line in the poem that is well perceived. The rhythm is a broken-down blank verse. The way to vary blank verse is not to throw in irregular lines all over the place, but to work within the line. Jonson and Milton can still be studied with profit. Free verse is not sloppy blank verse. If Reeve really admires Williams as much as he claims, he would do well to study him. The regular blank verse lines in the poem are dull as blank verse rhythm: they are heavy class room conceptions. You say Reeve has vigor, but I don't understand you. A poet displays vigor by writing good poetry. There is none here. Reeve talks about loud noises and bad smells, but it does not take poetic vigor to do that.

You say that you feel you ought to devote some space toward encouraging young writers. I think on the whole you ought. But you ought to know, or think you know, what you are encouraging. If you find a young writer who is imperfect, but who is trying to be intelligent and who displays talent at least by fits and starts, who as far as you can judge is endeavoring to raise all his work to the level of the fits and starts, not to reduce those fits and starts to the level of the rest, you might be justified in printing him. Reeve represents a dead level of worthlessness: to encourage him is to encourage him to continue where he is and either to encourage other young writers to emulate him or to confuse them.

[Winfield Townley] Scott's poem may illustrate my thesis further. I have seen a fair amount of his work: I took his magazine, *Smoke,* for a time, and he once sent a bundle of poems to Cunningham. I have not liked his work in the past. This poem, however, has definite virtues.

I am always suspicious of a wandering rhythm, but there is excellent precedent for it ("Lycidas," "Dover Beach"), and it is used here with a good deal of charm and some skill. The lines about the afternoon sun and the "illuminate hair" are striking, especially the latter. The conception is definite and serious. There is much that is just a little trite and inept: "alone before solitude," "precisely grown," "storming whirl of silence" at least. The general effect aimed at is a little too soft and slow for my taste. But there are certain definite things to be said for it. There is nothing to be said for Reeve or Macleod: their efforts are still-born efforts to be modish. If you feel that you have space for a poem of this sort, you could at least print Scott with some idea of why you were printing him. I think you have rejected better work: Ramsey, for example, has done three superb things, little short of major poetry, that you dropped like hot potatoes. But they are no longer available, so it doesn't matter.

Williams, I know, likes Reeve—more or less.[1] Far be it from me to deny that Williams ought to know something about poetry, or that every reader will be blind to a certain amount of good work. But before you take W.'s recommendations too seriously, you ought to cast your mind's eye back over the duds he has most enthusiastically backed: Wallace Gould, Carnevali, Alvah Turner, and McAlmon are his great favorites. Pound has done no better outside his own generation, the defects of which he shares and does not perceive. These gentlemen are not too old: the trouble is, that they will never be old enough. Our own generation, and the kids who are coming up, seem to be divided more or less clearly between those whose intellectual background is incomprehensible to the older men and who therefore remain largely meaningless to them, and those who imitate them feebly and flatter them in numerous ways (Zukofsky is the most shameless toady extant) and who are therefore praised by them.

I will start on Moore at once: I can use the Stanford library copies. But please try to bum review copies for me. I want the books very much, and can't afford them. I am going to praise Moore with more enthusiasm than he has ever received, and they can well afford to send me the books.

I wonder if you could get Morris Cohen to review for you. His book has been greatly overrated, I think, but he is a lively and intelligent man, and on the side of the angels: when he knows which side they are on. It is simply impossible for any one save a specialist to select authoritatively the best books in fields of special and difficult scholarship. It is impossible for a young man to do it. I should not even attempt to cover such a field as English scholarship: I am too closely tied down to particular work, at present, to begin to keep up with it.

Sincerely, / Yvor Winters

MS: Yale

[1]YW had written William Carlos Williams about Paul Eaton Reeve: "I am, as usual, wholly unable to grasp the significance of your critical and editorial activities. As editor of the *H. and H.* I recently examined a poem by a person named Reeve, an attempt to do Blake's 'Into the dangerous world I leapt' (I quote from memory) in imagery that was a stale imitation of 'Bateau Ivre,' and in a stale and bumpy blank verse. The poem was accompanied by a letter from Reeve, sloppy sales talk, and quoted at length a letter from yourself praising the poem in the most astonishing and fantastic terms. You really ought to know better than to write that kind of letter about that kind of a poem to that kind of a person" (August 18, 1932 [MS: Yale]).

Nov. 6, 1932 / R. 1, Box 363 / Palo Alto, Calif.

Dear Tate:

I have here your story "The Immortal Woman," sent me by Kirstein. I think it is very nearly a very fine story, but it seems to me to need—and need badly—a good deal of rewriting and clarification. My objections fall under two heads, narration and style.

Narration:

1. Near the beginning the narrator speaks of something as occurring during the ten years of his illness, as if he were now well, yet he speaks throughout from the wheel-chair.

2. The relationship of the people seen in the street to the people who lived in the house is totally obscure. It ought to be absolutely plain. A story is something you tell, not something you try to conceal.

3. As a result of the above obscurity, there are various incidental obscurities. The actions of the people in the street are largely meaningless. The football image at the end is meaningless and verges on the ludicrous.

Style:

1. The parts spoken by the narrator should be cleaned up a little, the occasional vulgarisms of idiom and construction removed. Mostly he is too sophisticated a soul for these things, and they jar badly. Or you might lower his level, except that I don't think you capable of it. And much that is valuable—in the way of the subtler Tatisms—would have to go. As he stands he is inconsistent and confusing.

2. The gossip's conversation needs to be freed of a good many stilted and excessively literary sentences which are improper to her. For example: "On the other side round the kitchen and the quarters grew in dense clusters bushes of flowering quince." This is a damned clumsy sentence in any context, and it is certain that the woman supposed to speak it would never have spoken it. No one speaks so. There are many other such accidents in her conversation.

3. Punctuation. If you bear the standard system any grudge, you should at least be consistent with some system of your own. Sentences of identical construction are punctuated in a wide variety of ways, with the result that one is perpetually confused in reading and frequently blames the actual writing unfairly. Often your punctuation leads to astounding ambiguities. Thus: "It encloses the garden and midway along it opens, or opened once an iron gate now a rusty green . . ." In connection with this sentence, note: (a) that there should

be a comma as a matter of course after garden (rule: independent clauses sep-arated by coordinating conjunctions should be separated also by a comma) and after gate (since the modifier is non-restrictive); and (b), what is more im-portant, that as you have written the sentence the word *it* is ambiguous when one comes to it, since it may be taken either as the object of *along* (which it is) or as the subject of *opens* (which leads to nonsense later in the sentence and forces one to go back and reinterpret, to the prejudice of whatever effect you are aiming at). The sentence should be written as follows: "It encloses the gar-den, and midway along it there opens, or opened once, an iron gate, now a rusty green." Please take this seriously: I am not nutty from teaching sophomore comp. Your prose is structurally rather complex, and inadvertencies of this kind produce the utmost confusion. The prose is swarming with them.

If you would go over the thing once more and clean it up, it would be one of the best stories in a long time.

Sincerely, / Winters

P.S. My wife agrees with the above.

MS: Yale

TO LINCOLN KIRSTEIN

Nov. 22, 1932 / R. 1, Box 363 / Palo Alto, Calif.

Dear Mr. Kirstein:

I can see nothing in Muriel Rukeyser. You sent me last summer a poem of hers about the sea that was better than anything since, at least as regards meter and organization, but it didn't impress me awfully. The stuff seems confused and repetitious and nowhere clean in detail.

Your rejection of [Albert] Guerard,[1] and the reasons you give for it, raise a critical issue that I think needs definition. The remarks I made about Miss Young do not apply to Guerard at all: in fact, he possesses precisely the virtues she lacks, and that one story is worth everything she has so far done. The ar-gument can be reduced to these principles:

1. A story may deal with a plot: that is, the interaction of character, or the influence of a situation on a character which leads to action.

2. A story may deal with a mood: that is, the influence on the feelings of a character of some situation.

1a. Stories of either of the above types may be treated logically: that is, the facts may be given in their natural order and may in addition be subjected to more or less analysis.

2a. Stories of either of the above types may be treated as a wandering mood dictates: that is, perceptions, recollections, odds and ends of consciousness may drift through the mind of the character, in the end leading us to guess the situation.

1 and 2 are questions of subject matter, and either is perfectly legitimate in a short story or sketch. Other things being equal, 1 *is likely* to result in greater power than 2, because it contains an additional principle of organization, an additional kind of material, or meaning. But other things are seldom equal, and a first-class story of type 2 is worth more than a second-rate story of type 1. To rule 2 out of the magazine arbitrarily is silly: it amounts to ruling out much of the best of [R. B.] Cunningham-Grahame in favor of Hemingway and of writers vastly weaker yet. It amounts to ruling out Baker's really great sketch "Freeze" (which is no longer available, and which I am not trying to sell you) in favor of tripe like "Off the Luke Road."

Types 1a and 2a are types of treatment. "Off the Luke Road," Flato's story, and all of Miss Young, in fact most of the fiction you have printed, belong to type 2a. Either type of treatment may be applied to either type of material, but when 2a is applied to 1 the power theoretically to be derived from a plot is nullified, since the plot is merely something disclosed, to be guessed, information in a footnote giving one a merely incidental clue to why so and so appears to be such a damned fool. Plot functions as a principle of organization only when its details are given in their natural order and the feeling is organized with relation to the action. The "plot" in Burke's novel, for example, is perfectly meaningless, a thin excuse for calling it a novel; ditto, the "logic" behind the *Waste Land*.

Yet to rule out 2a arbitrarily would be dangerous. Guerard's story actually belongs to types 1 and 1a: that is, it includes three separate plots—Mme. Lowen, Lia, and the boy—the first suggested merely, so far as action is concerned, the second and third actually given in action, all three influencing each other in an elusive but none the less profound way. The story, in other words, is formally very complex. Tate's story belongs to 2 and 2a. It is the sort of thing that ought almost always to be discarded on sight. It does not display a quarter of the skill of Guerard's story. Yet it is more moving and ought to be preferred to Guerard: its superiority lies simply in the superiority of Tate's mind, and the profundity of his comment. Guerard's story seems to me far superior to most of the stuff you have printed, however, and to all the stories you have sent me save Tate's.

All of this is of considerable moment so far as the magazine is concerned, but of little moment where Guerard is concerned. Guerard is young and will do better work: in fact he is improving with great rapidity.

I suspect you of finding Guerard's story slight because he does not muss it up with a lot of soft emotionalism and badly constructed sentences. I will send you nothing with those particular virtues: I am fighting them tooth and nail in the kids I am teaching or in any way influencing and for the most part have been successful. Guerard presented a complex story, with exactly the feeling appropriate to it, and with a good deal of incidental and very precise wit. His virtues are the sine qua non of distinguished writing, and the only sure foundation of greatness.

Yours, / Y.W.

MS: Yale

[1]Albert Guerard (b. 1914): American novelist, critic, and educator. A former student of YW and later a colleague, he dedicated to YW his book on Robert Bridges. YW was the first Albert Guérard Professor at Sanford, an endowed chair named for Guerard's father, Albert Léon Guérard (1880–1959), a former professor of general literature at Stanford.

TO LINCOLN KIRSTEIN

Nov. 25, 1932

Dear Mr. Kirstein:

I have read Burke's opus and advise against it. I shall present my case against Burke as briefly as possible, and then summarize the case against myself, in order to be perfectly fair.

Technically—as exposition—the piece is badly done. The numerous illustrations and excursions and parables in the first half or so get in the way and make one forget the argument. Many of them—the fire parable, for example—are very imperfectly relevant, and obscure the issue. The latter part is fairly free of these, but even so is extremely repetitious. Some of this semi-relevant material—the excursion on Whitman, for example—is good in itself, however. But if Burke would repress his personality a little, he could reduce his book by fifty pages and thereby render it incomparably more clear.

Burke's relativism seems to me very shoddy. This means, of course, that I am relatively an absolutist. Uncle Tom and Macbeth are not comparable in the way B. claims, and he continually shows himself unable to distinguish between the important and the unimportant: the chief instance of this is his writing the book in the first place, for the subject is secondary. I mean, that if an infatuation is corrupting Joyce, Eliot, and Crane, it is important, but that if it is corrupting Hicks and Cowley one may let it run its course with a clear conscience. The greatest tactical error of More and Babbitt was of this same kind: they wasted ammunition on irrelevant but "prominent" men, like Mencken and [Sinclair] Lewis, instead of studying the important men of their time. They were thus obsolete from the outset, as critics of contemporary literature. Burke's book seems to be some kind of Exhortation to Quiet Cowley, and is elaborately subtle and a trifle ungrammatically rhetorical about trivialities.

If you print it, go through it carefully and check over the "rather than" constructions. This is his formula: "I found I must eat rather than drinking." The error occurs repeatedly.

Burke's comments on the function of art are shifty, vague, and when definite shallow. His clearest ideas are slight; his attempts at handling serious ideas are confused.

There is much more discussion of Marxianism in general than is relevant to his critical issue: this is another instance of the way in which he wanders from his subject, almost as the hero of his novel wanders, and in spite of all his lists of categories.

Perhaps the above is a bit disorganized too. It is midnight, and I am tired.

As to my own shortcomings: I have never been east of Wolf Lake, Indiana, and have lived mostly in obscure and remote villages, in and west of the Rockies. There may be much in modern urban life that I do not understand. I find myself in general simply unable to understand most pragmatic and relativistic thought in the realms of ethics and aesthetics. I am not exaggerating. Dewey, for example, is largely incomprehensible to me. Burke, by failing to distinguish between what is for me the important and unimportant, by keeping what he would call an open mind and what seems to me in a way an empty mind, makes it very difficult for me to follow him at times. It is quite possible that he sometimes goes over my head. Further, I have acquired from his two published books a dislike for him that is both intense and personal, so that I may possibly be unfair. The novel seems to me simply contemptible, and the central doctrine of *Counter-Statement* (the doctrine of balanced excesses) is one of the shallowest things I have ever seen propounded. The hero of the novel goes insane because, by balancing one excess against another, he is relieved of the need of judgment; and while he is sane he is both unpleasant and uninteresting. Burke seems totally unsuspicious of all this, and propounds his hero's doctrines seriously and in his own name. Burke has all of the vulgar plausibility of a traveling salesman.

But I seem to be back on the subject of Burke again. At any rate, I have exhibited my feelings.

Nothing could have induced me to read the present book through, at any rate, had I come upon it in print.

Sincerely, / Yvor Winters

P.S. One might argue the other way thus: The thing is good pamphleteering, in the manner, say, of Thomas Nashe. It is verbose and scattered but often brilliant, and punctures the windy indignation of your attackers with much vigorous ridicule. If one is engaged in a Marprelate controversy, and finds Nashe on one's own side, there is much to be said for publishing him.

And as picaresque literature such a pamphlet is not without interest. Picaresque literature is always pragmatic.

MS: Yale

TO ALLEN TATE

Dec. 8, 1932 / R. 1, Box 363 / Palo Alto, Calif.

Dear Tate:

Thanks for your letter on punctuation. I knew my suggestions would make you sore, because it is traditionally insulting to mention a man's punctuation. Nevertheless, I hope you have recovered by now from your wrath and reread the story with an eye to my suggestions.

As to punctuation in general, there is a wide fringe of the subject that is controversial; but there is a good-sized core that is perfectly standard and is treated in exactly the same way in every text-book and printed examination from one boundary of our great republic to the other. This is one of [the] things one finds out by becoming an English instructor. And whether you believe it or not, the text-books are right. The most general of the rules, of which most of the others are subdivisions, is this: If any word or group of words is so placed in the sentence that, unpunctuated, it may appear momentarily to belong with an equal show of reason to what precedes or to what follows, it should be so punctuated that no doubt may even momentarily enter the reader's mind. The real reason for this is not pedantic at all: it is Aesthetic, with a capital *A*. If the reader is continually driven to going back over sentences to find out what the hell the construction really is, the rhythm, not only of the individual sentences, but of the entire composition, is wrecked utterly. You cannot spoil your rhythm with commas properly placed: a comma introduces nothing into the rhythm, but merely shows what the rhythm is. Your remarks on this subject sound as if you had acquired some kind of Cummingsesque neurosis. In poetry, where the syntax is usually simple, and in the simpler kinds of prose, loose punctuation does no harm. In sentences as elaborate as many used in your story, it is a major catastrophe.

As to the obscurity of the relationship between the people in the street and the former inhabitants of the house, it is, as I said in my second letter, perfectly legitimate if made explicit. That is, your narrator ought to know that he does not know the relationship and be able to state the fact: the fact is important with respect to everything he has to say—in fact, if that information is not stated, the reader is left, throughout the entire story, with the vague feeling that the relationship may be important and that he ought to have guessed it. Your story involves so many people that I had to read it three times to be sure you had not given me a clue. Further, the giving of this information is not, or should not be, a piece of obvious labeling. If you have half the sense you were born with, it is one of the best opportunities in the whole damned story for some valuable writing.

As to my remarks about style in general, they were not in the least pedantic. It is quite possible to stylize incongruities of speech: it is done constantly in Shakespeare, Fielding, Jonson, so on and so on. But the incongruities to which I objected were incongruities of style. This cannot be demonstrated logically, but is a matter of perception. If you don't see it you don't, especially if you won't.

The phrase "the time of my invalidism" is indeterminate as to tense, and as I remember the sentence (I returned your ms. long ago) there was nothing in the sentence, and there had been nothing in the story, to prove that it was past perfect, preterite, or imperfect, and one's understanding of it would necessarily be accidental. Unnecessary ambiguities, in structure as in punctuation, should be avoided.

Now the story, in the form to which I objected, and despite my objections, was one of the most impressive things I have seen. But there was suspended in it a certain amount of unnecessary mud that could be easily settled. I could have revised most of it out in about half an hour with a pencil, but I didn't dare attempt it. I therefore spent an hour writing you a letter about it.

I was not, as you strongly imply, reared in an aristocratic agrarian society, but in some ways this is fortunate: had I been, this letter would probably be compounded of the choicest profanity of a race-track tout instead of being merely further expostulation on the subject of commas.

You probably have received my letter explaining why we are not applying for a fellowship. Janet says she also wrote you on the subject many weeks ago, and wonders if you got her letter. Thanks, nevertheless, for your kind intentions.

You mention having sent me some poems. I have received only one poem, "The Meaning of Life." It is a good poem, very moving at times, and I have recommended it to K[irstein]. Nevertheless, the use of the fish at the end seems arbitrary: that is, they merely allegorize an abstraction, which could be more succinctly, and probably more powerfully, stated as an abstraction: the fish, as fish, are not perceived and so are not justified poetically. In this they resemble the Narcissistic Jaguar of the "Ode."

I hope you like my new poet, Don Stanford.[1] I have sent his three poems to K.

As ever, / Winters

MS: *Princeton, Allen Tate Papers*

[1]Donald E. Stanford (1903–1998): American poet, critic, scholar, educator, and co-founder and coeditor of the *Southern Review*, new series; poems included in *Twelve Poets of the Pacific*. He had been YW's student and became a lifelong friend (and correspondent).

TO LINCOLN KIRSTEIN

Dec. 20, 1932

Dear Mr. Kirstein:

*　　*　　*

I am glad you liked Louis Burgess. I like him myself, though I find him rather exhausting. Talking with him is a bit like arguing with a fire hose. If you are curious about his poems, you can find a good many short ones—amusing and lively journalism—scattered through *Poetry*. His best one was an epitaph for Senator Phelan, of San Francisco:

> Here lies a rich
> Son of a bitch.

It was never published. He has done a long poem in three Cantos, of which he doubtless told you, a poem dealing with the evolution of God. I have read the first Canto, which begins with something very primitively Hebraic, takes God into Egypt with the Hebrews and educates him in the temples there, brings him back through the Red Sea, and ends with the death of Moses. The last scene is really impressive, though it is very imperfectly handled. Most of the poem is very bad, and it is sometimes ludicrous in a very strange way, for the reason that B. is fundamentally a journalist and at the same time has an inordinate admiration for Milton. One of the minor animal-deities gorges on a sheep and ends up "gravid with mutton." God's education is largely sexual, and is very elaborately Egyptian. I never quite got the point of it all. The poem is really something of a curiosity, however, and it might amuse you to read it. Burgess knows more San Francisco scandal than any other man living, unless possibly it be Fremont Older, whom I have never met. He doubtless told you about his goats and mine. That was really how we became acquainted.

Sincerely, / Y.W.

MS: Yale

TO LINCOLN KIRSTEIN

Jan. 20, 1933

Dear Mr. Kirstein:

*   *   *

I think you would have acted more fairly to let Cunningham see Miss Monroe's letter before printing it, though it may have come too late.[1] Her corrections of fact are damned lies. Pound was foreign editor from 1912 to 1919, a few months short of seven years. Wescott worked in the office regularly one whole winter and received a small stipend: he was one of my best friends at the time, and one of my wife's, and I know. My wife worked in the office two weeks and was offered the associate editorship for one summer, but declined: she was very young at the time, and exerted no influence, and Cunningham should not have mentioned her perhaps, but Miss M.'s assertion of fact is incorrect.

Cunningham gave her the unkindest cut possible of course, and she always yawps, as a means to free advertising, but she also poured out on him a good deal of malice she feels for me. The recent deluge of bad Crane and Tate in her pages (and of others) comes after my having quarreled with her over her systematic ignoring of them (I have known the old woman for fourteen years and fought with her steadily and until fairly recently amicably). The sections of "The Critiad" devoted to her and [Morton Dauwen] Zabel made them both pretty mad, and they have been digging at me surreptitiously ever since. The dirtiest trick of all is in the critical note on Crane in her revised anthology. She quotes from a review I wrote of *White Buildings* praising it enthusiastically, and to which she appended a footnote objecting to my praise. She quotes a few sketchy and impressionistic sentences describing that part of the book which I disliked, and quotes them as if they were my description of Crane's entire talent. This is followed by a cumulus-cloud of praise from Mr. Zabel. Nothing could be more deliberately malicious. She is just as dishonest in her reply to Cunningham. Or else she is getting senile.

*　　*　　*

Sincerely, / Yvor Winters

MS: Yale

[1]Cunningham wrote a letter in response to Harriet Monroe. YW advised Kirstein that "Cunningham's letter should be printed. It would be fair to give Miss Monroe the last word had she not so elaborately perverted and obscured facts. But it is wholly unfair to let a person of Miss Monroe's reputation get away with such a piece of scurrility at the expense of a young and unknown writer" (Feb. 7, 1933).

TO GRACE HART CRANE

March 29, 1933 / R. 1, Box 363 / Palo Alto, Calif.

Dear Mrs. Crane:

Thank you for your letter, and for requesting that the book be sent to me. I shall be very glad to have it. Waldo Frank was probably the best choice you could have made for an editor.

Whenever there may be an edition of Hart's letters, I shall be glad to contribute my own collection, and, if the edition does not occur before I complete the extremely exhausting doctoral dissertation on which I am working, shall be glad to make such explanatory annotations as I can. Also, I have a copy of the poem to Emily Dickinson, in his handwriting, a very beautiful manuscript, which might some day be reproduced as an illustration.

As you probably know, I disagreed with most of Hart's central ideas, and disapproved of the general direction in which his poetry was working, but in spite of those facts he seemed to me one of the most powerful and at times one of the most perfect poets of the two last centuries. His greatness, and the certitude of his high place in the history of English poetry, should in time afford a kind of consolation for his loss. This may seem a cold consolation, but it is a great consolation, and one afforded few parents.

I am sorry I could be of no assistance with this book. If I can be of any assistance in the future, please call on me.

Sincerely, / Arthur Yvor Winters

MS: *Columbia*

TO LINCOLN KIRSTEIN

March 29, 1933

Dear Mr. Kirstein:

I can't see that [Mark] Schorer's story is any better. It is sloppy to the last degree.

John Vincent Healy, the graduate student, is a washout.

Scott's poem is a filthy mess. It is also a bad hangover from *Conquistador*. You have printed one rather poor poem by Scott in the interests of encouragement, and I think had better wait now till he sends in something good.

[David Cornel] De Jong's poems are diluted and insensitive Rimbaud. The meter is dull, the phrasing is blunt, and the method is obsolete. I gather from his letter that you are using his story. It is better than most that have come in, but if you are using it I am sorry. It is soggy and tiresome and De J. does not really know what the story is about. You don't really have to choose anything for a while yet.

Also, I have an idea which deserves a new paragraph. The stories you are getting are a rotten lot. This means that higher paying magazines are cutting in on you. *Scribners* and others are risking a few good stories, and they can naturally take the stuff away from you if they want it. The two fields in which you have no competition, in which you can get nearly anything you wish, are criticism and poetry. You could, by printing a little more verse than you have commonly printed, and possibly a little more criticism—though you print a lot already—and by reducing the size of the magazine a little, get by an issue or two occasionally with no fiction. It would be better, I think, than printing bad fiction: for one thing, you reach a pretty sophisticated audience which is in the main at least as interested in verse as in prose, and which is or should be more interested in good writing of any kind than bad writing of a particular kind. If the fiction field has been stolen from you, you could easily steal the two other fields completely. The *Symposium* is sophomoric, and the *N.R.* is handicapped for lack of space. I wouldn't abandon fiction, but I certainly wouldn't publish messy stuff in desperation.

I got the 3rd volume of Moore the other day. When the set is complete, I should like to do a very brief—one or two page—informative notice on the remaining volumes if you don't mind. The 3rd catches me with a very great poem which I had never read—nearly the greatest. The piece about Herod and Mariamne, at the end. Really colossal. Most of the other plays in the volume are really Vergilian Eclogues, and very beautiful specimens. If you could send a copy of the next issue to Moore I should greatly appreciate it. Send one of my copies.

Sincerely, / Y.W.

MS: Yale

TO LINCOLN KIRSTEIN

April 20, 1933 / R. 1, Box 363 / Palo Alto, Calif.

Dear Mr. Kirstein:

Miss Levine asks me if I have a paper called "Pessimism, Its Meaning and Consequences," by a man called Slochowar [Harry Slochower]. I have no recollection of such a paper and seem not to have it here.

I enclose Code's poem with a page of comment. I would suggest that you return the ms. with my marks and remarks, and ask him to consider them for a week and see what he thinks. I believe the poem ought to be printed whether he revises or not. The first section is pretty bad, but the other sections are in the main very fine.

"The Plumet Basilisk," by Miss Moore contains a few short but charming descriptive passages. I don't see why she wrote the poem, however, and don't think it worth printing. It appears to be wholly descriptive in its intentions, and most of the description is very poor. The sword image at the end is quite lovely.

Warren's essay on Ransom you have accepted and announced, so that my objections to it are not to be taken as a vote against its appearance. It seems to me, however, a very weak effort. The word "reason" is abused throughout: he employs it to mean imperfect reason, or half-educated reasoning, as when we speak of the Age of Reason (an age, really, of naive and unsophisticated reasoners, inadequately educated in the history of reason and the meaning of the experience that history formulated). This abuse of a good word is a sentimentalism that plays into the hands of the enemy (Satan, I mean, and [Eugene] Jolas, and Joyce and Dr. Williams). I believe his theory of a clean cut between the present and the past in all their aspects is a myth as naive as the myths of science: it really is a myth of a golden age, which justifies sentimental nostalgia for the unattainable and the resultant facile irony. Ransom's irony is exactly of the same kind as Laforgue's, Pound's, or Eliot's. So far as the detail of the writing is concerned, it encourages looseness; in the realm of morality it offers a politely weary excuse for the slackening of effort at a line chosen by the actor. To say that a secure and sane moral attitude is impossible because the agrarian south is destroyed is silly: We have Bridges, Moore, Tate (kicking but a convincing example), Baker, and others to prove the contrary. Really, the agrarian is used as an excuse for a literary habit that Ransom and others have not energy enough and understanding enough to shake off. It is facile and shoddy. The essay admits the nature of Romantic irony in general, but endeavors to prove Ransom's a special case by the mere and awfully vague assertion of the clean cut with the past and the resultant difficulty. There are other vague terms in the essay (lyrical and dramatic for example) but none so crucial in their location. The whole thing is nearly as vague, nearly as complacent morally, and nearly as imperceptive of literary values as most of the essays on Eliot by young scholars.

I like Red Warren, but not this essay.

The story, "A Man among Men," is a kind of tract for school teachers in western towns.

The poems enclosed by Carliner, Landers, Creekmore, Brynes, and Schubert, are all badly conceived and badly written.

I will do some sort of note on the [F. R.] Leavis[1] primer and on Pound's. The subject interests me. Probable title: "Poetry and Pedagogy."

Guerard has started a long story that will probably be his best. It will perhaps run to novelette length, however. He is going to develop very fast for the next few years, and I believe will go a very long way.

It is probably a sign of advancing neuralgia and increasing weight that I am becoming both vain and irritable about my students. Baker, Ramsey, Miss Lockett, Cunningham, Stanford, Guerard, and Holt make a rather impressive list for four years. I picked them all up before they had done anything decent, showed each one of them what he could do, and made him do it. I steered them all out of the morass of modern nonsense. I have four or five others almost as good as some of the above, and still developing: Dave Cooke (my wrestling champion), J. E. McGinnis (a medic with too little time for writing, but who will some day write good verse), Barbara Gibbs, and Eleanor Carlton. I picked Stafford up when he was trying to imitate "Prufrock." And the damned faculty here not only is blind to the fact, but regards me as an incomprehensible and probably dangerous influence on budding talent. When I have finished my degree, I shall probably be out on the world as a high school teacher. Guerard got a D on the best prose he has written in an advanced comp course taught by Edith Mirrelies. It gets on my nerves, especially as Guerard is easily discouraged and as I have had a very ticklish job in getting him clear of his papa's very muddy ideas without reflecting on his papa, whom I admire as a human being and for whom the kid has a little boy's devotion.

Sincerely, / Yvor Winters

MS: Yale

[1]F. R. Leavis (1895–1978): English critic and, with his wife, Q. D. Leavis, founder of the critical journal *Scrutiny*.

TO T. C. WILSON

June 24, 1933 / R. 1, Box 363 / Palo Alto, Calif.

Dear Mr. Wilson:

Your interest in my criticism is flattering, and I should like to correspond if I could. Correspondence, however, has the same defect as book-reviewing—excessive brevity—and the added defect of carelessness, at least where I am concerned, and clears up very little. I am working very hard on a volume of criticism, which I hope to finish in the next month or so, and at present simply have no time.

When you speak of stylistic advances, you perhaps inadvertently indulge in nonsense. There is no such thing as progress in literature after a certain degree of civilization has been reached. Williams is as fine a poet as you will find in English in a few poems and within a certain range; he has worked out a new technique and mastered it; but he is bound to certain limitations of subject matter by that very technique. Pound is a remarkable poet, but not much better than Swinburne, I suspect, and of much the same type. Stevens is occasionally as fine as Williams and covers more ground. Neither one appears to me as great as [T. Sturge] Moore by a very wide margin; and I prefer Bridges to Moore and probably Hardy, though I am not sure. A few years ago I should have placed Hardy above either. The poets you defend against me I have defended for years, and all poets, in so far as they are good, are defensible on the same general grounds. But the defects of these poets are not adequately recognized by the younger writers and the defects are of the utmost seriousness; I do not want to see them passed on.

Young writers have a way of seeing their difficulties as far more complex than they are. There is a general condition of hypochondria among the young and talented at present that requires a certain amount of cold water and common sense. The best way to come out of it is to read, on the one hand Aristotle, the Bible, and Irving Babbitt, and on the other hand the poets of the 16th, 17th and 18th centuries, and to try to forget Pound and one's worries. That program, with a deliberate effort to imitate Bridges for two years ought to make a poet of anyone who has the makings.

The young Englishmen do not interest me two cents worth.

Sincerely, / Yvor Winters

MS: Yale

Theodore Carl Wilson (d. 1950): American poet and critic.

.

TO THE *HOUND AND HORN*

July 23, 1933 / R. 1, Box 363 / Palo Alto, Calif.

To the Editors of the *Hound and Horn:*

I have recently been re-examining the last four issues of *The Hound and Horn,* and have arrived at a few conclusions and questions which may be worth the tentative consideration of the staff. The last four issues seem to me to show certain fairly definite changes in tendency.

The poetry in the last four issues reaches a higher level, I believe, than the magazine has previously reached. I can find only three poems that seem to me definitely and completely bad: those by Eliot, Scott, and Bishop. Of the rest, a few are weak, but have redeeming features or passages which justify their publication, and most are at a high level of competence. A few, those by Tate and Baker especially, and perhaps a couple by Blackmur, I believe to be major poetry. Cunningham, [Theodore] Spencer, Stafford, and Cuthbert all hit a very high level. It is regrettable that Stanford's later work did not get in, though his three poems in the current issue are worth printing.

There are no bad stories in the last four issues, and this marks a great advance over previous issues, some of which contained some very unpleasant fiction. "The Immortal Woman" is probably the highest point reached by the magazine in fiction since "Flowering Judas," and the other three stories are dignified and competent, Holt's, despite its slightly broken form, being to myself the most moving.

The small print section has had downs as well as ups, but has been preponderantly good and frequently very brilliant; it has, I should say, about maintained its previous level, which was very high. The work in this section which I have liked best has been that of: Cunningham, Clara Stillman, Owsley in the fall issue; Leighton, Blackmur, and Fergusson in the winter issue; Bernadete and Stillman in the spring issue; Blackmur and Warner in the current issue. This is a good bunch of reviewers, and should be worked as hard as possible. Mr. Bandler should contribute more frequently to this section. The film chronicle bores me, but is probably competent in its field, a field of which I know little and care less. I should like to suggest that as much poetry as possible be turned over to Cunningham. I hesitate to make this suggestion, because of his dilatoriness with the Catholic anthology, and I believe that he should receive nothing else till that review is done. He would work faster with books of modern poetry, however, and could be trusted to handle one or two large collections of books per year. He has certain defects of sensibility and of style, but is improving. He is more sensitive and more sure of what he is looking for than either Fitts or Tate; he is not more sensitive than Blackmur, but is probably more sure of his principles and less easily taken in by the vaguer forms of modernism. The fact that he is an undergraduate should not be held against him: he was forced out of school for five years by poverty; he is 22 years old; his scholarship is as good, in the field in which he may be regarded as a specialist for the moment, as that of most of your reviewers. He knows Latin poetry, classical and medieval, very respectably; he has a good knowledge of English poetry; and a thorough knowledge of contemporary poetry; his principles are in general those of the magazine, and his taste is in accord with his principles. Tate, on the other hand, enjoys most a type of work that runs counter to his principles: his recent praise of [Horace] Gregory and [Samuel] Putnam can do nothing but confuse issues.

The large-print essays in the past year have fallen off profoundly in quality, and I believe that something should be done about the matter. The only essay which has maintained the rather high level of the previous year or so was Mr. Bandler's. The summer issue alone for 1932 contained more first-rate criticism in the front section than all four subsequent issues. The essays—like that of Marsh in the current issue—have been frequently readable and informative, but have been shallow and journalistic. Sometimes they have been deadly dull: cf. [Max] Nomad on Marx and Bakunin. [Donald] Davidson in the current issue has sold you an essay that nearly every one of the agrarians has written and published at least twice, and has used 30 pages to spread out five pages of matter. The agrarian question should be definitely shelved so far as the *Hound and Horn* is concerned unless: (1) the critic in question works out a detailed economic and political program for the realization of his desire, or (2) unless he utilizes his position as a basis for a definite and detailed criticism of a specific and limited subject, literary, historical, or what have you. The agrarians all write badly except Tate and occasionally Ransom, and they should be viewed with suspicion. Warren's essay on Ransom is another case in point: it is as confused and as vague as possible.

I can do little or nothing as western editor to remedy this situation. Baker would make a good critic if he had time for it, but he is definitely occupied with a novel and a doctoral dissertation and has time for nothing else. Stafford is working on a long essay on the English sonnet, which he will not finish for another year. It will be a good essay, but only one essay, and is far from completion. Cunningham should be held down to reviewing till he is a little older. The only other possibility that I know of in the west—and he is the best of the lot—is Dr. Briggs, who refuses to contribute and whose refusal is inalterable: it is not the result of any ill-will toward the magazine, but of indolence and indifference. Baker knows nearly every one at the U. of California, and has found no one there. I am too busy and too isolated to look elsewhere, but imagine I should have little luck.

I can see only one remedy: to invite your best essayists from the past (an extemporary list: Blackmur, Tate, Parkes, [Etienne] Gilson, Bandler, Leighton, Fergusson, [S. Foster] Damon) to let you see as much of their work as possible. By concentrating on these men and a few others you would narrow the scope of the magazine a little, but would concentrate your influence and improve your quality. I believe it would be worth while. At any rate, the mild informative journalism, and the dawdling generalities of the recent essayists should be shoved out as quickly as possible.

Sincerely, / Yvor Winters

Copies of this letter for Mssrs. Kirstein, Bandler, Mayer, and Tate.

MS: Yale

August 8, 1933 / R. 1, Box 363 / Palo Alto, Calif.

To the Editors of the *Hound and Horn:*

Mr. Tate's letter of July 31 in reply to my letter of July 23, enforces that I offer a few notes in clarification of what I wrote.

1. Mr. Tate exaggerates when he says that my judgment of poets is always unqualified: let me refer him to my reviews and essays; there is seldom space for much qualification in a letter.

2. My objection to Warren's essay on Ransom was based primarily on the misuse of the word *reason,* as if it were equivalent to amateur reasoning, pseudo-reason, the reason of the Age of Reason, or something related. His essay, as it stood, was an effort to discredit the faculty of reason, and a very shoddy one. I believe the type of irony he praised in Ransom was vicious, for the simple reason that it weakens the style of Ransom and everyone else who uses it: my objection here is not abstractly or puritanically moral, but a matter of practical poetics. Mr. Tate, as I observed in my former letter, seldom notes virtues of style beyond a certain rough approximation of excellence, and consequently seldom notes their absence. I have no objection to Ransom's being praised in the *Hound and Horn,* however; many of his poems raise interesting questions and some are excellent. I regretted seeing him praised for his chief defect, and I objected to seeing him praised to the detriment of the rational faculty. Warren's essay was based solidly on the misuse of the term *reason:* correct that error and you erase nearly the entire essay.

3. I did not say that Mr. Tate *approved* of Putnam and Gregory (the italics are not mine), but that he praised them, and to praise them he must have liked them; to praise them as he did, he must have liked them a great deal. I am fully aware that he disapproves their ideas and tendencies. I said that he enjoys most that contemporary poetry which runs counter to his opinions: the reason for this is a taste for second-rate writing which is obtainable only from second-rate people, and an obliviousness to virtues of style which are cultivated by the first-rate. The whole tendency of Mr. Tate's criticism of particular poets is to encourage the sort of thing produced by Cowley, Cummings, Putnam, and Gregory, which is shoddy and empty, at the expense of the sort of thing written by Blackmur (in his sea-poems and a few things unpublished), Baker, or Stafford. There is a critical issue here of great importance; Mr. Tate will be as irrelevant a critic five years hence as Pound is at present. This objection to Mr. Tate is limited exactly to the terms I have herein used; the admiration for him

which I have expressed on other occasions and for other activities is undiminished, and this objection is nothing new, as Mr. Tate can assure himself by rereading my letters to himself.

4. My demand in regard to the agrarians was not with an eye to their revolutionizing the country (being a mere westerner, I am far more interested in what Roosevelt is doing than in finding out what they would like to do), but with an eye to their writing decent essays for the *Hound and Horn.* I have an academic prejudice to the effect that an essayist ought to say something, and Davidson's paraphrase of "The Deserted Village" seemed to me a good deal of an imposition on subscribers. If the agrarians mean to publish that essay thirty times more, as Mr. Tate says, they would do well to collaborate and get it into some final and presentable form. The fact that Davidson's essay was originally much worse does not comfort me. I enjoy Owsley, while commonly disagreeing with him, because he has something to say and says it with directness: that is the first virtue of expository writing.

It is with a good deal of humiliation, a sense of having been found out, that I confess to living in the West and in an academic atmosphere. But I am comforted by the feeling that Mr. Tate, on the other hand, lives in the South and in an unacademic atmosphere. I really mean this allegorically: his letter displays a greater depth of feeling than was necessary, and in his eagerness to reply to me, he took very little pains to read what I had said.

Faithfully yours, / Yvor Winters

P.S. This is my last encyclical for twelve months.

MS: Yale

TO LINCOLN KIRSTEIN

Sept. 5, 1933

Dear Mr. Kirstein:

While you are catching up with your work, do not fail to read carefully a story by Karlton Kelm (whoever he may be) entitled "Thoughts," and some sonnets by J. E. Scruggs (whoever he may be). I believe these things should be printed.

Guerard has one story (in an American setting) which might interest you. If I can reach him, I'll have him send it. I think he has gone off on vacation, however, and I am not sure of his address, nor am I sure he will have taken any mss. with him. "Davos in Winter" is better than you think, however: it is not great, but is expert and very lovely, and displays a very unusual gift for pure story-telling. Actually, it is based on personal experience and is not derivative from *The Magic Mountain*, which G. has not read and probably wouldn't understand.

I should be more than pleased to see Cunningham get the poetry prize, though of my two chief candidates my own favorite is probably Stanford. Who is judging?

I enclose another poem by Stanford, which is purely descriptive, but which seems to me very lovely.

Auden and his friends strike me as pretty muddled. The best poets in England are Elizabeth Daryush[1] and Viola Meynell.

Cunningham's review of Gregory, I believe, should be published. Gregory *is* important because he has been widely praised, and by several important people who should have known better: it is highly important to offer an exact account of his procedure, which Cunningham did. Gregory is not worth much space, but C.'s review will take very little.

I did not object to the essays in question because they were not literary, but because they were not critical: they were hardly more than good term papers.

I should be more sorry to have angered Tate, had he not insulted me with such unction, but one cannot regret giving pleasure. For the rest, he needs shaking up. His recent essay called "Poetry and Politics" in the *N.R.* is the worst mess I have seen in that eminent critical organ since Cowley's obituary on Crane. I should rather lose his friendship than see him go on making such an ass of himself.

Thanks for your good wishes, except as they extend to the goats. Fat milk animals give little milk. Good goats, like good cows, are lean. Don't learn your agriculture from the Agrarians.

Baker and I are introducing two six-months-old bitch pups to the Airedale fancy next Sunday—sired by my old dog and out of one of his litter sisters. By rights my pup should beat Baker's and beat most of the mature entries from this part of the state, but may not, as she is pretty young. It is the first time I have had time to exhibit a dog in three years.

I am glad you had a pleasant trip.

Sincerely, / Yvor Winters

P.S. In regard to my long essay. I have revised the thing, straightening out a certain amount of careless detail, especially some confusing remarks about Gay and Pope, and adding a short paragraph on *The Testament of Beauty*. If you decide to use the thing, I shall want to send the revised version. Do not hesitate to reject it, however: I shall probably send you more of my own work than you will be able to use, and for the following reason. I probably have a higher opinion of my own work than most people have, and so long as I am connected with the magazine I shall, as a matter of routine, send you what seems to me the best of it before sending it elsewhere. I enjoy being published, of course, but my regrets at not being published are not very profound; and as I have a steady job, you might, if forced to choose between myself and some one like Tate or Blackmur, give the other man the preference.

MS: Yale

[1]Elizabeth (Bridges) Daryush (1887–1977): English poet; daughter of Robert Bridges. Daryush corresponded with YW and Janet Lewis, who also sent frequent packets of foodstuffs and so on to her during and just after World War II. More to the point, YW wrote on her work in the *American Review* (1937) and *Forms of Discovery,* edited her selected poems (Swallow Press and William Morrow, 1948), and included her in *Quest for Reality.*

TO DONALD E. STANFORD

Sept. 13, 1933 / R. 1, Box 363 / Palo Alto, Calif.

Dear Don:

I will send "Noon at Neebish" to Kirstein. I may write you later of the present version.

R. P. Blackmur's winter address is 332 Waverley St., Belmont, Mass. I have written him that you would look him up. I trust you got my note regarding Theodore Spencer, who expects you to look him up at Eliot House, Harvard, before you register. Blackmur is probably still in Maine, but is likely to be back in Belmont at any time now.

The Magazine is still up in the air, but we ought to know something definite about it before long.

Jim is visiting Howard for this month, and returns to his job on the campus in a couple of weeks. He did not touch his bicycle all summer, nor did he finish the Catholic essay, though he claims, on whatever grounds, that he will finish the essay soon. I hope to heaven he can act his age next year and keep his job, for I can't help him further financially, and I can't take him in again: he has worn my nerves too thin.[1] I have an idea he is scheduled for the *H. and H.* prize. I hope not, because I think you deserve it, but I suspect he will get it.

Tex Holt was here for a week or so. It is too bad you missed him. He is a fine person.

Next year at Harvard, take as many solid historical courses as you can get. Fill your head with facts: never mind the appreciative stuff. The scholars who appreciate heavily usually do it badly, and you can do that for yourself. You need history, philosophy, and language, and need them badly. For God's sake prepare yourself to teach; get good grades so that you can get a job. There is nothing more pathetic and in a way contemptible than the free-lance writer who tries to live by writing and actually lives by borrowing from his more provident friends.

As ever, / Arthur Winters

MS: Stanford

[1]Cunningham's presence had placed a burden on the Winters family. As YW had written earlier to Howard Baker, and in a somewhat understated manner: "I think we shall have to chase Jim over to the campus to live next fall, though I haven't yet spoken to him of it. In spite of his dish washing, he complicates life vastly more than he simplifies it, and Janet and I are both pretty tired. We can probably lend him a little money, and if he will write two or three essays this summer instead of sleeping as he did last, I imagine he can get through the year and graduate. He is a good kid and ought to be got through, though few people are so exasperating, I imagine, at close quarters" (March 13, 1933).

TO R. P. BLACKMUR

Sept. 13, 1933 / R. 1, Box 363 / Palo Alto, Calif.

Dear Blackmur:

The history of *The Magazine* to date is briefly this: It is owned by a man named [John] McAllister. His original acting editor was a man named [Fred] Kuhlman, a bright boy just out of college. They wrote [Richard] Perry, a close friend of McAllister, who lived a few doors from Baker, to solicit mss. Baker was asked to help by Perry, and he wrote me. I wrote Kuhlman that I would help to the utmost if he would let Baker actually edit the first two issues and get them started properly, but that if they would not do so, I would have nothing to do with it, being tired of little magazines run by amateurs. Kuhlman refused and thought it a good joke.

Perry then went to L.A., and when he came back he was acting editor and K. was business manager. Perry gave Baker permission to go ahead, and that was where you found us a couple of months ago. McAllister then went to Europe, leaving Perry in charge. Perry and Baker got two issues together, and were ready to send one on to McAllister when he returned a couple of weeks ago. When McA. got to L.A., however, K., whose plans for typography etc. had been vetoed by Baker and Perry, began talking to him, and the two of them started soliciting mss. without consulting Perry. Since it appeared certain that the initial issues as made up by Baker and Perry would be diluted by their *trouvailles* in Hollywood, and since Perry was being obviously double-crossed, Baker withdrew all the mss., and Perry resigned. This a few days ago.

In reply to Baker's letter, McAllister wrote Baker asking permission to come north and consult him and go over mss. with him. This consultation will take place within a week or so, I believe. I shall be present. We shall let him have your poems, and ask him to pay you at once, regardless of the outcome: if you wish not to let him have them should we withdraw, inform us at once. Without us, the magazine will be a small *Pagany;* with us, it will be a small, and, I believe, greatly improved and essentialized *H. and H.*

Baker and I are disgusted and will drop the whole affair with very little provocation, so far as our own work is concerned and that of the group of our immediate friends here. But it may go through, and I suspect we shall sell him your poems anyhow if you want him to have them.

As to your Pound essay. Only a small part of the criticism is sent on to me for reading. If your essay comes, I will inform you. If it is rejected, send it to me, and let me read it and send it back to Kirstein. I will do all in my power to get it in. The worst I know to date about Kirstein's trip is that he met Spender and Auden and is much taken by them. They are to send him their poems and advice. I don't know if they are to be English Editors or not. That whole bunch of young Englishmen stink to heaven. They can neither write nor think.

If we do not sell McA. your poems, I will send them at once to Kirstein. You may easily withdraw them if you have other plans.

Don Stanford is to be at Harvard next year. He gives me as a permanent address, the following: c/o Joseph Earl Perry / 18 Holt Street / Belmont, Mass.

I shall give him your Belmont address and ask him to look you up. He is only twenty, but a charming kid, with the makings of an excellent scholar and critic. He is already an excellent poet, though his best work is unpublished.

I am sorry this magazine adventure has been so slow and muddled. I still believe we can get you a check for the poems sooner than you would probably have got it from the *H. and H.,* however.

Sincerely, / Winters

I forgot to say that of Kuhlman's two great literary discoveries in the south, with whom he hoped to impress McA., one turned out to be my brother-in-law

[Wessel Smitter] and another one of my favorite and most carefully educated ex-students.

MS: Princeton, R. P. Blackmur Papers

TO R. P. BLACKMUR

Sept. 23, 1933 / R. 1, Box 363 / Palo Alto, Calif.

Dear Blackmur:

I have just seen a letter McAllister wrote Baker, saying that he had sent you a check for your poems. I hope it is for the full $20 we calculated on. And I am sorry the whole affair has been so delayed and confused. My guess is that you can sell them more work rather soon if you wish to do so: verse, that is; they don't like criticism. What they are going to do in general, I don't know.

I have read your essay and cast my vote for it. K. wrote as if he regarded its publication as a matter of course. It is a very good essay, though at the moment I like it less than the two last. Your opening remarks about masks and voices are a little fanciful and obscure, and the essay never quite escapes from them. Also, if, as K. says, you are not much of a Latinist, your remarks about the subtler qualities of Propertius are pretty rash. I am not much of a Latinist myself, but Propertius looks better to me than Pound; in fact, the comparison seems to me to illuminate precisely the defects in Pound's texture, which you, along with nearly everyone else, regard as his great virtues: namely, the substitution of a degree, sometimes fine, usually rather obvious, of floridity and facile over-statement for genuine elegance. The eraser-pumice line is a good example. With all due respect to you, the Latin version is fine and Pound's is sophomoric. Also, you are wrong about my having missed what happens in "Mauberly"; you merely missed what doesn't happen. You will almost certainly discover what I mean in the due course of time; Tate certainly will not—for I am sure that he reads each poet only once, with one eye on the history of the Civil War, and then theorizes about the poet for the rest of his life.

My private feeling is, that the definitive study of Pound will consider in de-tail the work of Sandburg and of MacLeish, who parody Pound rather broadly and drag his methods to daylight. I don't mean that Pound is not better than they, or that you can invariably damn a man through his disciples, though usu-ally a first-rate poet is too difficult a master for such small fry to fiddle with.

As ever, / Yvor Winters

MS: Princeton, R. P. Blackmur Papers

Sept. 27, 1933 / R. 1, Box 363 / Palo Alto, Calif.

Dear Blackmur:

I enclose a five-dollar check the *N.R.* paid me for a poem which I had withdrawn in disgust because of their delay, or rather had tried to withdraw. I didn't expect the five bucks, so may as well lend it to you—to be repaid in ten years if you prefer. It is a small loan, but may help out if you are strapped, and I am still worried about McA. and Co., as they may have paid you less than I led you to expect. I would suggest that you send more verse to them at once if they paid enough to make it worth while.

The poems seem to me quite simply second-rate. Your method is bad, and inevitably draws out the weaker aspects of your matter. A shifting evasive rhythm is proper when you are describing the sea, but when you are writing relatively abstract statements of moral experience, it loses significance and merely leads to sloppiness; the Yeatsian echoes lead the same way, being diffuse and affected, whether in Yeats or in yourself. The same goes for the word-within-a-worry trick of repetition you borrowed from Eliot. This kind of thing *has to be* compact and swift or it is nothing: you will succeed in handling such material exactly in so far as you depart from your present models. There is only one way to get one's balance if one has been formed (as most of us were) on the moderns: that is to stop reading both the moderns and the poets (like Webster and Donne) whom they have mussed up in our minds, for a year or two, and read good sound traditional poets: Pope, Gay (try "The Birth of a Squire"), Churchill, Gascoigne, Greville, Jonson, till one gets the feel of precision in one's blood again. It is largely a matter of literary habit. It is a habit which your best work proves you could acquire quickly enough if you only saw its advantages. This relaxation, or giving way to one's material, is immoral, profoundly so: it is the central vice of modern poetry, and rests, whether the writer subscribes openly to the principle or not, on the fallacy of expressive form, that is, on the notion that the form should express the quality of the material, that the rhythm should follow the mood, or what-not. This boils down to the Whitmanian trick of writing loose poetry about a loose country, or the Joycian trick of going crazy to express madness. One writes well, not in so far as one acquiesces in one's matter (which is by nature formless) but in so far as one resists and reforms it. This you will doubtless agree to: but you are guilty of the sin in question nevertheless, in a sufficient measure for these and a good many other poems to be robbed of any real distinction. It is a damned shame, because your work at its best is very beautiful.

Do look Stanford up if you get a chance. I am sure you will like him a great deal.

Yvor Winters

MS: *Princeton, R. P. Blackmur Papers*

TO LINCOLN KIRSTEIN

Oct. 13, 1933

Dear Mr. Kirstein:

I meant to say in my last letter that I think you wise to shift the policy of the magazine back to literature. Also, it seems to me bad policy to order articles unless you are pretty damned sure of your writer. Get the best men you know to send in what they are interested in doing, and choose the best of it. Tate will be sore as hell, but with the *American Review* at his disposal, he has a fair enough organ for propaganda.

*   *   *

Perhaps I ought to give you a brief account of my own condition and attitude at the present moment. I am sick of contemporary literature, and, having finished my grand critical opus and sent it off to a couple of publishers, do not wish to say more about contemporary literature, except occasionally where some first rate writer is not getting fair attention and should be dragged to light. I am also extremely tired and have not the moral courage to face a very ambitious review. The job of finishing my examinations, finishing my book, and looking after Cunningham for the past 20 months has left me very done up. I have got to the end by increasing my coffee supply till at present I drink fourteen and fifteen cups a day and it has little effect on me. This means little except that I have to cut out coffee, endure headaches, and sleep twelve hours a day for a couple of months. This, with a heavy teaching schedule, will keep me very busy.

Cunningham lived with us for 20 months and was a good deal of a drain in several ways, but mostly nervously. He is a hypochondriac, a blind egotist, and in his personal behavior a hopelessly unmannerly and silly ass. He has a lot of fundamental good qualities and extraordinary talent, and now that he is living away from us and I don't see him often, I feel a good deal of affection for him, but I have seldom known anyone whom I have so consistently desired to like and whom I have found so consistently exasperating and even repulsive. In the course of two years this gets one pretty tired.

All of this means that if you send me books for review, I shall probably pass them on either to Stafford or to Cunningham if they appear interesting. Possibly to Baker, but not likely, for he is awfully busy. Stafford will make a fine critic: he is sensitive and a very clear thinker, and he writes a beautiful prose; he has remarkable personal dignity and integrity, which show in his prose. Cunningham is without dignity and there is something about the feel of his prose which I don't like, a faint cast of vulgarity, but it is a superficial quality, and he has a very penetrating mind, a mind which at the present juncture is simply invaluable. Both he and Stafford are perfectly indifferent to making enemies and will not evade issues in the interests of diplomacy, as, for example, Tate commonly evades them. They are men whom you should cultivate.

As ever, / Y.W.

MS: Yale

TO LINCOLN KIRSTEIN

Oct. 21, 1933

Dear Mr. Kirstein:

Of your English friends I have read *The Ecliptic* by J. G. Macleod, a book by Auden which was out at around the same time, and Spender's latest book, in addition to the volumes of Lewis. I have also seen poems in *The Criterion* and elsewhere. These young men all have a little talent, but they have no knowledge of style and no desire to acquire any; they are more concerned with stimulating the serious young critics (Leavis, your Ohio correspondent T. C. Wilson, and the like) to serious discussion than with anything else. They do not, as you say, irritate me; I simply have no respect for them. It irritates me a little to see people in responsible editorial positions taken in by them.

Your remarks on poetry are simple nonsense. All writing has a conventional base, which must be firmly defined. The personal contribution is in the nature and skill of the variations. Extreme variations are usually self-destructive, since they destroy convention. I will send you my chapter on poetic convention. You need to read it.

Do not let my remarks about Cunningham prejudice you against him. He is going to be a very important man in the course of the next decade and will probably outgrow most of his defects, personal and literary. Had he not such remarkable virtues, one would probably lay his defects to his age and forget them. He arrived here, for example, at the age of 19 with a very keen critical sense, an extraordinary knowledge of Latin and English literature, and a perfect inability to write three consecutive grammatical sentences in English prose: in this last respect, he was literally much worse than the average freshman. He mispronounced about every third word he used. He desired to become an English teacher; he was on my hands; and I had to straighten him out. He had, literally, not the slightest suspicion of his deficiencies, and regarded—as he still does—all corrections as personal affronts. I have spent hours correcting his published essays, and Baker and I have spent hours trying to force him to accept the corrections. I would have kicked him out on his ear at the end of a week, had there been any place to kick him to, but there wasn't. Add to that a complete social insensitivity, which allows him to harangue one's guest almost to extinction, a mistaken notion that he is witty (he mistakes silliness and unbridled rudeness for wit) and he can be pretty irritating. He is too frail to take a smack on the nose; one night at Baker's he made me so angry that I vomited my entire supper: that, I suppose, is an example of what happens when an irresistible force (my temper) meets a considerable check (inner check). Yet he has, within certain limits of perception, one of the three or four critical minds for which I have any respect whatever, and, in spite of the dead spots in his verse, he has written some rather grand poetry. His defects may be laid largely to his past history: shanty Irish family of a somewhat unusually disreputable sort, I gather, though he admires them all fervently, and five years of hardship, over-work, and undernourishment when he should have been in school. He really is improving.

The thing that perplexes me is that Cunningham should write such good verse and such intelligent criticism, when a person like Warren, who personally is charming beyond most of the people I know, and who in conversation appears intelligent to the last degree, should write so vilely.

As to your comment on Miss [Jean] Stewart. She is extremely shy, or at least has a very genuine and innocent desire to be unobtrusive. She is not "superior" if you use the word to describe an attitude. You are right about her being more interested in literature than you are. Your remarks about poetry are proof of the fact: you come to poetry, I suspect, for something other than poetry. This is a plagiarism from Eliot, of course, but a pertinent one.

Sincerely, / YW

Thanks for showing Spencer the essay. I may accept his offer.

MS: Yale

Nov. 3, 1933

Dear Kirstein:

Miss Hoyleman's performance is lunacy, but is scarcely unprecedented. I'll return it presently; I am out of big envelopes. As a matter of fact I thought the stuff of hers that you printed was pretty lousy.

I did not say that I went to poetry for something else than poetry; I said you did. All the best poetry is largely corroborative, to employ your term, because as Babbitt remarked all the most intelligent experience is corroborative of Christ and Aristotle. A poet, like Wordsworth or Rimbaud, who conquers new worlds, commonly loses the old—which is the most extensive and interesting world in spite of its age. All poetry is conventional: convention is the basic tone, the norm of feeling which the poet builds from. Without convention there is no poetry, since without the norm there can be no departure, that is, perception. Most modern poetry tries, vaguely or violently, to escape convention, and ends up by being sloppy. When one dislikes slop one is called insensitive. It takes real sensitivity, however, to perceive the variations in a Bridges or in a John Gay, because they are the variations of a civilized man. The easy floundering of your friend MacL. (who, if he were half a man, would have called me by name and have really written directly about my criticism instead of using Spender as a stalking-horse) is simply not interesting. Unless you can realize the role of convention in poetry and take it as a matter of fact and use it, you are wasting your time with poetry. Convention, not as a norm of reference, but for its own sake, is dull, but even that may have interest if one is really concerned with the art. I venture to suspect that you have never gone through the 16th century song books, poem by poem, marking the good songs, the songs that show a fine variation of feeling worth saving, for future reference; that you have never gone over the volumes of heroic couplets of the 18th century in the same fashion, or over the volumes of early Tudor doggerel. It is by so doing that one learns something about poetry; you are doing it unwillingly now for your own age, and are surprised that you like so little. Most modern poetry (like most other poetry) is not conventional but cliché. Unless you have studied conventions—and there are many conventions—you will confuse the conventional with the cliché very often, and you will mistake the attempt to establish a new sort of convention for intrinsic superiority, for a new revelation. It is new revelations that you seem to be looking for. A poem like Tate's "Shadow and

Shade" (in spite of the two outrageous revisions in the printed version) or like the sonnet on "Silence" which I quoted from Moore will stand beside the best work of any period. So will Frost's "Acquainted with the Night," or, within a narrower scope, his "Spring Woods." And this is not the end of the list.

WHAT ARE YOU PLANNING TO DO ABOUT STANFORD'S POEMS?

Sincerely, / Y.W.

MS: Yale

TO R. P. BLACKMUR

Dec. 4, 1933 / R. 1, Box 363 / Palo Alto, Calif.

Dear Blackmur:

I am glad you like Don, for I judge from his letters that he has seen a great deal of you. Your present view of me as a kind of Caligari is somewhat unjust, however. A year ago this time Don had just transferred to an English major from Chemistry and to Stanford from the College of the Pacific. He knew nothing whatever about English poetry, past, present, or to come. He had a small college aesthete's contempt for scholarship and ignorance of it. He was in a fair way to make a mess of himself in several distinct fashions, and, though his native good sense and rather considerable talent would eventually have come to his rescue, it is more than likely that he might have squandered quite a few years and a good deal of health and happiness in nonsense. Last winter Cunningham used to amuse himself by reading poems like "Dover Beach" and "Ode to a Nightingale" to Don, to see if Don recognized them: he almost never did recognize them. His having read anyone thoroughly is due largely to his having been taken in hand by Cunningham (primarily) and myself. Had I had him around for three or four years instead of one, I should have given him a much more thorough education in English poetry; but even in one I got things pretty well started and I suspect he'll take care of himself. Everyone at that age is dominated by some one or other for a time, and I don't believe I can possibly do Don as much harm with my orthodox academicism as my own masters did me with their half-baked modernism. Remember that he is not yet 21.

As to your fears that I am manhandling the rest of the people out here, they are sheer nonsense. The present bent of my wife's talent, which, I admit, has points of similarity with my own, she inherited as her birthright; I arrived at my own present attitude by arduous laboring and by more arduous blundering. Lyrics like "Going Home from the Party," and "The Candle Flame," she was writing when I was writing some of my earliest free verse. Baker is about as easy to influence as one of the California mountain ranges. The only things I have ever tried to teach him are, specifically: that mixed metaphors are bad; and that when making a trisyllabic substitution in iambic meter the two light syllables should be exceptionally light and short and that trisyllabic substitutions should be avoided anyway. And I have never succeeded in teaching him those principles. Cunningham is neurotically jealous of his independence; strictly speaking, he discovered me, and not the reverse—he started corresponding with me when he was about 16, and his intellectual principles (plain Catholic ones) were pretty well established before he arrived here: I showed him a few poets he had missed and convinced him of a handful of discrepancies between his tastes (such as that for Eliot) and his principles. My influence on Stafford has probably been greater than on any of these, but it has been only in a small part personal, for I see him no more than three or four times a year, and it is not very great anyway.

My real genius as a teacher lies in this: that I can distinguish teachable talent under a denser screen of faults than can anyone else I know of, and I can succeed in making young people with disparate faults and talents to pocket their private animosities and put up with each other long enough to make a few exchanges. Beyond that I have a handful of workable formulae, in the way of composition assignments and reading assignments, and a fair eye for revising mss. As a teacher I am, in spite of my public detractors, not a formalist but a rather sensitive opportunist. I have spent two years trying to undermine Cunningham's faith in concepts and in doggerel meters, while, at the same time, working in the opposite direction on various others.

As to Moore, you might try to get used to him. I have been reading him for fifteen years. Spencer's remarks on the two kinds of poetry give me a bellyache. He uses revery as an invidious term for meditation (which all poetry of necessity is) and then praises that poetry which pretends to be something it cannot be. Yeats's "Leda" is a great poem, but the ghost of melodrama is in it, and many of the poems are nearly all melodrama. Had Spencer quoted in full Moore's first sonnet on "Silence" and Yeats's "Leda" for comparison, he would have had a just basis, both men being there at their best. I believe Moore's poem to be a shade sounder, a shade more profound, and a shade more complex (it is, among other things, rather witty). To read Yeats in bulk is to habituate oneself to a strained and somewhat neurotic way of feeling; Moore is sane, and he is sometimes very great. For the defects (and virtues) of Moore's long poems, see my review.

I am glad you like the poems, though I had about decided to discard "The Prince" and the "Elegy" as too loose. I enclose another that you have not seen, though it is not especially new.

As ever, / Yvor Winters

MS: Princeton, R. P. Blackmur Papers

TO MARGARET LAMSON

March 27, 1934 / R. 1, Box 363 / Palo Alto, Calif. / Telephone: 6012

Dr. Lamson:

The survey of the trial and conviction of your brother[1] [*The Case of David Lamson*] will be completed this evening, probably with all corrections and revisions. It covers the evidence for and against your brother's character, all of the physical evidence of the incident, an analysis of the theories of motivation, a short summary of the most obvious injustices of the trial, in connection with the judge's rulings and instructions, the behavior of the prosecuting staff, and the conduct of the jury, a complete list of all the reasons given by the jury, and the obvious answers to them (all provided by the preceding text), and a very brief general summary.

Now I have a suggestion; namely, that you see Mr. Vollmer *today* and ask him to arrange as quickly as possible an afternoon or evening meeting at Berkeley, at which this statement could be read. I would be glad to do the reading. I should like to have the big scale drawing of the bathroom on the wall at my back, with Mr. Vollmer seated somewhere close to it with a pointer.

The meeting should be a *private* one, and a *small* one; not over fifteen or twenty persons. They should be persons of some academic rank, and should be selected on the basis of definite knowledge that they are humane, impartial persons with some training in thinking. It would be well to have one or two medical men and one or two chemists in the group, to catch any actual errors that may have slipped into the pamphlet.

I would request that the following persons be requested to come *at my very urgent personal request* as well as at Mr. Vollmer's: Professor Adams, of the Department of Philosophy; Professors Durham of the History Dept., and also T. K. Whipple, and if possible Mr. Bronson, of the Department of English; and

Professor Max Radin of the Department of Law. I know all of these gentlemen personally, and believe they would come, if they could, at my request. I am certain of their feelings when the review shall have been completed.

If Dr. Reinhardt could come, it would be well also. I might add that Professor E. O. James, of the Department of English at Mills, might be invited at my request.

After the reading, I would make a plea for the individuals present to sponsor the pamphlet. If this can be done at all, it should be done as quickly as possible.

Sincerely, / Yvor Winters

MS: UC

Margaret Lamson: David Lamson's sister, a physician.

[1]David Lamson (1902–1975): American fiction writer and, at the time of this letter, a Stanford University Press employee convicted of the murder of his wife and on Death Row in San Quentin. YW became involved in his case by accident. Janet Lewis had been asked to put Lamson's appeal in better prose. (Lamson was convicted in his first trial in September 1933.) Looking over her shoulder as she worked, YW became interested in the material, taking over the work. He became convinced of Lamson's innocence and devoted great time and energy to working for Lamson and his lawyers. For an intense year, he worked on the appeal as part of the Lamson Defense Committee, writing and publishing *The Case of David Lamson,* delivering speeches, and so forth.

When the California Supreme Court heard the appeal, there were questions about circumstantial evidence and a juror discrepancy (a deputy sheriff sat on the jury). A second trial in 1935 ended in a hung jury, as did a third trial in 1936. (There had been a mistrial between the second and third trials.) More details are included in letters to Maxwell Perkins, below.

It would be difficult to overrestimate the importance of this incident for YW or his wife. Because of the widespread assumption of Lamson's guilt, not least on the Stanford campus, YW undertook this work at serious risk to his academic career. In many ways, the incident underlines elements of YW's character: his tenacity for a cause in which he believed, however unpopular; his egalitarian sense of justice; his championing of the underdog. As is well known, someone sent him *Famous Cases of Circumstantial Evidence,* which he passed along to his wife with the suggestion that she consider it for material for a novel. (In fact, Janet Lewis wrote three novels of circumstantial evidence: *The Wife of Martin Guerre, The Trial of Søren Qvist,* and *The Ghost of Monsieur Scarron.*) Beyond that, the case led to three poems by YW—"To a Woman on Her Defense of Her Brother Unjustly Convicted of Murder," "To David Lamson," and "To Edwin V. McKenzie"—that are among his early occasional public poems. No one seems to have considered in any detail YW as a public poet, and yet it seems to me that he was not only a fine one but that the occasional public poem was important to him and is important to any consideration of his work.

March 28, 1934

Dear Howard:

Janet discovered that she was very anemic, and is now getting better as a result of treatment.

I am up to my neck in Lamson defense work, and in a worse nervous state than I have been in since my mother broke loose. I have just completed a 108 page ms. survey of all the aspects of the case to be published in booklet form some time next month. Vollmer is arranging a private reading of it before a Berkeley faculty group, Thursday, April 12. I did the survey in less than two weeks and hardly got five hours sleep a night in the period. Not that I invariably had to work that late, but I couldn't sleep when I went to bed. The thing is a nightmare. Lamson is beyond a question innocent and broken-hearted. He was railroaded by the O'Neal political gang in San Jose because the Lamsons refused O'Neal's offer to get him off for $45,000. This is strictly private. IT MUST NOT BE MENTIONED TO ANYONE.

The appeal lawyer, MacKenzie, is a grand man and probably a great lawyer, but is a terrible stylist.

If I can manage it I'll come up early the day of the reading and see you. May get up sooner, but don't know just what I may have left to do down here between the final cleaning up of the ms. today or tomorrow and the reading.

I am glad you like the new poems, though I was surprised to hear of their existence, I had so utterly forgotten them. And I am glad you like the children. *The M.* has accepted "Miss Prindle's Lover" and "Logan Grey's Land of '49," so are not quite *Pagany* yet. I am sorry about Smitter, though. It was a good story, and his family need the money.

I am enclosing a very remarkable document. I don't know whether it is literature or not. What do you think about sending it down? The author is an engineering student, and did this in his first quarter. It is a true narrative.

Arthur

MS: Stanford

March 29, 1934 / Palo Alto, Calif.

The Editor / *The Hound and Horn*

Dear Sir:

In your October–December issue for 1933 Mr. Theodore Spencer reviews Mr. Yeats's *Words for Music Perhaps,* and in so doing raises certain objections to comments of my own upon Mr. T. S. Moore, which I made in a review of the first two volumes of Mr. Moore's collected works, published in your issue for the previous spring. I had hoped to point out Mr. Spencer's misunderstandings and misconceptions in a review of the last two volumes, which are now published, but have been prevented by academic and other work. Let me list Mr. Spencer's errors very briefly, then:

1. Mr. Spencer takes for granted that I consider Mr. Yeats a bad poet, whereas I called him a great poet. To refute this supposed opinion of mine, he quotes four lines from one of the three or four best of Mr. Yeats's pieces and sets them against four lines from Mr. Moore which I had admitted to be faulty. This is hardly worthy of Mr. Spencer.

2. Mr. Spencer differentiates between poetry of revery and poetry of immediacy, classifying Mr. Moore's poetry as the former and Mr. Yeats's as the latter. But Mr. Spencer uses the terms very carelessly. *Revery* means *day-dreaming,* the irresponsible progression from image or idea to image or idea. This is precisely what I tried to show that Mr. Yeats is guilty of: the book which Mr. Spencer reviews illustrates the defect in nearly all of its contents, and shockingly in some. Mr. Spencer praises as "immediacy" the quality of false excitement with which Mr. Yeats sustains poems of this kind: needless to say, in a writer of Mr. Yeats's skill such false excitement is very consistent in its texture and may easily mislead a reader who began to admire it early and grew up with it—as I did, and, I suspect, as Mr. Spencer did.

Mr. Spencer uses the word *revery,* in connection with Mr. Moore, as an invidious synonym for *meditation.* This is a very serious fallacy. Mr. Moore's poems rarely indulge in revery, and when they do so, it is consciously and with no pretense of doing anything else. As to meditative poetry, the class probably embraces three-fourths of the greatest poetry in the language. Mr. Moore, in writing of a past experience writes *of his present experience of his past experience* ordinarily: that is, his poem is an act of comprehension, an attempt to understand something past. He does not try to "step up" or dramatize his feeling, as Mr. Yeats commonly does: that is, to *re-experience* it, which is impossible.

3. I have no desire to belittle Mr. Yeats, but I feel that his admirers in the main prefer his defects to his virtues; and they in so doing, confuse critical issues, damage contemporary poetry, and fail to do justice to writers like Mr. Moore who may have the virtues without the defects.

Mr. Spencer would do well to read Mr. Moore carefully; he shows little evidence of having done so. I have been reading him for fifteen years, and my admiration is of no sudden growth. All four volumes are now available, the two latter containing much that I referred to in my review.

Sincerely, / Yvor Winters

MS: Yale

TO MRS. GEORGE OSBORNE WILSON

May 25, 1934 / R. 1, Box 363 /
Palo Alto, California

Mrs. George Osborne Wilson /
344 Serra Road / Stanford University
Dear Mrs. Wilson:

Thank you for your letter of May 24. The material concerning which I enquired will not be printed since you request it.[1]

It is only fair to you to state, however, that Mrs. Russell believed this series of statements a correct summary of her interview with you; and further, that these stories, in essentially this form, have traveled very widely in Palo Alto, with your name as their sources—I myself have encountered most of them more than once. Since, as you say, they misrepresent your views, it would be well, I think, if you could counteract them, for they can do little good either to Mr. Lamson or to yourself, and far less to the cause of justice.

With your letter as my assurance, I will, you may rest assured, do everything in my power to discredit them wherever I may chance to meet them.

Faithfully yours, / Yvor Winters.

MS: UC

[1]YW had confronted her with the remarkable (and lengthy) document mentioned here, which attributed to her many statements damaging to David Lamson.

TO HOWARD BAKER

July 8, 1934

Dear Howard:

I think I had better ask you & Dorothy not to visit us for 6 or 8 weeks. Janet's present situation is precarious. She either will improve greatly in the next couple of months or she will be in serious danger. Her cough retards her recovery, & talking or any small excitement stirs up her cough. If she can stay almost entirely flat & quiet for 2 months, I believe she will be in pretty good shape.

I think I personally shall give up *The Magazine* as a bad job. They are all of them unpleasant fools. I take no pleasure in appearing among their selections, & I believe on the whole that they are likely to damage my reputation, or what is left of it. As to writing kindergarten articles for them—& for them to comment upon—it is out of the question.

Arthur

MS: Stanford

TO LINCOLN KIRSTEIN

July 23, 1934

Dear Kirstein:

It is too bad you have to give up [*Hound & Horn*]. It was a charitable enterprise for which you and such supporters as you may have had—I suppose your chief supporter must have been your father—ought to receive due credit in Paradise. I retain my opinion, however, that you have made many more mistakes than you should have made.

*　　*　　*

Sincerely, / Yvor Winters

MS: Yale

Jan. 10, 1935 / R. 1, Box 363 /
Palo Alto, Calif.

Mr. Maxwell Perkins /
Charles Scribners Sons / New York City
Dear Mr. Perkins:

A few years ago I used occasionally to offer you excellent advice which you never accepted. I am now going to offer you some which I am pretty certain that you will accept.

Within a day or two I will send you or have sent you the ms. of a book (as far as completed) on life in the Condemned Row at the California State Prison at San Quentin.[1] The book is written by David Lamson who over a year ago was convicted of murdering his wife and spent 13 months on the Condemned Row. The verdict convicting him has recently been reversed by the supreme court of California and Lamson has written the book while awaiting a retrial in the jail at San Jose. Lamson's attorneys have advised him that the book must not be published while there is any danger of his returning to San Quentin, because the prison authorities might choose to be irritated and make life unpleasant for him there. But as he is fairly certain of being acquitted within the next couple of months, this difficulty is a very minor one.

Lamson did not murder his wife. He was convicted on perjured testimony in one of the most scandalous trials ever held in the state. The trial was the result of the failure of an extortion plot on the part of the chief political boss of the county.[2] I will send you a booklet [*The Case of David Lamson*] on the trial prepared by myself and one of my older colleagues in the Stanford English Department, Professor Frances Theresa Russell. Lamson is personally a fine and intelligent man. The book is brilliantly written and intelligently conceived. As a social document its value is very great. As a series of narratives and character sketches it is extremely interesting reading. I believe it will be as permanent an addition to American literature as *The Oregon Trail* or *Two Years Before the Mast*. These qualities would make it a very profitable investment. Further, in this part of the country, at least, the case has had so much publicity that the publicity alone would make the book sell, I believe. Finally, Lamson has a future as an author.

Within a week or so, I will write an introduction to the book and send it on separately. Do, please, consider this matter seriously. You will make money on it.

Sincerely, / Yvor Winters

MS: *Princeton, Archives of Charles Scribner's Sons*

Maxwell Perkins (1884–1947): editor.

[1]The book, *We Who Are About to Die: Prison as Seen by a Condemned Man,* was published by Scribners (1935).

[2]For an explanation of the extortion, see YW's letter to Howard Baker, March 28, 1934. See also YW's letter to Maxwell Perkins, May 19, 1935.

TO MAXWELL PERKINS

R. 1, Box 155 / Los Altos, Calif. / Feb. 21, 1935

Dear Mr. Perkins:

Your letter arrived yesterday and your telegram today, the latter having arrived in Palo Alto, I am informed, on Feb. 14. I am very sorry about the delay.

Your letter contained a good many questions that I can scarcely answer; so I turned it over to Lamson last evening and asked him to write you at once. You can address him in care of his sister, Dr. Margaret Lamson, the Medico-Dental Bldg., Palo Alto, Calif.

I am glad you like the ms. and would like to try it. I still think it will sell. Also, I was hoping that you could manage to publish some of it in *Scribners Magazine:* Lamson, in his present predicament, needs every dollar he can get, and I should think the magazine would be none the worse off for some of it.

I will write a brief foreword for the book at once, answering the obvious questions regarding it; the foreword can then be used or not, as you and Lamson see fit.

And I wish to thank you finally for your kindness in reading the ms. and reaching a decision so quickly. It was very good of you.

The new trial began the 18th, this week having been spent in the selection of the jury. I am, by this time, pretty deeply in the confidence of Lamson's chief attorney, McKenzie, and am pretty certain that Lamson will be acquitted: nothing can prevent [it], at least, save a solidly packed jury, and that is hardly likely, although the prosecution are doing their best: 7 deputy sheriffs have turned up thus far on the venire, and also the wife of another. Deputies of the old regime, that is; for the famous Emig was beaten at the last election and a decent man elected.

Sincerely, / Yvor Winters

MS: *Princeton, Archives of Charles Scribner's Sons*

May 19, 1935 / R. 1, Box 155 / Los Altos, Calif.

Dear Mr. Perkins:

Here is the long-delayed foreword for Lamson's book, containing the sad story of the retrial. Lamson hopes that you can use this, and so do I. It seems unfair to send his book out on the world without an explanation, and it seems to me that these facts are sensational enough to add considerably to the interest of the book, whether regarded as narrative or as social study.

This has been checked by Mr. McKenzie for error, and there is none. If there is anything that you fear as grounds for libel action, let me know, and I'll have it rechecked. I am dead sure of all my facts, however; I have had this case at my fingertips for over a year. The stuff from the trial record is all correct. I witnessed most of it and then examined the record and then had both Lamson and McKenzie recheck. The story about Meyer I have already published. He threatened to sue me, threatened to embroil me with the Stanford authorities, and threatened me in general, and did nothing—for the simple reason that the story is true.

If you ever hear of a story more unlikely than this one, let me know. I have not recovered even yet.

The key to the situation, McK. will not let me publish. It is this: when Lamson was first arrested, Dr. Lamson was advised to hire Louis O'Neal as a lawyer. O'Neal is chief boss of the county and owner of Emig and the D.A. He demanded a fee of $45,000. When he didn't get it, he gave Lamson the works. It was foolish to go to him, but the Lamsons knew nothing of county politics at the time, and were utterly bewildered with grief and terror.

Sincerely, / Yvor Winters

P.S. I desire no payment for the preface if you use it. The book is to help pay Lamson's bills, and you have already been very generous.

MS: Princeton, Archives of Charles Scribner's Sons

June 20, 1935 / R. 1, Box 155 / Los Altos, Calif.

Dear Mr. Perkins:

I enclose a revision of the appendix.[1] The whole thing is reorganized. All statements of personal feeling are omitted. So far as possible generalizations have been abandoned in favor of their factual basis: this is not wholly possible in a short summary of a long trial, however. I have simply done the best I could in this respect. The appendix is a little longer, chiefly as a result of your attorney's finding the first version unconvincing.

I have omitted as many of the objectionable passages as possible. For those retained, I have given, in most cases, my proof. I am enclosing, in addition, a number of passages copied from the record, which may help to clear up a number of points for you.

I am certain that there is no danger of libel suits on the basis of anything herein stated. I have checked it very carefully, most of it many times. And besides that, most of the worst of this stuff, or quite enough of it, appeared in the Lamson booklet, which had a wide circulation locally, and we were not sued nor even threatened by anyone save Meyer, who had no ground for action and ultimately did nothing but write letters and discuss the case in his classes. I enclose a copy of the Lamson booklet, in case you have lost the first. Read over what I said of Proescher therein, for example. There was never a peep from him. And there never will be, for it would center attention on him instead of on Lamson and mean Quentin for him beyond a doubt.

If you wish to inquire about my veracity or my knowledge of this case, write any of the academic sponsors of the book, all of whom know me, some of whom know me very well and know the case very well. Try Vollmer and Blackwelder in particular. Also, one of your men wrote Lamson that he would be out here shortly and would visit Lamson. Lamson can show him the transcript —he has it in his cell. And the gentleman can check up in other ways if he wishes to do so.

I enclose your attorney's memorandum and my memorandum upon it. The memorandum was very valuable to me and I am very grateful for it. Nevertheless, some of the remarks were pretty hasty and based on a very careless reading of what I had written.[2]

* * *

The publication of this appendix would be of incalculable value to Lamson, and I should think would add to the interest and general value of the book. I am dead sure it will add to the California sale. I hope that the revision will prove satisfactory. I will gladly try again if you wish it and if there is time.

Sincerely and gratefully, / Yvor Winters

P.S. When you have done with the enclosed passages copied from the record, please, if you can, return them. If this thing goes into politics, presently, as I think it will, I am slated to be chief stump speaker, and shall need the pages.

MS: Princeton, Archives of Charles Scribner's Sons

[1]It was decided that YW's introduction would be used as an appendix.

[2]There follows a lengthy response by YW, "A Memorandum on the Memorandum sent me on the first draft of my appendix for Lamson's book," to twenty-seven items raised by the Scribners attorney. I have asked a lawyer familiar with the Lamson case, and he affirms that in practically every instance YW was correct, the Scribners attorney excessively cautious.

TO MAXWELL PERKINS

June 21, 1935 / R. 1, Box 155 / Los Altos, Calif.

Dear Mr. Perkins:

Here is Judge Syer's precious ruling. If I didn't summarize it fairly, I'll eat it. To agree with Syer one has to assume: (1) that Seawell would hang a man on insufficient evidence, or (2) that the presence of the deputy sheriff on the jury influenced his opinion of the evidence. Either implication is libel on Seawell, in spite of everything I know against him, and I know plenty.

One of the sponsors of our Lamson book was Professor Hardin Craig, of the English department, whose office is next door to mine, and with whom I am personally very well acquainted. He informs me that he is well acquainted with Mr. Darrow, of your company, who wrote Lamson recently that he would be out here shortly. If you want any information about me or the case, it occurs to me that you might get it through this connection. Professor Blackwelder, head of our department of Geology, and Professor Vollmer (Criminology) of the University of California, know the case in greater detail than Professor Craig, however, and both would vouch for me.

I will send you three or four minor insertions and corrections in a day or two—no question of libel involved.

The publication of this appendix would probably do more for Lamson than anything else could do. It would circulate the essential facts of the case. Without that circulation he is a doomed man, beyond the shadow of a doubt.

The newspapers won't do it for us; the magazines are either afraid, or not interested, or can't give us the needed space, or can't give us the circulation. Private printing doesn't circulate adequately. The appendix, joined to the book, would just about suffice, I believe, to wreck the case.

And I don't believe there is an error in the thing now except one very small and unimportant one which I will correct. And one couldn't libel those devils sufficiently to give them grounds for suit. After all, if a judge's or jury's count of Proescher's changes of testimony on Exhibit 39 showed only 6 instead of 12, what difference would it make? I don't mean that I have been careless on any such grounds, but that is the situation. And they didn't raise a hand against Mrs. Russell and myself for the book, anyway; and they knew we had very little money with which to fight them if they started anything.

Incidentally, that book as it stands, was written almost wholly by myself. I used a very little material from an earlier summary by Mrs. Russell, and she lent me her name as moral backing. I state this merely to assure you that I am familiar with the material.

Sincerely, / Yvor Winters

MS: *Princeton, Archives of Charles Scribner's Sons*

TO MAXWELL PERKINS

August 15, 1935 / R. 1, Box 155 / Los Altos, Calif.

Dear Mr. Perkins:

I received the galley sheets today, corrected them, and took them to Lamson, who will write you of what he desires to do. Any decision that he makes is agreeable to me. This letter is not a reply to your offer, then, but an unofficial commentary upon it.

The revised appendix contains no hint of perjury, corruption, newspaper falsehood, popular hysteria and malice, or of any kind of injustice whatever. It treats the case as if it had been fairly tried in a kind of social vacuum, and as if it were still fairly a controversial matter. But with this qualification: that Lamson was once convicted, was saved from execution by a Supreme Court divided as to the value of the evidence, and was then nearly convicted again; and with the additional qualification that the revised appendix is patently incomplete in its treatment. Anyone who knows nothing of the case will feel in reading such an appendix that there was probably a fair case against Lamson and that he is probably being defended by a prejudiced and sentimental friend. Lamson's enemies on the coast will be just as angry at this defense as at any other, and the defense, since it is timid and evasive, will be easy to attack and to ridicule. I believe personally that it will damage not only Lamson's chances—for one thing, it constitutes a tacit admission that the trial was fair and the case against him strong—but that it will seriously damage the book. If left upon my own responsibility, I should be ashamed to put my name to such a document, knowing what I know of the affair. If Lamson thinks it will help him, however, I will go ahead. But I don't think he will want it.

I am aware of your desire to be of help and am grateful for it. I am also aware of the effect that Mr. Darrow's brief experience with the case must have had upon him. I am aware of the difficulty of judging a mess of this sort on brief acquaintance and at a great distance. This is, however, the sort of thing that should be treated openly and without timidity, or else left to the dogs. My personal opinion—which is not an official decision—is that the appendix ought to be printed as I wrote it, or, if you don't wish to risk it, omitted entirely.[1]

Sincerely, / Yvor Winters

MS: Princeton, Archives of Charles Scribner's Sons

[1] The appendix was, in fact, omitted.

TO R. P. BLACKMUR

Dec. 12, 1935 / R. 1, Box 155 / Los Altos, Calif.

Dear Blackmur:

The copy of your book came today. It is a very handsome book; you are to be congratulated on your publisher. I looked over two of the essays that were new to me—the Crane and the Moore—and liked both a great deal; though I think you underestimate Crane, through refusing to consider the exceptions to which, as you say, I called attention: "Voyages II," and in the main "Repose of Rivers," are successful and, so far as I am concerned, unforgettably lovely; and I think you overestimate Miss Moore, through having overlooked two of her central defects. The conclusion of the next to the last paragraph on Miss Moore is fine; the last paragraph obscures the whole statement. Your statement that Crane read the French poets stemming from Baudelaire is scarcely true; he read no more French than my Airedales; and the French of the Symbolists is probably the hardest French to read that there is. Also, Crane wrote "The Hurricane" a year and a half or two years before he had read Hopkins, though he may have seen quotations here and there sufficient to give him the idea. And I resent mildly your comments here and there on Baudelaire: I wonder, frankly, how much better your French is than Crane's, or, say, than your own Latin. Baudelaire is one of the four or five most finished poets in French, and one really needs to know the language in some detail to criticize him. And, while I am objecting, I don't like your comments on Shakespeare's sonnets: they are sound, if you are trying to understand the sonnets as a group, which is pointless and hopeless, and they are sound where many of the sonnets are concerned. But many of the sonnets are wholly comprehensible individually and are incomparably great.

But these are small matters, and the book is very fine. Your prose, in the matter of the more beguiling graces and subtleties, is beautiful. I am greatly indebted to you for the copy. This is not the most propitious time for such a book to appear, for I fear it will be snagged in the Marxian mud; but it won't be lost forever.

Sincerely, / Yvor Winters

MS: Princeton, R. P. Blackmur Papers

TO R. P. BLACKMUR

Jan. 6, 1936 / R. 1, Box 155 / Los Altos, Calif.

Dear Blackmur:

Under separate cover I will mail you my first four books, if that is the word for them.[1] If I had it in my power to destroy them effectively, I would do that instead, saving a very small handful of pieces, some of them in revised form. But as the matter is not in my power, I see no reason why you should not have the copies. Don't bother about the essay unnecessarily, however; I should feel somewhat put out to lose the distinction of being the most neglected genius of my generation. You probably won't be able to make much of this stuff, anyway. I know that I can make little of most of it, now; it represents everything I most loathe.

The Magpie's Shadow is supposed to have a blue card-board cover. This uncovered copy is the only extra copy I possess, and the book is out of print. The copy of *The Proof* is the worse for wear. I am sorry.

I offer the following summary as a kind of apology. My childhood and adolescence were curiously unguided and misguided affairs. My father was a self-made business man, a handsome and gentle Irishman, who never got around to educating himself till he was dying of angina at the age of 50; his progress at that date was so rapid that I imagine that he might have done very well had he had a little more time and health. He died at 55. My mother was and is a paranoiac termagant, with whom I have had no commerce since my father's death. Crane met my father a few years before his death, and was very much charmed by him.

Throughout my childhood I was obsessed by certain solipsistic convictions, the obsession amounting at times almost to a mania; the first of these poems deal in a large measure with this material in retrospect. The texture of my poetry throughout a good deal of these first four volumes is probably affected by this.

In high school I went scientific, or specifically biological. I belonged to the State Microscopical Society of Illinois. I knew a hell of a lot about protozoology, and a good deal about several other and unrelated fields. I had a passion for the study of classification; at the age of sixteen, and quite incidentally to my main interests, I knew Jordan's *Manual of the Vertebrates* practically by heart. I took all of this far too seriously; I read outmoded philosophers like Spencer and Huxley; I became an unusually muddled mechanistic determinist; and the effect of that is to be seen at least half way through *The Proof,* in varying degrees.

When I was nineteen, after a year at the U. of Chicago, I found myself with TB, the result largely of having pickled my lungs in zoological laboratories. This sent me to bed for three years in Santa Fe. It was during the last year and a half in bed that I wrote the first two of these books. For the next two years I taught school in the coal camps south of Santa Fe, non-union camps full of bohunks, polacks, and god knows what, along with degenerate Mexicans and renegade Indians: Yaquis, Navajos, and all the varieties of pueblo peoples. You will observe that I had no access to libraries during this time, no instruction, no contact with any really educated mind. I knew the painters in Santa Fe, learned something about painting, had known Glenway Wescott and Elizabeth Roberts at Chicago, and knew Wescott for a year in Santa Fe. He was a few months younger than myself, less educated, and far more erratic personally.

At the age of 23 I entered the University of Colorado as a second-quarter sophomore and did two years intensive work in Romance languages—a useful subject but not a civilizing one. I got my M.A. in 1925 and went to the University of Idaho, where I taught French and Spanish for two years. It was while there that I began to think my way out of the muddle that these early collections represent, though there was little there to prompt thought. The attempt was fostered in part by a correspondence with Tate and Crane, both of them being, however, somewhat wavering guides.

At the age of 27 I came to Stanford as a graduate student. I was fairly on my way by that time, and gained access to a good library. I was greatly aided further by the seminar lectures of W. D. Briggs, the head of the English department, a man of great learning and a very brilliant analytical mind, who refuses to publish, either from contempt or from indolence or from a combination of the two, and who is therefore practically unknown.

You will observe that the literary criticism of my *H. and H.* days, and the much greater body of unpublished criticism on which that is based, was primarily a process of self-analysis. If we regard, as the best poets of my generation, Tate, Crane, yourself, Louise Bogan, and Damon, you will observe how much more deeply I was immersed in the experimental procedure of our forebears than any of them, and how much more completely I have departed from it. The greater part of the stuff through the first section of *The Proof* is insane. I do not mean that I was insane, but that by using a certain method, which acted as a kind of strainer, I isolated certain aspects of experience, which, when presented in isolation, constituted a kind of formalized madness. There are only two things to do with this kind of method: to succumb to it, as Crane did, and go under, or to understand it and get away from it, which I believe I have done. I had a capacity for going under, and might have done it. My analysis of technique has thus been an analysis of moral attitudes and procedure, with ramifications in general moral experience; it has not only modified my method but has helped me to understand my subject matter.

Most of these poems, as I say, I now all but loathe; they seem to me to reek with a kind of diseased nonsense. I still like a few things in *The Bare Hills* and the first part of *The Proof,* chiefly "March Dusk," "The Barnyard," "The Goatherds," and "Song of the Trees," the last for its meter primarily. The second and third parts of *The Proof* contain a few things that I like better: "The Moralists," "To W. D. Briggs," "The Empty Hills," "The Fall of Leaves," "Inscription for a Graveyard," "The Last Visit," "Moonrise," "Epilogue." The work in *The Journey* is mostly sound but is sometimes a trifle loose. *Before Disaster* I think a very good collection, and I like a few later things at least as well. But it is appallingly little to come as the result of so much labor and personal fury. Providence, in all decency, ought to permit me to do something very great, by way of recompense, in my declining years.

I threw together a ms. of my later poems the other day: *The Journey* group minus "The Critiad" and "December Eclogue," and opening with "A View of

Pasadena," "Before Disaster," and certain later things, and sent it off to Scribners, who will no doubt return it. I may send you a carbon of the ms., partly because of revisions in some of the poems you have seen, partly because of new poems, and partly to learn if you have any idea as to who might publish them. My great critical opus on the experimental movement I sent likewise to Scribners, requesting them to pass it on to the Oxford people. I wonder if your publishers would be interested in either.

Do not, for God's sake, write me a five page letter on all this stuff; I shall feel as if I were stealing food from your mouth and wisdom from posterity, if you so waste your time. And, as I said before, there is no real reason for bothering about an essay. I have sent you the books because I have extra copies and because you have expressed an interest; and I have written the present document largely in discouragement at reexamining the poems before wrapping them up and to explain to you why they are such a curious and inconsecutive mess.

Sincerely, / Yvor Winters

MS: Princeton, R. P. Blackmur Papers

[1]YW here fails to mention or include *Diadems and Fagots*.

TO R. P. BLACKMUR

Sept. 8, 1936 / R. 1, Box 155 / Los Altos, Calif.

Dear Blackmur:

Thanks for your note. You misunderstood my last. I was not demanding an immediate essay on my poems. I was curious to know what you made of the later and more ambitious work. Don't worry about the essay. I am sorry you have had so many distractions and difficulties. I'll tell you a secret, however. The damnedest of all distractions is book-reviewing. I wasted more blessed time while I was reviewing books than I ever mean to waste again.

I am glad you admire my criticism, and appreciate the great measure of praise you give it. As usual, however, I am irritated by the censure, particularly because the same objection has been made by others, and I believe unthinkingly and unfairly. Roughly, you say that I tend to be too clear and hence exclude too much, am relatively insensitive. Now that is where you are cock-eyed. I am a genuinely sensitive soul. You exaggerate your own lack of rational clarity, but roughly you lay your finger on your own weakness (and that of our period). You are, relatively, a sentimentalist. Now the sentimentalist is insensitive, in the main, because he is inadequately equipped to criticize and extend his sensibility. You (and of course it will be far more true of herds of others) will object to my low opinion of Yeats or Eliot or what have you, and you will lay it to insensitivity; you will overlook the fact that I have probably made more major discoveries than any other critic of our time (I believe that my remarks on Gascoigne, Churchill, Bridges, Moore, and Very deserve to rank as such), not counting the large number of young talents that I have discovered in embryo and trained. You (or the others) will discount these discoveries because you are too insensitive to see them; and you will thus fail to see that my objections to your favorites rest on a comparison of those favorites to a sounder and more sensitive art. To appreciate at full value such writers as Bridges or Mrs. Daryush requires real sensitivity, for they simply do not stoop to the heavy and melodramatic strokes that gain the "sensitive" writers their reputations.

I wish to make a few small changes in the ms. before and if it is printed, especially in the remarks on Bridges's meter, which are very badly stated. Many thanks for your good offices.

Sincerely, / Yvor Winters

MS: Princeton, R. P. Blackmur Papers

TO R. P. BLACKMUR

Sept. 26, 1936 / R. 1, Box 155 / Los Altos, Calif.

Dear Blackmur:

I have been reading your essay on Yeats. I like it a good deal, but can't help feeling that it was intended as a kind of covert reproach to me, the reproach, of course, to be visible to no one but me. So I offer these tentative comments.

I agree with your objections everywhere, and with much of your praise. I have never felt, myself, any objection to his magic on the grounds that I couldn't believe in it. As a matter of fact, I could believe in a great deal of it with very little effort. The notion that there are spirits meddling in the offing is not inconceivable to me. My mother, for example, who is a violent and somewhat unbalanced person, has had a series of telepathic experiences, perfectly verified, so far as I have ever been able to see, on which one could erect a whole philosophy of something or other if it seemed to one necessary. The point to all that, as I see it, is that it is unimportant in ordering one's affairs, and if gone into uncritically may be deleterious. Yeats's notion of surrender, for example, as a virtue (see that vicious and nasty little poem, "Leda," a beautifully written study in obscene demonism) is simply abominable. He has, in the first place, no notion of what kind of creature he surrenders himself to; he has an indiscriminate curiosity. I feel as Chesterton felt about Blake, that if he is really bent on keeping company in the other world, he ought to be more particular about the company. It is not dignified of an old man with a heroic cast of mind to humble himself before hobgoblins that play practical jokes on him, say one thing when they mean another, and leave him with his beard full of burs. I mean this in perfect seriousness, and taking his spirits as an allegory that may be more than an allegory for all I know or care. I don't think he gets much morality out of his allegory. "The Second Coming" is a great poem, all right, and your account of it is fine. "The Wild Swans" is nearly as fine. "The Magi" is incomprehensible, and a failure. One can find a few good minor pieces. But the objections that you make I should make stronger and apply more generally. Also, I find him a very bad metrist in his rhymed poems: that is the poems are insensitive and clattering. The blank verse, curiously, is very fine from a purely technical point of view, finer than any blank verse of our time outside of Bridges. But the loose noisy meter of most of his work, coupled with the willful emotionalism (the deliberate surrender to demons is merely the allegorical equivalent of romantic emotionalism), results in a tone that is, for me, false and unhealthy. He makes me sick, and I don't like him. I am aware of his virtues, I imagine, such as they are.

Your essay is fine, however. The Adams gets even better with thinking over.

I have been revising my ms. for Miss Codman [of Arrow Editions]. I guess I am more dogmatic than your Adams essay, all right, but my dogma seems to cover the subject of the limitations of dogma, notwithstanding, and I'm damned if I see anything I want to back down on. I have been working over the essay on meter chiefly, and nailing down loose boards. It is a pretty good essay, I think, by this time.

In regard to Yeats's offer to any government, etc., to which you call attention, might one not say fairly that it indicates that he himself not only lacks all conviction but is also full of passionate intensity? What could be worse, really, in a man of his years?

I am now chairman of the membership committee of the local teacher's union. That is the polite way of naming me chief organizer, without pay. I am the red that bores from within. I mean to start on the Los Altos school district shortly, in which we have no members. Across the street from me, in the midst of a 20-acre orchard, lives a man named Straub, who is on the local school board and who is also attorney general for the Pacific Gas and Electric Company, the outfit mainly responsible for Mooney's misadventure. So if you hear that I am in San Quentin presently, don't be surprised.

One thing and another reminds me that I predicted to all my friends hereabouts that Randall Jarrell would get that poetry prize. The style that that bunch are cooking up amongst themselves down there, is one of the most astonishing things I have ever witnessed. It would amuse me if Tate were not involved, but Tate makes me sick, somehow. He is a fallen angel, whether taken as poet or as critic. I cannot see how a man with his mind and genius can go to such lengths to make himself a fool.

And I feel that I ought to apologize to some one—you will do as well as another—for that essay on Bridges by Al Guerard. That was worse than Jarrell.

Sincerely, / Winters

MS: Princeton, R. P. Blackmur Papers

TO DONALD E. STANFORD

Oct. 23, 1936 / R. 1, Box 155 / Los Altos, Calif.

Dear Don:

Tex [Holt] has had a pretty thorough-going nervous collapse. His delusions in regard to Ruth [Lockett] have become acute. He has had a "feeling" that she was in Palo Alto, walked the streets for days last week, and nights as well, looking for her, following hunches, and asking for her at different houses. The thing has been developing rapidly into general persecution delusions, and what with walking several days and nights running, and no sleep, he had begun to act rather wildly in other ways. I hunted him all over Palo Alto Wednesday night, after some foolish behavior that had frightened his landladies, finally got the cops out and got him in the hospital about 3 A.M. His family arrived this morning and we have called in Dr. Cutting of Agnew, who wishes to see more of him before diagnosing or prescribing definitely.

I want you to write me at once and in detail anything relevant to this matter that may have occurred last summer; a statement that I can show to his family and to the doctor. He says that Ruth's mother told him in your presence that Ruth was in a certain town, that the two of you drove through it, and he looked for her there but failed to find her. He says he profoundly suspects that you went back later and saw her. The town was about 100 miles north of Taos, and in Colorado. He refuses to name it. The man who lives in his boarding house, across the hall from him, he is convinced is Ruth's uncle. This also is merely a feeling, except that he offers as evidence the statement that the man has a book with the name of this town written in it. The man is out of town at present, so I can't inquire of him.

It is a very bad situation. I have had a long letter from Ruth giving me more detailed information than I had had. His behavior has frightened her for a long time. It is no new development, but came most awfully to the surface this time and was spreading. A good specialist can probably stop it. Please write as soon as possible.

As ever, / Arthur

MS: Stanford

TO GEOFFREY STONE

Dec. 24, 1937 / R. 1, Box 155 / Los Altos, Calif.

Dear Mr. Stone:

I have to thank the *American Review* for two recent checks. I should also like to lodge certain complaints.

There are a good many alterations in the text of my essay on James ["Henry James and the Relation of Morals to Manners"] which are obviously editorial and not the work of the printer. They appear to me to be definitely alterations for the worse, and in a good many cases to be little short of barbarous in point of style. What, for example, is the justification, moral, intellectual, grammatical, for the phrase "on the contrary," fourth line from the bottom, page 491? You seem to have found my sentences in many cases too long; but the sentences were correctly constructed and said what I had in mind fairly accurately and concisely. Your shortening of sentences results in sloppy relationships, redundancy, and from time to time nonsense such as that just mentioned. These things are published over my signature, and I must really insist that they be published as sent you unless I give specific permission to make specific changes.

In the Hawthorne ["Maule's Curse: Hawthorne and the Problem of Allegory"] there were several typographical blunders, two of which resulted in nonsense: I would greatly appreciate your correcting these two in a future issue if you can do so. They are: Page 341, fourth line from bottom, "who" should be stricken out; page 360, lines 15 and 16, "inconceivable" should read "conceivable."

The sentence, incidentally, carried a footnote, originally, which you scuttled, which referred to an article by Katherine Simonds in *The New England Quarterly*. My sentence merely took over the conclusions of the Simonds article, which was extremely able, so that the loss of the reference leaves me pretty high and dry as a plagiarist.

I have just read Horton's book on Crane very rapidly. It is an astonishing performance. The clairvoyance with which H. understands the private thoughts and motives of everyone in the book is dumbfounding. I for example had no knowledge of Crane's homosexuality till after his death. I heard one or two very tenuous rumors shortly before his death. When I met him, he appeared anything but homosexual: rather, the talented and slightly spoiled little brother of Mickey Walker. And poor papa Crane is the most unsatisfactory villain I have ever met in melodrama. His paternal patience and common sense are really very touching. Having read the book, I wished that I had kept track of the sums of money Crane collected and disbursed during the years of his neglect and mistreatment. My off-hand impression is that his income during the black years was better than mine has ever been, but maybe a count would make it appear more modest.

I am sorry to object to the alterations, for you people have been very kind, but I am afraid that I do object very strenuously, and shall have to request that my work be accepted or rejected exactly as submitted.

Sincerely, / Yvor Winters

MS: Yale

Geoffrey Stone: American poet, critic, and editor.

TO GEORGE DILLON

April 3, 1938 / R. 1, Box 155 / Los Altos, Calif.

Dear Mr. Dillon:

It occurs to me that there is an outside chance that you might be interested in seeing an essay that I have had lying around for a couple of years. It is an attempt to revise the customary historical and critical estimate of the 16th century lyric ["The 16th Century Lyric in England"]. It runs to about 30 pages, typed, which is too long for you: you would have to serialize it to run it. I will not shorten it, however. It is apparently too critical and theoretical for *Modern*

Philology, and not gossipy enough for the *Southern Review.* It does not even mention Marxism or Auden. I think it has considerable bearing on the practice of poetry, however. I don't want to send it on, however, unless an essay of this length would be of interest to you. Personally, I think it one of the four or five best essays I have done, but that may not mean much.

It has long been my intention to do three other such essays on the three subsequent centuries, and write a kind of condensed history of the English lyrical rhetoric, but I seem to have mapped out a good deal of work on American literature which for practical reasons must be done first.

After all the trouble about the poems, [James] Laughlin decided to postpone the publication of my verse for a year; he will bring out a volume of seven essays on American literature this year instead. I am sorry to have bothered you about it.

Sincerely, / Yvor Winters

MS: Chicago

George Dillon (1906–1968): American poet and, at this time, editor of *Poetry: A Magazine of Verse.*

TO JULIAN SYMONS

Nov. 15, 1938 /
R. 1, Box 155 / Los Altos, Calif.

Mr. Julian Symons /
Twentieth Century Verse / London
Dear Mr. Symons:

Your American issue is sufficiently entertaining so that I am very glad to have had a share in it, but I fear that it throws very little light on American poetry.

It seems to me that in your foreword you are inclined to make an international incident out of the deficiencies of your own taste. As to that poem by Williams,[1] it is scarcely more popular on this side than on yours, but that is not Williams's fault nor mine. It is one of the really achieved compositions of the century. You may wake up to this fact when you discover that Auden and his group are merely the diluted backwash of the American Experimental movement of 20 years ago; when you discover the importance of two recent British poets, Elizabeth Daryush and Ruth Pitter; and when you discover the virtues of Robert Bridges. I don't expect much on any of these counts before the close of the century.

Poetry, you know, is an art; it is not a mauling contest. One of the most fascinating British contributions to culture in my day was a lightweight boxer named Freddy Walsh. He was so good that no champion ventured to engage him till he was nearing 35 years of age, but when he got his opportunity, he won the championship, though well past his prime. I saw him, a few years later— about 24 years ago, alas—box a rough boy from Chicago, who possessed great determination and a good left hook. Had you seen the bout, I feel sure that you would not have realized that Freddy was moving at all; you would have been bewildered by the expression worn by his opponent. But the fact of the matter was, that Freddy was winning the fight.

With sincere regard to you and the British Isles, / Yvor Winters

MS: Yale

Julian Symons (1912–1994): British poet, novelist, editor, and critic, best known for his crime and detective novels. He founded and edited the literary magazine *Twentieth Century Verse* (1937–39).

[1]The poem is "By the road to the contagious hospital." Symons had complained that he failed to understand Marianne Moore and William Carlos Williams; they were too American. Having said he read YW's comments on the poem in *Primitivism and Decadence,* he continued: "I regard his [YW's] analysis, not in its terms but in its nature, with a bewilderment which I am persuaded is due not wholly to stupidity; I do not at all understand why Mr. Winters thinks valuable a poem which seems to me after half-a-dozen careful readings such a piece of secondhand and commonplace observation as might be turned out by any good poet on an off day. I am quite sure though that Dr. Williams' and Miss Moore's poems could not be imitated and would not be attempted by any Englishman (as many Englishmen have grown up imitating Eliot and Pound): whatever good qualities their poems possess are qualities not shared and not likely to be shared by poets writing in England now or for some time to come" (*Twentieth Century Verse* 12–13 [October 1938]: 83).

TO MARK VAN DOREN

Feb. 5, 1939 / R. 1, Box 155 / Los Altos, Calif.

Dear Mr. Van Doren:

A week or so past, I received a copy of your *Collected Poems,* preceded by a note from the publishers stating that this book had been sent at your request. I am greatly indebted to you for your kindness. I have not as yet had time to read the whole of the volume, but I have read much of it, & believe that I had previously read most of it in other books & magazines.

I bear you a grudge, I think, for the tendency of your critical ideas. I do not believe that a man can really make his peace with Emerson & remain with soul uncontaminated. And you seem to me to derive from Emerson, by way of Frost & it may even be in part by way of Sandburg, a slightly casual attitude toward your art which I think is bad for it. Large numbers of your poems seem to me almost self-consciously loose, in spite of a certain discretion in the looseness. I could pass these over without comment for the sake of the poems I like—which are fairly numerous—did I not have a very deeply implanted feeling that the attitude inhibits—must inhibit—your full development or that of any man.

On the other hand, the poems that I like, I confess to liking very much. Such a poem as "Man" contains in perfection the qualities of style that I most admire. The poem has stayed with me since I first read it years ago in—I think —the *Dial.* It seems as lovely now as then.

It is with regret & a certain amount of confusion that I admit that no living American—questions of scope etc. aside—exhibits these particular qualities to a comparable degree, & in the traditional forms, which I prefer, unless it be Frost in the later lyrics, especially those of *West-Running Brook,* lyrics of which the symbolism is consistently & regrettably romantic. You show Frost's influence, but not in these best lyrics—for in them you achieve a pure & impersonal style, just as Frost achieves such a style in his best. Your second-best work shows the influence of Frost's second-best, I believe, & the attitude that gives rise to the mannerisms is, I am convinced, as I said above, an attitude that lets one's strength escape inefficiently.

But so much for objections. I shall not finish my initial perusal of the book for weeks, for I am midway in the busiest quarter of teaching in the year. I shall certainly read it all, however, & most of it many times, & much of it—I can promise that on the basis of past experience—with unqualified enjoyment. It will be a great advantage in my teaching, to have this work in a single volume, & the book will be a part of my graduate course in American poetry regularly in the future.

Many thanks, again, for your kindness.

Yvor Winters

MS: Columbia

Mark Van Doren (1894–1972): American poet, critic, and educator.

1940–1949

Yvor Winters / Box 155, Route 1 /
Los Altos, California / Nov. 15, 1940

Dear Howard:

I am glad you like the book [*Poems*]. The printing was considerably short of perfection, but I learned a good deal and ought to do a fairly neat job next time. As to the circulation of the book, I shall run a half-page announcement in the next *Kenyon Review,* and shall run a subsequent one of each book I finish, listing previous publications. I shall sell all copies direct, none through dealers, though I thank you for your offer. The price of the book, should anyone inquire, is two dollars.

I have small desire, I fear, for the admiration of the young men you mention. Laughlin's reason for postponing the publication of my poems indefinitely was that pressure had been exerted upon him to publish more experimental work in place of it. Who exerted the pressure, I don't know, but what he published was Schwartz and Patchen.

The New Orleans group seems to me unsuccessful. I see no unifying theme beyond the superficial one of the festival, which provides only a factitious unity for unrelated ideas. And I don't like most of the writing. "The Birth of the Blues" seems the most successful, but is pretty slight. "The Birth of Phebus" has a better theme, but is overloaded with talk, and the second stanza is solidly bad, I think. You simply cannot use words so clumsy as "simpered," or a line so clumsy as the third one.

I am working—or ought to be working—on a book on modern American critics: Henry Adams, Babbitt, Eliot, the hedonists (Stevens and Ransom, and possibly Blackmur), and Tate. With a theoretical introduction, and a conclusion disposing of several topics. The Eliot is finished and will appear in the *Kenyon Review* for winter and spring. If I could find the time or the moral energy to work without much time, I could clean the rest up in a few months, for I have mastered all the material. The critics in question, I may say, though the best we have, are a disgrace to civilization.

We are extremely pleased to hear that the baby is doing so well. The [Bertrand] Bronsons showed us some pictures of her the other day, and she appeared thoroughly charming. And it is nice to hear that you are doing well at Harvard.

Our best to all of you, / Arthur

MS: Stanford

Yvor Winters / Box 155, Route 1 / Los Altos, California / Dec. 1, 1940
Dear Mr. Van Doren:

Many thanks for your very kind letter. I am very glad that you like the poems. There is one thing I should like to do with the book, if possible, and that is place a few copies in library collections of modern poetry where they will have some chance of receiving better than average library care and perhaps surviving till some one begins to feel a little interest in them. Foster Damon is arranging something of the sort for me at Brown, I believe, and C. D. Abbott, of the Lockwood Memorial Library at Buffalo, asked for a copy some months ago, and should now have it. If you should happen to think of any such collection that would value a copy sufficiently to give it space, I should appreciate your suggestion. I don't want to send copies at random, however, to libraries that don't want them, and since my poetry, where it is known at all, has to combat the well established theory that it died when I abandoned free verse and modernism in favor of the kind of poetry recommended in my criticism, that my later work at best is a kind of defunct and transparent husk or cast-off snakeskin, I dare say that few libraries would be interested.

A young fellow named Alan Swallow,[1] who is beginning to teach English this year, and at the U. of New Mexico, may possibly print some of the people whom I was planning to print. His publishing projects are more ambitious than mine, I believe. He has just done a volume of poems by Lincoln Fitzell, which contains at least six or eight very fine poems.

Unless you get bored and protest, however, I shall send you any future volumes that I may print. I am starting now on my wife's poems.[2]

Sincerely, / Yvor Winters

MS: Columbia, Mark Van Doren Papers

[1]Alan Swallow (1915–1966): American poet, critic, scholar, editor, publisher, and educator.

[2]YW had planned a number of volumes of poetry that he would hand print and issue through his Gyroscope Press imprint. However, only the previously mentioned *Poems* was produced, although he did print a few sheets of the Janet Lewis book before abandoning it.

TO HOWARD BAKER

Dec. 12, 1940

Dear Howard:

In the current issue of *American Literature* I have an essay, one of three essays in that issue discussing the possibility of a co-operative history of American Literature. These essays are supposed to serve as the basis of discussion at the Amer. Lit. section of the MLA meeting at Cambridge this month. If you or Al could find time to drop around and hear what they say, I should appreciate it. I'll send you an offprint of the essay when the things arrive. I am afraid it will make the good gentlemen angry, and I am curious to learn what they have to say. If you don't see Al often, I wish you would forward him this note. Don't let the business inconvenience you, however, or Al either.

Arthur

MS: Stanford

TO THEODORE ROETHKE

[1 Feb. 1941]

Dear Mr. Roethke:

I have meant for some time to send you a copy of the book, but did not know how to reach you. I have liked a good deal of your work, as I have read it in magazines, & I have not liked much of the work of the young men of the past decade or so. I'll get a copy off in a day or two. If it does not arrived fairly soon, let me know.

Yvor Winters

MS: UW

TO THEODORE ROETHKE

March 6, 1941 / R. 1, Box 155 / Los Altos, Calif.

Dear Mr. Roethke:

Many thanks for your letter, and for the book of your poems [*Open House*], which I received a few days ago from your publisher. I sent you, the other day, the complete collected poems of my friend Clayton Stafford, now about 36 years old, the most reticent of poets, but I think a very fine one. Stafford is a former seaman: 5 years on a destroyer and 3 years on merchant and passenger ships; and is at present a technical expert employed by the telephone company in San Francisco. He is the most diffident soul that I know, and one of the two or three most serious; and in spite of his nautical mastery of strong language, which he does his best never to exhibit, the most respectable.

Your book reimpressed me with the distinction of your work. The poems I like best are these: "The Adamant" (a really superb piece), "The Heron" (mere description, but beautiful description), "Long Live the Weeds," "Against Disaster," "Reply to Censure," "The Reckoning," "Lull," "Night Journey," and perhaps "Highway: Michigan." There are a few other things of the same general sort that I like nearly as well, but these strike me as the best. It is a great relief to read a poet who has something genuinely serious on his mind and who is trying to say it as sharply and compactly as possible. The young southerners (see Laughlin's 5 *Young Poets*) are, I fear, getting on my nerves. I do not really like your ironical jingles, which concentrate in the fourth section, but appear elsewhere; they strike me as too easy and fundamentally somewhat stereotyped. "The Gentile," however, is almost good enough to justify them.

I should like to be explicit about what I like, however: I really think your best pieces hard as rock. Whether you are a "major" poet I don't know, but you are certainly in a way to be, and the thing you need most to do is to continue. There is very little being done as good as these things.

With best wishes, / Yvor Winters

MS: UW

TO HOWARD BAKER

April 16, 1941 / R. 1, Box 155 / Los Altos, Calif.

Dear Howard:

Many thanks for the pamphlet [*A Letter from the Country & Other Poems*]. My feelings about the various poems are about what they have been, but here they are for what little they are worth.

"Advice to a Man etc." seems to have been revised a little since I originally saw it, and improved. It is charming, verges at moments on a slightly sentimental-romantic doctrine, appears somewhat more loose than your best work. It is well worth keeping.

"The Passing Generation." The close is one of the greatest passages in its way I have ever read; but it is too great for the narrative, which is slight and casual. Yet it could not stand alone. This poem, like the long ones in general, strikes me as remarkable for fragments—in this case a fragment—rather than the unit.

"Destiny" is still a great poem, though I still think that your predestinarianism toward the close is philosophically, even logically, unsatisfactory and unnecessary, and in spite of the revised stanza. The revised stanza in some ways is an improvement, though you chucked some fine phrases. The revision of the sun image is justified by the formal rules, but the fourth line of the stanza is a trifle hard to say—the consonants get stuck in one's teeth. This matter of consonants, and the related matter of juxtaposing syllables which are long or accented or both, is a matter to which you are in general very insensitive and which you ought to watch. I think the whole matter derives from your manner of speech. You speak slowly, pausing more than most people between words, and drawing your words out; you read poetry in much the same way. The result is that the language does not, for you, move at its normal rhythm, and that syllables which are normally awkward in sequence are so slowed and separated that you do not perceive the difficulty. This whole matter, however, is real, and more people than I have noticed it: it bothered the life out of Mrs. Daryush, to name only one.

"Pages for a History" and "Dr. Johnson" are both fine, "Psyche" and "Pont Neuf" still seem to me very great, and "Violation of Logic" is nearly as good. In the last I don't quite like the word *interweaves*. It is pretty trite, even when applied to physical phenomena, as in my "Moonrise"; but when used for logic, plots, and such matters, it seems to me even worse. It is a favorite on student compositions. Here and elsewhere, I wish you had a less obvious tendency to the colloquial phrase and construction "who've," etc. Poetry can be formal without being affected, I believe, and this sort of thing increases one's exasperation, sometimes, at your occasional metrical difficulties: it gives a faint feeling of laziness to the composition.

"Patria" is good in general effect, but a bit slow and cluttered, I think.

"The End of the Year 1939" seems to me worth very little. The twig-earth symbolism is trite and sentimental. Twig and earth as such are perceived with no distinction. The political references, even five years hence, will require footnotes of much greater bulk than the poem. The feeling was in the air at the time, but it is still in the air. You merely referred to it; you didn't do anything with it.

"Faith" is beautifully executed, but the doctrine, I confess, strikes me as scandalous. It is the tail end of New England voluntarism, as it appears in the Unitarians: knowledge dependent wholly on faith, but nothing definable in which to have faith. One gets the same things in the later Babbitt: a habit, generated by a social structure, which in turn was created originally in conformity to a scheme of ideas, is identified with divine grace, and the mind goes out the window. If the faith collapses, you get Henry Adams; if it remains till the habit fades out too thin, you are likely to get Hart Crane. Do you know Gilson's *Unity of Philosophical Experience*? If not, take a look.

"Ode to the Sea." I feel about this as before. I like a few passages very much: stanzas 2, 3, 4, or most of them; 6, 7, 8, 10, 11, 17. For the rest, the writing seems to me undistinguished, the subject matter mostly negligible, and the structure repetitious.

My feelings about the last poem are much what they used to be, in spite of improvements. It contains fine stuff, but is, I think, pretty awkward.

You are a very great poet, beyond a doubt, and it is for that reason I ride you. Your long poems contain magnificence beyond even that of Crane, but they are as badly constructed and thought as "The River" or "The Bridge" ("Destiny" mostly excepted from this accusation), though for different reasons. As a critic and philosophical thinker, you seem to me slow and somewhat fumbling, though admirable in general intention, and you constantly, as in "Faith" or to some extent in the first poem, display a sneaking distrust of the reason which is characteristic mainly, I think, of people who have serious difficulties with their own reasoning. It has not done much harm to date, but it is a worm working at your core, nevertheless. I think your metrical difficulties are probably physiological in their origin, but they could be reduced notwithstanding. The best of the short things and the best passages in the long tower over most contemporary work. Tate in "Shadow and Shade" and "The Cross," Stevens in four or five of his early things, are the only living poets comparable; but I hate to see you, like them, dissipate so large a proportion of your effort.

Our best to you and Dorothy and the baby.

Arthur

MS: Stanford

Stanford University / Department of English /
Stanford University, California / May 26, 1941

Dear Louise:

Thanks many times for your letter. The mystery was pretty well cleared up before it arrived, as a matter of fact. The note in *The New Yorker* was very kind, and, along with your letter, raised me greatly in my own esteem. You are one of the very few living American poets for whom I retain, in my old age, any very profound esteem, and of the lot you are certainly the finest master of style, perhaps the only consistent master of style; so I value your good opinion.

Mark Van Doren seemed to think the best poems toward the last; perhaps you are both right, and it would be nice to think I have improved steadily; but I still feel that the second and third parts of "Theseus" and the "Heracles" are probably the best, and that I have perhaps thinned out a little since.

What I would like to know about Aiken is where in hell he got the book. I gave none to him, to Cowley, or to the *N.R.*, and if I knew who lent them one, I would scratch his name off my calling list. As to Cowley, I have known for years that he was not only a fool but a good deal of a sneak, and after the way his hatchet-men lied about the contents of my two books of criticism—in simple and obvious matters of fact—I should be an idiot to nourish any doubts on the subject.

As to Ransom, he has an honest preference for bad poetry and for a certain type of very confused thinking. Philosophically, he is hard to summarize, because his thought contains so many disparate elements: I am doing a long essay on him now, and have him all dissected on cards. He really tries to explain himself, however, which almost nobody else among our great critics does, and he never sets out to libel anybody. And at moments he is fairly good.

My book was advertised once in the *Kenyon*, at $2.00, with no discounts for dealers. That is still the rule. There are only about 80 copies left for sale, so I am in no great hurry.

Best wishes from both of us, / Arthur

MS: Amherst

TO THEODORE ROETHKE

Oct. 19, 1941 / R. 1, Box 155 / Los Altos, Calif.

Dear Mr. Roethke:

Of your two poems, I think the one called "My Papa's Waltz" extremely good of its kind. The other—"I stood near the top of a ridge"—strikes me as pretty formulary in detail and conception. The sentimental irony of "a fat man poised like a bird," and such is too easy.

You are more to be congratulated for Mr. Untermeyer's disapproval than for my approval. I should think it would fortify you against anything. As to Blackmur, he is an ass. He has written a few lovely minor poems that almost evaporate when breathed upon, and his first book of criticism had a certain value in its sensitivity to detail; but he has never understood anything in his life, and his last book of prose is the most appalling mess of contradictions, bad taste, and incomprehensible sentences that I have ever laid eyes on. The man writes as if he were drunk or well gone in schizophrenia. Stevens, in commenting to Don Stanford on B.'s essay on himself, said: "B. is like a bad lawyer; he tries to make a hundred points and doesn't succeed in making one."

You ought to buckle down and write some criticism. You could probably do it well; it would clarify your ideas and improve your poetry; it would force you to recognize the defects of your sacred contemporaries, with the result that their failure to review you would not distress you; and it would be good in the long run for your academic status.

My review of your poems appears in the current *Kenyon Review.* I trust you have seen it. I believe that my young friend Cunningham will drop you a note presently.

Best wishes, / Yvor Winters

P.S. I had another curious comment on B. from a man whose name escapes me, who was out here in connection with the Rockefeller Foundation. As an undergraduate he had been a roommate of Hillyer and Damon. He said: "Dick B. is a queer fellow; he never seems to understand anything, and yet he's a very understanding kind of person."

MS: UW

March 27, 1943 / R. 1, Box 155 / Los Altos, Calif.

Dear Mr. Abbott:

My wife has suggested that I answer your letter of March 22.

As regards goats, I advise you strongly not to get Nubians. Nubians are the handsomest of the goats. They are tall, long-legged, and because of their size and their drooping ears, very impressive to look at. Their milk is said to be very rich. But I have never seen a Nubian that gave better than 3½ quarts when fresh, and that is damned poor, especially when you consider the size of the goat and what it will eat. Further, Nubian milk is stronger in taste than any other, and if you are not used to goat milk, you would not like it.

There are three other breeds. One of these is the Swiss Alpine. I have never laid eyes on one, and I have never met anyone who has laid eyes on one.

One is the Saanen. The Saanen is a white goat, very large, when pure bred, and a very heavy milker. I am told that the best Saanens give seven or more quarts when fresh. They are very good lasters. They give the mildest flavored milk of all the breeds. I once owned a grade Saanen (she was actually about a quarter Tog) who gave five and a half quarts (which is extremely good in actual practice). She was a fine goat, not large, and not a heavy eater.

The other breed is Toggenburg. The Toggenburg is brown. Its characteristic marks are wattles under the throat. These wattles in any goat of mixed blood, regardless of size, shape, or color, indicate Tog blood. The best goat I ever owned was a Tog. She was pure-bred, not much bigger than a very big Airedale, and gave six and a half quarts when fresh. She was a very good laster. The milk of the Tog is a shade stronger than that of the Saanen when the goat is fresh, but the difference is hardly discernible after six or seven weeks. If I were getting goats again, I would look for Togs or for Tog-Saanen grades.

The lop ears in a grade indicate Nubian blood, but I would not worry about it in a grade if the goat looks good in other respects. In general look at the size and shape of the goat's bag, not at the size of the goat. Some of the biggest goats are poor milkers; some of the smallest are wonders. When the goat is going dry, it is hard to estimate the bag; but if the upper part of the bag seems to cover a large part of the goat's belly, it is probably a good bag, and if the bag narrows toward the top and covers a small part of the belly, it may not be so good. Most of the best milkers have very big teats, but if the split between the teats goes extremely high the goat may not be so good when the goat is nearly dry; however, the split may seem to go very high on an extremely good goat. And a few of the heaviest milkers I have ever seen have had teats no bigger than warts. The trouble with these last is that they are hard to milk, though one can acquire a kind of two-fingered technique with a little practice.

The milking of a goat, even the worst goat, is very easy as compared to the milking of a cow. Your children ought to be able to do it. I have milked a very great many of both beasts in my time, and know what I am saying. If the goat has large teats, the job is easy. The teats are soft, and the amount of milk is relatively small.

I advise you to pick your goat on its looks, not on its breeding. As to using your goats to clear land, there is no real harm in it, unless the eastern U.S. breeds especially unpleasant shrubs, which is more than likely. Green food makes any milk, cow or goat, a trifle stronger than dry, but the difference is slight, and no farmer worries about it. Our goats always grazed as long as there was any grazing. Be sure you get expert advice about milking: the goat must be milked DRY, after it has been fresh ten days to fourteen: before that, a little milk must be left in the bag, or there may be a case of milk-fever.

Rabbits are a simple problem. The medium sized breeds, Belgians and New Zealands (regardless of color), are the most practical. The big ones (Flemish) are less hardy and less prolific, and the small ones, though more decorative, produce less meat. Get advice about care and feeding from the man who sells you the stock. It is all pretty simple. I picked up a fine medium-sized grade doe the other day, and expect to have meat all winter.

The Army turned me down because I had a touch of TB almost 22 years ago. Such is war.

If you want any more advice about farming, let me know.

Sincerely, / Yvor Winters

P.S. For God's sake don't enquire of Robert Frost.

MS: SUNY

Charles D. Abbott (1900–1961), American librarian.

Stanford University / Department of English /
Stanford University, California / May 10, 1943

Dear Louise:

Thanks for your letter & for reading the kid's poems.[1] She will be very pleased indeed to receive a letter from you.

The book to which I referred is not a book of poems but a book of criticism [*The Anatomy of Nonsense*]. It is now out. The collection of poems which Laughlin is doing for me later will contain only a few things you have not seen. I have been pretty much paralyzed by the war.

I tried to get a commission in the army, but was turned down because I had a touch of TB over 21 years ago. I could probably go into the merchant marine as a crew member, but I can hardly take a job voluntarily that will pay me too little to support my family. Janet is not strong & the children are young. My friend Clayton Stafford is now a captain in the Signal Corps. Meanwhile I sit around & watch the kids go. About all I can do for civilization is try to counteract a little of the effect of Lewis Mumford & our new School of Humanities, which is a god-awful mess.

I am glad you liked Janet's new book [*Against a Darkening Sky*]. I do not think it quite so successful in its total effect as the other two [prose books], but think it contains much of her best work notwithstanding.

As ever, / Arthur

MS: Amherst

[1]The poet is Ann Hayes, whose work appears in *Poets of the Pacific,* second series.

TO DOROTHY M. WESTPHAL

June 5, 1943 / R. 1, Box 155 / Los Altos, Calif.

Dorothy M. Westphal / Editor,
The Los Altos News / Los Altos, Calif.

Dear Mrs. Westphal:

As the result of a recent criminal case in Los Altos, I was asked a few weeks ago whether the Auxiliary Police in Los Altos could not give some assistance in the general police protection of Los Altos. I was forced to state that they could not. The Auxiliary Police, as such, have no police powers except in connection with blackouts, dim-outs, bombings, or other defense emergencies. Auxiliary Police, as such, have not even the right to carry arms.

However, the increase in recent months of criminal cases has been real; the sheriff's office has not enough men to police regions like this one adequately and cannot get them; many women, with or without children, are living without the protection of husbands now in the armed services; and the community should no doubt do what it can to meet the situation. Technically, the problem does not come within my jurisdiction as Zone Warden; morally, it probably does.

At any rate, I put the matter up to Sheriff Emig a couple of weeks ago, and he said that he would deputize a few responsible men of the community to serve as emergency police. Today, I and two others, Mr. P. J. Denand and Mr. Irvin Chilcote, were deputized. Mr. Harold Danforth has already been deputized; Mr. L. G. Broadus will be deputized within the next few days. At some time within the next few weeks there will be an additional deputy in the hill country in the back part of the Zone.

These deputies are unsalaried volunteers. All are well armed and are familiar with the use of their weapons. They will not engage in patrol duty, but as far as it is possible they will be on call for emergencies. All will commonly be available at night. Mr. Broadus and the man whom I expect to have presently in the hill country will be available, ordinarily, day or night. I am usually at home on Saturdays as well as Sundays; I get home as a rule fairly early in the afternoons (ordinarily between 3 and 4 o'clock), and I shall probably be home fairly late in the mornings during the summer.

Anyone needing police assistance should call one of the following numbers: Ballard 1500 (the sheriff's office); Los Altos 4597 (the Zone Warden's home—that is, my own); Los Altos 4752 (the Assistant Zone Warden's home—that is, Mr. J. C. Ford's); or Mountain View 2176 (the number of Mr. Chris Madsen, Constable of the township).

We do not promise to be a perfect police force, for we are all engaged in earning our livings in other ways, but we shall do the best we can to help the regularly constituted authorities in protecting the community.

Sincerely, / Yvor Winters /
Zone Warden for Zone 3 of
Santa Clara County

MS: Stanford

June 12, 1943 /
R. 1, Box 155 / Los Altos, Calif.

Mr. O. W. Helena / Postmaster / Los Altos, Calif.

Dear Mr. Helena:

I have your letter postmarked June 11. I shall take the liberty of leaving this letter and the accompanying materials at your home; my doing so will save a good deal of time.

I have no file of Civilian Defense Council Instructions. I should have thought that the Post Office, as a Federal Institution, would have been supplied with directions from Washington; but upon your request I shall be glad to give you what I have: namely, certain mimeographed sheets which I used as a syllabus for courses which I gave last winter to Civilian Defense workers in Los Altos. The sheets contain a few statements about Zone and County personnel which are now obsolete, but as regards protection measures they are perfectly up to date.

Your letter has more or less the tone of a complaint, and I should like to explain a few matters briefly for that reason. The printed matter available on these subjects is not issued in quantity sufficient for general distribution, and much of what was issued early in the war is so obsolete as to be misleading and dangerous. I have a complete set of the best government handbooks (and have also some of the worst), most of which were issued to me at the War Department Civilian Protection School at Stanford; these handbooks are issued only to instructors, however, and to a few people fairly high in county and city organizations. If, after reading the material which I am giving you, you care to examine any of these books in connection with the protection of the Post Office, I shall be glad to let you look at them; but I cannot give them to you.

As nearly as I can make out a good many people think the local C.D. organization is doing nothing in particular. I should like to disabuse them, if possible, to this extent: it is doing about as much as it can in the face of a community which is in general highly critical and very largely unwilling to help. I gave ten days of my time last September to take the War Department training course. I spent over $60 of my own money getting these sheets mimeographed. I had previously spent all my spare time for about three weeks writing up the material in the sheets from my course notes and from the government handbooks. I gave courses at the Los Altos grammar school, which 35 C.D. workers out of a possible 200 completed. Since I have been Zone Warden, I have spent on an average of 12 or 14 hours a week driving about the Zone, or on trips to San Jose, on problems of organization. Most of the Precinct Captains have contributed a good deal of time and some money; and the same can be said of Elmer Lenzen, the bomb reconnaissance agent.

This is a volunteer organization, with no funds except such as come from the pockets of the members of the organization.

If the community cares to pay for the printing of the instructions on these sheets, I shall be glad to cut the sheets down to a bare minimum, make a check with the War Department School at Stanford to make certain that no important matters have developed since I wrote the sheets (I have been keeping pretty well posted, and am reasonably certain now that none have come up), and turn the sheets over to the printer designated. Or if any limited group wants copies of the sheets, and cares to pay for the mimeographing, the stencils are still on file at the Stanford mimeograph office. But I cannot pass these things about generally: I had them done for workers in the organization and I cannot afford further expense in connection with them at present.

I might say that a few days ago I sorted out fifty sets of these sheets at my Stanford office, from which fifty I am now giving you three. The job of sorting took about two hours.

Sincerely yours, / Yvor Winters / Zone Warden, Zone 3

MS: Stanford

TO POETRY

Feb. 22, 1944 / R. 1, Box 155 / Los Altos, Calif.

The Editor of *Poetry* / Chicago, Ill.

Dear Sir:

In your issue for Feb. 1944, you print a letter written by myself in regard to a review of my book, *The Anatomy of Nonsense,* the review appearing in your issue for November 1943, and having been written by Mr. Thomas Howells. You print likewise a reply to my letter by Mr. Howells. It is with some regret that I ask you to give more space to this argument, but the whole matter transcends the issue of my private irritation.

Two of the issues which I raised, those relating to Adams and Eliot, Mr. Howells declines to discuss; Mr. Howells merely says in his letter: "He"—that is, myself—"says nothing in his letter to facilitate comprehension of these or any other matters." On the contrary, what I said was perfectly clear; Mr. Howells merely resorts to a gentlemanly sort of abuse because he lacks arguments.

With regard to another issue, that of the primarily conceptual nature of words, Mr. Howells merely reiterates his original and wholly obscure assertion in new words; that is, he declines to risk discussion. If he can cite words which are not conceptual but which may be symbols of emotion, or which can communicate emotion without relationship to their conceptual meaning, he will be doing a great deal to settle in favor of romantic theory one of the most vexed and confused critical issues of the past hundred years. I wish you to note, however, that he makes no attempt, but merely makes a dogmatic assertion.

In regard to "Sunday Morning" and its various dates and versions, he appears now to consider the date of 1923 unimportant, though he considered it important in his review. To explain the obscure remark in his review that my supposed error with regard to dates invalidated my conclusions, he now says: "My point was that a poem which becomes better artistically at the same time that it becomes more explicitly hedonistic cannot be used, as Winters uses it, to illustrate the debasing effects of hedonism on the author's work. That is still, I think, a valid point, even though with regard to the evolution of this poem, Mr. Winters's ignorance and my own seem to complement one another." I am not aware of my own ignorance in this connection; nor does Mr. Howells indicate its nature. I did not use the poem to indicate the debasing effects of hedonism on the author's works; I used it to indicate that he held a hedonistic view of art and experience, and I traced the gradual debasement of his art, under the influence of this view, in his later work. I discussed in some detail the manner in which an unsound, though still comprehensible, philosophy might result in a great poem, not only in my essay on Stevens, but in my essay on Eliot, and particularly with reference to this poem. Mr. Howells neither admits this fact nor tries to refute me. His letter is aimed at the reader who has not read my book. It is an attempt to salvage a few shreds of dignity as he retreats toward the wastebasket.

In brief, Mr. Howells is a fake; and if the evidence of his letter is to be trusted, he knows he is a fake. He finds consolation in the fact that I find him representative of a widespread incompetence. If he wishes to take refuge among the generality of critical writers in this age or any other, he is welcome to do so. It is a refuge from which he will never emerge: its name is Oblivion.

He is representative, however, both in his incompetence and in his disingenuousness; and it is for this reason that I insist on keeping the issue alive.

Until critics are held strictly to account for what they write, and until editors are willing to consider themselves accountable, within the limits of reason, for their selection of critics, contemporary literature will remain the morass of young wise guys on the make, with neither scholarship, intelligence, nor principles, which, very largely, it is at the present time.

Sincerely, / Yvor Winters

MS: Chicago

TO THEODORE ROETHKE

August 12, 1944 / RFD 1, Box 155 / Los Altos, Calif.

Dear Mr. Roethke:

I am not teaching this summer and get over to Stanford only about once in ten days. Your letter must have been lying there for several days when I found it this morning.

Cunningham's address is 1423 Emerson St., Palo Alto, Calif. He is finishing his doctoral dissertation this summer and tied down pretty tight. I don't know how you could interview him as things stand, but I wish I could persuade your department to try him. He has been teaching for six or seven years as a regular instructor and can teach anything or anyone. He is at his best with intelligent students, but is patient and hard-working with the poor ones. The late W. D. Briggs, head of the department until his death a couple of years ago, had the highest opinion of Cunningham and gave him various advanced and graduate courses. Briggs's successor is a very limited little man, a bibliographer and philologist, who is afraid of all ideas and all judgments, and upon Briggs's death he took Cunningham's good courses all away from him. Stanford is going into the hands of a group of academic politicians at the moment, and a lot of us hope to get out, myself included. I have been teaching here since 1928, and like the kids, the country, and the climate, but the academic atmosphere has changed so radically that it is pretty distressing. But to get back to Cunningham: he is a first rate poet, critic, and teacher; and in ten years he will be one of the best known Renaissance scholars in the country. He is about 32, has had his career slowed up by his wife's going off with a cheap scoundrel and leaving him upset emotionally and with a small daughter to look after. But once his dissertation is killed off and he has time to publish the Renaissance material he is gathering, he will become quite a figure among the orthodox scholars. This is not my opinion alone, but that of a good many people. You might write to the following, in addition to A. G. Kennedy, head of the Stanford English Department: Herbert Dean Meritt, Associate Professor of English; Margery Bailey, Associate Professor of English; Raymond D. Harriman, head of the classics department; Herman Fränkel, Professor of Classics; Philip W. Harsh, Associate Professor of Classics; F. W. Strothmann, Associate Professor of German.

Don Stanford is teaching in the Army. His status is that of an enlisted reserve, so that he is out of civilian circulation.

We have two graduate students here who will be first rate men for some one, but the present Stanford administration is unlikely to realize it. They are John Conley[1] and Thomas Carpenter. Both are interested in writing fiction; Conley, the more talented of the two, has published a little. Both write well and teach well. You can find Conley represented in a collection called *Great Modern Catholic Short Stories*—a fearsome title, but a fine collection. My copy is in my office, and I cannot remember the editor (a nun) or the publisher.

As you wander about among the more orthodox universities (I am probably too old and sot for a place like Bennington) you might drop a good word for me if you get a chance. I really want to move on.

Best wishes, / Yvor Winters

MS: UW

[1]John Conley (1912–1999): American scholar and educator who also wrote some fine short fiction early in his career. He had taken undergraduate courses from Howard Baker and subsequently took graduate courses from YW.

TO WHOM IT MAY CONCERN

September, 1944 / Department of English / Stanford University

Data Accompanying an Application by Yvor Winters
for a Position as a Teacher of English

To Whom It May Concern:

The following mimeographed pages will accompany a formal application for a position in your English department. I hope you will pardon this manner of conveying the information. There is a good deal of information to convey, and I cannot afford the time to do it in any other way. My family responsibilities and salary are such that I cannot afford to travel about to make application in person. I am dissatisfied with my present situation at Stanford and with the future outlook for me at Stanford, and am anxious to leave. I am therefore employing this method, which is the best I can think of, to seek a position elsewhere. The following pages will contain a brief biography, an incomplete but representative bibliography of my published work, a list of books dealing with my work at greater or less length, an incomplete list of reviews of my books with excerpts, a brief list of comments upon my work found in articles on other subjects or reviews of other books, a brief list of personal references, and, at the end, an explanatory note.

* * *

Explanatory Note

There is a large element of vulgarity in the composition of any such sales pamphlet as this, and I deplore it, but I have not seen any way to avoid it. I wish to leave Stanford. To leave Stanford I must leave the state, for there is, I believe, an agreement among the institutions within the state, not to hire each other's men. Personal contacts are impractical, and I have made few in the past, largely out of a kind of social indolence and preoccupation with my work. I have been able to devise no better way than this to proceed.

In the past, my wife's health has been such that the climate either of California or the Rocky Mountains seemed necessary. I believe that other climates would be safe enough now, provided other conditions were adequate. The Rocky Mountain climate (since we must leave the California climate, if we leave Stanford) would still be a real inducement, though not a determinant one. Any kind of urban life, however, is out of the question. We must live in a small town or better still on the edge of one. Such a location combined with a civilized salary would be sufficient for our purposes.

Sincerely, / Yvor Winters.

MS: Winters

I have used only the opening and conclusion of this lengthy (12 typed pages) document. I have omitted a brief biography and extensive bibliography, including quotations from published commentaries on YW's work.

Yvor Winters / Route 2, Box 625 /
Los Altos, California / Jan. 30, 1945

Dear Grove:

It was very good of you to take so much trouble for Jim. He is very pleased with the prospect of his new job, and all of us here feel very grateful to you for what you have done.

I am proceeding slowly with a book on E. A. Robinson, but am nearing the end. I unfortunately have a pretty heavy program this quarter. I am still looking about for a job elsewhere; I have nothing definite as yet, but I think there are about four or five possibilities at the moment, either for next year or the year after. I am pretty sick of Stanford, but I do not mean to leave unless I get exactly what I want. If the right offer arrives I shall accept it without any bargaining here.

I shall be greatly honored by the dedication of your book [*The Sky Clears*]. Please give our regards to your wife. Best wishes from all of us,

Yvor Winters

MS: Odell

A. Grove Day (1904–1994): American scholar, editor, and educator. He was a former student of YW, and his book mentioned in this letter began as a dissertation that YW directed.

Yvor Winters / Route 2, Box 625 /
Los Altos, California / Oct. 16, 1946

Dear Mr. Nims:

Perhaps I should not have told you that my essay on Frost was first delivered as a talk. All of my essays are written in the same way: I use them as lectures in my classes, and normally stop and explain rather often. It is, unfortunately, written in the form in which I wish to see it printed, except for the omissions which I indicated. I am now busy with other work, and can scarcely find the time to do a special version of it for *Poetry*, even if I wished to see it published in a special version, as I do not. I am afraid I do not share your belief in the intelligence of the readers of *Poetry*. It has been my experience that if one explains ten ideas in the greatest of detail and with the fullest of illustration, one is lucky to learn that one idea from the lot has been approximately grasped by the most learned and talented audience that one can discover. One can do better with a university class, because the class has to pay attention or fail. Most contemporary criticism has been written according to the formula which you recommend in your letter; and as a result, most contemporary criticism, including that in *Poetry,* is in a fog.

Sincerely, / Yvor Winters

MS: Chicago

John Frederick Nims (1913–1999): American poet and, at this time, editor of *Poetry: A Magazine of Verse.*

TO MR. AND MRS. RAYMOND HOLDEN

Yvor Winters / Route 2, Box 625 /
Los Alto, Calif. / Dec. 12, 1946

Dear Mr. and Mrs. Holden:

I will try to answer all of your questions in a single short answer. I believe that group activities in connection with the writing of poetry are beneficial provided the group is fairly small and is sufficiently intelligent to begin with. When I was an undergraduate at the University of Chicago we had a small poetry club, unsupervised by the faculty, which was a very fine thing. Among the members were Elizabeth Madox Roberts, Glenway Wescott, Maurice Lesemann, myself, and my wife (Janet Lewis). We learned a great deal from each other, and would have developed more slowly without it. In later years the group apparently became larger and more miscellaneous, and fruitful communication between the members more difficult. A group made up of all comers is hopeless: either the incompetents are put in their places and feelings are hurt, or the group functions at their level and is worthless. I have observed this difficulty in student organizations over many years. As to poetry classes, I believe that they are successful if the teaching is adequate, but I do not believe that it is often adequate. Among my own students in the past have been J. V. Cunningham, Don Stanford, and Ann Stanford. I have had other more recent students of promise who thus far have published little or nothing. Frequently a student of marginal talent will develop surprisingly under pressure, and then either deteriorate or lose interest when the pressure is removed; but as good poets are rare, I suppose this is not surprising.

Best wishes, / Yvor Winters

MS: Princeton, Raymond Holden Papers

Raymond Holden (1894–1972): American poet (and first husband of Louise Bogan, who is not the Mrs. Holden herein).

TO ALLEN TATE

R. 2, Box 625 / Los Altos, Calif. / May 5, 1948

Dear Allen:

Many thanks for your very kind letter. I have been very remiss about writing you. I appreciated your hospitality a great deal, enjoyed the afternoon and evening, and envy you the small Italian restaurant. I find myself growing more and more remiss about everything, however, as I grow older. I have a pile of letters eight inches deep demanding immediate answer, and I shall probably forget most of them.

As soon as I got back I was in a mess of dogshow business, three shows on three successive week-ends, which meant hours of work on my dog. On the first occasion my dog was first winners, his litter brother (who beat him in San Francisco in February) was reserve winners, and their litter sister took best of winners. The second time, at the big Airedale specialty show in Los Angeles, my dog went to best of winners, beating 38 Airedales from all over the United States and Canada, his brother and sister among them, and under the judge who is reputed generally to be the best man in the United States. Last week-end, at a small show, a punk local judge knocked him down to reserve winners, and put a couple of lanky cow-hocked hounds over him. The last judge was an old woman, weighing about 300 pounds, and since she couldn't move very fast, she tried to make us show Airedales as if they were setters: set them up, cheek by jowl, pose them for five minutes, and so on. My dog, unfortunately, is an Airedale, and is as restless as if he were on a hot stove, and will kill any dog within grabbing distance; it was pretty hopeless. The life of art is a hard one.

I try to find some good excuse at least once a year to drive to Los Angeles. If you are ever out this way I would like to take you over the route. From Los Angeles north through Santa Barbara and over the Gaviota Pass (about 125 miles) you are in southern California, red granite mountains, sparsely covered by brush, with rock jutting through everywhere, citrus groves in the foreground, and much of the time along a bright blue ocean. It is impressive if you like it. From the Gaviota Pass to San Luis Obispo, you go through a kind of transition country, fifteen or twenty miles of it covered with dust and oil wells, the rest cattle country. And beyond San Luis, you go into the Salinas Valley and are in it for a hundred and fifty miles, the first half of it cattle country, the rest the richest truck farming country in California, thousands of acres of lettuce, spinach, and the like, much more impressive to see than to hear about, with the tremendous desert mountains back of it on every side. And then at San Juan you come over into my valley, the Santa Clara, cattle and truck for a little way, then a few pears and apples and cherries, and after that prunes and apricots (thousands of acres of them, more than in any other part of the world). The whole trip comprises 400 miles of the most magnificent country I have ever seen. It is hotter than hell, but well worth the heat.

I think you over-estimate Cunningham's indebtedness to me. The three or four poems immediately following the first one in his book, were written when he was about 16 years old, at a time when I was writing the sonnets and songs immediately following the translations in my book and when he knew little or nothing of my work. The genesis of his manner is there. His interests in scholarship and philosophy diverge a good deal from my own, and I confess that I see little similarity between his poems and mine. Examine the epigram on the calculus, the last epigram, and "Plato, despair" carefully once a month for a year, and then see what you think.

When I get a few inescapable letters written, and a couple of promised book reviews, I will settle down to a serious reading of your new book of poems, and will write you when I finish. I am still impressed by my old favorites; I am impressed by "The Seasons of the Soul," but feel that I would be more impressed if I could understand it all; but I shall perhaps be able to speak more intelligently later.

Our best wishes to you and Caroline, /
Yvor Winters

MS: Princeton, Allen Tate Papers

TO DONALD E. STANFORD

March 30, 1949 / R. 2, Box 625 / Los Altos, Calif.

Dear Don:

I should have written you long ago, but it has not been possible. I am much busier than I was a few years back. I am also getting older, and in the main I do not feel too well. In addition, I was in a crack-up on the highway early last month, had no car for over a month, and am not altogether recovered from the effects.

In general, however, much as I regret it, I cannot exchange friendly letters with people, or write letters criticizing poems. My old students send in stuff by the carload, and I simply cannot take care of it. I have been so busy that I have not succeeded in writing a poem of my own in almost three years. This is not a matter of personal preference with me; it is simply a matter of fact. I am tired and busy, and I would like to salvage a small part of the time remaining to me for myself.

I do not think your poems in general were too good. They are boyish and enthusiastic and over-rhetorical, even when they are being cynical (I think that is the correct word). They are a dilution of your best work of eight or ten years ago. You had, and still have, a real gift for language, but after a certain point a poet either grows up or is washed up, and so far you have not grown up. I do not think you are beyond hope, but unless you make some effort to learn to think, and start thinking about topics of interest to adults, you will not accomplish a great deal.

Best wishes, / Arthur

MS: Stanford

TO ALLEN TATE

Sept. 29, 1948 / R. 2, Box 625 / Los Altos, Calif.

Dear Allen:

Your book of essays arrived yesterday. I wish to thank you very much for it. I think I am already familiar with most of the material, but this will be a good occasion to reread it.

Many thanks also for your kindness to Wes Trimpi.[1] He is a very intelligent kid, and I think is less likely than most to fade out.

I have gone on from triumph to triumph since I last wrote you. My young dog finished his championship in June; his litter brother finished in August; and their litter sister is only four points away. Three champions in one litter is very rare, and all three have placed one or more times in the terrier variety group, something which few individual champions ever do.

An unreconstructed New Yorker like yourself may find these agrarian details inexplicable. The fact of the matter is, that I am older than my years. You should not be too surprised by an occasional symptom of disintegration.

Best wishes to you and Caroline, /
Yvor Winters

MS: Princeton, Allen Tate Papers

[1]Wesley Trimpi (b. 1928): American poet, scholar, and educator; former student of YW who became a colleague and was a lifelong friend. Although his poems were few in number after his first book, Trimpi's later poems are distinguished. YW included his work in *Poets of the Pacific,* second series, and mentioned him briefly in *Forms of Discovery.*

TO ALLEN TATE

Sept. 21, 1949 / R. 2, Box 625 / Los Altos, Calif.

Dear Allen:

Thank goodness you have moved. I don't really approve of Princeton, but I like it better than anything I have ever seen east of Nebraska. Its advantages for you and Caroline are obvious.

As to the Hillyer affair, I would be glad to write the letter, except for one thing: The second article appeared after I left Los Altos; I did not see it at Gambier, and I have not seen it since; that copy of the *SRL* is missing from the Stanford library, and so far I have not been able to lay my hands on one. If you can find me one and send it, I will read it, write the letter, and return it. Meanwhile, I shall continue my search.

I sent the examination to poor Nancy [Tate's daughter], but have not heard from her. When you write her, please tell her to take it as a game or else to throw it lightheartedly in the waste-basket. My students invariably disgrace themselves in the examination on that course. Pearce was frightful. Nancy, with her limited experience, probably thinks she ought to have it cold if she is not to appear illiterate. As a matter of fact, three or four of my most learned colleagues at

Stanford flunked (in private) the examination which I sent Nancy. Tell her to cheer up, take it in her stride, and act the way I do at a bum dog show.

Black Jack was best of breed and second in the terrier group at Petaluma ten days ago. He is a classical terrier if I ever saw one. On the same day his litter brother was best of breed at Santa Monica.

Alan Swallow was here during the MLA meeting. He told me a curious tale about our first $500 poetry prize award. You were invited to judge and declined for reasons which I remember. The judges were Blackmur, [Arthur] Mizener, and Swallow. The prize went to a perfectly illiterate freshman girl. The students all over the department were indignant; so was [Wallace] Stegner [chair of the Stanford creative writing program]; so were most of the faculty. B. and M. had agreed on the girl, and Swallow had not considered her, and the theory was that B. and M. had conspired to keep any student trained by myself from winning the award. Swallow wrote me the same theory. I did not believe it. But Swallow was at a dinner with Mizener recently at a writers' conference (I think in Kansas) where Mizener told the story of how he and Blackmur had held several long distance conversations to prevent any of the "little Winterses" from winning. He apparently had forgotten that Swallow was the other judge, and he thought the whole tale very entertaining. In my book they are both of them sons-of-bitches from here on. I may or may not influence my students to write as I write: I try not to. But I try to teach them the mechanics of style and the great models. If they learn something from that, they will stand apart from most of the illiterates of our time, Blackmur among them. If Ed Bowers's[1] poem on a mountain cemetery were published anonymously in one of our quarterlies, and the readers were asked to guess the authorship, no one would guess me, but a number would guess you. I have been trying for two years to iron your individual eccentricities out of his style without damaging what he has learned of you that is impersonal. In any event those two eminent authorities behaved as gentlemen should not behave, and they convinced about fifty of our best students that they were damned fools.

Now that you are on the verge of being domesticated again, I will send Caroline the nearest thing that I can to my recipe for meatballs. However, I cook much as Rimbaud wrote, and the recipe can be taken only as a general guide. Give my regards to Caroline, and, when you write, to Percy and Nancy and the babies.

I have a southern magnolia just outside my study window. It blooms from April to November. *Ha!* (quoted from W. C. Williams.)

In spite of the quotation, I feel my age. I am tired as hell, am baffled by metaphysical speculations of which there is no end and no solution, and on which no comment seems possible.

As ever, / Arthur

P.S. One of Stegner's students, Boris Ilyin, has just published a novel entitled *The Green Boundary,* which I think extremely fine. If you or Caroline should get a chance to read it, don't pass it up. I don't like the short stories that have come from Stegner's classes, as I think I told you, but this novel is an extremely civilized performance. It may have limitations, but so far as I can see it is without flaws.

MS: Princeton, Allen Tate Papers

[1]Edgar Bowers (1924–2000): American poet and educator. Bowers was a former student of YW and a lifelong friend. YW included his work in *Poets of the Pacific,* second series, and *Quest for Reality,* and wrote about it in *Forms of Discovery.* Bowers was awarded the Brandeis Creative Arts Award and, in 1989, the Bollingen Prize.

TO HAYDEN CARRUTH

[undated]

Dear Mr. Carruth: This has just gone off to the *SRL.* Tate asked me to send you a copy. Too late for your pamphlet, I fear, but please keep this copy for the present, and I will notify you of further developments.

Y.W.

Hayden Carruth (b. 1921): American poet and critic and, at this time, the new editor of *Poetry: A Magazine of Verse.*

Oct. 9, 1949 / R. 2, Box 625 /
Los Altos, Calif.

The Editors / *The Saturday Review*
of Literature / New York City
Sirs:

Last June, before I left for a summer of teaching at the Kenyon School of English, a friend called my attention to Robert Hillyer's first article on the Bollingen award. It struck me as both malicious and stupid but unimportant, and since I am not a regular reader of your journal and was not interested in the business, I did not get around to reading the second article until recently. As to my opinion of the whole affair, it is essentially similar to that of Malcolm

Cowley (*New Republic,* Oct. 3, 1949), except that I do not go all the way with Cowley on his poetic judgments, and feel that the Fellows of the Library of Congress had no choice except between Pound and Williams, both of whose books contain major faults and real virtues. It is not this aspect of the matter which concerns me at present, however, but another, which touches me personally.

In 1941 John Crowe Ransom published a book entitled *The New Criticism.* This book discussed at some length the work of four critics: I. A. Richards, T. S. Eliot, William Empson, and myself. The term *new criticism* as it has been used in our decade appears to have been derived from the title of Ransom's book, a fact which would identify the four critics mentioned as "new critics" to a certainty. Ransom, as the author of the book, is usually so identified; so are a few others who have been personally associated with him, among them Allen Tate, Robert Penn Warren, and Cleanth Brooks. Unless my memory is at fault, Tate is the only one of these critics who was on the Bollingen award committee, but Hillyer appears to equate the committee and the "new critics," and he makes certain statements about the group as a whole.

He uses these expressions: "The party line . . . is merely the old doctrine of art-for-art's sake titivated with plumes of voodoo jargon to overawe the young." "They have pooled their separate timidities and frustrations, gaining strength from each other's weakness, and have succeeded in an age unprepared by education against pretentious cheek." "Their current preoccupation is a new vocabulary that has no purpose but its own creation." "Pound and Eliot are their unquestioned and almost their single point of reference." " . . . they are neither scholarly nor deeply read." " . . . the clouds of the new Fascism and the new estheticism have perceptibly met in that award." "A mind seeking the advantage of superiority over others. . . ." "this common snobbery. . . ." "What I have been leading up to in this sketch of the new estheticism is that its sterile pedantry, based on a sense of personal inadequacy, and its failure to command our common English, result in a blurring of judgment both esthetic and moral. I have said that in the Bollingen award to Pound the clouds of an intellectual neo-Fascism and the new estheticism have perceptibly met and on a horizon too near for comfort." "Half the committee were disciples of Pound and Eliot and sympathetic to a group which has a genuine power complex." "The performance of the Bollingen committee is disagreeably reminiscent of what happens when a dictatorial will moves through a group wherein right and wrong are no longer clearly distinguishable from each other." " . . . a spiritual morass where language, ethics, literature, and personal courage melt into something obscure

and formless ... something shaped out of stagnant art by groping Fascism. ...
It is not genteel authoritarianism or the desire for order in a disordered world,
as polite critics have called it. It is the mystical and cultural preparation for a
new authoritarianism."

According to these passages and the contexts from which they are taken,
the people discussed are timid, frustrated, cheeky, unscholarly, snobbish, sterile, pedantic, personally inadequate, morally confused, disciples of Pound and
Eliot, dominated by a power complex, devoid of personal courage, and Fascistic.
These accusations involve among other things intelligence, professional competence, mental and nervous stability, personal character and motive, and political bias. If Hillyer and the editors of the *Saturday Review of Literature* have
knowledge on these matters with respect to particular persons, knowledge which
will stand public scrutiny (i.e., scrutiny in a court of law), they should name
the persons and make the accusations definite. If they have no such knowledge
they stand convicted as public liars. If they refuse either to make their accusations definite on the one hand or to retract them on the other, they stand convicted not only as public liars but as pillaried cowards.

I demand that this letter be published in the *Saturday Review of Literature*
without alterations or omissions, and with an adequate reply. If it is not so
published there, it will be published elsewhere.

Sincerely yours, / Yvor Winters /
Professor of English / Stanford University

MS: Chicago

Published in *The Case Against* The Saturday Review of Literature (Chicago: Poetry,
1949), pp. 69–71.

TO HAYDEN CARRUTH

Oct. 19, 1949 / R. 2, Box 625 / Los Altos, Calif.

Dear Mr. Carruth:

I received the enclosed yesterday. I had wired the *SRL* some days ago, and
told them to wire me collect, but I got no wire. If you have no need for this, send
it to Allen and ask him to return it. I am not really sure that the bastards are
worth all the trouble, but anyway I would just as soon chuck my half a brick.

If it is not too late, you might change one word in my letter, in the interests
of a better sentence: at the end of the next to the last paragraph, the letter reads:

" . . . , they stand convicted not only as public liars but as pilloried cowards." Change *convicted* to *exhibited*. It makes more sense.

As to my reply to your editorial, I would like to withdraw it, and let you enjoy the field, provided it has not gone to press.[1] It is too much in the way of a personal confession, and I don't really like it. It is, however, about the only answer possible. Your editorial struck me as foolish: as if you were taking upon yourself the neurotic burdens of all the spoiled children who think themselves poets and who believe that the world owes them a living. What if there were some odious drudgery in teaching? Who expects to get by without odious drudgery? My wife, who has never been strong, has gone through 23 years of the odious drudgery of keeping house, and has managed to produce three novels, a novelette, a book of short stories, and a book of poems; she thinks I lead the life of Riley, and in comparison, I do. If you have gone too far with the thing to allow me to withdraw it, however, please make one change. On page 3, where I assert (about two-thirds down) that I had about 1000 people working under me in C.D., I let my enthusiasm run away from me. Change it to 400. During the whole business, I had well over 2000 in the organization, but probably no more than 400 to 450 at any one time. I no longer have my records, and so cannot check it.

Sincerely yours, / Yvor Winters

MS: Chicago

[1]Published as "The Poet and the University: A Reply," *Poetry* 75:3 (1949).

TO HAYDEN CARRUTH

Oct. 29, 1949 / R. 2, Box 625 / Los Altos, Calif.

Dear Mr. Carruth:

This letter is in reply to several of yours, and I shall have to make it brief. As to my epistolary style, when it shows obvious traces of high-flown rhetoric, you may safely take it as a specimen of my curious variety of humor. I know that I ought to reform in this respect, but I have never been able to reform. I bear you no real grudge; I was only mildly exasperated; and since most of us are in a state of mild exasperation most of the time, you may fairly neglect my condition. I am sorry if I bothered you.

I am returning your letter of Oct. 21, with comments, in order to save you trouble in connection with your reply to my reply.

(1) The question of most of all poets. This depends on what you mean by poets. If you mean all those who think they are poets, or all those who contribute to *Poetry*, you mistake my intention. There are hundreds of people publishing verse whom I should hate to see in any English department. On the other hand, there are many people of real poetic talent, who (I suspect) would have been good scholars, good teachers, and better poets if they had been caught young and had not been trapped in a sentimental aversion to the teaching profession. Tate, for example, is a great poet (greater than Crane); he is a brilliant teacher; I know that, because I have talked with his students, both at Chicago and at Kenyon; but he is only on the fringe of the profession and has been there only lately. Had he not been turned aside from the profession in his youth by sentimental nonsense, he might have been a more learned man, a better critic (his criticism is marred almost brutally by bad exposition, the result of utter obliviousness to the difficulties which will appear to minds other than his own, difficulties which he could easily have eliminated had he had ordinary classroom experience with friendly adversaries), and a cleaner and less perverse poet. As to Crane, he is not the greatest talent of our time (you are guilty of romantic foolishness there); Tate, Stevens, Robinson, and J.V.C. all have greater gifts, and there are doubtless a few others. He is an extreme case of temperament; he may have been incurably psychotic, or so nearly that, that he could never have dealt with other people, but neither you nor I can tell now. There are more men of genius, however, who are comparable to Tate than to Crane. As to Jim, he was a brilliant teacher at Stanford; if he has not been one at Chicago, I think it is probably because of the personal difficulties of the past couple of years; and if he says he is not, I think it is because of a streak of hypochondria and of inferiority complex, the result of his early life, which invariably comes to the surface whenever he is under personal stress. He is before anything else a scholar and a teacher, and he could never have been anything else. He likes to kid himself with the thought that he might have been a business man, but you know him well enough by now to realize that that is bullshit. If he can get his private life straightened out, his professional life will take care of itself, in spite of his bad manners.

(2) Alcoholism and megalomania occur in every phase of intellectual life. Furthermore, I suspect that neither is new.

(3) "Technique is valueless." You are going out on a Romantic limb. The more a poet knows (a) about his material (that is, the critical understanding of human experience) and (b) about his medium (meter, metaphor, rhetoric, etc.) the better equipped he is. Joe Louis learned to box by the book, learned so

well that his learning was second nature in the ring, so well that he might be able even to improve instantaneously on his learning; but that is only the greater justification of his learning. I can teach a great deal to young poets which will be of the utmost value to them, and may make the difference between their being vulgarians and classics (minor classics, perhaps), or the difference between their being messy geniuses like Wordsworth and really great poets. Naturally, I cannot give them genius.

(4) The poet in the university, if he has his wits about him, should bring to bear on the problems of teaching and scholarship the special talents which he has. This paragraph in your letter is obscure to me. The poet, if he is an able man, has the same talents which any other scholar has, plus greater perceptivity. I see no reason why he or anyone else should suffer from this fact.

(5) "any poet who allows critical doctrine, etc." Bushwa. Study the Renaissance in general and Ben Jonson in particular.

(6) What you think about my good fortune is nonsense. I was 40 years old before I earned $3000 a year. After the death of Briggs I fought for my life for about seven years. I fought with the phonies. But I walked into them and knocked their teeth loose, and I stayed on the job till we had a new department head and a new administration. As of this year, I am a Professor; as of last year my salary is $6000. Of course I am a good teacher: to be a good teacher one needs to know one's subject, to be able to expound it clearly, and to be reasonably unpretentious and courteous in dealing with students. Any poet who is really a poet has an initial advantage in the first matter, and if he is a normal human ought to do well enough in the rest.

(7) See (1).

I send you this letter merely to keep you out of deep water if possible. Please don't take it amiss.

Yours, / Y.W.

MS: Chicago

TO HAYDEN CARRUTH

Nov. 13, 1949 / R. 2, Box 625 / Los Altos, Calif.

Dear Mr. Carruth:

I still think you were pretty Romantic, both in your editorial and in your letter. However, there is no great point in arguing the Points.

The trouble with this sort of argument is that it remains in a state of glorious generality unless one names names and events. One cannot do so in public. When I came to Stanford in 1927 as a graduate student Briggs was head of the department. He did not like my poems (I can sympathize with him now, for I no longer think much of what I had done then). He distrusted modern poets in general, and perhaps with some reason. He had no great critical sensitivity with regard to matters of style, but he had inhuman learning and [a] philosophical mind the like of which I have never seen equalled in another man. When the men he had assigned to direct my dissertation made certain stupid comments upon it, which showed that they had not taken the trouble to read simple and careful sentences before jumping to conclusions, he took over the direction himself, even though he knew very little of the materials (the dissertation was *Primitivism and Decadence*). He told me that so far as he was concerned, he would have accepted Matthew Arnold's first collection of essays as a dissertation if [it] had been offered him, in spite of the fact that it would have been an irregular sort of dissertation; and that he was willing to give me my chance. I was the last man in the Stanford department ever to have to defend my dissertation in a special and second oral examination: when the examination was half done, Briggs had taken up the defense and was arguing down a hostile board. You must bear in mind that he was not an enthusiastic man or an especially friendly one. I never got to know him well, and I think he was always a little sceptical about me; he had a real affection for Jim, but little that I could discover for me. After I had been here for a year, however, he made me an instructor; and I was promoted twice under him, but the two promotions were slow, and to get both I had to go to him, lay the cards on the table, and tell him I would walk out if not promoted. When he died, Kennedy, a fourth rate little bibliographer and philologist took over. Kennedy was consumed with jealousy of Briggs and hated every man that Briggs had liked. He fired Jim, but I was an associate professor and he could not fire me; so he tried to squeeze me out; and he gave libellous reports on my work to Tresidder, who was Stanford's worst president. Tresidder was snatched away to Valhalla and Kennedy retired (after about 7 years), or rather these events occurred in the other order. Jones became head of the department, and began working on my behalf; after Tresidder's death, and during Faust's interim as acting president, Jones got my promotion. The new president seems to be a good man.

I fought this old two-way prejudice between the artist and the professor for years; it is beginning to break down here and there as a result of my work and the result of the work of a few others. I have trained young people who (believe it or not) will be among the permanent poets of our time and among the distinguished scholars of our time; I have caught them young and shown them the foolishness of being irritated with professor so-and-so because he is not as fine a critic as God-Almighty, when he can teach them something about Renaissance texts and the language of Chaucer. I have civilized a lot of young geniuses who could easily have blown their tops at an early date. I get irritated at outbursts like yours for that reason. I know more about the problems involved than you are ever likely to know; and I have spent the better part of a lifetime working at them. As a critic, I shall win out over my rivals in the next fifty years or so, mainly because of my teaching. I have had my hands on a fair number of very good people, who are going out into other universities, and as a teacher I have had a far better chance to explain things to them than I should ever have as a critic alone.

Your unhappy young poets are most of them, I suspect, as anachronistic as Shelley. They don't want to work at anything, either studying or teaching, and least of all at thinking. I know who some of them are. And why should they not be unhappy? Most of us are unhappy much of the time. Why get excited about it? And how happy do you think John Berryman would be in the engine room of a tanker? Try to be reasonable.

As to the deletion, I hope you can manage it. I don't mind taking a swing at John Dodds and Hubert Heffner, so far as they are concerned, but it may kick up a mild ruckus for poor old Jones, who has worked miracles here and who is in extremely bad health. My two poems (in *Poetry* ["A Song: From an Academic Bower" and "An Ode on the Despoilers of Learning in an American University"]) paid my respects adequately to the people in question.

I am afraid that Stanford would not subsidize you. Its enforced salary-increases and enforced building program have kept it, I gather, on the ragged edge. But if you really want to try, I'll recommend you—on the supposition that you are to remain editor for a while. It would be purely a dream, however.

Sincerely yours, / Yvor Winters

MS: Chicago

Dec. 31, 1949 / R. 2, Box 625 / Los Altos, Calif.

Dear Allen:

If you dislike writing letters as much as I do, I have probably seemed a trial in the past few weeks. Don't bother about me. All serious business is now clear unless you object to that poem. Jim will not like it, but he sometimes comes up with objections which I don't accept.

I have seen the *Nation* editorial. It is very good. I will look for the next one. Meanwhile, I will try to keep my temper in hand. I did not see why in hell Smith sent me that letter to Berryman anyway, since no explanation came with it, and I was busy and was sick of Smith. So I tried to explain to Smith quite privately and personally that I was sick of him. I thought he would understand.

As to my Phi Beta Kappa key, I shall be glad to rid myself of it in a good cause. The society has always seemed to me a pretty feeble affair, and if they are setting out to substitute name-calling for the discussion of ideas, I would like to be clear of them. Whether the Colorado chapter will back me up is more than I can guess, but I think the Stanford chapter will, in spite of the fact that I have never attended one of its meetings. The current vice-president is one of my oldest friends, Virgil Whitaker of the English department; and I have long been suspected in these parts of being pretty leftish, and once was suspected of being pretty red; so the whole thing will probably strike the boys as somewhat grotesque. About the time Gregory was calling me a fascist in the *New Masses* (because I liked the poems of Robert Bridges, which resembled Hitler's early Paintings), old Percy Martin of our history department called me into his office one day for a little friendly advice: he said that I was known as something of a red, and that if I was a red I ought at least to be pretty discreet about it.

Anyway, I am getting tired of this nonsense.

Best to you and Caroline, / Arthur

MS: Princeton, Allen Tate Papers

1950-1959

Jan. 8, 1950 / R. 2, Box 625 / Los Altos, Calif.

Mr. Hiram Haydn, Editor / *The American Scholar* / New York City

Dear Mr. Haydn:

I wish to thank you for your letter of Jan. 3, and for your promise to publish my protest. However, I wish to make myself clear with regard to the chief point in my original letter. I do not consider that I am on trial, and I do not consider that a retraction with regard to myself is adequate. I consider that Mr. Davis and *The American Scholar* are on trial, and I still consider the method of Mr. Davis's article disgraceful.[1]

The method was to list a large number of writers living and dead and from various countries and to imply that they were in essential agreement with each other and were part of a single movement; to offer a few quotations and misrepresented quotations from some of them and endeavor to put them together as if they were part of a single program with regard to which all the writers were in agreement; to assert that this program was opposed to constitutional democracy as we know it in this country; and to assert that these writers were therefore of no value in dealing with American literature and culture. I will grant you that he did not apply the term *fascist* directly to any living American or English writer mentioned, but the implication of fascism was clear from beginning to end of his essay. This is the kind of thing which any self-respecting teacher would fail if he received it from a student. It is the old technique of smear, sneer, and a quick getaway, which has been the familiar technique of literary adventurers from time immemorial and of the left-wing press, both literary and political, for the past thirty years. When the official organ of Phi Beta Kappa substitutes name-calling for the responsible discussion of ideas, I wish to get out.

Perhaps I should amplify briefly, for your own personal enlightenment, the second paragraph of my original letter. Of the people named by Davis, I have never read: De Maistre, Maurras, Robert Heilman, G. R. Elliott, Donald Davidson (except for a few poems which strike me as bad), Graham Greene, Evelyn Waugh, Reinhold Niebuhr, Barres, Drumont, or Sorel. I have written complete and wholly unsympathetic attacks on the literary theories not only of Ransom and Eliot, but of Poe. I have read a little of Norman Foerster and find him pretty vague and extremely vulnerable. Babbitt stimulated me when I was young, but I am twice on record in print as disagreeing profoundly with his positive program. Lionel Trilling I know only as a reviewer in the *Nation*. (What ominous inferences are we to draw, incidentally, from Trilling's having appeared in the *Nation* or—I believe I am right in this—from his being a Jew, or from my having appeared in *The New Republic* during the same decade in which I appeared in *The American Review*?) Of C.S. Lewis I have read *The Allegory of Love,* which seems to me one of the great works of our time both in scholarship and in criticism, though I think Lewis over-rates Spenser; I have also read parts of the *Screwtape Papers* [*sic*]: I found the first twenty or thirty pages amusing and fairly sound satire, but the book became tedious through repetition and I dropped it. What is the harm in Lewis's being an orthodox Anglican? Davis mentions it as an ominous fact. I have had the impression, I hope a true one, that every man has a right to his own religion and a right to endeavor to make converts. What the devil is Davis getting at? Of Auden I have read very little, for he strikes me as dull, and I know nothing of his political ideas. T. E. Hulme I have read carefully and disapprove thoroughly: it is very easy to demonstrate that Hulme is the tail-end product of the associationist and romantic tradition of the 18th and 19th centuries, and although I have never published on him I have dealt with him repeatedly in those terms in my yearly seminar in American criticism. H. M. McLuhan I have read occasionally and find wholly confused: I have criticized his essay on Hopkins in my essay on Hopkins which appeared a year or so ago in *The Hudson Review.* If you polled the other living writers mentioned by Davis you might find many who have read more than I have read, but you would certainly find as wide a range of disagreement as I have indicated here. Neither you nor Davis know a damn thing about their political affiliations. Davis guessed and you guessed he was right, and I have called your attention to your error in connection with myself in order to point out to you the unscholarly element in guess-work.

Near the end of my original letter, I listed organizations to which I belong. In my exasperation, I forgot to mention the AAUP and The United World Federalists.

Since you have promised to publish my original and long letter, I cannot ask you to publish this; but you have my permission to use any part of it if you see fit. I enclose a separate copy for forwarding to Davis. I am sending additional copies to the Colorado and Stanford chapters.

Sincerely yours, / Yvor Winters

MS: Columbia, Random House Papers

Hiram Haydn (1907–1973): American scholar and educator.

[1]Robert Gorham Davis, "The New Criticism and the Democratic Tradition," *American Scholar* 19 (1949–50): 9–19. Davis argued that the New Criticism was part of an international movment that was fascist and anti-American.

TO HIRAM HAYDN

Jan. 10, 1950 / R. 2, Box 625 / Los Altos, Calif.

Mr. Hiram Haydn /
The American Scholar / New York City

Dear Mr. Haydn:

In my exasperation, which I think you understand, I failed to list one reference to my own published works in my first letter. It is a matter of indifference to me whether you publish this reference, and I do not feel obligated to keep a card catalog of subjects discussed by myself in print for the benefit of those professional scholars who choose to smear me in advance of reading me. Nevertheless, I think that your contributor Davis is on the spot and that he had better read this passage before answering my protest and not after. And I think it would be a good thing if you would read it.

The reference: *Edwin Arlington Robinson,* by Yvor Winters (New Directions, 1946); pp. 52–57.

Sincerely yours, / Yvor Winters

MS: Columbia, Random House Papers

TO DONALD DAVIE

Jan. 16, 1950 / R. 2, Box 625 / Los Altos, Calif.

Dear Mr. Davie:

*   *   *

As to the poems you have sent me, I think they show both talent and intelligence, and I really like them, but with reservations. From the poems, and from your letters, I think you are sweating unduly about what the "attitude" or the "approach" of the poet should be. My own theory is, that there should be nothing of the sort, that the poet should be as nearly impersonal as possible, and should concentrate on his subject. Many years ago, I was a baseball coach in the mining camps of northern New Mexico. The basic aphorism in baseball is: Keep your eye on the ball. As soon as you start to think about your own relationship to the ball, the ball has either passed you or hit you in the jaw. This is not quite a fair parallel with regard to poetry, for the ball (in poetry) may vary considerably; but I am objecting to what I suspect is a tendency toward a theory of an invariable attitude on your part. I think Ransom is talented but worm-eaten with mannerisms. I think most of the young British poets are worm-eaten with mannerisms (and frequently, though this does not seem to be true of you) with downright clichés.

*   *   *

Sincerely yours, / Yvor Winters

MS: Stanford

Donald Davie (1922–1995): English poet, critic, scholar, and educator.

TO HARRY DUNCAN

March 9, 1950 / R. 2, Box 625 / Los Altos, Calif.

Dear Mr. Duncan:

I have your letter of the fourth. I have not yet received the pamphlets [*Three Poems*], but they will doubtless arrive tomorrow or the next day, and I will write you when they get here. From what I saw of the proof sheets I am sure I shall like them very much.

As to our controversy, there is no point in continuing it indefinitely, but I confess that your letter causes me a certain mild irritation on several counts, and I might as well indulge in a little self-expression.

Your letter contains more emotion than reason. You refer ironically to my "own wealth," etc. I will grant you that it may seem wealth in comparison to what you listed for yourself, but it is, by and large, a lower middle-class kind of wealth. By the time my income has been nicked for income tax, property tax, life insurance, automobile insurance, retirement annuity, contributions to charitable institutions, etc., I have maybe $4000 a year on which to support a wife and two children. And three or four hundred a year out of that for books is a big item. And I have to have the books to earn the money. Furthermore, the tone of your letter indicates that you feel there may be something degenerate in my having such "wealth." Let me assure you of two things: (1) I have worked for what I have (except for a small portion of it, for which my parents and my wife's parents worked), and have really come by it honestly; and (2) I have not compromised either my art or my scholarship in coming by it (in fact both were for many years a handicap). When I retire, I may have an annuity of $2000 a year (if I live long enough to get it).

You seem to resent my Airedales especially. Why, in God's name, should you resent my enjoying the company of five of God's most charming little creatures? Breeding and showing Airedales is a minor art; quite as much so as making fine furniture or making fine books. You may not realize this, but that is doubtless because of your ignorance of animals. I have two dogs on the place who are beautiful to watch in every movement and position, and I have two others who are almost as fascinating; and the fifth is not bad. I would rather have these dogs than, say, masterpieces of furniture or silver—as works of art they are quite as admirable and quite as serious and much more to my taste. As to the matter of book-making, I shall put that off to another paragraph.

In giving you an account of my own situation, I was merely trying to point out to you that I have to buy books in quantity on an income of such a nature that I have to be careful of the cost of individual books. You appear to have mistaken the point, either emotionally or willfully.

As to the Taylor edition,[1] the book came out about ten years ago, when costs were much lower than they are now. Whether it was a "fine" book or not, a barbarian like myself would not know, but it looked like one superficially, and it cost $7.50. During the same decade, my first three books of criticism were issued in smaller editions, with more pages and with vastly more typesetting, sold out, and paid for themselves and a little better; and they were decent looking books so far as I am concerned. The Taylor would have sold 2000 or more copies (probably many more) by this time if it had been priced so that university students could buy it. University students, like the rest of us, have their financial problems; and when they become interested in the metaphysical poets and discover that Taylor costs as much as almost any three of the others, they buy the others first. As to this particular volume, like many others which I have thought priced too high, I bought it and do not need to borrow a copy; but I think the editing, the book-making, and the pricing represent a needless barrier to the spread of civilization. "Lycidas," for example, is just as good a poem in the *Oxford Book of English Verse* as it is or might be anywhere else.

You ask what kind of Airedale could one get for $7.50? A very poor one, obviously. But I don't need a basic library of 5000–6000 Airedales. And I could get along without any in a pinch. Your question is silly. I can get a very decent edition of Donne or Herrick or Milton or even King or Vaughan (complete) for from three to six dollars. The poems are there, the text is good, the print is readable. It is the poems I want.

If I were to follow your advice to the utmost, I should buy not only the finest works of printing, but the finest furniture, silverware, chinaware, draperies, etc. These arts (printing included) are all minor arts, real though they may be. I cannot afford them. As I said before my art is poetry and my profession is scholarship. My minor art is Airedales, and it is just as good as any of the others.

My complaint against fine printers is not confined to the cost; it extends very often to interference with the text. [William] Meredith's statement[2] seems to me foolish, but your job on Blackmur still seems to me bad. I see no reason in God's good earth why I should spend hours familiarizing myself with Victor Hammer's eccentric brainchild so that I can read a small collection of Blackmur's poems. The poems may or may not be worth it (I still don't know), but they will eventually be published in readable type, and meanwhile I have other reading to do. In looking at the book, I found that I had to spell out the words and read the words one by one. The poetic structure of the line was lost. The structure of the poem as a whole was smashed. Normal type can be distinguished, clear, and unobtrusive; and I still believe that the printer's job is to render the work of his betters, not to obscure it for his own glorification. This is a harsh way of putting it, but it is a traditional and perfectly defensible view.

You say your partner paid $7.50 for Taylor. So be it, and all honor to him. But if the book trade got its support from people in his situation and yours, it would not last long. It gets a large part of its support from people like myself, people who are seriously interested in the art of literature and in the history of literature and who have to buy large numbers of books in the course of keeping themselves going, who have to support families (immoral though it may be), and who cannot afford objets d'art (that is, not beyond the number of five or six).

I will venture to name one book of verse which seems to me satisfactory in all important respects (as regards book-making): *The Sleeping Fury,* by Louise Bogan. I am sure this is not a fine work of art from your point of view. But one can read it easily; the type, though familiar, is distinguished; one can see the shape of the poem on the page, and can get an idea of what one is moving into before one spells it out. I should like my own poems, when they appear in definitive form, to be published as well and no more elaborately.

Frankly I think you and your partner would do more for civilization and for yourselves if you were working for a big firm and improving its products within practical limits. If you were doing that, you would probably be in a better position than you are now to indulge yourselves on the side in the kind of printing you really like, and you would certainly be doing no harm.

You seem to be very angry with me already, and this will doubtless make you angrier. I am not really angry with you; merely a bit irritated. I am trying, incidentally and in all honesty, to explain a point of view which is not merely my own but that of nearly all of the serious and distinguished writers whom I know (and the number is fairly large, if you consider the limits of the class).

Incidentally, if you are not too exasperated, I would like to make a deal with you. I have mislaid your partner's name and cannot remember it. If you will send me his name, and will also send me a list of your publications, I will send you two copies of my poems (1940), printed by myself on my own handpress, one inscribed to you and one to him. Your sufferings over these books will be intense but I daresay enjoyable. You may write me whatever you think, without reservations.

Best wishes, / Yvor Winters

P.S. Don't worry about "bullying" me. I am hard to bully.[3]

MS: Duncan

Harry Duncan (1917–1997): American printer, editor, and publisher. His Cummington Press published YW's *Three Poems* (1950).

[1] *The Poetical Works of Edward Taylor,* ed. Thomas H. Johnson (New York: Rockland Editions, 1939). The book was published in an edition of 925 copies and printed at The Spiral Press.

[2] Harry Duncan had written YW that Meredith, too, had objected to *The Good European,* not on typographic grounds but because all books of poetry should look as "'ordinary' as a cheap novel" (4 March 1950).

[3] Harry Duncan had written that he wouldn't send YW a list of Cummington publications because he didn't want to appear to be bullying YW into buying.

TO HARRY DUNCAN

March 24, 1950 / R. 2, Box 625 / Los Altos, Calif.

Dear Mr. Duncan:

Thanks for the dope. I enclose a check for $24.50. This is to cover the following items:

1. The six copies of my poems which you say you have mailed me: . .$6.00
2. The Tate pamphlet which you sent me some time ago but which
   I wish to buy: 1.00
3. One copy of the Tuckerman pamphlet: 1.00
4. The next four pamphlets, regardless: 4.00
5. *Three Academic Pieces* (Stevens): 12.00

I am at present in the midst of grading bluebooks, and have a deadline to meet, but I will get a copy of my poems off to you in the next few days. Meanwhile, I will meditate on what I should send to Mr. Williams. I have several examples of fine printing here, but will think it over, decide and act within a week. There are a couple of other items on your list which I should like, but it will be necessary to postpone them for a month or so. Meanwhile, I will try to get a couple of the items at least for the Stanford Library. As to the six copies of my poems which you mailed me, I asked for them, and I had intended to order them as soon as I got your post-card. Our agreement with regard to royalties was that you should pay me if and when the pamphlet produced them.

My wife informs me that I underestimated our income from unearned increment by about $1000, as far as the past two years were concerned. She takes care of the income taxes. I was going on my memory of the war years. I didn't want you to feel sorry for me. I was just giving you a portrait of your average practical and vulgar customer.

I think that our controversy ought to have an end fairly soon, but you produce, I confess, an almost unending series of temptingly weak arguments. Let me assure you that I feel no bitterness toward you. You seem to feel no bitterness toward me at present, but rather a kind of sanctified compassion. My real feeling toward you is that you are dedicating your life to a lost (and essentially pointless) cause; and although I feel that you are quite within your rights in doing so, I see no harm in trying (at no length beyond the limits of this letter) to persuade you of your error.

Your remark about Taylor's having been bought up and priced down is irrelevant. I cannot afford a private detective to keep track of that sort of accident. Theoretically I ought to read all the catalogues that come in, but actually I teach in a post-war university of considerable reputation and too damned many students, and in the past ten weeks I have accumulated a pile of catalogues over a foot deep which I have not had time to look at. I have recently had a graduate helping me in this work, but he has to be paid for his time, and the available money is limited. Had the book been made and originally offered at a reasonable price, it would have sold out, and a complete edition at a reasonable price would be a great success now.

As to [Victor] Hammer, we did not bully him. He offered us two types [for Janet Lewis's *The Earth-Bound*], and we chose the one he used, although he wanted the other. As to the price of the book in relationship to his labor you are quite right. I sold copies of my poems for [$]1.00 each, but if I had priced them to pay for my labor $20.00 would have been insufficient. But this is the fault of trying to pursue hand-printing in a mechanical age.

As you have discovered, I am very ignorant. But I can see few real advantages to a hand-press. These, perhaps: you or I can afford to buy one and we can afford to operate one in a very small way provided we have another source of income. You or I may have better taste in poetry than some bastard in the editorial department of a big publishing house. But there it ends. I know little of handprinting and nothing of bigtime printing, but in general the machine is more precise than the hand, in matters of evenness of type, regularity of impression, etc. This should be no different in printing than in the manufacture of fine guns or fine engines. And the machine in the long run is far more economical. This last is a simple matter of history.

For the rest, my ideas about the printing of poetry are as follows: immortal paper and binding, and non-corrosive ink, are highly desirable if not too expensive; but by and large they are too expensive. For you or anybody else. As to type and format, I will briefly defend the job which [S. A.] Jacobs [of The Golden Eagle Press] (L[aughlin] told me he was a Persian and also a genius) ended by doing for me [*The Giant Weapon*]:

The type should be large enough for easy reading but no larger. 8 pt. is ideal. The format should be such that the metrical and stanzaic structure can be taken in at a glance, and unless the poem is a very long one, the over-all shape. The sound of poetry is an integral part of the poetry. One must hear with the mind's ear when reading. The ability to cast the eye quickly ahead and estimate provisionally the coming movements is extremely important. If the type is so large (even 10 pt., to say nothing of 15, is bad) or so unfamiliar that this is difficult, then the printing is an obstruction rather than an aid. The stanzas should be as compact as possible without crowding. The poem should start high on the page, in order to prevent run-over pages as far as possible. Run-over lines are invariably an obstacle to reading and should be avoided as far as humanly possible. The job which Jacobs did respected all of these principles, and I consider it wholly satisfactory. The job which he wanted to do would have violated most of them.

Now with the typical self-righteousness of an artist, you inform me that I have no right to interfere with a printer; yet you say that it is the printer's job to interpret the poems, or present them, or something of the kind as clearly as possible. That is well enough in a vacuum. But what does Jacobs know about poetry? Or what do you? I have no way of knowing, except that both of you are ready to defend a format which would make it impossible for me to read any poem except with difficulty and extreme irritation. And make no mistake about it, I know a great deal about poetry: about the writing of poetry, the exegesis of poetry, the evaluation of poetry, the metrics of poetry, the rhythm of poetry, and the reading (audible) of poetry. Few people know as much; few people even know the issues involved. How can Jacobs render my poetry properly when (as I suspect, though I may be wrong), he does not even know what poetry is, or what the issues are? I may have no right to tell Jacobs how to print, but if I am certain that he will butch[er] my own life work I have the right to withdraw that life work and look for a practical tradesman who will take advice. Jacobs took advice in the end, and did a job which I think about as good as I could have asked.

You remind me of the amateur poets who think they can write good poetry without being able to understand their subject-matter, since they know the principles of scansion (or think they do) and have mastered a few of the rules of rhetoric; of the professors of Education, who believe that it is unimportant to know much about English literature if one is to teach it, but important to know only the method of teaching it; of the professional handlers on the coast who have begged me to let them handle my young champion free of charge, but who cannot trim an Airedale properly or handle him properly in the ring because they do not understand the essential nature of the breed. (Mostly they trim Airedales as if they were wire-haired fox terriers and handle them as if they were spaniels.)

This last paragraph is over-emphatic. I made it so not to insult you but to press the point.

Now then, I should think that you and Williams could find a place either on the designing staff or on the editorial staff of a big house. Both of you obviously know more about both items than most of the people engaged therein. But if you feel that you must come up through the print-shop, there are obvious ways of learning how to use the machines, and if you will only consider the people who are using them, I am sure that you will not find the difficulty overwhelming. I suppose you will continue to fight your losing war, however, and I will argue with you no further on the point. When I first started insulting you, I thought you had some sort of practical and workable arrangement there; I did not realize that you were sailing so close to the wind. I am sorry if I have at any point hurt your feelings. But since I started, I felt that I might as well finish, especially as you seemed to be so good at defense and infighting.

Anyhow, please try to forgive me and accept my best wishes.

Yvor Winters

MS: Duncan

TO DONALD DAVIE

April 10, 1950 / R. 2, 1950 [sic.] / Los Altos, Calif.

Dear Mr. Davie:

I have your letter of April 1. If you care to discuss my students in England, I shall naturally be glad to have you do so. I have no objection to your discussing my poems if you wish, provided only you make it clear that the homemade volume I sent you is no longer publicly for sale: I simply don't want to be bothered with answering requests for copies.

If I were to select a small handful of my poems which I think the best, they would probably be these: "Theseus," parts II and III, "Heracles," "Time and the Garden," "The Marriage," "A Prayer for My Son," "Sir Gawaine and the Green Knight," "To the Holy Spirit." If I were to extend this list, it would contain two or three that you dislike in preference to those you like. It seems to me that your remarks about perfect rhythm and riming are unsound. If the perfection is perfection, you have no case; if it is something else, you have not stated the case. In general, however, the current theory of "roughening" for which Ransom is the chief spokesman over here strikes me as silly. I see no reason why I should be any rougher than Ben Jonson. I suppose you don't like Bridges, since he is nothing more than a respectable Briton. I would suggest, however, that you examine carefully "Dejection," "Low Barometer," and "The Affliction of Richard." They are very great. There is not much greater.

As to my personal struggle with the temptations of the romantic tradition, I think the struggle has been more intensely realized in this country and in France than in England. The British always took the issues placidly; we took them religiously; the French took them logically. It has been a desperate matter in our tradition, however, and I might add in my personal life. I am constantly being bewildered by romantic lovers of the bucolic who have never milked a cow or a goat, who have never trimmed a terrier, who cannot tell a finch from a thrush, who have never pulled a carrot fresh from the ground and eaten it raw, who have never had to battle with a natural and impulsive love for too much alcohol, and who have never got any pleasure out of a fight with their bare fists. These things and others loosely related to them have been the great temptations of my life. Well, well, leave us leave the subject.

Best wishes, / Yvor Winters

MS: Stanford

April 11, 1950 / R. 2, Box 625 / Los Altos, Calif.

Dear Caroline:

I have not started to look for a house for you, so don't be forehanded in your thanks. I merely had a sudden feeling that you ought to be warned about certain matters. I will look, however, when the proper time arrives, and any information I may have about your desires will be all to the good when I start.

Since last writing you I have talked to a neighbor, Mrs. Mary Minetor. Mrs. Minetor lives about three blocks from us, on San Antonio Road, which is the main road from the highway to Los Altos Village. She is about two short blocks from the highway and from two large grocery stores (stores that would have been large in Mount Vernon and that would have supplied 20 Gambiers apiece). She has the best Bedlington Terriers in the west; if there are any others in the country as good they belong to Wm. Rockefeller, but she has consistently beaten all the Rockefeller dogs that have come west, and last winter she showed at a Bedlington specialty show in Chicago and got best of breed with her young champion bitch and best of winners with a 7 months old male puppy. When you walk into her place four or five Bedlingtons rush at you and leap on you, and they look and feel like little clouds or bouquets of asphodel; you scarcely know they are there. Bedlingtons are the only dogs that Black Jack does not attempt to kill on sight. He is devoted to them, and by and large they try to put up with his somewhat strong-armed affection.

Mrs. Minetor has a husband who is a sergeant in the regular army and is mostly away from home. She has a married son who lives in San Jose but who occasionally blows in for a week-end. He and his wife are very quiet and civilized. She has a 17 year old son who lives at home (very quietly) and who is very practical and decent. He works for me a few hours a week, and last summer took care of my dogs, and held Back Jack's show coat for me. She has a seven year old daughter who is a little hellion, but very smart, and no worse than other little hellions of the same age.

She has an upstairs apartment which at present she rents for $65 a month. If rent controls go off, rents may go up, this along with others; again, they may not, for there is a tremendous amount of building going on around here. The apartment has a living room, a bedroom, a small (but adequate) kitchen, and a bathroom. The apartment is furnished, and the rent includes utilities. To get into it, you have to enter the main house: there is no outside entrance. It would be impossible to engage this place now, for summer after next; I simply mention it as a typical case. You could be comfortable there, but would not have great room. The family and the dogs alike would be quiet, friendly, and considerate. It may or may not be available.

Another neighbor, a little closer to us, is fixing an upstairs apartment in his house, which will be larger and will have an outside entrance. I do not know the price.

Then here is another story. Gabor Szegö, who lives near me, who is the head of the department of mathematics, and who is Hungarian in origin, has been invaded every summer by visiting mathematicians, mostly European and impecunious. Last summer, he had over three most of the time, in a house which for practical purposes is smaller than ours, and he could neither eat, sit, nor sleep in private. So, I have just learned, he has rented a fraternity house on campus for next summer, in which he plans to house all the visiting mathematicians. He gets the entire house for the entire summer for $140. I don't know the real details. This may or may not include use of the kitchen equipment, it surely does not cover water, light, gas, and electricity, it probably involves his responsibility for taking care of the lawn and such garden as there may be, which would involve close to fifteen bucks a month in water bills alone. I will find out the details of this deal eventually and let you know. You would have plenty of room in such a jernt, God knows, but you might have plenty of housekeeping and the Lord knows what else. However, it is something to think about.

I shall probably never get around to *The Cocktail Party*. I feel that I have done my duty by Eliot, and for almost thirty years I have found him a bore. The sentiments expressed in my poems are deplorable, I know. They have made me sick for a year or more, or at least I think they have had a large part in it. But they are the best at which I have been able to arrive. The Dove has never descended upon me, and I fear will not at this late date.

As to [F. O.] Matthiessen, I was sorry to hear of his death. I did not know him personally. For years I have thought him a classical example of the academic phony. I hope I was wrong.

Best wishes to you and Allen, / Arthur

MS: Princeton, Caroline Gordon Papers

Caroline Gordon (1895–1981): American novelist, short story writer, and educator.

May 6, 1950 / R. 2, Box 625 / Los Altos, Calif.

Dear Mr. Davie:

My remarks upon romanticism were hasty and not very clear. I am sure that many a Briton has abandoned himself to sin—we at any rate claim no monopoly on sin—and some may have done it under the influence of Romantic doctrine. I was really thinking of two things, and I telescoped them. I am always mildly irritated with Romantic nature lovers who have never looked at nature: Wordsworth is a case in point; except for a dozen or so lines and short passages there is nothing to indicate that he ever observed a natural object with precision. The other matter that I had mainly in mind was a realization of the theoretical import of Romanticism. I doubt that there is much of that even in Lawrence, and Lawrence is late. If you compare Wordsworth to Emerson, for example, you find that Wordsworth almost never pushes his pantheism and anti-intellectualism to a real issue. He fades and fuzzes and strikes postures. Emerson, of course, did not realize the ghastly implications of his doctrine, but he accepted the doctrine fully and in statements of ultimate meanings. Whitman was quite as wholehearted, but of course wrote so badly that one has to be a true scholar to find out what he was talking about. You get nothing in England even today comparable to the pedantic thoroughness of Mallarmé in disorganizing poetic logic; or of Rimbaud in disordering both his poetry and his life. These men worked on principle: this theory is true; these are the consequences; ergo, here we go.

In this country Romantic pantheism began to be a genuine religion (not merely a theory of literature) with Emerson or thereabouts. It had the true-blue Yankee Calvinistic drive behind it. Only four writers of the century who had the imagination and the religious sense to be moved by the religion understood it and rejected it: Jones Very (I am not too sure that he really understood it or was even tempted, but Emerson tried to tempt him and failed), Emily Dickinson, Melville, and F. G. Tuckerman. Again, you get nothing in British literature comparable to the careful and at times almost hallucinated explorations of Romantic possibilities (along with the criticism and ultimate rejection of them) that you get in Melville. It is hard to think of Emily Dickinson's "Farther in summer" being written in a British context, and still harder to think of "The Cricket" by Tuckerman.

This brings me to the real occasion of this sermon. A few days after I last wrote you, I received a copy of *The Cricket* from the Cummington Press. This poem had never been published. It was printed from a pencilled copy; then a later and better copy was turned up, and they printed a short list of errata based on the 2nd. They have since seen four or five others. As to later improvements, I suggest that you write in "laugh and blush." for "tittering blush." (I have ordered a copy sent you.)

The poem is an irregular ode, much more carefully put together than may appear at first reading. The first two sections put the cricket in his natural setting, and expand him indefinitely through acres of crickets, with a sound like the sea (the traditional symbol for nature); the next section relates him to death (as of the earth and nature); the next relates him to antiquity (so that, like Melville's whale, he becomes ubiquitous in space and in time); and the final section then explores the evil and the fascination of the surrender to nature, and ultimately rejects it as impracticable at any rate, and needless since death arrives anyhow. It seems to me a very great poem; great as "*Le Cimetière Marin*" was great, or "Sunday Morning." Tuckerman published a volume of poems in 1860, which was twice reissued, and then sank without a trace. In 1930 Witter Bynner (through Alfred Knopf, N.Y.) published a collection of his sonnets, some from the *Poems,* some from the notebooks. I believe that this book is still obtainable. It contains a few very beautiful sonnets, and quite a few beautiful lines.

At any rate, what I was getting at in my last letter was this: that I do not believe that the British have gone through the complete cycle that we have gone through: utter surrender, realization of consequences, criticism, and rejection. What may seem to you merely baldly theoretic in my "Sir Gawaine" is something quite different to me: it is a statement about a serious matter (serious in my life and in my literary tradition), and no more bald than Donne's "Thou hast made me" (which incidentally is a great poem, possibly the best of Donne).

As to T. S. Moore, try "Titian's Bacchanal" and the first sonnet on "Silence." As to Bridges, try "Low Barometer" again, and "Dejection," and "The Affliction of Richard," and "Eros" (he writes it in Greek letters). These are not "Georgian"; at any rate not unless Ben Jonson is Georgian, or Greville, or George Herbert, or the late Sidney.

Best wishes, / Yvor Winters

P.S. There is a bare chance that my wife and small son may be in England for a couple of weeks a year or more from now. If you are still there, I would like to have them meet you.

MS: Stanford

May 27, 1950 / R. 2, Box 625 / Los Altos, Calif.

Dear Mr. Davie:

I am glad you liked the Tuckerman poem. The English edition of his poems was an exact reprint, I believe, of the volume which was printed three times in this country. Tennyson was probably responsible for it, so don't be too hard on Tennyson. I have not seen this volume, though I have tried for years to get hold of it. By the intervention of the Cummington Press, I think I shall be able to borrow a copy from Tuckerman's grand-daughter, as soon as the present school-term is over and I have time to read it. I wonder whether it contains the sonnets beginning: "An upper chamber in a darkened house" (I think it must contain this), "Under the mountain as when first I knew," "And change with hurried hand has swept these scenes." I will copy any of these out for you that you have not seen. The 1931 edition of the sonnets, edited by Bynner, published by Alfred A. Knopf (New York), is still available, if you can persuade your library to get it. This volume does not contain all that was in the *Poems*, but contains a considerable amount of later work; it also contains a more or less informative introduction.

I did not wish to imply that the exact description of natural detail is a *sine qua non* of good poetry; I have been arguing against such a notion for years. I am merely bored with romantic lovers of nature who have never looked at nature. If you are basing your career in a large measure on natural description you ought to be good at it. The "Intimations" ode is a tissue of clichés; there are about six or eight respectable lines in the poem, and they are little more than respectable. The "Ode to Duty," on the other hand, which relies on something else, is one of the few great poems of the 19th century, in spite of a few bad lines (don't tell me about the first line—I already know about it). Incidentally, tell your student that Tennyson does not look so damn sick if you take his best poems. "Tiresias" is pretty impressive in spite of the Tennysonian close; the vision of Athena, the naked truth, and her striking Tiresias blind, is great poetry. "Demeter" is quite a poem also, and, in a smaller way, "Tithonus." Nineteenth century poetry is a matter of poems rather than of poets. Browning's "Serenade at the Villa" is a great poem, for example; and so is Christina Rossetti's "A Pause of Thought." I could name a few others.

Best wishes, / Yvor Winters

MS: Stanford

June 1, 1950 / R. 2, Box 625 / Los Altos, Calif.

Dear Mr. Duncan:

I am sorry to have kept the ms. so long. The problems involved in trying to adjust my eyes to a new and unsatisfactory pair of glasses (I am a little tired of being told to adjust myself), the increasing academic pressure as the quarter nears its close (in addition to teaching three classes, I have 11 doctoral dissertations either under way or started, and have or have recently finished some six or seven masters' theses, and I give the departmental examinations in Romance Languages for M.A. candidates, which have been coming in pretty thick and fast). As nearly as I can figure it, I am directing twice as much graduate research as my nearest competitor in the department, and three to five times as much as most. Somehow this will have to be straightened out. We have a good department, on the whole; offhand, I doubt that any single department in the country has so many men who are not only distinguished scholars but men of sound general intelligence; but I am the only one who can be of much use in helping students interested in critical theory beyond the usual history of ideas business on a superficial level, and we have about 15 extremely brilliant graduate students, plus perhaps 20 more who are above the average (almost any of these 20 would have looked like geniuses at the Kenyon School of English last summer, and in fact the only one of the 20 who was there was regarded as one of the two or three top students), and a lot of run-of-the-mill students besides.

As to your typographical habits in relation to my reading habits, I have given up advising you to do anything, because it will accomplish nothing. I shall have to continue, I fear, to admire your work from a distance and do most of my reading in the kind of format and type that you deplore. The average "good" or fairly good commercial job I can read with little or no difficulty and with no sense that there is a veil between me and the text. However, if you can settle on the type used in *The Cricket,* I may be able to go along with you.

Many thanks for the comment on my poems and on my students, and also for the poems. There is bound to be a measure of imitation and of what you call brain-picking in this sort of relationship. Young poets always start out by imitating somebody, and if my students don't imitate me they are at least likely to imitate my favorite poets, which may get a more or less similar result. Any collection of that sort is more or less of a compromise. Some of the poets have no future for lack of any real talent; e.g. [R. K.] Arnold, [Colgate] Dorr, Miss [Melanie] Hyman, and, I fear, [Pearce] Young. Others have been sidetracked:

Frances Crawford, for example, was one of the most brilliant students I have ever taught—as a 16 year old freshman she began taking my advanced courses, and was invariably at the top of her class. But she is now a Ph.D. in psychology and a practicing psychologist of some kind, and her verse, although she still writes it, is deteriorating horribly. [Donald F.] Drummond has a streak of genius combined with a streak of simple-minded grotesque clumsiness, and both combined with a gift for blowing himself up personally. "The Froward Gull," I think, is a tremendously impressive poem; but I don't think the man has it in him to develop. Ann Hayes is a sweet little girl, happily married to a brilliant young scholar in classics and philosophy (they will be at Princeton next year); she was the best secretary our department has ever had; she has written some of the best critical papers I have ever received. She will write a dozen or more extremely distinguished minor poems in the course of her life, I suspect, if she lives her life out. They will be occasional, somewhat limited, and very feminine; but she may turn out as well as Alice Meynell, with a little luck. What she lacks in fiery genius and a capacity for alcohol she makes up in part in solid character and common sense. Christian Rasmus Holmes, Jr. is the son and heir of a man very famous in this part of the world; Holmes, Sr. had immense sugar interests in the Hawaiian Islands, and other business interests scattered clear across the American continent. From what I can gather by way of gossip he was mildly manic-depressive and extremely alcoholic, with a monstrous nervous and physical energy. Chris, Jr. seems to be like him, except that his taste for alcohol is still under control so far as I know. Chris was judo champion of the Islands at 17, and holds some kind of a championship swimming belt won at the same time. He can split a good fresh one inch plank with a blow from the side of his hand. He came out of the war as a sergeant in the Marines, and served through some of the nastiest campaigns. Toward the end of the war his father killed himself, and Chris inherited the entire mess. He was administering the estate when he first came to Stanford, flying every week-end either to New York or to the Islands or to Nevada. He has gradually been selling the remoter interests and concentrating his activities in California. But he will never write again; the rest of his life will be divided between business and politics.

For the rest, you underestimate Bowers, who has one of the best minds I have ever met. He is a slow developer in some ways but he has a mind which is both comprehensive and brilliant, and he has a solid Presbyterian character. Miss [Helen] Pinkerton[1] is doubtless the best at this moment, and may remain so. [Lee F.] Gerlach has been developing fast, but is still awkward. Trimpi has swiped more from me than most, but he is not yet 21, and he is both skillful and sensitive; and he has a very good brain in general.

The bright boys who make bad jokes about the fruits of one's labors over ten years or so, might well try the job. Most of them would simply be laughed off the campus if they tried to teach here. One takes the people who come and does what one can for them. Most of my poets will never be poets, but they know a damned sight more about poetry right now than most of their critics. Meanwhile I taught Cunningham, Miss Pinkerton, Bowers, and Gerlach. They are better poets than the imitators of Tate, Ransom, and Eliot, such as Warren, Randall Jarrell, and Berryman. When somebody else comes up with a better kennel-full I shall be glad to see it.

Best wishes, / Yvor Winters

MS: Duncan

[1]Helen Pinkerton (b. 1927): American poet and (as Helen P. Trimpi) scholar. She was a former student of YW and became a lifelong friend. YW included her work in *Poets of the Pacific,* second series, and *Quest for Reality;* he wrote an essay on her poetry for the issue of *Sequoia* devoted to him and discussed her work in *Forms of Discovery.*

TO ALLEN TATE

Dec. 19, 1950 / 101 West Portola Ave. / Los Altos, Calif.

Dear Allen:

Needless to say I am sorry you are not coming, but what must be must be.

Thanks for your information about Catherine [Davis]. I knew she had had a bad life, but I didn't know it had been that bad. I really don't know how to estimate her present condition. We seem to be back on good terms again, had her out for supper two nights running a week or so ago, and shall have her for Christmas dinner. But it is impossible to see more than so much of her, and all the rest has to be done by telepathy. She wanted grades of incomplete in two of her courses, so I gave them: the make-up in one of these will mean merely the reading of a couple of volumes, and ought to be easy except that I don't see why the reading wasn't done last quarter. In the other course, I will try to persuade her to attempt a critical essay aimed at publication, instead of the usual class exercises. If she could pull herself together to the point of doing something of the sort successfully, it would be good for her in more ways than one. She is not going to get her degree, and I don't know that she has any practical use for it, though she could use the coincidental education. About the best I can hope to do, I guess, is get her working at something that will bring her talents into play and get her interested and that may possibly be of use to her later. Your idea that I find a young man to love her is a good one, but: most young men of 26 or more have already found some one else, at least around here; and if she will not show herself in public her chances of meeting anyone or getting acquainted with anyone are almost nil. However, Lee Gerlach is back from Michigan, where he passed his comprehensive examinations, and Lee knows a lot of people and usually ends up by persuading people to do what he wants them to do. His wife worked on Catherine in his absence but didn't get very far. Maybe the two of them can now get her to come to their house on an occasional evening and meet a few people. Anyway, they are going to try. It would be a good thing to have someone other than ourselves dragging her out, and especially someone younger.

Alan Swallow wants to publish my complete selected poems, and I promised him long since that he could, but I have been waiting for *The Giant Weapon* to dwindle out of print and also to find time to make a selection. I have been going over the home-made volume [*Poems*] which I sent you some time ago, and am seriously considering the following eliminations: page 3 "The Fragile Season" and "The Impalpable Void" and perhaps "The Moonlight"; pages 8 and 9 "The Cold Room" and "The Dead, by etc."; page 16 "Threnody"; page 33 "The Werwolf," "A Petition" (I have thought about "The Prince" and "Phasellus Ille," too, as a matter of fact); page 56 "A Dedication in Postscript" (for personal reasons I hate to drop this, but there are aspects of the poem which I dislike). *En revanche,* as the French are supposed (according to Henry James) to say, I would add at least seven or eight later poems, and perhaps a dozen, but again I am unsure. Some of these last are in *The Giant Weapon.* The last three poems would be the Cummington poems, though I would reverse the order of the short ones, ending on the song.

As I look over the stuff, it strikes me as one of the most miraculously modest life-offerings in the history of literature; and yet I have worked at it very hard and have tried to achieve the kind of style which is perhaps the hardest to achieve (it may or may not have any other virtues) and which is certainly the least likely to be liked. I think the book would probably sink without sound, and I wonder if it is worth the trouble.

If you have any useful advice it would be gratefully received; but don't try to talk me out of Swallow. If the book is published Swallow will get it if he wants it. He has done a great deal for me and Janet, and I like him, and I would rather be published in Denver than in New York.

Best wishes to you and Caroline and Percy and Nancy and the babies for Christmas and the new year.

Arthur

P.S. I turned in my grades yesterday. I think I am more nearly exhausted than I have ever been in my life. Partly a very heavy quarter and partly the state of the world and above all of the nation. I hope to God that little Harry gets some stuff moving on the assembly lines in one hell of a hurry.

MS: Princeton, Allen Tate Papers

TO DONALD DAVIE

Jan. 7, 1951 / 101 West Portola Ave. / Los Altos, Calif.

Dear Mr. Davie:

I am indebted to you first for the Christmas greeting with the charming view of Trinity College, and second for the review of my children, with the other enclosures. Trinity College appears small but charming in the picture. I sometimes wonder about the relative merits of British and American university systems. One of my most brilliant graduate students recently met [David] Daiches, who is returning either to Oxford or to Cambridge. My student asked him why. He said he was returning because he could earn a living by lecturing five or six times a month, or something of that sort (maybe it was more or maybe it was less—you would probably know). Last quarter I taught a course in the American novelists—Cooper, Hawthorne, Melville, James, Wharton, Glasgow—in which I lectured four times a week for ten weeks. My students wrote a mid-term examination and a final examination which I graded, and wrote 4 critical papers of 2000 words or more, which I graded. There were about 55 students. They were about half graduate and the rest upper division majors in American literature. I also taught a course in the criticism of poetry, in which I had over 25 students; here the students wrote similar examinations and six critical papers, all of which I read and graded. I taught a course in the writing of poetry which met twice a week and had five students. This quarter I have a course in the American poets from 1630 to the present, which will work like the course in the novelists, but in which I have only about 35 students, a course in the American historians, with 5 or 6 students, and a course in the writing of poetry with 5 or six students. In the spring it will be a seminar in the American critics (limited to about 15 students) and a lecture course on the history of the English lyric (about 25 students, probably, and conducted in the same way as the other lecture courses), and of course the writing of poetry. In addition I am directing 12 doctoral dissertations, five or six masters' theses; and I am serving on almost every department committee. I think I lead a rougher life than you people do; but so far as I can judge from the evidence available, I think we are giving our students a better education than they get at Oxford or Cambridge.

I mention this for two reasons: the air of leisure expressed in that picture of Trinity College made me jealous, and I recently read an article in *Scrutiny* by a young English woman (whose name escapes me) about education in this country. She had taught at a middle western institution (I gather a state college or university) and at another like it in the Pacific Northwest. Nearly everything she said was true, I believe, about such schools all over the country. But they are giving something to students who probably would not get anything at all in Britain, or so I suspect. What educational opportunities are open for example to the average (I do not mean the exceptional) child of a farmer or coal miner in Britain? And exactly what "cultural" heritage does he have which is above and beyond that of the son of a Missouri farmer or a California orange or cattle rancher, provided the children in each case do not go on to higher education than our high school (which is mostly, but not invariably, poor) or your grammar school (which may well be better, but which is not, I take it, open to the public without tuition)? The young woman saw the surface of things in the communities in which she lived for two years, and heard the radio, and suspected the worst; but there was more in the background, I think, than she discovered.

Our universities and colleges might be divided roughly into three groups: private institutions, like Harvard, Yale, Princeton, Chicago, and Stanford, which endeavor to accomplish the same function accomplished in England by Oxford and Cambridge—they do it by different methods, but I suspect (from the evidence) more efficiently; the smaller state institutions, with inferior faculties and inferior students, which do what they can; and the larger state and public institutions, such as California, Michigan, Ohio, and Columbia, which have exceptionally brilliant faculties but which have to accept all kinds of students and then shuck them off later.

You saw two of our products recently. Wes had just completed his B.A.,

Helen her M.A. Both of course were exceptional; but laying their poetic gifts aside I could show you almost 20 other Stanford products of the same ages and classes as well educated and almost as intelligent in a general way. Wes comes of a very wealthy family: his father appears to be a north Italian type (bull-chested, bullnecked, shrewd-faced, and blond); his mother is, I should judge, of old Anglo-American stock, small, pretty, delicate, spoiled, possessive, and pretty hard to take. His parents were divorced years ago, both were remarried, and both redivorced; enormous wealth all over the place in all the connections. Helen's family were copper miners from Montana: I mean mine-workers, not opera-tors; some of them were killed in cave-ins, etc. etc. Yet Helen got her B.A. at Stanford, an expensive university, with a little help from her family, with the help of a good many jobs, and with the help of scholarships which she earned. And she got her M.A. through a $2000 fellowship in the writing of poetry. And both kids, in spite of their amateur status, are, I believe, pretty damn well edu-cated; better educated than most of the young English poets and critics who have come to my attention. What baffles me about the young English poets and critics is that most of them seem to have devoted so little attention to the his-tory of their own literature. The poetic tradition begins with Yeats and culmi-nates in Eliot; and of course there was Donne. My children get an education in the English poets, big, little, and medium, and in how they worked. And these poets are not "foreign" to them; they are less foreign to them than they are for-eign to MacNeice and MacTreece and MacDylan MacThomas and all their de-scendents.

Well, well.

I was grateful for the review of my children. I think you chose to quote one of the worst poems by Wes: it tries to be epigrammatic but is pretty soggy. I don't know quite what you mean by Georgian (I understand the dynastic ref-erence of course, but am vague about the rest). The best of Bridges and Moore is neither Georgian nor Victorian nor anything else; it is, quite impersonally and untemporally, good poetry. As to the worst of these poets or of any others, I am not greatly concerned with it. I left the magazine, letter, and poems at my office the other day, and so cannot refer to them intelligently, but your young poet does not seem to me to differ much from the poets in the magazine: loose meter, loose and unachieved description employed, apparently, for no particu-lar purpose, and a loose grasp of his theme. I will read the pieces again more carefully and then send them back to you. I merely submit this proposition to you: A good writer is an intelligent man saying something worth saying about something worth discussing. Loosely described landscapes, with cynical or sentimental overtones (faintly discernible), done in loose meters, are scarcely worth the trouble.

Now as to that Wyatt sonnet. 20 or more years ago Miss Foxwell, in her edition of Wyatt, suggested that the strange meters in his attempts at iambic pentameter were due to his failure to understand the use of the French mute *e* in Chaucer:

> Whán that / Apríl / le wíth / his shóur / es sóut / e;

that he read such a line as follows:

> Whán / that Á / pril wíth / etc.

By this time of course a good many Chaucerian scholars are saying that Chaucer read the line in the second way, but since the reading makes hash of most of Chaucer I think they are wrong. But I suspect that Miss Foxwell was right: her theory would account for the unpredictable and frequently awkward monosyllabic feet that occur all over the place in Wyatt's five-foot lines.

Wyatt's first line is troublesome. "Whoso" means "Whosoever," and the accent should be on the first syllable. If we put it there, we get this:

> Whóso líst to húnt, I knów where ís an hínd,

or a matter of six feet, the third of them monosyllabic, whereas the rest of the poem is pentameter. We can read "Who só list to húnt," with an iamb and an anapest, and get the thing down to five feet. I doubt that W. pronounced "Whoso" as "Who *so*" (I will not now go into my reasons), but we might well have a misprint or a case of primitive spelling. The remainder of the poem through line 10 is fairly regular iambic pentameter. 11 goes as follows:

> And grá / ven with dí /amónds / in lét / ters pláin /

and 12:

> Thére is / wrítten / her fáir / neck róund / abóut /

and the rest:

> Nóli / me táng / ere; / for Cáe / sar's I ám /

And wíld / for to hóld / though Í / seém / táme. /

Thus it is only the last line inescapably, and possibly the first, that indulge in any irregularities of a radical nature. This poem is not written in accentual verse, but is written in iambic pentameter, ineptly and ignorantly, but with some taste for rhythm. Your poem was written in regular four-beat accentual verse and bore no relationship to this.

If you wish to see a poem which bears some relationship to this, examine my translation of Ronsard in the home-made book which I sent you. I did this piece at the age of 19, when I had learned what French I knew without help and read French verse with heavy accents as if it were English:

Ah, lón / gues nuíts / d'hivér, / donnez mói, / bourrélles,

etc. And so went Ronsard's alexandrines, and I got a new and irregular rhythm from them. I have often wondered how good Wyatt's French was.

Best wishes, / Yvor Winters

MS: Stanford

TO HISAYE YAMAMOTO

Jan. 24, 1951 / 101 West Portola Ave. / Los Altos, Calif.

Dear Miss Yamamoto:

My wife and I both liked your story ["Yoneko's Earthquake"] in the last *Furioso,* and I obtained your address from Reed Whittemore so that I could tell you. If you should ever have any business up in the pleasanter regions of California, we would like very much to meet you. (You might want to come up for air, for example.)

I wonder if you have ever tried for one of the Stanford fellowships in writing. I have nothing to do with the awards in fiction—they are handled by Wallace Stegner and Richard Scowcroft—but I should think you would have a very good chance. Next year will be the last unless we get a new grant. The fellowship is for $2,000, and you are required to attend at least one class per quarter in the field of writing for which you receive the fellowship. The deadline for applications is some time next month.

Of course it might not be possible for many reasons. For all I know, you may be Mrs. Yamamoto instead of Miss Yamamoto, with no end of commitments. But I thought it worth mentioning.

> Best wishes, anyway. /
> Yvor Winters / Professor of English, /
> Stanford University.

MS: DeSoto

Hisaye Yamamoto (b.1921): Nisei short story writer.

TO HISAYE YAMAMOTO

Feb. 1, 1951 / 101 West Portola Ave. / Los Altos, Calif.

Dear Miss Yamamoto:

Thanks for your letter. I ought, perhaps, to apologize for a few of my remarks. I have no desire to hurt the feelings of anyone, even a Southern Californian, but a Southern Californian *as such* presents a moral problem which I have never been able to settle to my own satisfaction. On the one hand there is truth, on the other hand there is gentility. Well, suppose we leave it there.

As to the Stanford fellowship, the adopted son would be a problem. Since your fellowship runs out in July, and the Stanford fellowship would not begin till the end of September, I see nothing irregular in applying for the latter this month. There would be no overlapping in payments. You could hardly take him into a Stanford dormitory, and you would have trouble getting into an apartment or rented room, and if you did you would still have the son to cope with. You might conceivably find a family who would take the two of you in and look after him when you were away, but it would take some looking. I would be glad to do some preliminary looking for you, however, and I have a few connections which might lead to something. But the idea probably would not appeal to you. If you are interested, in spite of all this, you should write me at once, so that I can have the forms sent to you. You could withdraw your application later if you wished.

Frankly I don't think you stand in any great need of the training that you would get here in short-story writing, at least if that one story is a fair sample. But it is a good university if you know how to find your way around; there are good people on the faculty and there are a good many intelligent students. I liked your story for several reasons: it dealt with a serious and moving situation; it did not conform to any current machine-made pattern of short-story writing (Stegner, alas, has a fixed pattern, and most of his students follow it); and the prose was good. The prose was, in an utterly unpretentious and quiet fashion, perceptive and charming and witty. The last adjective may startle you, but nevertheless the wit was there and was wholly in keeping with the subject and was controlled in tone.

I am a quiet and inarticulate rebel against the current conventions in fiction. I think that the point-of-view technique is the bunk, purely and simply; that the fictionist should deal with a serious subject, in prose which is flexible and intelligent; and that most contemporary writers of short fiction would do well to start all over again from a consideration of Melville's "Benito Cereno" and "The Encantadas," and from W. H. Hudson's "Marta Riquelme" (see *Tales of the Pampas*).

I may get south to see my mother during the spring vacation; or I may get down to one or more dog shows in the summer. Either way I will drop you a line in advance, on the chance of talking with you for an hour or so. You will have to write me explicit directions, however. That place is a jungle to me. I know every cowpath that existed there fifty years ago, but that was long before you were hatched.

Best wishes, / Yvor Winters

MS: DeSoto

TO HISAYE YAMAMOTO

Friday, Feb. 5th or 6th or so, 1951 /
101 West Portola Ave. / Los Altos, Calif.

Dear Miss Yamamoto:

You might possibly get by up here on the fellowship with the child, but it would be a problem—both as regards living quarters and the expense. You doubtless know the child and his needs better than I do. You probably wouldn't get enough out of it to justify the struggle, but I would still be glad to help you work it out. There are other fellowships, however, which do not involve a change in residence. Do you know about the Phelan fellowships, for example? Stegner keeps up with these things, and I don't, but I will speak to him about some of them when he gets back next month.

I did not mind the intrusion of the narrator in your story and did not think it coy. The story would have been a very different story without the narrator, and probably not so good. The point-of-view technique, which began with Flaubert and James, and which is now standardized, seems to me a very limiting technique. For very successful violators of it, see Melville (*Shorter Novels*); W. H. Hudson (*Tales of the Pampas*); R. B. Cunningham-Grahame (especially "Hope"); and Edith Wharton (the *Old New York* series and the story called "Bunner Sisters" in *Xingu and Other Stories*).

Your directions, alas, mean nothing to me. Don't bother about that unless I write you that I am coming down. I may be down late in March to visit my mother, or she may come up here; but I shall probably be down to one or two dog shows in the summer. In any event, I shall be staying either with my mother in Pasadena or with some Airedale-breeding friends in San Marino, and shall need explicit directions from Orange Grove and Colorado to wherever I may need to go.

My father built the 6th house in Eagle Rock (his uncle had built the 2nd about 20 years before). That was in 1906, and I was born in 1900. My father owned what is now North Highland Ave. in Eagle Rock, on both sides, and beyond that to the ridge of the foothills. It was all apricots except for our house. Glendale, in those days, was a short main street with a couple of grocery stores and two blacksmith shops; we used to take the two hour drive over about once in six weeks to have our horse shod. Later, one of these shops became a garage. I used to climb over the hills when I was about ten and wander around in La Cañada, which was uncontaminated live-oak forest, not a house in miles, and almost knee-deep in leaf-mold.

Best wishes, / Yvor Winters

MS: DeSoto

TO ALLEN TATE

Feb. 15, 1951 / 101 West Portola Ave. / Los Altos, Calif.

Dear Allen:

Harry Duncan wrote me six or eight weeks ago of your conversion; so I was not surprised. I congratulate you and envy you, and I am grateful for your prayers. I now have some five or six Jesuits praying for me, and more than a dozen nuns, but perhaps the prayers of so notorious a brand as yourself will have greater efficacy. Let us hope so.

However, I would like to enter a mild and charitable sort of protest. My intransigence, if that is the word for it, is not Protestant (please discount the *rime riche*). (I mean almost *riche*.) Recently I was invited by a local emissary of John Pick to contribute to *Renascence* and support the neo-Catholic revival in criticism (I am sure Pick didn't know of the invitation), and more recently a certain Father Berrigan (apparently a very good man) at Weston College Mass. (whatever that is) wrote me a very expansive letter, apparently under the delusion that I was a Catholic of long standing. I'll bet that nothing of that sort ever happened to you. Protestant, my eye.

I wonder whether your conversion is due more to the reasoning of Newman or to the prayers of Caroline. Far be it from me to go into this, but Caroline is a subtle character. I still resent the incident of the fish at Gambier. All I did was take it out of the ice-box in Peto's presence, open my mouth wide, and roar until Peto screamed, and then I put it back in the ice-box. Caroline ate it for breakfast the next morning, and though she went through the motions of confessing to Peto, he never believed her, and was always convinced that I ate it raw. Furthermore, she knew this.

As to my poems, the Gyroscope edition which I once sent you—I will send you another if you have lost it—contains everything up to that point which I will include and a few things which I probably will not include. As to the other stuff—mostly later—there isn't much, but I will try to send it off in the next few weeks.

I am busy and tired to the edge of real sickness, but the situation here in some respects is improving. That is, the hope for a real program in American literature here seems to have collapsed; so I shall stop carrying two men's work in the hope of getting help. Next year I am dropping a seminar, and I will accept no more Ph. D. dissertations till I get my list pared down to five or six. Right now I am engaged in 12, am committed to two more, and will almost certainly inherit another as a result of Clarence Faust's leaving us. No one else has more than 5, and only two have that.

Give my regards to Percy, and my love to Caroline, Nancy, and the babies.

As ever, / Arthur

MS: Princeton, Allen Tate Papers

Feb. 25, 1951 / 101 West Portola Ave. / Los Altos, Calif.

Dear Miss Yamamoto:

I can understand your feeling about fellowships. However, you had better continue to write on Sundays and to do a little reading in the evenings.

"The Spark" is the weak spot in that series. I should have warned you. Your comments on the Melville are childish, however. In the first place the story is based on a real incident actually reported by Captain Delano. The incident occurred at a real period, when people really had certain beliefs about Negroes and acted upon them. The Negroes themselves actually practiced slavery, and most of the Negroes brought to this country were bought from Negro traders. If you were suddenly transported into that era you would dislike it, but if you had been born into it, who knows? In any event, Delano is carefully portrayed by Melville as the blandly mediocre man of good will and no perception (he misunderstands everything); Cereno as a man of too good a heart to operate within the framework of a slave society—that is, he should either have improved his mind or hardened his heart; and Babo as a man of ability in whom evil becomes dominant as a result, if you like, of injustice, but of injustice which neither he nor anyone else in the story understands. The story is one of the most curious and profound studies of evil I have ever read. To "root" for Babo is silly; you might just as well root for Charlotte in *The Old Maid*—both of them are stuck in history. And you, too, will be stuck in history until you learn to understand it.

Under separate cover I will send you a couple of reading lists which I use in my courses. Also a couple of books. Don't be disturbed by this. I have extra copies of these items, and you do not have to tell me that you like them or even that you have looked at them.

Best wishes, / Yvor Winters

MS: DeSoto

March 15, 1951 / 101 West Portola Ave. / Los Altos, Calif.

Dear Allen:

Life goes from bad to worse. As you may recollect, Janet got a Guggenheim fellowship last year. She planned originally to go to France on March 30. I had this pretty well squelched, but the international situation seemed to be a little more stable, Janet became a gloomier and gloomier Griselda, and a few days ago I capitulated. I am not too happy about it, but I suppose she (and Danny, who is going with her) will get back. I mean, I hope so.

They leave here by plane the 20th, and after a couple of stops will arrive in N.Y. on the 24th. They sail on the Queen Whosit on the 30th. Janet would like to meet you and Caroline if possible, though she will have to see a number of people and you will doubtless be busy. It may be impossible to arrange a crossing of paths. I don't know where she will be staying, but she may be staying with Isabelle Taylor of Doubleday. Anyway, the Doubleday office will be her first port of call and they will have the dope on her. Isabelle Taylor and Donald Elder are most likely to know the score. If you think you could arrange a meeting, you might leave a message there in advance. If you can't, don't let it worry you. The notice is short, the time is short, and life is short, and all of us are aware of these facts.

Give my love to Caroline, Nancy, and the babies; my esteem (mingled with a mild and non-poisoned kind of jealousy) to Percy.

And for the rest, please accept the prayers of your unregenerate friend and admirer,

Arthur

MS: Princeton, Allen Tate Papers

TO HENRY RAMSEY

July 8, 1951 / 101 West Portola Ave. / Los Altos, Calif.

Dear Henry:

I have your letter of June 28. I am very grateful for your kindness to Janet and Danny. From all accounts they had a marvelous time.

I confess I should have been nervous about leaving Danny over there; not so much because of the international situation, since he would have been in the hands of the State Department, but because of the complications of getting him home. However, I gave my permission. Two days later I had a cable from Janet saying that Danny would return with her, and a few days later a letter saying that she had counted on me to veto the plan and that Danny was mad as the devil at her. When I cabled my permission I had the situation pretty well figured out and was reasonably sure of what would happen. But I am tired of being the villain in the family. And as you say, it would have been good for him. For one thing he is too dependent on Janet.

I had a pretty heavy schedule last quarter, and had Janet's work as well as my own, and I am tired as the devil, so I will not try to write much of a letter. But I am very grateful for your hospitality to both of them.

My best wishes to all of you, / Arthur

MS: Stanford

TO THEODORE ROETHKE

Oct. 14, 1951 / 101 West Portola Ave. / Los Altos, Calif.

Dear Mr. Roethke:

I am sorry to have been so slow in replying to your letter. Last summer was technically my "quarter off," but I did nothing all summer save read doctoral dissertations and assist in doctoral examinations. We are short-handed in American literature at present, and I am the only hand in criticism, and as a result I have about three times as much graduate research as anyone else in the department.

As to the poems:

"Winter Words" I do not like at all. It is compounded of unrealized figures of speech, and is trite as regards the figures and vague as regards the theme, inch by inch. It is a perfect example of the modern fallacy that everything must be stated in terms of the concrete, even if the statement be both trite and vague. There is no harm in using the concrete if you make it work—as Valéry does, for example—but it is not a sine qua non of good poetry: some of the greatest poetry ever written is all but devoid of it. And as Ezra Pound remarked many years ago, if you are going to use a symbolic hawk, the hawk must first of all be a good hawk; he might have added that it must secondly be an exact representation of that which it is supposed to represent. In "*Le Cimetière Marin,*" Valéry makes the sun his symbol of the Aristotelian prime mover, and the sea his primary symbol of the material universe. When he writes:

> Midi le juste y compose de feux
> La mer, la mer, toujours recommencée

the description as such is startlingly exact, and the description carries an immediately perceptible charge of abstract meaning. In this poem of yours, you fail in every respect.

"Elegy for Jane" is pleasanter as regards the details, but it is merely an impressionistic bit of prose broken up into lines. You do not understand free verse, and the poem is loose rhythmically and too long.

I found approximately these same defects throughout your second book. I am sorry but so it is.

Best wishes, / Yvor Winters

MS: UW

TO SEYMOUR GRESSER

Stanford University / Department of English /
Stanford University, California / Nov. 20, 1951

Dear Mr. Gresser:

Your poems strike me as worth very little. I am too busy & too tired to try to criticize them & I could not explain much to you by writing letters anyway. I assume, for example, that you have read my criticism, since you sent me these, yet these represent the kind of loose writing to which I have been objecting for years, & the fact has not, it would seem, occurred to you. About the best advice I can give you is to read as many poets as you can, especially in the 16th & 17th centuries & try to find out what poetry is.

Sincerely yours, / Yvor Winters

MS: UConn

Dec. 17, 1951 / 101 West Portola Ave. / Los Altos, Calif.

Dear Mr. Gresser:

My letter to you of last November was neither pompous nor rude. Yours to me is both. However, I am not shocked, for I have had so many letters like yours over the past 15 years that I am used to them, and merely find them an irritating bore. I have shown your letter to the secretary of my department, and she has promised to write me a form letter to deal with such situations in the future.

Let me rehearse the situation briefly, however. You sent me some poems and asked my opinion of them and I gave it. If you had not been willing to accept an adverse opinion you should have had the ordinary wit not to send them.

I said that I could not write you a detailed criticism. This is a matter of fact. I am 51 years old, the worse for wear, and overworked. Furthermore, I believe that nothing can be explained in brief exchanges, either of letters or of conversation. You say that you have read my criticism. I reiterate, that if you have read it, you ought to know that I would not like the poems. I have published several hundred pages of criticism, and anything that I could add in a letter would be worth very little. If you were here and could attend my courses for a year, I might be able to help you.

As to Crane, my opinion of him is in print. He was born with genius and threw most of the genius away, as a result of a preposterous philosophy and an unsound conception of poetry. You appeared to be imitating his weaknesses in a pretty feeble manner and to be unaware of his virtues. The poems which you sent me appeared to be about very little and to be badly written in detail.

If I answered all the people who write me as you wrote me, I should have to neglect my professional duties rather seriously. Nevertheless, had your poems shown any talent, I would have answered you in detail. I gave you the best advice which I could give you in brief space: to study the poets of the 16th and 17th centuries. Take it or leave it.

You appear to be young. I trust you will grow up.

Sincerely yours, / Yvor Winters

MS: UConn

Jan. 19, 1952 / 101 West Portola Ave. / Los Altos, Calif.

Dear Miss Yamamoto:

Many thanks for the picture of Paul. He looks fat and happy and charming. If that thing in his hand is a sandwich, part of the reason for his expression is clear. I once saw a photograph of Henry James at a garden party; he was similarly fat, he was holding a cup in one hand, a large old-fashioned cruller in the other, and he looked quite as happy as Paul and in much the same way. And not a bit subtler.

Our writing fellowships here have been renewed for another five years, in case you should ever feel inclined to try for one. Next year we shall start using the first fellowships of the renewal. Have you published any more stories? If so, where? I can find most of the normal publications (and some others) in the Stanford library.

I hope that your friend, the Zen mystic (his name escapes me), has managed to maintain his physical health.

Last summer was my quarter off. This means that I received no salary for it and was supposed to devote myself to writing and research. Actually I did nothing but read doctoral dissertations, give doctoral examinations, and do a little reading for the fall quarter. Perhaps I can do better next summer, but I am carrying the work of two men, or near it, and old age is catching up on me rapidly.

I was in Pasadena on the day of the Stanford-USC game, but not for the sake of the game. I was down for the funeral of my sister's husband [Wessel Smitter], and I had no time to look you up. I have not exhibited a dog in more than a year: my best dog, Black Jack, is so powerful, and in the ring he becomes so savage, that I have about decided to retire him. Anyway, he has his championship and won a good deal of glory over a number of years. I have bred his three-year-old daughter to a very fine dog, and if I get a good bitch pup, I will probably start invading the south again. In which case I'll try to look you up.

Best wishes to you and Paul, / Yvor Winters

MS: DeSoto

TO VAN WYCK BROOKS

Stanford University / Stanford, California /
English Department / March 4, 1952

Mr. Van Wyck Brooks /
National Institute of Arts & Letters / New York City
Dear Mr. Brooks:

I have just received your letter notifying me that I have been awarded a grant of one thousand dollars by the National Institute of Arts & Letters. Naturally, I am gratified, & I will try to be present at the annual ceremony. I will write definitely of this matter in a day or two.

Please inform me, however, of the nature of the costume I am supposed to wear. I am a country boy & do not own a tux & do not like to wear one. But I will do my best to make myself respectable for the occasion if you will instruct me. These remarks about costume are written in dead seriousness.

One other matter: You people have me attached to the wrong university. I would be grateful if your press announcement were correct in regard to this.

Sincerely yours, Yvor Winters /
Professor of English / Stanford University

MS: Academy

Van Wyck Brooks (1886–1963): American scholar, critic, and educator.

TO FELICIA GEFFEN

March 11, 1952 / 101 West Portola Ave. / Los Altos, Calif.
Dear Miss Geffen:

Many thanks for your letter of March 7. It relieves me of a vast weight of uncertainty and perturbation.

Forgive me if I ask you one or two more questions. If I am to be there on Wednesday, May 28, I shall have to fly east on Tuesday night, and I shall have to be back in the class-room at Stanford the following Tuesday. Even this will involve my cutting classes for three days. I would prefer to fly west Monday morning rather than Monday night, for two reasons: I would like to look out the window at North America as I pass over it; and I would like to get a night's sleep before I start teaching again. This will give me four days (after Wednesday) in or near New York. I would like to see a few of my friends, most of them faculty, or graduate students, at Harvard, or else members of the Airedale Terrier Club of America. Will there be any additional business after the Ceremonial? Or will that be the end of my formal obligations? This may sound harsh and practical, and I don't mean it that way. But if there are any social complications connected with the business, I would like to know about them before I make other plans.

I am sorry to bother you with so many questions.

Sincerely yours, / Yvor Winters

MS: Academy

Felicia Geffen (1903–1994): executive director of the American Academy of Arts and Letters.

TO HISAYE YAMAMOTO

March 20, 1952 / 101 West Portola Ave. / Los Altos, Calif.

Dear Miss Yamamoto:

I have just read your misguided letter, and am asking you to reconsider. Don't go Zen on me; don't go Whitmanian on me. I phoned Stegner and warned him that you might withdraw, so that he could choose a reserve in case you were in the top four; but I said that I was going to write and try to change your mind. Stegner says that no decision will be reached in all likelihood before the end of April; he himself has not even looked at the mss. yet. So you have a little time to think it over.

I don't know exactly what is eating you, but you sound a bit panicked. Maybe you have heard things about Stanford. It is a big, tough university. It is a rich kids' playground. And so on. As far as the undergraduates are concerned, most of them are rich, but some go through on scholarships and odd jobs. The graduates, who constitute almost half of the population, and with whom you would be associating if you were here, are mostly rather poor. Some veterans, many intelligent kids from all over the country, who come in and get part-time teaching jobs and fellowships of various kinds and struggle through. Next year there will be two former holders of the poetry fellowship on the campus, one working for the Ph. D., one holding down a job in the Press, both of them nice girls; there will be a very intelligent former holder of a fiction fellowship working for the Ph. D. I have already picked my two fellows in poetry for next year, and they are both fine people. There are other extremely intelligent students

interested in writing. They probably know more than you in the way of scholarship; but they have no more talent. They are nice people, I give you my word
of honor: not rich bums, not snobs, not nasty wise-crackers, but nice people,
and you would like them and they would like you. Furthermore, they would be
good for you. You could learn more from talking with them than you could from
most of the courses. And they would admire your work.

The land is not the only fundamental. It is O.K. if you don't get mystical
about it. But your mind is important, too. A year here would do a lot for your
mind and your art; and at the end of the year the land would still be there, and
you would be better prepared for it and for other things. I am beginning to
think that it is you and not Paul who are afraid to go away from home.

If you get the fellowship and come up here, we will put you up for a few
days; we won't leave you and Paul in the gutter. And we'll help you to find a
place to live.

Think it over once, or twice, or three times, again.

Yvor Winters

MS: DeSoto

TO FELICIA GEFFEN

March 20, 1952 / 101 West Portola Ave. / Los Altos, Calif.

Dear Miss Geffen:

Many thanks for your second letter, with all the detailed information. You
may be sure that I will attend your party and will stay to the very end. Furthermore it will be a great pleasure.

Your information, however, will enable me to plan in advance. A few years
ago I gave a couple of lectures at Princeton and had a few days there. I was treated
very kindly, but everything I did was planned for me, and I had no opportunity
to do several things that I wanted to do. This time I intend to plan for myself.

I have written the secretary of the Airedale Terrier Club of America to learn
if there will be a dog show within reach, so that I can see a few of the eastern
Airedales and meet some of the breeders. After that I will arrange for a visit to
Harvard. And by the time my friends know that I am coming back my schedule will be made up. My literary and academic friends regard my interest in
dogs as trivial and are inclined to assume that I will push it aside for any little
literary gathering. They are wrong. I have bred dogs since I was 14 years old, I

am good at it, I am known clear across the country as a breeder and fancier, and I like to meet dog people. The members of the Airedale Terrier Club will take me in as an old friend anywhere I go, even though they may not have met me personally. There is one enthusiastic and elderly lady in N.Y. whom I wish in particular to circumvent without being forced to overt rudeness. The last time I was back she took up an entire day dragging me around to places which I would have preferred to avoid.

If there is anything which you think I ought to do in N.Y. in the way of meeting literary people, beyond the limits of the Ceremony and the following party, please let me know, and I will endeavor to work it in.

Many thanks for your kindness.

Yvor Winters

MS: Academy

TO HANNAH JOSEPHSON

March 28, 1952 / 101 West Portola Ave. / Los Altos, Calif.

Dear Mrs. Josephson:

I have your letter of March 21. I am sorry that I cannot provide you with any mss. of the sort you request. I seldom write an essay on anything until I have lectured on the subject in the classroom for two or three years. After that I have the subject down pretty firmly in mind and sit down to my typewriter and run off a draft. After that I read the draft, put check-marks in the margin, and retype the draft, expanding, cutting, correcting. When this is done, I burn the first draft and revise portions of the second. Along about there I am through. I have no more sentiment about my old mss. than I have about my old socks, and I never save them. I have not the vaguest idea of what may have become of old galley proofs. It is my devout hope that they are lost. I ought to have gone through my books and made notes for future corrections, for I know that there is reason for corrections. But I have been so busy and so tired that I have not done it. If I live to the age of retirement, 13 years hence, I may have time and energy left to attend to this genuinely serious business. But for the past ten or twelve years I have been living on the ragged edge of my health and my strength, and I have not been able to do it.

I can provide you with first editions of some of my books if you want them. In all likelihood you can pick up enough there for your purposes, but if not, please let me know. I promise you that I will do my best to co-operate so far as co-operation is within my power.

Best wishes, / Yvor Winters

MS: Academy

Hannah Josephson: American Academy of Arts and Letters librarian.

TO FELICIA GEFFEN

March 28, 1952 / 101 West Portola Ave. / Los Altos, Calif.

Dear Miss Geffen:

I have a letter from Mrs. Josephson, which I have answered to the best of my ability, a letter from your publicity directors, which I will presently answer to the best of my ability, and a letter from you which I herewith answer to the best of my ability.

My schedule is now shaping up as follows: I will fly east the night of May 27th and be with you for everything on May 28th. On Saturday the 31st I will be in Dedham, Mass. for the specialty show of the Airedale Terrier Club of New England. I shall be the guest of the club for lunch and for the special ceremony of drinking punch out of the Airedale Bowl (Airedale Terrier Club of America) after the judging. This item is my concession to what you people will doubtless regard as my lower nature. But I am a member of the Airedale Terrier Club of America, as I think I have said, and a member of the California Airedale Terrier Club, and a member of the Southern California Airedale Terrier Association, and I shall be an honored guest. I detect a fine undertone of very gentle irony in your letters. Spare me. The breeding of Airedales is quite as fine an art as the creation of miniature sculptures. The products are impermanent, but may be nonetheless beautiful. I have bred many show winners and my share of champions and group winners, and I have bred one best-in-show winner, but I have bred only one whom I consider a fine work of art. I am grateful to providence that he is still with me and that I can still look at him. And I am grateful to providence that I now have six of his grandchildren, not quite four weeks old.

As to the matter of invitations. I confess that I am more or less baffled by the problem. I have spent my entire life in the remote west, where men are civilized but never get within gunshot of each other. I had never been east of Gary until about three years ago, when I flew back to give a couple of lectures at

Princeton; and up until that time I had never been so far east as Chicago since 1921. I simply don't have any personal friends among the literary people in N.Y. The few acquaintances I have back there, except for reservations which will follow hereinafter, are people whom I would just as soon duck.

As to the oldest generation of American poets, the only one who moves me very profoundly is Wallace Stevens; but he is more than 20 years my senior and is not even mildly interested in me, and I would feel it presumptuous to send him an invitation on this occasion. I have a limited admiration for W. C. Williams, but again see no reason why he should be interested in me. I would like you to send an invitation on my behalf to Miss Marianne Moore, provided she will not be there anyway. Many years ago, when I was stuck in the coal camps of New Mexico, Miss Moore used to write me letters and send me books from the N.Y. Public Library. I have never met her face to face, but I have always been grateful for her patience and kindness, and I think she would understand my reason for sending her an invitation.

As to the people of my own generation, I would enjoy seeing Louise Bogan, whose poetry I admire very deeply, and whom I knew slightly more than 25 years ago, Stanley Kunitz (if you know where to find him), Allen and Caroline Tate (except that they will be embedded in the deep southern spring in Minneapolis), and K. A. Porter if she is not lost in South Africa or her dreams. I would enjoy seeing Robert Fitzgerald once more: he was my guest in California a good many years back, and I met him again at Tate's apartment when I was last in N.Y. And please send an invitation to J. V. Cunningham, Dept. of English, U. of Chicago. He will not be able to come, but he is the greatest poet now writing in English and one of my few close friends. I have some acquaintance with all of the above save Kunitz. I admire his poetry a great deal, and would enjoy meeting him.

In addition, I would be grateful if you would send invitations to the following. I doubt that any of them can come, for practical reasons, but they are old friends and I would like to send them invitations.

Professor & Mrs. Albert J. Guerard / 18 Hilliard Ave. / Cambridge, Mass.

Professor & Mrs. Albert Léon Guérard / The Ambassador / Cambridge 38 / Mass.

Mr. and Mrs. W. W. Trimpi Jr. / Molder Hall B-11 / Harvard University / Cambridge, Mass.

Mr. and Mrs. Lee F. Gerlach / Taber Academy / Marion, Mass.

To return to my schedule, I will probably go up to Harvard Thursday morning; then to Dedham for the show on Saturday morning. After the show I will return either to N.Y. or to Harvard—as yet I don't know. I shall fly west Monday morning.

Many thanks for your patience.

Yvor Winters

MS: Academy

TO HISAYE YAMAMOTO

April 5, 1952 / 101 West Portola Ave. / Los Altos, Calif.

Dear Miss Yamamoto:

Since you appear to be sot in your way, I have notified Stegner. However, I asked him to read your material, anyway, and he said he would; so you may not get it back immediately.

I have never seen *The Catholic Worker* and have never heard of the Catholic Workers. I hope you have checked up on them and made sure that they are solvent, really Catholic and not something else, etc. If you have done so and wish to go ahead, there is no harm in trying it, except that you will be a long way from home if you change your mind. I hope that you have considered the fact that you will be at least five feet away from The Good Earth during five months of the year. I hope you can use snowshoes. However, you may like it. Me, I am a Californian, and I don't like anything about the country back there.

I will wish you luck and give you my blessing on one condition: that you write me occasionally and tell me how you are getting along, and whether you have published anything and where.

You will be a Catholic in less than two years.

My very best wishes and affection
to you and Paul, / Yvor Winters

MS: DeSoto

June 29, 1952 / 101 West Portola Ave. / Los Altos, Calif.

Dear Miss Geffen:

I arrived safely among my little works of art on the Monday after the Ceremony. Flew the whole trip by day and had a window seat. It was really wonderful. Unfortunately the end of the spring quarter is pretty hectic at best, and I was almost a week behind on a lot of business when I got here, and my capacity for work is not what it once was, and I am just beginning to crawl out from under the papers. I had meant to write you sooner than this and thank you for your kindness, but I have had no opportunity.

The whole trip was pretty strenuous. On May 27th I ate a light supper at 6 P.M. and got my plane at 9:45. At 3 A.M. California time, dawn came up over Des Moines, and they served us two small sweet rolls and a couple of cups of coffee. Sweet rolls nauseate me, but I ate them. At something after 8 Chicago time, we got some more coffee and more breakfast of which over half was sweet rolls. This time I passed the rolls up. The plane was late in N.Y., and I barely had time to get to a hotel, get cleaned up, and get over to the ceremony. Because of the peculiarities of plane seats and the state of my health, I cannot sleep in a plane. The result of all this was that by 6 P.M. of May 28th I had had no food except that which I mentioned for a matter of 24 hours, and had had no sleep for 36 hours. Furthermore I had not had a chance to get a drink, and I discovered too late that only cigarettes can be smoked on a plane, and since I derive about half my nourishment from a pipe, I was all in all in a bad way. The party after the Ceremony was so vast that I was lost, and I was so tired I could hardly stand. So about 6 P.M. I gathered up two of my friends and went to a nearby bar for a couple of bourbons and then got back to my hotel for some food and sleep. I was sorry to miss you in the mob, but I was so bushed that I couldn't stay around.

The dog show in N.E. was excellent, and I saw some old friends at Harvard. The Ceremony was interesting, but the mechanics of it and the quality of the oratory could unquestionably be improved. I think I have never heard so many discredited ideas expressed in such astoundingly cliché language. I don't want to sound harsh or ungrateful, but it was really very bad.

Best wishes, / Yvor Winters

MS: Academy

August 14, 1953 / 101 West Portola Ave. / Los Altos, Calif.

Dear Louise:

I am doing something which I hope you will forgive. I am sending a young woman to see you in the hopes that you will be able to give her a little advice about how to get along in New York. The story follows.

The young woman is Miss Catherine Davis. She is about 28 or 29. She held one of our $2000 fellowships in writing a few years ago, and is one of the four or five best poets I have taught in about 25 years at Stanford. In my opinion she is one of the really fine young poets in the country, but she is a pretty rigid perfectionist and has published very little. She grew up in extreme poverty and in pretty rough surroundings and has had a hard life all the way. She is slightly spastic, though if you saw her you would think that the trouble came from polio. At any rate, the entire left side is somewhat affected: left eye about worthless, left hand, arm, leg and foot, somewhat shrunken and only semi-efficient instruments. She has supported herself thus far, as best she has been able, by library work and office work, but office work is now largely conducted by machines, and with only one really good hand she can't operate the things. The only thing that she or I could see that might work out is some kind of editorial work— magazine or publishing house—where her handicap wouldn't matter and her really remarkable intelligence would matter. She has a first rate critical mind, but at the same time has the sort of practicality which would enable her to judge a ms. in terms of the audience at which it is aimed, so that I don't believe her literary gift would handicap her as a reader for a publisher. She would be extremely valuable in judging almost any kind of expository work and in suggesting revisions if they seemed in order.

From time to time, as she has had a little money, she has taken university courses, but she has no degree. At one time or another she has studied under R. P. Warren, Tate, Jim Cunningham, and myself. During the year she was at Stanford she picked up all the poetry prizes, and if I remember rightly you were one of the judges for the main prize and placed her first.

She is extremely small, but is rather pretty, and if she could afford good clothes would be very pretty. When you first meet her she is likely to be tense and shy, but when she relaxes she is very good company.

She would be a very useful person in some publishing or magazine office, or perhaps in the office of a good agent—provided only that she could get in.

If you could give her any advice, or could introduce her to some one who could help her in any way, I would be extraordinarily grateful.

Best wishes from Janet and myself, / Arthur

She worked for about ten months at the Stanford press as a copy editor, and is very capable at that kind of thing, but I think she deserves a slightly better job. She will probably stay temporarily with another former student of mine, Miss Marion McClanahan, 42 Union Square West (I think it is West, but the name is in the phone book).

MS: Amherst

TO THEODORE ROETHKE

Sept. 19, 1953 / 101 West Portola Ave. / Los Altos, Calif.

Dear Mr. Roethke:

Many thanks for your note and for the book.

I don't like "The Waking." It seems pretty facile, and repetition of lines is almost always the last resort of the desperate poet.

"Four Poems for Sir John Davies" contains nice work: stanza 2 of I, for example, and the last three lines of III. But Yeats did you no good. My own opinion of Yeats, of course, is heretical and incorrect; it is one of the more obvious evidences of my pedantic simple-mindedness. Nevertheless, I believe that Yeats is fantastically overestimated; that his worst faults are facile emotionalism, foolish self-dramatization, trite language, and a complete inability to think. The first and third of these faults appear in your four poems rather obviously. The poems are not tough enough, not compact enough, not definite enough. It is easy to go on a binge and even to display a certain amount of talent while on a binge. It is damned hard to write a good poem.

"The Heron" is much less ambitious than these last poems, and the rhythms are much more naive. Yet the poem does what it attempts; it is fine description, with no funny stuff; it seems to me more honest.

My opinions, you may be sure, will not be those of your reviewers. Whether they will be those of posterity, and if so of how remote a posterity, are matters of opinion. But I honestly don't think you realize as yet what poetry really is.

Best wishes, / Yvor Winters

MS: UW

Feb. 21, 1954 / 101 West Portola Ave. / Los Altos, Calif.

Dear Miss Yamamoto:

Thanks for your N.Y.'s Day note. I wonder how you and Paul and the little rabbits are making out in the cold weather.

I saw your review.[1] It was very kind, but when you set out to praise me with such enthusiam, why did you spend four-fifths of the review enumerating your causes for exasperation? I must be very irritating. I have always regarded myself as a gentle and fatherly soul. Most of the reviews have been similar, and I am a bit perplexed by it all.

I don't know whether you have access there to any literary periodicals or not, but there are some good poems from time to time in the *Hudson Review* and the *Western Review*. Keep an eye out for Edgar Bowers, Margaret Wilson Peterson,[2] and H. A. Pinkerton. All former students of mine.

You have my blessing. But I still don't understand why you went there. If you do, however, and are reasonably satisfied, it is all right.

Our best to you and Paul, / Yvor Winters

MS: DeSoto

[1]"Yvor Winters: California Poet," *Frontier* (December 1953): 13–15
[2]Margaret "Jan" Peterson (1929–1992): American poet.

TO DONALD HALL

March 20, 1954

Dear Don:

Now that I have done wearing myself weak over Snodgrass, [Cal] Thomas, and Gunn, I have begun on you.

First of all, you sometimes write very good light verse: "The Lone Ranger," for example, and epigrams xi and xii. "Epitaph" is good but is unpublishable (it would require too long a footnote, and if you published epigram and footnote, Barney [Childs] would publish a dirtier epigram and a longer footnote, and this sort of thing ought to be nipped in the bud). Epigram xv is amusing but clumsy: the idea is a pearl of great price, but the form is a run-of-the-mill oyster.

Light verse can be distinguished in this way as well as others from serious satiric or ironic verse: it employs careless rhythm and diction in a manner at once light-hearted and conscious. It is the light heart, I suppose, which makes it light verse. The consciousness keeps it from becoming bad light verse.

When similar qualities of style are carried over into serious verse, you get a kind of journalism, or an admixture of journalism, such as occurs in Auden and often enough in Yeats. I am marking what seem to me some of the more obvious examples.

I like "Rhyme of Appointed Death" less and less on reconsideration. What Bentley and Craig did was simple, brutal, and stupid; likewise the penalty. The crimes of which you accuse yourself are presumably psychological, subtle, subtly punished, and in the long run more devastating. You therefore evade the real problem [word obliterated] with these crimes: you compare them to something obvious, uninteresting, and violent: the result is melodrama.

"A Novelist": I still do not like the last stanza. I know that the suicide occurred, but you have not prepared for it, and the result again is melodrama; and in spite of the admiration of the class for the last line, I think that the diction and image are only indifferently interesting. Definitely weak lines: line 2 of st. 5 (pure redundancy); all of last stanza. The rest seems to me pretty sharp.

"The World, the Times": Stanzas 1, 4, 6, and 7 have a great deal of force. The other stanzas are passable, I suppose, but are nowhere more than passable, and the facile rush of easy magniloquence in these stanzas is a bit irritating and damages the effect of the other stanzas.

In all of the poems which I have listed there is one pervasive weakness: a mechanical and monotonous rhythm. You do not vary your line; it is heavy, obvious, and violent, and this insistent quality contributes to the effect of melodrama.

The best poems in the collection seem to me to be "Abroad Thoughts from Home" and epigram xiv; xiii is good, but less good. I have no quarrel with these poems either in execution or in conception. Both seem fine.

In general, however, you write too easily and are too easily impressed with your own resonance, or so it seems. It is a radical fault, and if uncontrolled could dilute your talent past usability. On the other hand the talent is very real, and I am sure that you can control this tendency if you can see it clearly. This is not a project for the spring quarter, but for the rest of your life.

Your work shows vigor of thought and frequent vigor and compactness of expression; but it shows very often a kind of coarseness of execution. This is your problem.

Yvor Winters

"At Delphi" is nicely done, but is little more than pretty.

MS: UNH

Donald Hall (b. 1928): American poet, critic, and editor.

TO CHARLES GULLANS

August 4, 1954 / 101 West Portola Ave. / Los Altos, Calif.

Dear Charles:

Thanks for your communication of July 29. You, like some of the others, seem strongly inclined to teach your grandmother how to suck eggs. I suspect that I know more about all of you than you know about each other; and sometimes I think I know more about the important aspects of each than he knows about himself.

This Great Man business gives me a pain in a place which I won't mention. There are two views of the principles which I have taught you kids: (1) they are correct, in which case they are not my property but are universals and are in the public domain, for anybody to use who has the talent to use them; (2) they are wrong, in which case it is up to you to work out something better. Jan [Margaret Peterson] seems to feel that they are largely correct but that they should be treated as if they were wrong: the result is bound to be frustration and neurosis. And it is a damned fool attitude in general. As nearly as I can make out, Jan thinks I have damaged all of you. What I was trying to do was knock a little common sense through your skulls.

If I took the same attitude toward you kids which you take toward each other, I would work myself out of a job within a year. And when I say you, I mean all of you back to the beginnings, with the possible exception of the Trimpis, who seem to have some common sense. I honestly wonder what kind of teachers you will make. Each one of you sees the flaws in each of the others. As nearly as I can understand you, you derive a kind of self-defensive gratification from this, and do your best to see little or nothing but the flaws, and you are all of you too inclined to dump each other cheerfully into the waste basket. This attitude carries over all too often into the teaching career. It has damaged J.V.C. as a teacher, and I suspect that it will damage Edgar. It damaged Don Stanford for years, but I think he has outgrown it. I take it for granted that most of the kids who fall into my hands will be largely ignorant and rattle-brained: my job is to look for any trace of intelligence which I may find and try to extend it. I am sorry that the traces are not all in the same places in the various kids, but they aren't, and we had all better try to make the best of it.

Wes imitates me, sure; and I know about his run-overs. But some of the imitations are good poems in their own right, and that makes them legitimate. The "Perseus" imitates me much less than you seem to think. The blank verse is very different from mine, and far more violent. The compression of statement, he got from me, but that is legitimate: I learned it from other people. The poem is a damned impressive poem. Jan thinks she imitates me but doesn't. I think you do occasionally in a slight degree, but I see no damage resulting. Edgar does not, but perhaps he tries almost too hard not to. I cannot see that Barney imitates me at all.

As to Barney, he is a stubborn and excessively emotional man, and he may destroy himself. Your estimate of him, however, strikes me as almost devoid of insight. You and he apparently got in each other's hair, and neither knows much about the other. As to his music, I cannot judge it professionally and neither can you. Neither can Jan. Neither can Doug [Peterson], who is a good trumpet player but little more in music. I suspect it is diffuse and perverse, but I have heard only two pieces. If my suspicion is right, the reason may be: (1) that Barney has no talent for musical composition but has some kind of emotional commitment which he has not overcome; (2) that musical composition involves problems very different from those of poetic composition, and a transfer is not easy. Or both reasons may be operative. I think it foolish to mix his music with his poetry, however, in any evaluation of his possibilities. He has written two of the best poems that have ever come from my students, and some others are respectable.

I am glad that your affairs are straightened out and that you can finish your work properly. Please bear in mind that I love Jan. She is one of the best poets I have ever taught, and by that I mean one of the four best at the largest estimate. She is a nice girl. And she is very pretty. She has everything in her favor. But I wish to God she would stand up and shake the dust out of her curls. And I wish that all the rest of you would do the same.

Best wishes, / Yvor Winters

MS: Gullans

Charles Gullans (1929–1993): American poet, critic, scholar, and educator. He was a lifelong friend of YW, although there were rifts in the friendship. YW wrote about Gullans in *Forms of Discovery* and included his work in *Quest for Reality.*

August 28, 1954 / 101 West Portola Ave. /
Los Altos, Calif. / Phone: WHitecliff 8 4597

Dear Mr. Gunn:

I have your letter of Aug. 22. Your address in Palo Alto will be 334 Lincoln Avenue. It is only a few blocks from the station, and a taxi can take you there in a few minutes. Nevertheless, I hope that you will let me meet you (if you get in before 10 P.M.). If you get in at a reasonably early hour, I would like to bring you to my house for supper. I am not a Don; I am merely a professor. My most intimate friends are Airedales, but I enjoy my poets, and during the school year I have not the time to see as much of them off the campus as I would like.

Your house is listed in the phone book under the name of Mrs. Lettie Hinds. But the woman who runs it (the one with the wig) is Mrs. Hyde. This is confusing, but this is the way it is.

I don't know whether to be pleased or not that you will see the Atlantic seaboard first, but I don't know how to prevent it either. It is a dismal province, and you will like the west the better, I suppose, for having seen the worst the first.

There is a small university in New Jersey which is called Princeton. I gave a couple of lectures there about six years ago, and the professor who introduced me said that I was the best literary critic west of the Mississippi. This was true, but it was only two-thirds of the truth. On the other hand I would have given him far more territory if he had asked for it. If you will ask your hosts for a map of the United States—I am sure they will have one—you might do this: Find the Mississippi and trace it north to the point where the Missouri comes in on the left; then trace the Missouri to the point where the Platte comes in on the left; then trace the Platte to the point where the North Platte and the South Platte join to form the Platte. Through that point draw a line directly from north to south. On the left of that line is everything that matters. On the right are the provinces.

In New Mexico and Arizona (which you will miss unless you come by the Santa Fe) the earth is red. These are good states. In California the earth is red on the western slope of the Sierras, and when you get down into the great valley, the grass will be dead and the air will be yellow. I find that I cannot endure to be far from the yellow air for very long. It is like gold to airy thinness beat, but it smells better.

Give my regards to Don and Kirby [Hall].

Yvor Winters

MS: Gunn

Thom Gunn (b.1929): British poet, critic, and educator; lifelong friend of YW.

TO LOUIS KRONENBERGER

Jan. 24, 1956 / 101 West Portola Ave. / Los Altos, Calif. /
(after Feb. 1 this address / will be 143 West Portola)

Mr. Louis Kronenberger /
National Institute of Arts and Letters /
633 West 155th St. / New York, N.Y.
Dear Mr. Kronenberger:

I wish to thank you for your letter of Jan. 16 last, and to thank the members of the Institute for electing me. Two photographs have been sent you by the News and Publications Service of Stanford University, Stanford, Calif. If you wish more they will send them. They will help you in any way that you may request with your publicity. They do not, at this writing, know what it is all about, and are a trifle indignant.

One aspect of the business bothers me. I do not know whether I can pull myself together and get back to your ceremony or not. If my presence there is essential, I shall have to think it over. I do not wish to be evasive about this: I shall not be teaching in the spring quarter and shall have no commitments. But I shall be on sabbatical leave and working on a book, and the trip will be an interruption right in the middle of things. Furthermore, I have always hated to travel, to visit, to stop at hotels, and to appear in public; and this feeling has increased to an intensity by this time which might, I suppose, be described as neurotic. Furthermore, my two brief visits to New York have left me with a hatred for New York: I do not like the size, the noise, the dirt, the smell, or the calculated rudeness of the mass of the citizenry.

And the one ceremony which I attended a few years ago left me exhausted by three hours of excessively bad oratory and rather angry at the rudeness of the various masters of ceremonies. I was irritated, for example, to be introduced as one of a number of young artists (I was past 50) by a man only five or six years older than myself, whose name I had never heard before and have never heard since. And there were others in the group as old as myself and older. And I could not understand why the gentlemen reading the citations had not learned to pronounce the names of the people whom they were publicly honoring: a dozen times, I suppose, they asked for help in public, and a few other times they ought to have asked.

Well, I am getting old, and, as you can see, am the worse for wear. I will try to organize myself with respect to this decision. Meantime, I will be grateful for such advice or information on the point as you can give me. And I am grateful for your letter.

Sincerely yours, / Yvor Winters

MS: Academy

Louis Kronenberger (b.1904): American editor, scholar, and educator.

TO HANNAH JOSEPHSON

April 6, 1956 / 143 West Portola Ave. / Los Altos, Calif.

Dear Mrs. Josephson:

Please note my new address. Same house, new number.

I appreciate your letter of April 13. You wrote me a similar letter three or four years ago. As I wrote you then, I would no more think of saving old manuscripts than of saving old socks. This whole thing strikes me as undignified, as ridiculous, as contemptible. Who in hell do writers think they are? If a writer can write something let him write it, and write it well, and set it on the record, and then withdraw from the scene.

I enclose a poem ["A Tentative Draft of an Academic Eclogue"] which I have written. It was published a good many years ago in an earlier version: I will not tell you where. This version has never been published. If you wish to pin it up on the wall, why God be with you.

Best wishes, / Yvor Winters

MS: Academy

TO ROBERT PENN WARREN

April 18, 1956 / 143 West Portola Ave. / Los Altos, Calif.
Mr. Robert Penn Warren /
National Institute of Arts and Letters / New York City
Dear Red:

I have your letter to members of the Institute regarding grants in literature.

I wish to nominate J. V. Cunningham, who is now Chairman of the Graduate School of English, at Brandeis University, Waltham, Mass.

Cunningham is about 43 or 44 years old. I enclose an incomplete list of his publications. All of the books are obtainable from Alan Swallow, 2679 South York, Denver 10, Colorado.

A good many years ago Cunningham was one of my students. I am quite aware that my students are still considered to be quite as comical as I was supposed to be a couple of years ago. I doubtless taught Cunningham something. I have learned at least as much from him as I taught him, and probably more. In my opinion he is the greatest poet now writing in English, in spite of the brevity of his poems. His prose publications are technically scholarly rather than critical, but they exhibit one of the most learned minds in the English Renaissance now writing, and perhaps the best critical mind in this country.

It would do the members of the Institute good, I believe, to study him carefully, even if they voted against him. It would do him more good to be honored by the Institute now than to be so honored twelve or fifteen years from now.

Sincerely yours, / Yvor Winters

MS: Academy

TO MALCOLM COWLEY, LOUISE BOGAN, ALLEN TATE, AND ROBERT PENN WARREN

April 28, 1956 / 143 West Portola Ave. / Los Altos, Calif.
A letter addressed to:
Malcolm Cowley, Louise Bogan, Allen Tate, and Robert Penn Warren.
Dear Malcolm, Louise, Allen and Red:

Please forgive me for addressing you in this conglomerate and carboned manner. I am old, tired, and busy. Now that I find myself a member of the Institute, it looks as if I shall have to hire a private secretary or withdraw. Yet I would like to live up to my duties as a member, if it is humanly possible, in spite of my reputedly (and really) unsociable nature. This letter may be an improper one, in some respects, to address to two of the officers. I really don't know. But a couple of the questions I shall ask should be answered by an officer, and for the rest, you are the only people in the Institute whom I feel inclined to address on certain other matters.

A couple of weeks ago, I received a formal notice from Professor Warren, asking for nominations for $1000 grants. I nominated J. V. Cunningham, and gave my reasons. Then I received a notice calling for nominations for elections to the Institute. And a day or two ago a request for nominations to honorary memberships. This is rough going for a professor of English (not a resident poet), who is on every important committee in his department, and who is pretty goddamned tired. But this is the way it is.

First of all, can a man receive a grant and be elected to the Institute in the same year? Can a member of the Institute recommend more than one recipient of a grant in the same year? Can a member of the Institute nominate more than one person for election in the same year? Can a member of the Institute nominate one man for election and second the nomination of another in the same year? These are questions for one of the officers to answer, or perhaps Miss Geffen, who, I suspect, is better informed than any of you.

If I can nominate two members for a grant in the same year, I would like to nominate J. V. Cunningham as my first choice and Stanley Kunitz as my second. If I can nominate two persons for election, I would like to nominate the same two, provided I can get seconds. If I cannot nominate two but can nominate one and second another, I would like to nominate Cunningham and second Kunitz.

There is then a legal question: can officers nominate or second? And then the personal question: would either of the officers addressed, or the other members addressed, be willing to second Cunningham or nominate Kunitz?

Stanley Kunitz is not a friend of mine. I have never met him, and I have exchanged only two or three letters with him, and those on matters of business. I just happen to admire his poems, and I think that you people have been overlooking first-rate writing in a major way for a good many years. His first book, *Intellectual Things*, appeared, I believe, in 1930, and I seem to recollect that I reviewed it in *The New Republic*. His second book, *Passport to the War*, appeared in 1944. I believe that a later book was announced a year or so ago, but I have not seen it, or any notice of it. Three of his poems—"For the Word Is Flesh,"

"The Words of the Preacher," and "Ambergris"—seem to me among the absolutely first-rate poems of our time. Kunitz is about 50 years old, or maybe more. You would do well to consider him seriously before he has a heart attack. He is—believe it or not—one of the four or five best poets of our generation. Henry King wrote only two poems worth remembering, and not one of you knows the second.[1] The first is "The Exequy." I will bet each and every one of you one dollar that you cannot name the second. The terms of the bet are these: you name your poem, and if I think you are right, I will pay, but if I think you are wrong, I will name the right poem, and if you think I am right you will pay, and if you think I am wrong I will pay. Henry King will be around for quite a while on the strength of one poem that you know and on the strength of another that your grandchildren will know. How many of the little poets in the Institute will be here that long?

Cunningham has published three books, all of which may be obtained from Alan Swallow, 2679 South York, Denver 10, Colo.: *The Helmsman* (verse), *The Judge Is Fury* (verse), *Woe or Wonder* (a critical and scholarly study of certain aspects of Shakespeare). I can have copies sent to any of you if you wish them. You should read at least the first two of the following three articles in addition: "Essence and 'The Phoenix and the Turtle'" (*A Journal of English Literary History*, Vol. 18, No. 4), "Logic and Lyric" (*Modern Philology*, Vol. LI, No. 1), and "The Literary Form of the Prologue to the *Canterbury Tales*" (*Mod. Phil.* XLIX, 3). Cunningham is a very great man. His verse is great and his prose is great.

If one has to choose between a grant and election, I myself would vote for election, simply for the honor of the Institute. These elections have been too long deferred.

Your country cousin, / Yvor Winters

P.S. If any one of you knows how to break into Glenway Wescott's house and would get all of my early poems out and burn them, you would earn my undying gratitude. I was appalled to see that some of this trash had been exhibited at the Institute. This is a violation of privacy, and it is an activity beneath the dignity of serious adults.

MS: Academy

[1]The poem in question is "The Dirge." See *Forms of Discovery*, p. 88.

May 2, 1956 / 143 West Portola Ave. / Los Altos, Calif.

Dear Malcolm:

Thanks for your paternal letter. It isn't so much a matter of mood as of facts. The goddamned book I am working on now is something that I started in my late twenties and have had to keep putting aside for other jobs. It will be dull reading. But it will be useful to the young who are trying to find out something about the nature and the history of poetry. I know it all by heart, because I have been teaching it in a course for years, and for that reason, I suppose, I hate the bother of writing it. If I can just get through the later seventeenth century, which I find exasperating, I can handle the rest of it more rapidly. But for several years I have found it hard to concentrate in the company of a typewriter. As to poetry, I am nearly written out. I have no intention of kidding myself, as Stevens did in his last 25 years or as Allen seems to be doing now with his curious terza rima slip-slop. I would be willing to settle for a few very minor poems if they were good, but no ambitious hogwash. In fact no hogwash. And I suspect that everyone has just about so many poems in him. Stevens really could handle only one theme: that of the isolated nominalist, in an impersonal universe, confronted by death. It is a major theme, but you can't do it over and over. He did it superbly in "Of the Manner of Addressing Clouds," in "Of Heaven Considered as a Tomb," in "Domination of Black," and in "The Course of a Particular" (the one great poem of his old age, which he didn't include in his final volume). In "Sunday Morning" he sugared the situation with hedonism, and this led to his downfall (see my essay). The fake Platonism of his last years is simply an attempt to disguise his own convictions from himself.

It is a fact that I have become bored with people. I had to learn many years ago not to discuss literary matters with my colleagues: a casual expression of like or dislike would arouse festering resentment, simply because I "thought I was" a poet or a critic or something. My contemporaries in the Stanford department have outgrown that now, and I like all of them except one son-of-a-bitch whom you probably didn't meet, John Dodds. But the habit is fixed. On the other hand, you people, my literary colleagues, in the main just don't know enough: about the history of ideas, the handling of ideas, the details of the history of poetry, and so on. Louise, for example, was given by God one of the finest poetic talents of our time; but she is ignorant as the devil, and she remains ignorant on principle, and she has remained a minor poet (though a fine one in a dozen poems), and she prefers her bad poems to her good. I feel lost in either camp. I can talk with Jim Cunningham or with Edgar Bowers about the things that most interest me, and there it ends. I cannot discuss poetry with old R. F. Jones, although he invariably tries to force me to discuss it; but his book *The Triumph of the English Language* casts more light on the critical problems which most interest me (problems which he does not understand) than do all the critical works of Brooks, Blackmur, Tate, and the rest, which I find pretty damn muddled. I say this regretfully, because I am fond of Allen; but he again has refused to learn the obvious—about ideas and about the writing of poetry—all the way through his career.

[Jackson] Matthews was through here a few years ago, and talked about his project. I would never undertake a poetical translation of Valéry. I could do a prose translation, to serve as a guide to the reader with a little French, but I don't believe that he wants that. And I wish to finish my damned book on the history of the short poem before undertaking anything else. At the rate I am going, it will take me the rest of my life.

You will learn more about my neuroses when you read my long essay in the Fall *Hudson* ["Problems for the Modern Critic of Literature"].

Our best to both of you, / Yvor Winters

MS: Newberry

TO MALCOLM COWLEY

May 4, 1956 / 143 West Portola Ave. / Los Altos, Calif.

Dear Malcolm:

The letter I wrote the other day may have seemed unfriendly to you and others. I did not mean it to be so. I was trying to clarify things.

I am very fond of R. F. Jones, for example, and I owe him a great deal. When W. D. Briggs died, he was succeeded by Arthur Garfield Kennedy, as head of our department. Kennedy was a very patient bibliographer and philologist, and a stupid and malignant man. When Herb Meritt first came here as a young philologist, Briggs said to him: You will be working in a large measure under Professor Kennedy; I feel that I ought to say something about him so that you will understand him: he has filed and kept all of his laundry bills for the past thirty years. Briggs died early in 1940, as nearly as I can remember, and Kennedy succeeded him, and was head of the department for about five or six years. Kennedy hated Briggs and everyone whom Briggs had liked. Briggs had managed to have me promoted to an associate professorship just before he died, and Kennedy couldn't get rid of me without an AAUP scandal. John Dodds was already dean of humanities and already hated my guts because I thought I was a poet and a critic. Dodds, as dean, made himself more bitterly hated all over the campus than anyone save the president whom he maneuvered into office and controlled: Donald Tresidder. Kennedy and Dodds reported my faults, real or imagined, to Tresidder in great detail, and did the same for Cunningham. Cunningham was a mere instructor and could be fired: he was fired. Briggs, a few months before his death, had told me that he considered Cunningham a very great scholar, and hoped that he could be kept in the department. Tresidder died after a few years in office, and there is some reason to believe that it was suicide. He had muffed his job, and knew it, and admitted publicly on one occasion that the faculty had no respect for him. Tresidder was succeeded by Alvin Eurich as acting president (for about a year), and Eurich by Clarence Faust, who was acting president for about six months, before Sterling became president. Dodds was out of his deanship by this time, and Faust had succeeded him. Old R. F. became head of the department in about 1945, and retired five or six years later. When he came, he had Tresidder as president, Eurich as vice-president, and Dodds as dean. He was the shrewdest academic politician I have ever seen in action. He set to work at once to have me promoted, but did not succeed until Faust became acting president. He managed to get my salary raised each year, but no promotion. He put me on a professor's teaching schedule at once; Kennedy had kept me on the schedule of an assistant professor. This was quite an accomplishment, for a year or so earlier Tresidder had told a group of protesting students that he would do nothing to force Mr. Winters to leave and nothing to encourage him to stay. When Jones arrived, my salary was $3,500 a year. Bear in mind that I was 44 or 45 years old, and that most of the verse and prose which I now have to my credit was then in print. During these years my literary colleagues ignored my work, or misrepresented it demonstrably, or referred to it occasionally as a joke. They provided weapons, in brief, for Kennedy, Dodds, and Tresidder. The people who came to my rescue were R. F. Jones and Clarence Faust, and later Virgil Whitaker, the present head of the department. Believe me, I am grateful to these people, and I am fond of them. But they are children when they talk about poetry, and I am literally afraid to get into a discussion with any of them (or any of my colleagues), except Whitaker, who is tough of mind and of temperament and has at least a few perceptions. On the other hand, Jones, Whitaker, Meritt, Ackerman, and Johnson could make better critics of you and Allen and Louise and Cleanth Brooks and Blackmur if you could study under them for about three years and adapt some of their knowledge to your own purposes. I have learned a great deal from them.

Just after you arrived I stepped into your office to greet you and you said something for which I have not quite forgiven you yet; you said: "You disagree with everybody." This was almost a direct quotation from old Pa Kennedy: "Waal, Winters, everybody seems to be out of step but yew."

I am a little tired of being brushed off this way. I am a better scholar than any of you people, by a wide margin; and I suspect I am a better poet, though that is hard for me to judge. I have explained my beliefs, both theoretical and particular, in some detail. If there is something wrong, it is a matter for demonstration not for a superior remark. I have laid my cards on the table, and I shall be laying more on it this fall. Furthermore, you would be surprised how many people agree with me: mostly young scholars and poets, who will be taking over the situation within the next decade or so. Well, so much for my irritation.

At any rate, it is this kind of thing that has driven me into a sort of spiritual isolation and, I suppose, depression. There is no real cure for the situation now, but I shall not commit suicide or go mad; so don't be disturbed about me. I shall merely try to go ahead with my job as best I am able.

And I really became very fond of you and Muriel when you were out here. So did Janet.

Dixi. No more of this.

Yvor Winters

MS: Newberry

TO MALCOLM COWLEY

May 6, 1956 / 143 West Portola Ave. / Los Altos, Calif.

Dear Malcolm:

Thanks for your composition on folkways. I may say that I dislike most folkways, but I don't expect to reform the Institute immediately, and have so much work laid up that I shall doubtless stop trying after one or two more blasts.

Some of your folkways seem remarkably like those of departments of English. For example: we will hire, fire, and promote or refuse to promote on the basis of book-reviews; of course we know, perfectly well, that we would not trust one in ten of the reviewers to handle a class in freshman composition, but we are too lazy to evaluate the work of our colleagues, and, after all, publicity is publicity. Since I became a professor, a couple of years before I received my grant from the Institute, I have been working on this one in the executive committee of our department, and I have just about got it discredited. For example: we don't like people who are hard to get along with. But what does this mean? Obviously a man must do his teaching, committee work, and so on, and discuss departmental business with his colleagues without violence. But if he has a sharp tongue, in meetings or at parties, what then? The department is a social club among other things, and each one of us is a part owner. Well, I have pretty damn near got rid of that one too, though it is common in the universities generally. It seems to me to represent not merely a dereliction from duty but an active betrayal of duty. The duty is to maintain the department at the highest possible intellectual level, and let personal irritation go to hell. For example: Pa Kennedy had no racial or religious prejudices, but he felt that the introduction of a Jew into his department would diminish the community of feeling. Well, Pa has gone to his reward, whatever it may be, and we have two Jews and are considering another, and everybody seems to be happy.

As I told you, I know nothing about Kunitz, except that I am told that he is doing a good job at Washington this year, where he is substituting for Roethke. And I know that when you have bad administration, the air gets full of knives. I note in the little purple book, however, that among your members is a man who did a stretch in San Quentin for homosexual relations with grade-school boys. He lived here at the time, and a lot of boys were involved. Now frankly, I consider this behavior immoral, and I wonder if Kunitz has done anything worse. Since the Institute is not a university, and Kunitz's temperament could not trouble anyone very much, I should think that the quality of his poems would be the sole issue. What would you people have done about Baudelaire? Jim Cunningham would probably irritate you all worse than Kunitz. Worse even than me. Jim has a way of saying what he thinks in the fewest possible words, whereas I waste words and dilute the effect.

If the Institute has any excuse whatever for being, it is this: to keep up with the art that is being produced and discover what is best before the *Sat. Rev. of Lit.* gets around to it. If the members of the Institute are insufficiently interested to do this, then the Institute is a pretty dismal organization: little better than Phi Beta Kappa or any other self-congratulatory social group.

Well, such are my sentiments. I hope you can disentangle them from my redundant style.

Yvor Winters

Don't bother to answer this, but please meditate on it. Stay with Valéry. I have to get back to Crashaw. You are in far better company.

MS: Newberry

TO LOUISE BOGAN

July 17, 1956 / 143 West Portola Ave. / Los Altos, Calif.

Dear Louise:

I cannot do any translating for Matthews. I told him that two or three years ago. Neither can Janet. I am working as best I am able on a book of criticism. Janet is working on a novel. Valéry's poems, like any really great poems, cannot be translated. French and English are so close to each other that I see no reason for translation. My opinion of poetic translation is perfectly expressed by Nabokov in the last *Partisan.*

Recently I took the liberty of giving Thom Gunn a letter of introduction to you. Thom is a young Englishman, about 26 years old, well known in England as a poet and critic. He won the Levinson Prize last year. Last year he was teaching in Texas. The year before he was at Stanford on a poetry fellowship. Next year he will be back here working for a Ph. D. I think him a fine poet at his best, and a very intelligent man.

The other day I met Stanley Kunitz for the first time. He was batting for Roethke in Seattle last year, and drove down the coast on his way east. I got him down here for lunch and dinner, and confess that I liked him a great deal. He is a kind of finicky Jewish bachelor of a type I have met before; but his learning is extensive, and he knows a hell of a lot about the nature and history of poetry. And I still think him one of the very few first-rate poets now writing.

I saw by the paper the other day that Jo Miles had received a grant from the Institute. I do not know who may have received the others, but I suppose I shall learn. Miss Miles is a heroic woman, God knows, and I wish her well. But as a poet she is little more than a tadpole.

Janet has been in Denver this past week teaching at a writers' conference. I expect her home in a week.

As ever, / Arthur

MS: Amherst

July 21, 1956 / 143 West Portola Ave. / Los Altos, Calif.

Dear Thom:

Cowley writes that the best way to get in touch with him is by phoning him at the Viking Press on a Tuesday. He earns his living by going to his office every Tuesday. The rest of the week he spends on his 20-acre estate in Connecticut. He is a pleasant and friendly person, but don't expect too much from him in the way of literary intelligence. Or from anyone else, for that matter. Allen and Louise have more talent and are more perceptive in spots, but are less perceptive in spots. And the ignorance of all three will surprise you if you have a chance to explore it.

Cunningham is teaching at the University of Washington in Seattle this summer, and will drive down the coast at the end of the session. You might be here in time to meet him, but probably not. Don Stanford started a swing around the country from Baton Rouge at the end of the spring term. I had a card from him the other day from northern Michigan, where he claimed he caught seven bass. He might stay around here long enough for you to meet him. But I don't know. I gather that you have had correspondence with Bowers. His address for the summer is Route 2, Stone Mountain, Georgia. Stone Mountain is near Atlanta, I think a bit to the north. You had better look him up if you can.

As to your poems, the melodramatic sometimes appears, and also the Picassoesque. But not invariably. The Picassoesque does not have to be melodramatic, although it inclines that way. "The Corridor" is mildly Picassoesque but not melodramatic. The method is essentially the same as that of "Les Éléphants" or "Les Hurleurs" by Leconte de Lisle, of "Le Jeu" by Baudelaire, or if you like of my "John Sutter." In "The Wolf Boy" the final stages of the incident were pretty violent in relationship to the earlier, and you didn't get enough out of them to justify the violence of the raw material. This may not be very clear.

Beware of rattlesnakes, copperheads, cottonmouths, alligators, Mississippi dogfish, bad liquor, and characters out of Faulkner. Beware also of tellers of tall tales. Do not allow your speech to be corrupted, no matter what strange predicament you may encounter. And above all, keep a diary, so that you may read it to me next fall.[1]

Yours, / Yvor

MS: Gunn

[1]Gunn was preparing to leave San Antonio to do some traveling before eventually returning to Stanford.

June 13, 1957 / 143 West Portola Ave. / Los Altos, Calif.

Mr. Malcolm Cowley, President /

The National Institute of Arts and Letters / New York City

Dear Malcolm:

I wish to resign my membership in the National Institute of Arts and Letters. There must be some provision somewhere in the Constitution or Laws for such resignations; if not, I should think that provision could be easily made. After watching the proceedings for a year, I find that I disapprove of the organization for reasons which I will explain below. In connection with my disapproval I experience a kind of distaste which I would not care to describe, *mais c'est plus fort que moi.* I desire to be clear. I will send you my diploma and boutonnière under separate cover.

The trouble with the organization is briefly this: the membership—and this is especially true of the literary portion—is much too large; and as a result the group is predominantly undistinguished. Any such group of people has to conduct its business on a democratic basis—this cannot be helped. But the arts, curiously enough, are not democratic. The result is that decisions are a kind of statistical average of mediocre minds. The Institute, so far as I can see, imposes a penalty upon distinction and places a premium upon mediocrity. The literary people whom I respect most highly are not in the Institute and are unlikely ever to be there. There are only three or four members of the Institute (literary members, I mean) whose work interests me even a little, and they and I have no critical principles or judgments in common so far as I can see. I live too far away to meet other members and try to persuade them by conversation; I have no time to try correspondence; and neither method is worth anything anyway. My work is done in the classroom and in print, and I do not wish to continue as a member of an organization which is supporting the kind of writing which I most dislike.

I hope you will be able to understand me. I appreciate the efforts made by yourself and Louise and Allen to get me into the Institute. They must have been heroic; but they were misguided.

My very best personal regards to all the Cowleys.

Yvor Winters

MS: Academy

TO MALCOLM COWLEY

June 25, 1957 / 143 West Portola Ave. / Los Altos, Calif.

Dear Malcolm:

Your letter came today. I was expecting it. In fact I could have written it. You ought to have been my grandfather. But even if you had been, it wouldn't have done any good. I don't want to argue the matter. I can't say any more than I said in my previous letter without going into particulars.

I like you personally and I want you to do me just one favor: put my resignation through. I enclose the rosette. I can't find my diploma, but it will turn up eventually and when it does I will send it in.

My best as always, / Yvor Winters

MS: Academy

TO MALCOLM COWLEY

July 16, 1957 / 143 West Portola Ave. / Los Altos, Calif.

Dear Malcolm:

I have found the diploma, at last, and here it is. I had stashed it away among my old dog-show ribbons. I sent you the rosette some days ago. I hope that it will now be possible for you to process my resignation. I am sorry about this. I suppose that I should not have accepted in the first place. But I didn't know much about the Institute—at the time of receiving my grant had never, in fact, heard of it—and it seemed only fair to find out. It is not merely last year that depressed me; it is the entire record in the little purple book. Also it is the critical record of the only three or four people in the Institute who might by some wild stretch of the imagination be considered my allies. I am not interested in the Institute, and I have no time to argue with it; and I don't want to be connected (even nominally) with its decisions.

Yours, / Yvor Winters

MS: Newberry

July 31, 1957 / 143 West Portola Ave. / Los Altos, Calif.

Dear Malcolm:

Thanks for your two recent letters and for the return of the diploma, which I shall put back into the morgue. My two great champions are now dead, and I have no energy or enthusiasm for further breeding or showing or for anything else. When Sally (Champion Buckthorn Sal to you) died almost two years ago, I cried for almost three days. When Black Jack (Champion Buckthorn Black Jack, the best dog in every way that I have ever owned) died a few weeks ago I merely became more securely and permanently depressed. I am not a real dog fancier. A real dog fancier takes this sort of thing in his stride. I can't take it. Both died of old age, and there was nothing surprising about it. I have three little bitches left—one the mother of a champion, but now old; the others not good enough to show or breed.

Well, as to trochees. You strike me as insane. I said very little about trochees, and that little can be found in Webster. The trochee consists of two syllables, the first accented; and the normal position for the trochee when it is substituted in an iambic pentameter line is in the first or third position. Everybody knows this—even Hopkins. What is eating you? That it can be substituted elsewhere with great success I am fully aware. I wrote one line (toward the end of my first "Theseus" poem) which contains trochees in every position except the third. In one of my poems called "The Fable," there is a trochee in the last position. In a poem called "Summer Commentary" (tetrameter) there is a trochee in the second. All handled with great success. But one has to know what one is doing and why. When people merely throw trochees around they get into trouble. Although no one seems to recognize metrical trouble any more.

As to Kunitz my claims for him were modest. I merely stated that he had written three poems better than all except perhaps a dozen poems by living members of the Institute. Like most poets, he repeats and dilutes himself. It is the business of the good critic to rescue the good poems from such a mess. Cunningham and Bowers are another matter: they are the two greatest poets now writing, although Thom Gunn, the young Englishman, is pushing them, and so is another poet of whom you have never heard, Alan Stephens.[1] But you and Allen and Louise will need twenty years to get used to these men, and twenty years from now you won't be around, but Ciardi and Wilbur and Jarrell will be around and will be running the show. Why did the Institute wait to elect Stevens until he was 65 years old? When I was 21 I reviewed E. A. Robinson's collected poems in *Poetry* and stated that R. and S. were the two greatest Americans then writing, and S. the greater. *Harmonium* did not appear until two or three years later. I was grateful for Allen's high praise of my poems in 1953. But most of the poems which he cited had been in print and in his possession for twenty years or so. If they were so good, why was Allen so slow? And why do you elect punks like Wilbur and Ciardi in their thirties, when you pass up great men until they are almost dead?

I know that you all regard me as an eccentric. But you are the eccentrics, or rather the provincials. As I have said before, you don't know enough. You know damned little except each other's opinions and the prejudices of your generation and of the preceding generation. And you have never examined these with any care, or considered their implications. For years I have been teaching a graduate seminar in American criticism, devoted mainly to modern criticism. My students come in convinced that I am Yvor Winters and therefore wrong. They go out completely bewildered by the utter incoherence of our most eminent men, and I let them demonstrate most of it in their own papers. If there were more brute historical knowledge among the great of my generation, there would be much less bullshit written about what poetry is. I have read a good many of the best books and have directed a good many of the best dissertations. I am not ignorant. I have been grubbing in this stuff professionally, while you people have been agreeing privately and publicly with each other.

But I can't convince any of you by this kind of letter, and even if I could, none of you will be around much longer. I would rather work with my boys, some of whom are bright and most of whom have a good many years before them.

But in spite of this, I am fond of Allen and Louise and yourself. In fact you seem the most human of the lot. I am sorry that I have been a disappointment to you.

Yvor

MS: Newberry

[1]Alan Stephens (b. 1925): American poet, scholar, and educator. He was a student of YW, who wrote about him in *Forms of Discovery* and included him in *Quest for Reality.*

Oct. 17, 1957 / 143 West Portola Ave. / Los Altos, Calif.
Mr. Roger Boas, / Station KQED / San Francisco
Dear Mr. Boas:

Your telegram was so grimly serious and so righteous, that I thought I ought to explain.

In the first place I have absolutely no duties toward the public in general, save my duties as a citizen, and these I try to fulfill. My only other duties are toward my family and toward Stanford University in general and my students in particular. Everybody from here to hell and back thinks he has a right to a slice of my time: to appear in public, to criticize poems in private, and what have you. I get five or six requests of one kind or another every month. My work at Stanford is exacting and there is a good deal of it, and I am old, tired and nervous.

I have certain fixed habits, the disruption of which leaves me exhausted. I get up at 6 A.M. every morning and go to bed by 9:30 every night. I dislike driving intensely, especially in traffic. The little trip to San Francisco for your program, at best, would have left me ill. But it would not be at best, for I have an appointment with my dentist that morning which will probably be rather rough, and later I have a department meeting.

To discuss the people you mentioned, I would have to reread some and read one or two others for the first time. There would simply not be time for this. Furthermore, even if there were time, I would not do it, for the people in question bore me, and I have other things to do.

I am convinced that nothing can be explained about literature in casual conversation. If I appeared on your program I would merely infuriate [Kenneth] Rexroth and his crowd (which would not bother me in itself) and bewilder (or infuriate) the listeners. Nothing would be clarified. As to the public's having a right to both sides of a literary question, they don't unless they want to get out and root for it, and of course they don't. Nearly all of them are fools and ignoramuses, and that is why the Rexroths flourish.

There is a Rexroth every eight or ten years. When I was young it was Sandburg (cum Lindsay, cum Masters, cum Anderson). Then it was Cummings; then Archie MacLeish. More recently Jarrell. These people are not worth criticizing. They come up periodically like spring weeds, and you can't stop them. They don't last; they are merely replaced.

It is too bad, of course, that San Francisco has to be identified with the present plague. My heart bleeds for San Francisco. But if your heart bleeds in the same way, you might try to persuade Mr. Champion to persuade the *Chronicle* to stop giving free publicity to these punks and to put a civilized man in charge of the paper's literary policies.

I have other work to do which will accomplish more for civilization in the long run.

Sincerely yours, / /unsigned copy/

MS: Boston

TO ALLEN TATE

Jan. 13, 1958 / 143 West Portola Ave. / Los Altos, Calif.

Dear Allen:

This is the first I have heard of an English edition of my poems. I would be more than happy to have your review as an introduction, either in its published form or as you might care to revise it. Provided, of course, that you don't add too many cracks about my criticism.

I am sorry that I didn't send the book. I thought I had sent it. What happened was this: Last Feb. my daughter was married in Cambridge. I flew back, but I had to take night flights both ways in order to save time for my teaching. I cannot sleep on a plane, partly because of the seats, partly because of the racket. I spent two nights in a hotel in Cambridge. Cambridge was just moving out of an intense cold spell into a very sloppy thaw, and the hotel kept the heat on. It was like a blast furnace. I spent four nights without sleep, and I am too old for that. I got back here completely exhausted and got the flu, but had to teach anyway. Janet got back a few days later and got the flu from me, and I had to look after her and the house for a couple of weeks while I was teaching and convalescing. I was still exhausted at the end of last summer. Everything was neglected except what actually had to be done.

However, I did send you a copy of Bowers's poems, and you never acknowledged it. He is a great poet and a Southerner. You ought to read him.

As to Routledge Kegan Paul, Thom Gunn lent me one of their books recently: *Romantic Image* by Frank Kermode. It is a very good piece of scholarship and pretty fair criticism, though he seems to over-rate Milton and when he has Yeats all set up for the kill (well-deserved) he says "But aren't these wonderful poems?" They aren't. In fact they ain't. This book would be good for you.

Yours, / Arthur

P.S. What became of your anthology?

MS: Princeton, Allen Tate Papers

TO ALLEN TATE

Jan. 26, 1958 / 143 West Portola Ave. / Los Altos, Calif.

Dear Allen:

One thing occurs to me in connection with that English edition of my poems. In your review of my book you stated that the chief influence on my work was the Elizabethans, or maybe it was the early Elizabethans. I have written a little about these poets and intend to write more, and I admire a good many of them very deeply. But the only English poets who have influenced my work very seriously are Ben Jonson (especially in the "Before Disaster" group) and Bridges (see "Eros," "Low Barometer," "Dejection," "The Affliction of Richard," and "Elegy: The Summerhouse on the Mound"). Sturge Moore was an influence on some of my very early work, but he was mainly part of a French influence. There are about a dozen poems by Wallace Stevens which I have always thought very great and which are probably a real influence. Otherwise, the main influences are Baudelaire and Valéry. If you will read the poems in my book which you like best—read them with a cold and dispassionate eye—you may see this. My style is not Elizabethan at all. It is strictly twentieth century, as are my themes.

But I don't object to your standing by your original statement if you really believe it.

Yours, / Arthur

MS: Princeton, Allen Tate Papers

TO ALLEN TATE

March 15, 1958 / 143 West Portola Ave. / Los Altos, Calif.

Dear Allen:

Since I gathered from one of your recent letters that you were revising your review of my poems, I thought it only decent to send you these notes. I would have done it sooner if I had had the time. At the moment I have a two or three hour lull in examination week.

I will separate my comments as far as possible into two categories: matters of opinion and matters of scholarship (fact). I would not mention items of the first category at all, except for two things: your opinions sometimes irritate me (this is unimportant) and I am pretty damned sure that they are sometimes wrong (this will be important to your reputation in the long run).

1. Middle of the first paragraph. "Crane being dead," etc.[1] This is a matter of opinion. You continue to over-rate Crane with a kind of 30-year-old enthusiasm. There are two impressive but inadequately intelligible poems in Crane: "Repose of Rivers" and "Voyages II." There are some fine fragments. There is a misguided effort. And there is an inordinate amount of horrific garbage. What you like, I believe, is the violence of the effort, even though you know it is misguided. You like violent writing even when it is obviously bad. I am a much better poet than Crane; so are you; so is Louise Bogan; so is Jim Cunningham; so is Kunitz; so is Bowers.

2. A few lines below: remarks about Tudor poets.[2] I have already written you in some detail on this matter, and I will not repeat. The peculiar facts of my life were such that I knew French poetry pretty thoroughly from Villon through Valéry, before I had even discovered the English 16th century. I also knew Spanish poetry from the *Cid* through the 17th century, and I knew a good deal of Old Portuguese and a little Old Catalán. I started reading systematically in the English 16th century about 1930, and by that time the poems in my collected poems, up to and including "The Grave," had been written. The main influences were Bridges and Baudelaire, with perhaps a little Valéry: the main influences, I mean, after the obvious imagistic influence on the early stuff. And if you read my poems, the fact is obvious. This is a matter of scholarship, and some one will jump you for an error like this if the error appears in book form.

3. "the dour polemics of his critical prose."[3] I suppose that this is a matter of opinion, but since it appears to refer to my critical manners, I refer you to some remarks on the same subject in an essay in *The Graduate Student in English,* a small journal originating in your department.[4] The legend of my bad manners, generally, originates from these facts: my critical position is opposed to that of most of my contemporaries; my critical position is sound; I defend my position so effectively that my opponents cannot effectively attack it; I write a much better prose than any of my critical contemporaries; my contemporaries are irritated by these facts and abuse me, and one of their favorite forms of abuse is to accuse me of an abusive style. In my old age I begin to feel tired

of this. I am not Peck's bad boy at the University; I am not Peck's bad boy on the literary scene. I am a first-rate scholar of my peculiar kind, and a major critic, and a major poet. I *know* more about the art of poetry, and the history of the art, and the history of the theory of the art than any of you people.

4. "his aloofness from the world causes."[5] I simply don't know what this means. If you know, you ought to explain; if you don't know you ought to drop the remark. If you will read through my poems you will find more concern for political, social, and historical events than in the work of most contemporaries. As to my prose it is concerned with something else, and, like most professional scholars, I prefer not to make an ass of myself by holding forth on topics on which I am not an expert.

5. "Winters, like Yeats before him" etc. (well along in the second paragraph). This is all a matter of opinion to me. First of all, Yeats is not one of my masters (I realize that I borrowed the figure of the tree[6] from him in the recent *Hudson* ["A Dream Vision"], but I did something with it, and he didn't). I think that Yeats is preponderantly a bad stylist, although he comes out with good passages. He is habitually violent (and tritely so), and you like the violence. But my style is not violent, whatever the themes may be, and this is why you were so slow in coming around to my poems. Neither is my style numb.[7] Every word in the Gawaine poem is working.

6. Next paragraph: "it takes an unviable gift."[8] This is a matter of diction. Consult *Webster* on *viable*.

7. The last few sentences of paragraph 4.[9] I don't know exactly what you are getting at here, but you seem to be saying that there is a wide discrepancy between my poetical theories and my poetical practice; and that I believe that poetry should moralize. If my interpretation is correct, you are wrong on both points, and both points are matters of scholarship. There is a very close and pretty obvious correlation between my theory and my practice, and most people who have read me carefully are aware of the fact. Furthermore, I have distinguished carefully and repeatedly in my prose between didactic (or moralizing) poetry in particular, and poetry as a moral judgment in general. I have no objection to didactic poetry: Jonson's "A Farewell to the World" is moralizing poetry; so is Louise Bogan's "Exhortation." Both are remarkably beautiful. But there is non-moralizing poetry as well, which is nevertheless moral judgment. I have written poetry of both kinds.

8. Near end of review. "He is a Renaissance humanist of the pre-Spenserian school of metaphysical rhetoricians, the school of Greville and Raleigh."[10] For general comment on this, see pt. 2 above. But in addition: G. and R. were

contemporaries of S. and outlived him. S. was in some ways quite as medieval as they, though much more lush. You are probably harking back here to my old essay on the Elizabethans; but you are not giving enough of the history of the period to protect yourself. You are writing like one of my students on a final examination.

Arthur

MS: Princeton, Allen Tate Papers

[1]"In his own generation he has the eminence of isolation; among American poets who appeared soon after the first war he is, [Hart] Crane being dead, the master" (*New Republic,* March 2, 1953, p. 17).

[2]"If he has been neglected—when he has not been ignored—the reasons are not hard to find. He has conducted a poetic revolution all his own that owes little or nothing to the earlier revolution of Pound and Eliot, and that goes back to certain great, likewise neglected Tudor poets for metrical and stylistic models" (17).

[3]"The dour polemics of his critical prose and his aloofness from world causes (not in itself a virtue) have set on edge the teeth of the fashionable literary world" (17).

[4]Refers to John Fraser's review of *The Function of Criticism: Problems and Exercises,* "A Great American Critic," *The Graduate Student in English* 1 (1957).

[5]See note 3, *the dour polemics.*

[6]This appears to be a reference to the tree in Yeats's "Among School Children." Of this tree and the question to it, YW wrote: "The question addressed to the tree is preposterous: the tree is obviously more than the leaf, the blossom, or the bole, but these all exist and can be discussed, and it is because of this fact that we have words for them—the implication of the passage is that the tree is an inscrutable unit, like the Mallarméan poem." (*The Poetry of W. B. Yeats* [Denver: Alan Swallow, 1960], 14).

[7]"But Winters, like Yeats before him, is a master of composition; he first deploys a force of 'numb lines,' and then, at the right moment, produces the explosion" (17). AT had quoted the sixth stanza of "Sir Gawaine and the Green Knight," which became his example: "The explosion here is the word 'swarmed,' but one needs the delicate radar system of a bat to hear it" (17).

[8]"It takes an unviable gift that can only be called genius to use the least figurative distortion" (17). My own speculation is that *unviable* is simply a typographical error; the word should be *enviable.*

[9]"We cannot read Winters if we decide in advance, as I once decided, with my mind on something else, that he is a gifted academic poet of the neoclassical decadence (roughly contemporaneous with [Samuel] Johnson)—a view to which some of his critical theories, notably in *Primitivism and Decadence,* lend a certain plausibility. We must try to distinguish what the poet does from what he says he is doing. His theory of the heroic couplet, for example, as a moral agency in poetry, though much is to be said for it, must not be allowed to convince us that Winters himself is a moralizing poet" (17).

[10]"He is a Renaissance humanist of the pre-Spenserian school of metaphysical rhetoricians, the school of Greville and Raleigh: a poet whose moral imagination takes, without didacticism, the didactic mode, striving for precision in language and, in verse, for formal elegance" (18).

TO ALLEN TATE

April 4, 1958 / 143 West Portola Ave. / Los Altos, Calif.

Dear Allen:

Thanks for your recent note. I am calm enough; don't worry about that. Furthermore, I don't think that I alone am right. You would be surprised to find out how many people, generally, are in agreement with me. The number increases yearly. If you attack my critical position at Brandeis, I hope that you will manage to get your remarks into print, so that I can look at them.

I don't object to your disagreeing with my critical position, but:

(1) I think that you should give some evidence of understanding it before you disagree;

(2) I do not feel convinced that an introduction to my poems is the proper place to express such a disagreement;

(3) I don't think that you can express such a disagreement intelligibly in so brief a space as you would have to give to it in an introduction to my poems.

Beyond this, I really don't want to be introduced by statements which are essentially unscholarly and which will appear comical to such Renaissance specialists as may read them.

I cannot send you a copy of my last letter, and I simply haven't the time or energy to write another—at least at present.

Yours as ever, / Arthur

MS: Princeton, Allen Tate Papers

TO ALLEN TATE

April 7, 1958 / 143 West Portola Ave. / Los Altos, Calif.

Dear Allen:

I have a brief breathing space, perhaps the last I shall have for ten weeks. Let me try to clarify a few points.

My Gawaine poem was written around 1936–37—quite late enough to have been influenced by my Elizabethan studies. But it is not very Elizabethan. Compare it to "A Valediction Forbidding Mourning": not with regard to which is the better, nor with regard to individual virtues and defects of writing, but with regard to method.

Donne's poem is typical of the high Renaissance in certain respects: the rational (almost logical) structure, which, in Donne as in Sidney and in others, is often perversely misused but is still there (see the books of Rosamund [Rosemond] Tuve, and see the essays by Cunningham listed in my recent book); the fact that the superficial or explicit subject of the poem is the real subject—the poem is a poem about the temporary parting of lovers.

My poem is narrative in structure (no serious divergence here, but one not common in the Renaissance). The superficial or explicit theme of my poem is not the real theme: the explicit theme is a curious adventure and love affair; the real theme is a relationship between what Aristotle and Aquinas would have called the rational soul and the sensory soul. Gawaine at the first level is the rational soul, but ultimately he is the whole man, and the Green Knight and his lady are a part of him, and he emerges at the end for a temporary respite. His first act, the beheading, might be called a premature and naive generalization with which he hopes to put an end to the real difficulties; the rest of the poem deals with the consequences of his error. This is nowhere stated explicitly, but it seems to me obviously implicit throughout, and the descriptive language implies it at every moment. When I said that my poem was narrative in structure, I meant at the superficial level: the narrative is condensed, and is used for an expository purpose.

There are important differences in the use of figurative language. Donne uses explicit similes and metaphors to develop distinct aspects of his argument. There is, I believe, only one simile in my poem: "like a forest vine." There are two explicit comparisons which can hardly be called figures of speech: "Green as a bough," "like a fool"; and I suppose you can add "Reptilian green." But the whole poem is a metaphor, not explicitly stated, but each detail supporting the other to the extent that any descriptive detail (e.g., "Where growth was rapid, thick, and still") means more in the poem than it does at the descriptive level in the passage.

This method is not Elizabethan or even 17th century. It is post-symbolist[1] and post-imagist. You will find it here and there in Stevens (see the pigeons at the end of "Sunday Morning"), occasionally in Louise Bogan (see "Simple Autumnal"), all over "*Le Cimetière Marin*" and the "*Serpent.*" I have used this procedure more consistently and more skillfully than any other poet in English. It is not the only procedure that I have used but it has been my favorite. The corresponding symbolist (or imagist) procedure occurs in Crane's "Repose of Rivers": The vehicle (to borrow Richards's jargon) is explicit and rich; the tenor is more than uncertain except in a vaguely general way. This unbalance never,

I think, occurs in my poems after the early and imagistic period. It certainly does not occur in the Gawaine.

I don't care, personally, whether my poems are published in England or not. The only Englishman who knows much about poetry right now is Thom Gunn, and he is a graduate student at Stanford. But such a publication would be good for my department and would please Virgil Whitaker, who is the head of my department and a very good friend of mine.

Whitaker, however, is a first-rate Renaissance scholar, and my department is a strong Renaissance department. I do not wish to be an accomplice in anything which would make me and my friends look silly.

Yours, / Arthur

Some day I will write you another letter about another poem.

MS: Princeton, Allen Tate Papers

[1]A few years later, YW would write Don Stanford: "If you ever write the book on French and American poetry, let me give you one word of warning. Leconte de Lisle influenced me (along with others) in what I have called post-symbolist method, and (along with Baudelaire) in a common 19th century method (the account of the scene or the action followed by the moral). But he contributed nothing to my unfortunate and ill-suppressed tendency toward solipsistic mysticism. That comes from my early childhood and appears in poems written before I could read French" (January 25, 1961 [MS: Stanford]).

TO ALLEN TATE

April 9, 1958 / 143 West Portola Ave. / Los Altos, Calif.

Dear Allen:

Please consider this a continuation of my last. As regards the single-metaphor construction, with its accompanying use of sensory detail, you might regard the following poems, at least, as more or less obviously of the same kind: "To W. D. Briggs Conducting His Seminar," "The Fable," "The Fall of Leaves," "The Slow Pacific Swell," "The Journey," "A Vision," "Midas," "A Sonnet to the Moon," "Orpheus," "Chiron," "Heracles," "Theseus," "John Day," ("John Sutter," perhaps, but other elements get into this), "The Manzanita," "A Spring Serpent," "Much in Little," "To a Military Rifle."

There is some variation among these poems, however, in regard to other matters. I will mention only one example: "The Slow Pacific Swell." The ocean throughout this poem is the familiar symbol of the eternal non-human and sub-human of the universe. It is seen from three points of view, and these are arranged in a properly rational order: first the remote view from the hill-top and childhood; second the immediate view of semi-immersion in the thing itself; finally from the relatively mature view of accustomed and occasional contemplation. This relationship is indicated only in the course of each stanza, however: not explicitly at the beginning of each, as an Elizabethan would do it. As one goes through the poem, the connection from stanza to stanza *appears* to be associationistic and within each stanza the movement from detail to detail is more or less associationistic; but the associationism is controlled, does not wander from the real theme. It seems to me that this method of treating this subject is better than any conceivable Elizabethan method. But in any event it is not Elizabethan. The mere bulk of sensory detail separates it from the Elizabethans by an abyss. Here as in the Gawaine, the sensory details *contain* the theme, but they are not illustrations or ornaments. Donne's gold and compasses are more quotable than any of my details: that is, they are more easily detachable. This is because they are, in a sense, attached, they are ornaments —extremely good ornaments, but ornaments. Donne is a typical Renaissance poet in this respect, just as I am a typical post-symbolist poet.

This kind of imagery, however, gets into poems which go directly to their subjects, which are not constructed as single metaphors. Consider "To the Holy Spirit." The structure of this poem from stanza to stanza is one of closely controlled associationism. Examine Donne's poem again: you will find that he states his subject in the first sentence, and then elaborates upon it point by point: this is typical of his period. The first stanza of my poem is pure description until the last two lines, but the description is preparation for the last two lines, which introduce the metaphysical question of the poem. The second stanza drops all metaphysical questions. There is only one figure of speech in the stanza: the word *irregular,* a play upon physical irregularity (now) and spiritual irregularity (in the past). But note that although there is a trace of sensory perception in all this, it is very subdued, and the sensory and denotative are inseparable. The sensory does not illustrate the denotative; where the sensory enters, it contains and continues the denotative. The language is quiet, and I suppose that the final word really makes the stanza, but the style is not numb, nevertheless; the whole stanza is good as one proceeds through it. The third stanza brings the first two together, and the fourth moves to its conclusion. I will call your attention only to the last six lines of the last stanza, which are of the same kind as the irregular lines. "Stir of age": confused movement of the process of aging, seen here in a desert setting, among distances, like the movement of dust. "Seem to fall": the falling of dust—desert dust and the dust to which man returneth. All of this is in the poem, I am sure. The method is indirect as compared to that of Donne, but not so indirect as to be difficult. It permits a subtler interrelationship of details. And I confess that I like it better.

I will now break off and perhaps write you one more letter.

Arthur

P.S. You might read my remarks on Valéry in my recent book and *The Mirror and the Lamp* by M. H. Abrams.

MS: Princeton, Allen Tate Papers

TO ALLEN TATE

April 10, 1958 / 143 West Portola Ave. / Los Altos, Calif.

Dear Allen:

I will continue. Please bear with me.

There is at least one of my poems which differs greatly from any that I have mentioned, but which is still farther from the Elizabethans: "On a View of Pasadena from the Hills." This poem compares the Los Angeles–Pasadena area as it was about 1929–1930 with the same area as I knew it about twenty years before, in my childhood. The poem is a comment not merely upon the change in the landscape but upon what the process of this change did to the men involved. The poem is loaded with descriptive detail, and in this it is utterly remote from anything you can find in the period from 1500 to 1620. The descriptive detail is also very literal, and in this it differs from anything that you can find down to "MacFlecknoe." The theme of the poem is different from anything that you can find until you get to Crabbe. If I were writing the poem now, I would try to cut the descriptive detail down somewhat, but I could not cut it down a great deal and still write the poem. There is no general metaphor or allegory in this poem; the poem is a general description of the alteration in a social situation. The subject may not be the greatest of all possible subjects, but it seems legitimate, and neither the subject nor the treatment is Elizabethan. There is one poem back of this: "Elegy: The Summerhouse on the Mound," by Bridges. The Bridges poem is similar in scheme, contains a large number of blunders in diction and versification, but is brilliant in some details and sound in conception. My poem is a better poem, I believe, in spite of certain flaws. The Bridges poem may have suggested a few details in the first stanza of "The Slow Pacific Swell," although

Crabbe may equally have suggested them: see *The Borough,* "First Letter," the passage beginning "Turn to the Watery World." I knew these things when I was very young. Thanks to Ezra Pound.

"A Summer Commentary" is largely descriptive, but not in the same way. The first two stanzas refer to my very early days, my imagistic days, when I was inclined to regard the landscape with a kind of pseudo-mystical intensity. The remaining stanzas bring the landscape down to earth. This is a minor poem, but I think a very good one. But it is all description, and the subject would have been unintelligible to Ben Jonson.

As to poems showing the Elizabethan influence. I think that I told you that I began my study of the Elizabethans about 1930. I had read the dramatists voluminously before this date, but the dramatists are irrelevant to my procedure and, so far as stylistic structure is concerned, to the masters of the short poem in the Elizabethan period. A few poems in the Before Disaster group show the influence of the plain-style poets of the early and high Renaissance, but I think only slightly, for my real talent did not lie in that direction. I had just discovered this body of poetry at this time, and I wanted to write a group of poems without any sensory imagery. I succeeded up to a point in some poems, but not brilliantly; I violated my intentions in other poems. Cunningham did what I was trying to do, and I shortly abandoned the effort. As to poems showing the intention, read: "To a Young Writer" (influence of Jonson, but the fifth line is not good), "The Prince," "A Post-Card to the Social Muse" (this comes straight out of Googe and Turbervile), "Dedication for a Book of Criticism" (Jonson and earlier plain-style poets), "On Teaching the Young." The plain-style poets at their best seem to me the best of the Renaissance, but my talents lay elsewhere, and my style was pretty well formed in ways that I liked better when I found them. I do not like the ornamental figure (the gold and the compasses); and I believe that Wyatt's "It was my choice, it was no chance," and Jonson's "To Heaven" are better poems than Donne's. The nearest thing to my use of imagery that you will find in the Renaissance is George Herbert's "Church Monuments." But his structure, for better or worse, is not my structure.

"Before Disaster" itself is a solidly balanced comparison; but this kind of comparison, as such, is more 19th century than 16th [YW's autograph marginal note: "also 'Time and the Garden'"]. As to the quality of diction etc. in the poem, I had four items in the back of my mind when I wrote it: Nashe's "Autumn hath all the summer's fruitful treasure," Blake's "London," Blake's unattached couplet "The harlot's cry" etc., and Sassoon's "The Kiss" (the best poem of the lot, and nearer in theme to my poem than the others). Make an Elizabethan influence of this if you can.

So much for now. There will probably be one more letter, if I can find time. If I write it, I will really curse you out in general terms.

Yours, / Arthur

MS: Princeton, Allen Tate Papers

TO ALLEN TATE

April 10, 1958 / 143 West Portola Ave. / Los Altos, Calif.

Dear Allen:

This letter will be the final one.

You will find in such poems as "The Wreck of the Hesperus" and "The Chambered Nautilus" a very common 19th century procedure: the account of an action, a situation, or an object followed by a moral tag. These poems are bad poems, but the method can be used well: see Baudelaire's "Le Jeu," "Une Martyre," and "Delphine et Hippolyte," for example, or Le Conte de Lisle's "Les Hurleurs." This is more or less the procedure of my "John Sutter," and with qualifications of "Before Disaster" and "Time and the Garden," although in this last poem, the application of the initial material in the second half is not really moralizing; the second half merely offers a parallel experience. In both of these poems there is another difference from the normal procedure: the fable and the application are equally balanced, half of the poem to each. You might say that the second and third of the poems just named have certain Renaissance qualities: they are rationally stated, are explicit about their topics, and are precisely written; but I don't know that these qualities are confined to the Renaissance. The poems do not state their real subject in the opening lines and then develop it, as the sixteenth century poems almost always do. And offhand I cannot think of a sixteenth century poem using this half-and-half structure, though there may be one.

I have not discussed or classified all of my poems, but I have gone over enough so that you ought to see the point.

I would suggest that you obtain and read two doctoral dissertations from the microfilm library at the University of Michigan: one a Harvard dissertation on Ben Jonson, by Wesley W. Trimpi;[1] the other a Stanford dissertation on the theory and practice of the plain and eloquent styles in the fourteen, fifteenth, and sixteenth centuries, by Douglas Peterson.[2] Both grew out of my course in the English Lyric. The first was officially directed by Bush, but actually and unofficially by Cunningham. The second was directed by Whitaker but I was the second reader and gave a good deal of advice. Peterson had advice also from Francis Johnson and from one of our medievalists, R. W. Ackerman. You would learn from these dissertations precisely what the poets discussed thought they were doing, and you would learn also that they were actually doing it. Your knowledge of the nature of English poetry would be greatly enriched, and it needs to be.

You put me in mind of a story I picked up some years ago in a book by a Mexican journalist whose name eludes me. The book is called *El Águila y la Serpiente,* and deals with the Mexican revolution from the overthrow of Díaz through the Madero, Huerta, Carranza, and Villa episodes down to the establishment of more or less order. The author had been in the fighting as a very young man, and served for some time with Villa. Villa conceived a great personal affection for the author, but the author became convinced (quite rightly) that Villa was a dangerous wild animal—savage, irrational, and unpredictable. He finally managed to leave Villa, and began covering the revolution as a journalist in Mexico City. Toward the end of Villa's career his paper asked him to visit Villa and write an account of him. He went with some trepidation. Villa had a way of shooting on sight any former friend who, in his opinion, had drifted away from him. However, Villa received him like a favorite son. A couple of days later, Villa took the journalist and his officers out for pistol practice. They nailed some pieces of tin about the size of pesos against a stockade, and shot rapid fire from the hip at about fifteen paces. Villa nailed all six of his targets, and his officers did almost as well. The author (his name now comes back to me—[Martín Luis] Guzmán) missed all of his by two feet or more. Villa turned to him with his jaw falling off, and said: "Son, how have you ever lived so long?"

Well, so far as this business is concerned, I guess that question is my final word to you.

Yours, / Arthur

MS: Princeton, Allen Tate Papers

[1]Published as *Ben Jonson's Poems: A Study of the Plain Style* (Stanford, Calif.: Stanford University Press, 1962).
[2]Published as *The English Lyric from Wyatt to Donne: A History of the Plain and Eloquent Styles* (Princeton, N.J.: Princeton University Press, 1967).

April 19, 1958 / 143 West Portola Ave. / Los Altos, Calif.

Dear Allen:

I add a couple of post-scripts in the interest of clarity, not for further objurgation.

I had read casually in the 17th century long before I got into the 16th. This was the result of the general misunderstanding of the Renaissance into which I blundered: a misunderstanding begun by Eliot, continued by Leavis, yourself, and others. One simply does not know what is happening in the 17th unless one knows the 16th well, and one ought to know the 14th and 15th. Eliot's remark that the metaphysicals are the heirs of the 16th century dramatists is silly.

But fairly early I stumbled onto George Herbert's "Church Monuments." This is the only great poem that Herbert wrote. In his other poems there is a kind of childish pietism which is very hard to take. This poem is absolutely serious; it would appear to come from another hand. The kind of diction employed in this poem probably influenced me; also, the management of sentence in relationship to line, stanza, and poem.

The diction is similar to that of certain poems by Bridges which I mentioned earlier ("The Affliction of Richard," "Eros," "Dejection," and "Low Barometer"). You might examine these poems in connection with what I have said about my own.

Donne is a greater poet than Sidney, but he resembles Sidney closely. In the "Valediction F. M." the emotion asserted is far in excess of the situation, and is melodramatic. The first 8 lines are a series of hyperbolic clichés, purely ornamental in intention. The poem comes through by the grace of God and by the grace of a few good strokes. The sound of the poem rattles like the sound of a Model T Ford. But in spite of the brilliance, it is a second-rate poem. S.'s command of sound is more civilized.

As to Herbert's poem, the overall construction is strictly 16th century. The quality of the diction is more subtle than one will often find in the 16th century. After Herbert structural control declines rapidly. New principles, at first bad, take over. Churchill operated on the principle of association, and for the most part badly. In the "Dedication to Warburton" he had it under control, and the diction was superb. Controlled association has its virtues, and I think great virtues. It is the principle of most of my poems except the very short ones. See once more "To the Holy Spirit."

Arthur

MS: Princeton, Allen Tate Papers

April 21, 1958 / 143 West Portola Ave. / Los Altos, Calif.

Dear Allen:

If you are not incurably angry with me by this time, you may have a mild interest in further ruminations. You have set my mind running on my past, and it continues to run.

Consider my poem "At the San Francisco Airport," in the *Hudson,* Spring 1955. I sent you this poem in typescript and you didn't like it. Morgan wrote me that it was the best poem the *Hudson* had published. My own opinion is in between: I think it one of my 15 or 18 best. But this is no matter.

Consider the procedure. The second and third stanzas are almost wholly in abstract language; they are a close and quick analysis of a certain moral situation, roughly similar to what one might expect to find in Wyatt or Jonson. The other three stanzas are largely a matter of physical detail (although the fourth stanza is partly abstract). The sensory imagery, however, is of the kind which I described in connection with my other poems, and is not Renaissance imagery. The closely ordered rational structure of the whole poem may resemble Jonson. But this is a late poem, where many influences are coming together.

"The Marriage," written before I had read the Elizabethans (including Jonson), in detail might seem to show the influence of a few plain style poems; but just on the basis of my personal history, I don't see how it can. The only influences that occur to me are a few Old Portuguese and Old Provençal love poems; but these, though they have something of the direct statement in detail which I tried to achieve, are ornate in structure, with elaborate refrains, echoes, semi-repetitions, and the like. See my two translations from the Old Portuguese (Old Galician),[1] and Pound's "Alba Innominata." For what little they are worth in this connection—and I suspect it is little.

By and large you do not like such of my poems as show any discernible Elizabethan influence. Yet you find such an influence in poems not so influenced. Can you explain?

Yours, / Arthur

MS: Princeton, Allen Tate Papers

[1]"The Lady's Farewell" by Nuño Fernández Torneol and "Cossante" by Pero Meogo. Both translations are in YW's *Collected Poems* (rev. ed., Denver: Alan Swallow, 1960).

May 4, 1958 / 143 West Portola Ave. / Los Altos, Calif.

Dear Allen:

A few more items have come to mind, which I should have mentioned. These have to do largely with my early and more or less imagistic verse.

Generally this kind of verse corresponds in my career to the work of Rimbaud and Mallarmé in the career of Valéry. That is (see my remarks on Valéry's imagery in my last book) I learned at this time the virtue of the precise sensory detail, tried to make it imply more meaning than it had (for I was unsatisfied with purely sensory detail), and then went on to write a more complete kind of poetry. The break between this verse and my first sonnets may seem more complete than it is, because of the sudden shift from free verse to standard verse. But the only possible shift from free verse to standard verse is a sudden shift, and the shift gave me the medium to do what I had been trying unhappily to do for two or three years.

There was no Elizabethan influence at this time. I had got my first clue to the kind of style I wanted from the poems by Bridges which I have named, and from a few poems in free verse by Williams which I named (along with others) in my review of Williams[1] in the first issue of the *Kenyon Review*. This was a style in which motive and emotion were precisely related, in which there was no hyperbole or melodrama. For reasons which I gave in my old essay on meter (*Prim. and Dec.*) ["The Influence of Meter on Poetic Convention"] I found that standard meter provided a better medium than free verse for the kind of honesty that I was trying to achieve. I later found this quality (in spite of structural differences) in certain poems of the 16th and early 17th centuries.

I had found this quality in Baudelaire even before I had shifted meters: see my early essay with the long title in the *Amer. Car.* ["The Extension and Reintegration of the Human Spirit Through the Poetry Mainly French and American Since Poe and Baudelaire"] and I shortly found it in a complex form in Valéry. I had found it in a few things by Stevens when I was about 17 years old, but at that time I didn't know what to do with it. Before I was 30 I had learned.

In these terms my Gawaine poem is more than a mere figure of the relationship of the rational soul to the sensible soul; it is that, but it is also a figure of the problem of poetic style, which in my terms (the correct ones) is the problem of moral judgment and moral integrity.

I can't help wondering how you thought me so simple. But that is not the real problem: I can't help wondering how you could have thought anyone so simple.

Arthur

MS: Princeton, Allen Tate Papers

[1]The poems YW named are "The Widow's Lament in Springtime," "The Bull," "A Coronal," "Arrival," "Portrait of a Lady," "The Hunter," "The Lonely Street," "To Mark Anthony in Heaven," "To Waken an Old Lady," and "Waiting." To these he added "By the road to the contagious hospital" and "The Sea-Elephant."

TO EUGENE SHEEHY

June 27, 1958 / 143 West Portola Ave. / Los Altos, Calif.

Dear Mr. Sheehy:

I have your letter of June 23.

There is no law against projects such as yours; therefore I cannot object. On the other hand I would prefer that you did not make such a bibliography;[1] therefore I will give you no help.

Furthermore, I do not see how I could give you any real help. I have been publishing here and there for almost forty years. I have never kept a list of my publications. I do not even have a complete file of my publications, and such material as I have is stowed in many odd corners of my small and over-crowded house and I would have to tear the place apart to find what I have. I have other and more serious work to do.

If you insist on this project, then, it will have to be your headache and not mine.

Sincerely yours, / Yvor Winters

MS: Columbia, Eugene Sheehy Papers

Eugene Sheehy (b.1922): American librarian and bibliographer.

[1]The bibliography duly appeared, without YW's assistance: Kenneth A. Lohf and Eugene P. Sheehy, *Yvor Winters: A Bibliography* (Denver: Alan Swallow, 1959).

June 27, 1958 / 143 West Portola Ave. / Los Altos, Calif.

Dear Malcolm:

I am sorry to be so irritating. I suppose that I can't help it. My idea of a writer is somebody who has something to say which will interest superior adults and who knows how to say it. This takes a good mind, and a good mind is something more than a native talent: there has to be reliable knowledge in the mind, reliably understood. Arnold had a point when he said that the Romantic poets didn't know enough. He didn't know enough, either, but at least he tried. Most novelists are simply dull ignoramuses. I am not the only one who finds the most famous contemporary fictionists unreadable. Most of my close friends (all of them scholars, of course, but interested in literature notwithstanding) are in the same predicament.

You seem to grant me the ability to write verse, but to deny my ability to write prose. My early prose was awkward but at least serious. *The Anatomy of Nonsense,* my third book, was pretty damned well written, and so was my last one. One of the real masters of contemporary prose is Jim Cunningham, but he is a mere scholar and you probably haven't read him with attention. Perhaps the greatest single masterpiece of American prose is Henry Adams' history, but that alas is another work of scholarship.

You said you were thinking of people who want to write professionally. What do you think I do? Or any other scholar? Or were you merely thinking of people who want to be popular with the median reading mind?

I don't know the details of your teaching career, but my impression is that you have been an occasional teacher. I have taught English for thirty solid years, and I taught French and Spanish before that. I have taught the writing of poetry and years ago taught a little of the writing of fiction. Mostly I have taught the usual lecture courses and seminars—without which I could not teach the writing of poetry. I have directed more dissertations than any other person in my department, and over a wider spread of materials than any three of my colleagues would attempt for himself. And I have watched plans for broadening general education come and go, and I have found them all bad. Any writer, like any scholar, needs to know one body of literature thoroughly, in order to have a scale for reference. After that he can branch out on his own, and perhaps do it intelligently.

I hate to come back to poor Allen, but why in God's name he thought such poems of mine as "The Slow Pacific Swell," "On a View of Pasadena from the Hills," "Heracles," "Theseus," and "To the Holy Spirit" were influenced by the Elizabethans I shall never be able to guess; nor why he thought that Greville and Raleigh were pre-Spenserians. One ought to know one's own literature better. It really helps.

As ever, / Yvor

MS: Newberry

TO DONALD DAVIE

July 5, 1958 / 143 West Portola Ave. / Los Altos, Calif.

Dear Donald:

*   *   *

St. Martin's Press recently sent me *The Less Deceived,* by Larkin. I cannot review it: I have too much other business on hand. But I offer you these observations. "At Grass" is a fine poem which is all but ruined, for me, by the last line of the fourth stanza. Larkin employs a beheaded tetrameter here after having used normal tetrameters previously in the stanza, and even one line containing a fairly heavy anapest. Furthermore, the beheaded line contains long syllables and heavy syllables in the light positions, and one of the worst consonantal sequences I have ever tried: cked, th. Why in hell couldn't he have written: In almanacs their names live; they? Maybe he is ignorant. Maybe he is just trying to be ugly. But he ended up ugly. And the poem should have been beautiful. "Lines on a Young Lady's Photograph Album" is the next best. It is skillful and amusing and slight and expanded beyond all reason. It reminds me of some of Ransom. You have some of the same faults, and these faults seem common in your generation of Englishmen. "The Wind at Penistone," for example, is deliberately diffused in much the same way. The subject is more interesting, but you were playing with the subject. Reread Hardy's "In Time of 'The Breaking of Nations.'" More is there in 12 short lines. All of you people strike me as afraid not to be clever. It is easy to be clever. I was clever as hell when I was about 25, but I gave it up.

My best wishes to all of you, / Arthur

MS: Yale

July 7, 1958 / 143 West Portola Ave. / Los Altos, Calif.

Dear Malcolm:

So far as prose is concerned, I think that you and I could be classified as members of two schools which among the sixteenth century poets were known as the courtly and the plain. You belong to the courtly, I to the plain. The plain style poets—Wyatt and Jonson, for examples—believed that poetry should say something efficiently, and they believed that such saying was an art, and in their hands it was a very great art. Sidney and Spenser, however, were less interested in saying something than merely in saying with grace and ornament, and their poetry was inferior.

Don't get the idea from the above that my verse is in the sixteenth century plain style, because it isn't; it isn't in the courtly, either.

When you say that I don't recognize prose as an art, you are dreaming. Adams' history is great art. So is Johnson's introduction to his dictionary.

What bothers me about your prose—not merely this one essay, but nearly everything I have read—is the elaboration of elegance, out of all proportion to what you are saying. I get bored very early, and stop. The same kind of poetry bores me equally.

You define a professional writer as a man who gains most of his living directly or indirectly from writing. And you exclude me. What do you think my living would be if I had not written? And published? Or don't you know how the universities work?

Your program would occupy about half the time of a department the size of ours. How many potential professional writers—not as you defined the term, but as you meant it—do you think there would be among the undergraduates in any major university? If the program were sound, which I do not believe, there might be room for one such program in the country. But I would sure as hell hate to teach in it or have any dealings with its products.

I don't think that your program would teach young critics to write in the various forms you indicate. It would put them through glib exercises and make them both ignorant and self-conscious. One can write only if one has something to say (and exercises on nothing in particular are a curse), has talent, and acquires scholarship.

I am sorry, but I have taken my stand. Dixi.

YW

MS: Newberry

July 8, 1958 / 143 West Portola Ave. / Los Altos, Calif.

Dear Mr. Allen:

I am sorry to have been so remiss in answering your letter of June 15. The fact is, that the summer quarter has now begun, I am not teaching, I live six miles from Stanford, and I am writing the paper which I am supposed to read at Hopkins. Consequently I seldom pick up my mail.

4:30 on the afternoon of November 7 is satisfactory to me. However, how much time may I have? I am now more than half way through my paper and think it will run to about 30 pages of typescript. If I read it complete, it will certainly take an hour and quarter. There are parts that I can cut, but the cutting will not improve the paper. I understand that you wish to publish the paper in some fashion.[1] If I cut for the reading, would you be willing to publish the entire affair? This last is important to me in a way, because the main body of this thing is revised very greatly from an essay that I published in *Poetry* about thirty— or was it twenty?—years ago. There is only a little of the original text left, but enough to make magazine publication difficult. And I have been lecturing on this material for years, and it has been draining away into doctoral dissertations at Stanford, Harvard, and elsewhere, and I would really like to publish this portion soon, so that my students will have to make acknowledgments to me instead of vice versa.

Also, would it be of any help to you to have an advance copy for printing? I shall finish it within ten days, but would want to keep it around for a couple of weeks at least for reinspection.

I cannot be present for your entire fiesta. As I told you, I believe, I work for a living and have responsibilities to my students. I will fly east on Thursday the 6th (this involves cutting one lecture), will read my paper on the 7th (one of our secretaries will administer an examination to my lecture class on this day), will read my poems on the 8th, sit in the audience on the 9th, and fly home on the 10th. This is the best I can do.

Sincerely yours, / Yvor Winters

MS: Hopkins

Don Cameron Allen (1904–1972): American scholar and educator.
[1]Published as "Poetic Styles, Old and New."

Nov. 16, 1958 / 143 West Portola Ave. / Los Altos, Calif.

Dear Mr. Allen:

I got home. I am just beginning to feel competent again, as there was much more society than I am used to during that week-end, and much more plane-trip. I got up at 5:40 A.M. on Monday to get my plane. That is 2:40 California time. And I arrived at my house at about 7:15 P.M. But whenever I begin to feel sorry for myself, I think of Mr. Coleman. I hope he has managed to get a little sleep since I last saw him, for he looked as if he needed it.

You and Mr. Coleman and Mr. Macksey were all very kind, and I wish to express my gratitude to all of you. I will write Mr. Coleman and Mr. Macksey within the next few days, but I would be grateful if you could show them this letter in the meantime.

I shall have Alan Swallow send each one of you copies of books of verse by Edgar Bowers, Alan Stephens, and Ellen Kay. And I shall send each one of you from here a copy of Thom Gunn's second book. Miss Kay is the least of these, but she is very good, notwithstanding. I hope you will like them. Thom's book may not be in stock at the Stanford Book Store. If it is not, it will have to be ordered from England, and this will take time.

I did not actually witness much of the program. I heard Miss Moore and Ransom read their poems, and that was all. I have heard Frost before, however, and I suppose it was the usual performance, loose tennis-net and all. Miss Moore gave me a short breakdown of what she was going to say about Dame Edith. I am, frankly, upset by this kind of thing. Poetry has always seemed to me to be the highest form of scholarship, and I hate to see it turned into a sideshow. Grateful as I am to Miss Moore for her kindness to me when I was young, I think that she traduced poetry. She did not read poems. She exhibited her personal eccentricities. Ransom did the same thing in a more genteel manner.

I know that I was not a success. This is partly because I was nervous, as I told you, and partly because I played it straight. I suspect that the *Baltimore Sun* spoke for 90% of both of my audiences. I have not the talent to be an entertainer, and if I had the talent I would refuse to use it.

I wonder what would happen if you introduced at least two serious and literate people into this program every year, even if they had small popular following. M. C. Croll, if he were still alive, or Jim Cunningham now? It might diminish the interest at first, but it would raise the tone. It might do a great deal of good in the long run. I have talked to a good many people about this kind of business, and I am not alone in my opinions. Even the Stanford undergraduates were angry at Frost, and I talked the other night with a young professor of English from Northwestern, who is exasperated with most of these people, and I gather that he felt that he was not alone.

I think that the generation preceding my own is incurably addicted to this kind of performance, and most of my own generation as well. But there are a few younger people who are serious, talented, and well-educated. I pin my hopes on them.

I enjoyed talking with you a great deal. And I enjoyed talking with Mr. Coleman and Mr. Macksey. I would have enjoyed talking with Mrs. Macksey and your three students at dinner Saturday night if conversation had been possible.

It turned cold here yesterday and is now quite as cold as it was at Baltimore, but the weather is unlikely to become much colder, and the cold spells will be brief. Once the rains come, it will be warmer. The frost finished my fig crop, but ripened my persimmons and pineapple guavas. The last of my Valencia oranges were picked recently, but we are still eating them (they ripen in May). My tangerines will ripen around Christmas. My strawberry guava crop has just come to an end, after about two months of heavy production. My pomegranates are ripe. Most of my olives are picked (a big cast-iron washtub full) and I am now engaged in putting them in rock-salt (for Greek olives) and in the lye-and-brine cure. In May my loquats will ripen (loquats are one of the finest fruits I know, but they deteriorate rapidly after picking and so are never marketed) and I shall have loquats for two months. In early June my cherries, nectarines, apricots and early peaches, and in mid-June my early figs (white) and my first crop of black mission figs. In July my late peaches and the end of the loquats. The black figs should continue through half of July and start their second crop late in August, at which time my late white figs and grapes will be starting. In addition to this we have quinces, limequats, and Meyer lemons. The lemons and limequats bear fruit straight through the year.

These are interesting facts, and I feel justified in mentioning them to you, as one scholar to another. There is a long-standing tradition, however, among Californians to the effect that they never brag about their home state. This is a tradition which I invariably respect.

Sincerely yours, / Yvor Winters

MS: Hopkins

1960–1967

Nov. 20, 1960 / 143 West Portola Ave. / Los Altos, Calif.

Dear Jack and Erma:

I should have written you sooner. Few things that I should do are done when they should be done. I should not be writing a letter of this kind on a typewriter, but my handwriting has never been more than barely legible, and I doubt that it would be that now. I cannot keep up with my work (lectures, grading, theses, dissertations, committee work), and still write letters to my friends. I am tired. I hope, for the sake of Janet and Dan, that I can get through the next five years. Joanna and her husband are almost on their feet now and will be shortly.

To tell you the honest truth, I cannot remember what I have ever taught you, nor can I remember any especial kindness that I have ever shown you. I have always been fond of you—more fond of you than all save a very few people, and quite as much as those. But this is a distinct matter.

I am skeptical about the value of my entire career. I do not say this with reference to you; I say it with reference to the entire literary situation: from Stanford to Timbuctoo. Don't bother to reassure me: I know the phrases.

My love to both of you, and many thanks for the gift.

Arthur

MS: Winters

TO ROBERT LOWELL

May 7, 1961 / 143 West Portola Ave. / Los Altos, Calif.

Dear Mr. Lowell:

Many thanks for your very friendly explosion in *Poetry.* I had meant to write you sooner, but the usual load of spring quarter examinations and dissertations has kept me steadily exhausted and behind in my work. I was amused that you found my little song ["A Dream Vision"] "magical." Most of my young friends were shocked by [it], turn slightly green when they refer to it. I doubt that I shall write any more verse.

Yours, / Yvor Winters

MS: Harvard, bMS Am 1905 (1514)

Robert Lowell (1917–1977): American poet and dramatist.

June 29, 1961 / 143 West Portola Ave. / Los Altos, Calif.

Dear Dick:

Your letter of June 22 is about the third I have had from you asking me to do something or other. I get on an average two letters a week asking me to write an article or to contribute a poem or to read my poems. This is doubtless flattering, but I have no time to do these things and in fact no time to answer the letters. I have only a little time left, and that time is *my* time, not the time of the public. I remember you with kindness, but please, for the love of God, forget that I exist.

Yours, / Yvor Winters

MS: Stanford

Richard Elman (1934–1997): American novelist, journalist, poet, and social worker. He was a former student.

TO ALLEN TATE

August 16, 1961 / 143 W. Portola / Los Altos, Calif.

Dear Allen:

I should have written you long ago to thank you for your contribution to *Sequoia*. My only excuse is the usual one: a kind of moral lethargy, the result of nervous exhaustion, which has been growing on me. Physically I seem to be O.K., if you consider my age. My M.D. knows that I drink too much red wine (it is innocent stuff, and we get very good red wine in this blessed state) and that I smoke too much (Comoy and Dunhill pipes, however, and very good tobacco —I have always considered cigarettes a filthy habit and was sorry to see you smoking one on the envelope of your Yale recording), but he (the M.D.) has had no luck with me. Recently he gave me the double cardiogram test, a triple blood test, and a urine test. He didn't tell me the results until I asked him. Then, rather bitterly, he said, "Mr. Winters, in spite of everything you can do, you are in good health." My real trouble has been blood pressure, but that is now down to normal, thanks to a pill which I am no longer taking, at least for the present. The pill contains serpasil (snake-root) and esedrix. The latter causes gout, and I had two attacks early last year, but no more. I cured it by eating less meat. Now that I am off the esedrix I should have no more trouble. But I am very tired spiritually.

I have a sabbatical leave next year and a Guggenheim grant, and hope to write my last book of criticism if I can pull myself together. I have made a start and hope to move faster now that I have done a lot of sleeping. I am somewhat depressed by my sudden accession to fame now that the fame will do me little good. I feel as if I were surveying the first stage of my posthumous reputation. My reputation will doubtless go down before it goes up again, but it will last. The worst thing about it is that my son Dan will have to live his life out in my shadow. Dan is very civilized and has a fine critical intelligence. He might have been a fine poet and critic if I had not been in the way. But I doubt that he will try. He will be a very good teacher of Romance Languages, probably in a state college or junior college, and will hunt continually for obscurity.

You are wrong about my criticism, but I am glad that you like the poems. Al Guerard was off target in his essay on the story (of which I don't think very much). The story is actually a study in the hypothetical possibility of a malign supernatural world. Al is a simple-minded naturalist and this didn't occur to him as a possibility.

This letter has been an experiment in controlled association. I hope that you are still with me.

Janet is in Cambridge to have a look at our grand-daughter (Sara Elizabeth Thompson, 3 months old) and to help Don and Joanna move to Madison, where Don will be teaching anthropology next year. I will visit them in the spring, but please don't mention the fact to anyone. I do not want to read my poems, read a paper, talk to graduate students, or go to a cocktail party.

If you see that unregenerate character Jack Levenson anywhere in the halls of your dark satanic mill, give him my regards.

Yours, / Arthur

MS: Princeton, Allen Tate Papers

[1]*Sequoia* 6 (1961) was devoted to Winters. Among the contributors were Cunningham, Gullans, Gunn, Marianne Moore, Swallow and Tate. Asked what he felt about being chosen the first holder of the endowed Albert Guérard chair, YW wrote the editor of *Stanford Today* (autumn 1962): "As to honors (blessed term), I wish that you would list the issue of *Sequoia* which the undergraduates published in my honor last year. The undergraduates got there ahead of you and ahead of my appointment to the Guérard professorship. Their project was well under way before I received the Bollingen award. In brief, they were more interested in my publications and in my teaching than they were in my honors. This strikes me as the more honorable interest. I consider it my greatest honor" (n.p.).

TO ALLEN TATE

Oct. 16, 1961 / 143 West Portola Ave. / Los Altos, Calif.

Dear Allen:

I ought long ago to have answered your letter of August 31. The fact is, that I am tired, as I said. Forget the rhetoric and remember the fact.

I am happy to hear of your marriage. I send my best wishes to you and your wife.

Now forgive me for what I am going to say. When I go to Wisconsin it will be a trip to Wisconsin only. I want to see my grand-daughter, whom I have never seen, and my daughter and son-in-law, whom I have not seen for about three years, and whom I may never see again. I am going by train, for two reasons: I have not crossed the country by train for a good many years, and I want to see the country from close up once again; I have responsibilities to Janet, Dan, and Joanna, and I cannot afford to be liquidated at this particular juncture. I shall be in Wisconsin for only two or three days, but the trip will take time; and I am supposed to be working on a book. I shall have to keep the trip short. Also, as I have said, I am tired. I have always been the retiring type, and I am not sure that I can keep going until I retire.

I would like to write a paragraph on behalf of California Wine. The stuff that is exported to foreign parts is pure shoe polish. I doubt that you can get any decent California wine in Minnesota. But when you are shopping look for Charles Krug's Cabernet Sauvignon and Grey Riesling. Wente Brothers put out good white wines. All of the Krug wines are good, but those I have mentioned are the best. I find little sustenance in white wines, but the best California white wines are supposed to be better of their kind than the red.

I must now return to the Elizabethan epigrammatists—who never influenced me.

Yours, / Arthur

MS: Princeton, Allen Tate Papers

TO GLENWAY WESCOTT

Nov. 3, 1962 / 143 West Portola Ave. / Los Altos, Calif.

Dear Glenway:

You are nervous beyond the occasion. We should be very glad to see you, if the matter can be arranged. The main problem with me is my health: shattered nerves and high blood pressure. I am normally in bed by 8 P.M. and cannot possibly sit up beyond 10. Extended conversation, even with my best friends, sometimes results in my fainting.

I may as well give you a brief résumé of this and that. I am a little tired of being regarded as self-centered and nonsensical in my criticism. I am neither. Most of my critics are both. I doubt very much that you could pass an elementary examination in the history of occidental critical theory or even English critical theory, or in the history of English and American poetry to go no further. I assure you that I could pass such an examination; I give such examinations. Most of the eminent critics of our time could not pass such an examination. Tate in praising the first edition of my collected poems very highly in the *New Republic* some years ago, showed a complete ignorance, not merely of my poems and their origins, but of the history of English and French poetry; he did not even bother to check dates in the *Oxford Companion to English Literature.* But he finds me an eccentric critic, and he regards himself as a kind of norm. I have devoted my life to scholarship and to teaching, and I am bored with professional ignorance. If the people who lift their eyebrows at my conclusions would take the trouble to examine my arguments and the texts which I discuss they might acquire a modicum of education.

You mention the dates Nov. 19–22. Nov. 19–21 are the dates of pre-registration at Stanford, and I shall have to spend a good deal of time in my office; but if I know a week in advance when to expect you, I could manage an afternoon off. We could easily put you up for a night if you will permit me to go to bed early.

Janet will doubtless write you if she has not already done so. We hope to see you.

Arthur

MS: Yale

TO CHARLES GULLANS

Dec. 11, 1962 / 143 West Portola Ave. / Los Altos, Calif.

Dear Charles:

I wish to thank you for the copy of the book [*Arrivals & Departures*]. I am honored by the dedication and by the poem addressed to me, which is a fine one.

The book is very distinguished from start to finish. I have read it about three times, but am not yet prepared to give a definitive criticism. I doubt that I had seen more than a third of the poems previously, and I cannot recollect having seen any of the poems that impress me most.

There is a heavy concentration of the best in the final section: "St. John's Hampstead," "First Death," "Autumn Burial," "Question and Answer," and the poems following, are, I suspect, great poems. Others are as well done and almost as fine, in this section of the book and earlier. The book as a whole strengthens everything contained.

"A New Scots Poem" and "The Second Draft" are the best things of their kind that I can recollect, but of course they are, in a way, a bit low. Of the other satirical or semi-satirical pieces, excluding the short epigrams, which are fine in their own kind, the best, as I see the matter at the moment, is "The New American Poetry."

I have a shrewd suspicion that the book will make you a very sudden reputation. It is a pity that it was published in December, for this fact, I fear, will prevent its coming to the attention of the various award committees. But maybe not.

Dan is in Bordeaux and enjoying himself. Janet and I are getting along as well as can be expected.

I hope that you will enjoy yourself and a little solitude (that is more than I hope for) over the holidays.

Yours, / Arthur

MS: Gullans

TO HOWARD BAKER

April 3, 1963 / 143 West Portola Ave. / Los Altos, Calif.

Dear Howard:

We have not seen each other for a long time. Perhaps I should explain a few things. I suffer from high blood pressure and from a chronic fatigue, both physical and nervous. I never go out and almost never invite people here. I find conversation pointless and tiring; if it continues for an hour and a half, or is more than usually a bore, I sometimes roll over in a faint. I especially dislike talking about my work with an eager questioner, and I think that an interview is a bad preparation for a critical essay. If Kazin wants to write about me, he should do it on his own power. I am not irritated by whatever he wrote about me years ago; I don't remember what it was. By this time I don't care what anyone writes about me. But I am tired and overworked and am trying to finish my last book before my eyes give out (they are bad) and before I check in. I am sorry, but this is the way it is.

Yours, / Arthur

MS: Stanford

TO POETRY:
A MAGAZINE OF VERSE

August 26, 1963 / 143 West Portola Ave. / Los Altos, Calif.

The Editor / *Poetry* / Chicago

Dear Sir:

Recently John Williams of the University of Denver has published through Doubleday Anchor a volume called *English Renaissance Poetry*.[1] It is an anthology from Skelton through Jonson with an introduction. It is pirated in a very large measure from my publications. It leans most heavily on an essay which I published in *Poetry* in 1939; it seems to have derived a good deal from my essays "The Audible Reading of Poetry" and "English Literature in the Sixteenth Century," both of which appeared originally in *The Hudson Review* and later in my volume *The Function of Criticism*. It may have derived something from an old review of the *Oxford Book of 16th Century Verse* which I published in 1933 in *The Hound and Horn* and from my essay "Poetic Styles, Old and New," included in a book called *Four Poets on Poetry*, edited by Don Cameron Allen and published by the Johns Hopkins University Press.

The evidence is obvious.[2] Williams' table of contents follows my lists of poems very closely, although there are a few variations. My lists were offered as the basis for a theory of the history of the poetry of the century, and Williams takes over this theory in his introduction. No one else, I believe, has ever expounded it, certainly no one before I did. The book was first called to my attention by a graduate student, who was dumbfounded. A little later a former student called on me for an explanation and told me that three of his friends had written him for information. Williams makes no acknowledgments.

I wrote to Doubleday on July 19th last and called their attention to the facts. After a good deal of delay they agreed to my minimal demand, a slip of acknowledgment pasted into the copies. Thus far I have not seen the slip and am beginning to doubt that I ever shall.

This letter is not for publication, and I have not time to review the book. But I thought that you might be interested in checking the matter, especially as my old essay in *Poetry* is chiefly involved.

Yours, / Yvor Winters

MS: Lilly

[1]*English Renaissance Poetry: A Collection of Shorter Poems from Skelton to Jonson,* ed. John Williams (New York: Anchor Books, 1963).

[2]YW's lengthy letter to Anchor Doubleday very carefully and precisely laid out the evidence, which is irrefutable, listing the poets and, especially, the poems he discussed that were taken over by Williams.

TO HENRY RAGO

Sept. 12, 1963 / 143 West Portola Ave. / Los Altos, Calif.

Dear Mr. Rago:

Doubleday finally came through with a statement from Williams[1] which I accepted. It was not a complete confession but it was good enough, I guess. The book is a simple act of burglary. The statement names the essay in *Poetry* in particular and as a paste-in will probably arouse interest in a few.

You may show Jim Cunningham my recent letter, if you wish, for I would like the news of the book to get around; but I don't believe Jim would be interested in reviewing it. The best reviewer would be Charles Gullans of UCLA. Gullans recently published a fine collection of poems through the U. of Minn. press. He is a very learned young Renaissance man and is thoroughly competent in modern literature, English, American and French. He taught at Stanford last summer, and I asked him to look over the evidence. He was probably more indignant than I was.

A review is probably superfluous now, however. I have expanded the old essay in *Poetry* and revised it, and it will be part of a book which I shall publish, I hope, within a couple of years. I shall have to mention the Williams book in self-defense.

Meantime the news is moving over the academic grapevine rapidly. Many of my former students have seen the book. The news is already in England.

I don't wish to seem unduly dramatic about this, for I have been pirated before and on a fairly large scale. But this was mainly a theft from an old and uncollected essay and the action probably seemed safe. And my new book is involved. And the little bastard will doubtless make a good deal of money out of my work.

Yours, / Yvor Winters

MS: Lilly

Henry Rago (1915–1969): American poet and, at this time, editor of *Poetry*.

[1]The following statement appeared as the "paste-in" under the title "Note": "The past two decades have seen a marked increase of critical interest in the poetry of the English Renaissance, an interest not, perhaps, so dramatic as an earlier concern for 'metaphysical' poetry, but one which in the long run may be more substantial. A number of valuable new authoritative editions have appeared, notable among them William A. Ringler's recent *The Poems of Sir Philip Sidney* (New York: 1962) and Geoffrey Bullough's *The Poems and Dramas of Fulke Greville* (New York: 1945); the Muse's Library has given the general reader inexpensive new editions of Wyatt, Ralegh, and Drayton; and Alan Swallow, in his *Men of the Renaissance* series, has made widely available for the first time in many years the work of such poets as Thomas, Lord Vaux, and Barnabe Googe. Among the dozens of critical essays that should concern the student of the period, of especial importance are J. V. Cunningham's 'Phoenix and the Turtle' and 'Logic and Lyric' in *Tradition and Poetic Structure* (Denver: 1960), and Alan Swallow's three studies of literary method, as well as his essays on Skelton, Wyatt, and Surrey, in *Editor's Essays of Two Decades* (Denver: 1961). And two very recent books by younger critics—John Thompson's *The Founding of English Metre* and Wesley Trimpi's *Ben Jonson's Poems: A Study of the Plain Style* (Stanford:1962)—attest to the continuing vitality and growth of this interest.

"No one has been more responsible for this increase of critical activity than the poet and critic, Yvor Winters. His essay, 'The 16th Century Lyric in England,' which appeared in the magazine *Poetry,* February, March, April, 1939, has had an influence far out of proportion to its general circulation; since its appearance, nearly all informed criticism of the short poem of the period has had, in one way or another, to take account of the theories and judgments enunciated in it. It should be clear to all that this anthology is deeply indebted to that pioneering essay, and to other aspects of the subject upon which Winters has touched in his other critical works: neither this work, nor the interest which occasioned it, would have been possible without Winters' efforts. *J[ohn].W[illiams].*"

TO CHARLES GULLANS

Nov. 10, 1963 / 143 West Portola Ave. / Los Altos, Calif.

Dear Charles:

*   *   *

You do not really understand the moon goddess.[1] The farther back you pursue her (in all directions) the more subdivided she becomes. But at a kind of classical point she becomes the triple goddess. Thereafter she becomes more complicated once again. Diana, approximately speaking, was the Roman equivalent of Artemis. In Italy she was, among other things, the patron goddess of any point at which three roads crossed, and at such points a small shrine was usual. In this aspect she was known as Trivia.

I myself have three names. At the dogshows the handlers used to address me as Professor.

Yours, / Yvor

MS: Gullans

[1]Presumably this exchange began with reference to YW's poem, "Sonnet to the Moon," where she is apostrophized "O triple goddess!" (line 9).

TO CHARLES GULLANS

March 31, 1964 / 143 West Portola Ave. / Los Altos, Calif.

Dear Charles:

Dan recently lent me his copy of *Poètes du XVIème Siècle* (Bibliothèque de la Pléiade). I have just been reading the introduction to the *Délie* of Maurice Scève. It seems that Scève devoted much of his career to struggling with the triple goddess (who was born at Delos). You ought to look into this. You don't know how much you have been missing.

* * *

Do you know what a runcible spoon is? If not, look it up in *Webster's Unabridged.*

Yours, / Yvor

MS: Gullans

TO CHARLES GULLANS

April 1, 1964

Dear Charles:

See reference to triple Hecate, in *Midsummer Night's Dream.* I owe this reference to Janet. (end of play)

Your Triune Tutor, / YW

MS: Gullans

TO CHARLES GULLANS

[April 9, 1964][1]

Dear Charles:

Janet says 3 cheers.

Yours in triplicate / A—Y—P

MS: *Gullans*

[1]The date is the postmark date

TO DONALD E. STANFORD

Oct. 26, 1964 / 143 West Portola Ave. / Los Altos, Calif.

Dear Don:

I enclose a check for a three years' subscription [to the *Southern Review*, new series]. The Prospectus looks very good.

The other day I was presented by the author with the following novel: *Catherine Carmier*, by Ernest J. Gaines (Atheneum). Gaines is a Louisiana Negro who graduated from S.F. State and held a writing fellowship in fiction at Stanford six or seven years back. He took no work with me (I was told that he was afraid), but he used to come into my office and talk. He is a very nice guy. The book is not a great novel but it is a real novel (not propaganda) and is very moving. The prose is simple but good; the situation and the people are complicated and realized. You had better get a review copy and review it; you had better order it for your library. And I think you would do well to try to get something from Gaines for your magazine. Address: Ernest J. Gaines, 998 Divisadero St., San Francisco, California 94115.

*   *   *

Last May I had an operation for cancer of the tongue. It was, as they say, successful, but it involved a good deal of plastic surgery, and I was under anesthesia for about two and a half hours. It left me in a state of exhaustion akin to severe illness. I am teaching again and am getting a little strength back.

Best wishes, / Arthur

MS: *Stanford*

TO ALLEN TATE

Jan. 27, 1965 / 143 West Portola Ave. / Los Altos, Calif.

Dear Allen:

You had better correct my address in your memo book. See above.

I cannot write anything on Eliot. I am not even interested in him as a bad influence by now. And I haven't much time left. I am trying to finish a book, which will be my last criticism. Last May I had an operation for cancer of the tongue. Too much pipe smoking. It was successful, but I was under anesthesia for about 2½ hours, and the experience did something to my chemistry. Blood pressure down, thyroid down. I now take thyroid pills instead of blood-pressure pills. My muscles are sore. I feel half asleep most of the time. No more tobacco, no more liquor. I drink Knox's Gelatin. I have one more year to teach, and shall be glad to be done with it.

I saw Eliot on TV, receiving the Presidential Medal in the London embassy. He was pretty obviously senile; he ought not to have been exhibited. I wonder how long that condition had existed.

Yours, / Arthur

MS: Princeton, Allen Tate Papers

TO GUS BLAISDELL

Feb. 26, 1965 / 143 West Portola Ave. / Los Altos, Calif.

Dear Gus:

I would be grateful if you would say as little as possible about my personal life. It is not scandalous, but for the most part it is irrelevant, and I do not like personalized critical essays. You may not quote this letter or any part of it. You may use the information contained in it, but please use it sparingly.

I was in bed for about three years with TB in Santa Fe, most of this time in Sunmount Sanitorium (now, I believe, a nunnery). Sunmount is located on the road to Lamy, and at that time was well beyond the outskirts of Santa Fe. I left there for Ranchos de Taos, where I stayed for a few weeks. I then went to Madrid, where I taught the fourth and fifth grades. Madrid is now a ghost town, I am told, but then it was a busy and filthy coal camp. The next year I taught in the high school at Cerrillos, a few miles down hill from Madrid, and on the railroad. Cerrillos was an adobe village, originally a Mexican village; I am told that the chief business there now is little restaurants and Giftie Shoppies. In my day the chief business was illegal liquor and whore houses. You will doubtless recollect that all liquor was illegal then, everywhere. It was legal, however, to buy a box car full of California grapes, and these came in rather often; the grapes started dripping and fermenting before they got out of California, and when they were coming our way we could smell them half way between us and Albuquerque. There was also the local white mule. And we were on a rum running line from Mexico to Denver, a line which provided fairly good (but expensive) stuff. Only two of the fifteen grocery stores in town could afford to handle the Mexican liquor. The "Fire Sequence" was written a few years later, in Idaho, but the setting was Madrid. As to my boxing, forget it. It is a legend that accumulated somehow at Stanford. I never boxed in public, either as a professional or as an amateur. For a good many years I was a social boxer; my talent was about B minus.

For dates see *Who's Who*. See also (for other reasons) a very bad essay on my poems by Alan Stephens in *Twentieth Century Literature* for Oct. 1963 and my reply to it ["By Way of Clarification"] in Oct. 1964. This may keep you from making a number of fool mistakes. In some of the poems preceding the translations, you can obviously see the NM landscape. Also in a few the influence of Indian poetry. I doubt that this had a formative influence on my work; I should have been about the same anyway.

What are you doing?

Yvor Winters

MS: Stanford

Gus Blaisdell (b. 1935): American educator, publisher, and writer. Blaisdell had discovered a copy of *Diadems and Fagots* and wanted to republish it in the *New Mexico Quarterly*. The information he sought was either to form an introduction or to be published in lieu of the translations. (YW refused permission to reprint.) Either way, the projected work seems never to have been published; there is no listing in Grosvenor Powell's bibliography of YW.

TO DONALD E. STANFORD

Sept. 7, 1965 / 143 West Portola Ave. / Los Altos, Calif.

Dear Don:

Thanks for the corklifter. I will cherish it sentimentally. It will always serve to remind me of your almost-destructive behavior in my kitchen.

I offer you a few of my recent meditations upon your problems as an editor [of the revived *Southern Review*].

Wes says that you insist on modern literature as the subject of your critical essays. Where do you draw the line? You are willing to publish an essay on T. S. Moore, even if you decide against mine ["The Poetry of T. Sturge Moore"]. Would you have published my essay on Tuckerman ["A Discovery"]? Or my essay on Churchill ["The Poetry of Charles Churchill"]? Or my essay on Jonson —the one that was part of the paper I read at Hopkins ["Poetic Styles, Old and New"]? If not, you would have missed something, and you may miss other good essays by other people, and good material is scarce. These essays are all relevant to an understanding of modern poetry.

The backbone of any literary quarterly is its reviewing staff. You should try to get my young friends to review for you, and maybe you can find some one else. You cannot use one more than once in a year and a half if he has other things to do and you expect good work from him, so you should line up quite a few. It is hard to get older men to do this kind of thing unless they are professional journalists and phonies like Howe and Kazin. But there are intelligent young men, and many of them would like to do this kind of thing occasionally for a few years. And this is one way of leading them on to more ambitious efforts in criticism; your problem is not merely to find contributors, it is to train them.

The Library of Congress puts out a journal of book-reviews. What do they call it? The *Library Journal*? Anyway they seem to have a rigorous policy: each of the very short reviews must give a concise but accurate description of what the book is about, and only a few sentences of evaluation. When Swallow was editor of the *New Mexico Quarterly* he had a similar policy. The result is a lot of reviews which are very useful to the reader. If the review is a little longer, there is more space for evaluation, but the evaluation should be preceded by careful description. 5 years ago Tate used to review for the *New Republic* and the *Nation*, and he used this method; the result was a good many very fine short reviews. I think that you would do well to establish some such policy for your reviewers, and to have a short statement of your policy printed on slips to be mailed out to your reviewers. Their opinions would be their own, but you should require an honest and careful account of the nature of the books. You would protect yourself in this way against a good deal of egocentric bushwa.

The first American magazine to be professionally critical (as well as other things) was the *Hound and Horn*. The *Dial* was edited and written by and for gentleman amateurs. The *Little Review* was the organ of the unlettered but sometimes brilliant geniuses. The *Hound and Horn* printed not only the best criticism going, but a lot of the best poetry and fiction. It published excellent critical work by two or three men who disappeared when it closed down, and excellent work by others. It was the best thing we have had. It was run by young men and in a large measure written by young men. You will fail or succeed because of the young men that you don't or do obtain. My generation is finished, and there is not much critical intelligence between my generation and the people who are now about 30 or 35—or even younger. The big names who are washed up or who give you the stuff they have written with their left hand while dozing off under the influence will only kill your magazine. There is no point in simply duplicating the *Hudson* or the *Sewanee*.

It was nice to see you. Our best to both of you.

Arthur

MS: Stanford

TO THE PALO ALTO TIMES

Sept. 10, 1965 / 143 West Portola Ave. / Los Altos, Calif.
The Editor / The Palo Alto *Times* / Palo Alto, Calif.
Dear Sir:

I would like to put in my bit about the Ravenswood School. The recent letters against eliminating the school have failed to deal with the issues.

First of all, the young are not as intelligent as they should be. In this, they resemble most of their elders. They are, alas, more or less herd-minded. This is true of Negro children; it is true of white children; it is true of nearly all Stanford students, whom I have taught for thirty-six years. The Negroes have been told for generations that they are inferior; they have been treated as outcasts; they cannot live or work among the rest of us. The children see no hope for their own betterment; their discouragement is deep and understandable; they communicate it to each other, with the result that they do not work hard in a school which is predominantly Negro and many of them drop out. White children would behave in the same way if they were in the same predicament; but as the world now is, white children see a future and are competitive and so learn more. The Negro children should be spread out through the white children's world; this would instill a more competitive feeling into them and would help to make them feel that they were a part of our society. It would also eliminate a school which is discouraging to a number of devoted teachers who cannot of their own power overcome this social disease.

I am not imagining this situation. My wife has helped with the Ravenswood literary magazine and has become acquainted with teachers, pupils, and parents. Besides, the situation is a common one; it is present in every school of this kind.

We are fond of saying that our people are our greatest natural resource, but we don't do much about it. We need people trained for work at all levels; untrained people are wasted in modern society; we cannot afford to waste the trainable. And we cannot carry the burden of 20,000,000 people who are discouraged and embittered, and an unnecessarily large number of whom are unemployable. The problem is not simple: it is social and it is economic; it involves national survival. It is also moral, but of course no one mentions moral issues any more, except when a few old ladies wish to censor books or night-clubs.

One other thing: this is not a local issue; it is a real part of a national issue. In brief, it is serious.

Yvor Winters

MS: Stanford

TO ALAN SWALLOW

August 2, 1966 / 143 West Portola Ave. / Los Altos, Calif. 94022

Dear Alan:

I have decided to use chapter numbers.

*   *   *

The reason for this is the same as the reason for the paragraph which I added recently to the introduction. The thing is turning into a very unified book and much more of a history than I had anticipated—a history of poetic method, which ought, in twenty years or so, to revolutionize the teaching of poetry, and a history of the best poems (not all the poems) which should accomplish something also.

*   *   *

Arthur

MS: Stanford

TO IAN WATT

Sept. 16, 1966 / 143 West Portola Ave. / Los Altos, Calif. 94022

Dear Ian:

*   *   *

I may visit the campus again some day, but it will only be from dire necessity. My freedom from academic society is a wonderful thing. Notwithstanding
this fact, I should be happy to see you some time—or sometimes—if you care
to drop by. But I should explain my habits. I go to bed about 7:30 P.M., and after
4:30 P.M. I am busy around the house and garden. Callers should come in the
morning or by 3 P.M. at the latest. I can be reached by phone around noon or
after 4:30. The rest of the time I am in my study on the back of the lot or in the
garden. If there is any theory among my former colleagues that I am lonely, or
depressed, or in need of visiting committees, please discourage the idea as gen-
teelly as possible. I never was an academic man; I merely had scholarly interests
—and I had to earn a living. I would like to enjoy my retirement as fully as
possible.

Yours, / Yvor

MS: Yale

Ian Watt (1917–1999): American scholar and educator.

TO ALAN SWALLOW

Oct. 20, 1966 / 143 West Portola Ave. / Los Altos, Calif. 94022

Dear Alan:

*   *   *

I think it [*Forms of Discovery*] is a good book. I hope you like it. At least
there is nothing else similar to it. I think it will be used for a long time simply
for the analysis of poems. Sooner or later some one should discover that it is a
historical and philosophical work, but that may take time.

Yours, / Arthur

MS: Stanford

TO DONALD E. STANFORD

Nov. 25, 1966 / 143 West Portola Ave. / Los Altos, Calif. 94022

Dear Don:

The other day I mailed back my proofs and the dope sheet. On the latter I forgot to mention: *The Early Poems of Yvor Winters* (Alan Swallow, Denver). If you can get it into my contributor's note without too much trouble, it would make Swallow happy. And he deserves to be made happy. He is a dead game publisher. Wait till you see *Forms of Discovery*.

The poems are now out. He sent me my author's copies which melted at once. I have ordered more, but they have not come. I will send you a personal copy as soon as I can. It is a damned good book, much better than you think. And much better than Pound, Williams, Miss Moore, and all save the best seven or eight of Stevens. It will have a funny career—watch it.

Arthur

MS: Stanford

TO MAE SWALLOW

Nov. 26, 1966 / 143 West Portola Ave. / Los Altos, Calif. 94022

Dear Mae:

Alan's death is a shock, though I suppose I was expecting it. Everybody said he had been working too hard for a long time.

I have written Don Stanford and have asked him to let me do an obituary essay for the *Southern Review,* preferably for the spring issue; I am sure he will let me do it. But I shall need information, the usual basic facts: Dates of birth and death, where born and raised, facts and dates of education and war service. I think it might help if you could give me a few facts (with permission to use them) about his early career as a trick motorcycle rider, flyer, or whatever it was, and about the accidents that brought on his illness. I would not play these up, but they throw a little light on the curious inner violence that contributed to his success and to his death. I would like one of the little booklets listing publications. I would submit anything I wrote to you before submitting it to Don. Perhaps Gus could put this together.

Alan was a great publisher and one of the most remarkable men I have ever known. I owe him a great deal, but so does contemporary literature in general. It is these facts that I would emphasize.

I don't know what the fate of the publishing house will be, or the fate of my book. The house ought to go on, if it can continue as intelligently as it has gone, but this may not be feasible for financial or other reasons. Gus would make a good editor and director, but the operation may be too small to support him.

Gus phoned me from Albuquerque shortly after I received your wire. He said he would see my book through if you would permit him. He is more than competent. But everything may be stopped legally; I don't know. Even if you plan to sell the business, I think it would be good business to finish my book: it is the best book of criticism I have done; it will more than pay for itself and a good deal of money must be invested in it already; this book and the *Early Poems* will bring my whole career together as a unit and should greatly increase the sales of my earlier books. Alan, now you, will then own my entire opus except for the little book on Robinson published by New Directions. If you sell, this should make me more valuable than otherwise. I have my selfish reasons of course, but they are not what I am talking about at present.

The state of the book is as follows. I have read the first galleys on the first four chapters and returned them to Alan; I have here the galleys for chapters five and six, have read them and had them ready to send when your wire came yesterday—after thinking it over, I will send them off today air mail special, along with this letter; I have galleys 110 through 115 of the seventh and final chapter—I will hold these until I have the entire chapter.

In addition I have the second (corrected) galleys for the first three chapters, along with the first set of galleys which I marked up, and along with a few pages of the copy which Alan sent so that I could check the worst errors—this means that your copy for these chapters will have some gaps in it until I return this stuff. I have checked the corrections; most are O.K.; some were completely overlooked; and there are new mistakes, some of them bad. Some one who knows the business will have to stand over the printer, because he is unreliable. It should be someone who knows what I am writing about; this is where Gus would be the best man I can think of. I wish to read through the new galleys carefully before returning them, but this should not take more than a couple of days. Alan wrote me that he would be sending revised galleys for the whole book very shortly; I don't know how long it might take now.

A few days ago I wrote Alan a letter enclosing a table of contents, a Prefatory Note, and the usual Acknowledgments. If the book is still going ahead, I shall wish to send a new prefatory note, which will include a statement of my indebtedness to Alan.

Alan was a great man. I cannot tell you how depressed I am.

My best to you and Karen and Bill.

Arthur

MS: Stanford

Mae Swallow: Alan Swallow's wife.

[1]YW did publish his tribute to Alan Swallow in the *Southern Review* (1967). He also paid tribute in a letter to Martin P. Miller: "Alan was an odd genius. He was a bad poet; the syntax of his prose was sometimes as incoherent as Ike Eisenhower's, but his prose was intelligent. He had a gift which is restricted usually to good poets: He could recognize good writing and recognize it at once (he recognized the same gift in Gus, and so do I). It was this that made him a success as a publisher, this plus the energy of three bull-mastiffs. He was almost ready to take Gus on, before he died, as a junior partner; but he had been a lone wolf for so long that he couldn't bring himself to it. Lone wolf, lone bull-mastiff. I begged him repeatedly to take Gus or somebody. I knew he was killing himself, and so he did" (April 29, 1967).

TO DONALD E. STANFORD

Nov. 29, 1966 / 143 West Portola Ave. / Los Altos, Calif.

Dear Don:

It occurs to me that my last letter may have given you the idea that Swallow killed himself. In a way, he did, but it was not suicide. From what I have heard I would guess that he had a very sudden coronary attack. You may know about his early career as a trick-rider of motorcycles at carnivals and his life-long passion for fast motorcycles and fast cars. A few years back he had a couple of very bad accidents from which he never recovered. I gather that he had been full of drugs, some curative and some pain-killing, for years. But he drove himself almost insanely. He was unable to get along with assistants and refused to think about a younger partner. I have not heard from Mae or Gus Blaisdell. Perhaps Gus could persuade the N.M. Press to take over the Alan Swallow publications and Gus could keep an eye on the business as part of his regular job. Any press that does this will get some awfully good books.

A few days ago I sent you my *Early Poems*. You should have them by now.

Arthur

MS: Stanford

Nov. 30, 1966 / 143 West Portola Ave. / Los Altos, Calif.

Dear Allen:

I have your recent letter and I understand the law on this point and the people involved are filthy bastards.[1] But one can do nothing short of a lawsuit or the threat of a lawsuit. I will not threaten anything that I cannot go through with. I have not the money, time, or energy for a lawsuit. I had intended to write the bastards and also the University of Michigan, but now I cannot do that. In a couple of days I undergo another operation, probably cancer again. I'll probably survive it, but I expect to be knocked out for some time. Alan Swallow died on Thanksgiving day; this was a great shock to me. Beyond that my latest and best book of criticism is set up in type and I have been correcting proofs for a bad printer. I don't know quite what will happen now.

A few years ago I asked you to destroy all of my letters and told you that I have always destroyed literary correspondence. You replied self-righteously that you were preserving my letters for posterity, or perhaps turning them over to some university. I don't remember. Your chickens have come home to roost.

This sort of thing will happen after we are dead if it doesn't happen sooner. The foolish ideas of your youth will be recorded; there is no help for it.

I hate people who do this sort of thing, but I don't care if they quote me personally about Zabel.[2] He *was* a sonofabitch and a slippery little rat. To hell with Zabel.

Yours, / Arthur

MS: Princeton, Allen Tate Papers

[1] Tate had written YW about Leonard Greenbaum's *The Hound and Horn: The History of a Literary Quarterly* (The Hague: Mouton, 1966). Without seeking permission from the authors, Greenbaum had included rather extensive correspondence to *The Hound and Horn*, including a number of Tate's and YW's letters. Tate was angry in general, but what particularly angered him was the publication of a long letter he had written Lincoln Kirstein about Negroes. The reference to the University of Michigan refers to the fact that the book originally had been a doctoral dissertation at that institution.

[2] YW had written Lincoln Kirstein: "[Zabel] is as foul and slimy a son-of-a-bitch as the good Lord ever made. He has camped on my trail for years, stolen my ideas (as far as he could understand them), adopted my opinions, and vilified me consistently. A month before my review of Bridges appeared, he was sweeping Bridges out in the dust-pan, along with Abercrombie and Binyon. A month after the review appeared, he was listing Bridges with Landor and Herrick. The Moore review had a similar effect" (December 3, 1933).

TO GUS BLAISDELL

Dec. 8, 1966 / 143 West Portola Ave. / Los Altos, Calif. 94022

Dear Gus:

*   *   *

I shall not have time to bother about the index for some time at this end. The operation will knock me out for some time. The book can survive without one. The chapters are arranged for careful thumbing.

I am not sure about contracts for *Forms* or the *Early Poems*. I will ask Janet to look. All of this business, both books, blew up in a kind of hurricane. Alan was pushing me like hell, I suspect because he thought he might not last; I was pushing myself like hell, because of doubts about myself. We may have glided over business details.

I do not understand whether you are financing the book or whether the estate is doing it. You can hardly afford to. I could at least lend you money if need be.

I am more indebted to you than I can say. I really wish that you would address me by my first name. All of my young friends do. There are few others left to do so.

Yours, / Arthur

MS: Stanford

TO GUS BLAISDELL

Dec. 30, 1966 / 143 West Portola Ave. / Los Altos, Calif. 94022

Dear Gus:

I came home on Tuesday—almost 3 weeks in the hospital. Medicare takes care of about $1,500 hospital bills as well as other matters. I have other insurance. All in all it may cost us $300.

It was cancer, but the pathologist found it to be strictly in one spot. There will be no radiation treatment, at least for now. My surgeon says that in a couple of years it will probably be possible to control this sort of thing with pills.

The surgery was what is popularly known as massive surgery. Most of the muscle up the right side of my jaw and my right collarbone was removed, with most of everything else within the triangle. There is still a little drainage from the wound but it should heal shortly. No pain worth mentioning, because all the nerves were removed. My general strength has returned. In a few more days I should be O.K. except that the right side of my jaw, neck and shoulder will be crippled somewhat for a good many months for lack of muscle.

I don't know whether you have had time to proceed with the book or whether the situation may be changing. There should be a contract, as you said, as soon as we know definitely who will be the parties to it. If I lend you money, this should be in a formal contract, also, to prevent the lawyers from forming their own ideas if they get into the picture. $5,000 without interest. I could go a little higher if need be. The money to be repaid from the sales of the book. You were wrong about one thing, I am sure: the book will be a good deal bigger than *The Function,* maybe 350 pages. Your estimate of cost may have been too low. And you may need to set a higher price.

Don't worry about my eccentric footnoting. If the notes are numbered properly and the numbers are properly attached, and if the printing is correct, all will be well. I never was a model for graduate students or for other scholars.

Yours, / Arthur

I can read proofs if you wish, or do other odd chores.

MS: Stanford

TO GUS BLAISDELL

Jan. 2, 1967 / 143 West Portola Ave. / Los Altos, Calif. 94022

Dear Gus:

Our recent letters crossed in the same mail. I will try to explain how things went.

Chapter I was put into its present form and much of it written in 1961–62, on a Guggenheim. Chapt. II (Churchill) and the pamphlet version of the Yeats essay must have been done in the summer of 1960; the original Cunningham was done shortly afterward. My health was poor and my eyesight worse; I could not reread these things to refresh my memory about footnotes, etc. I could not work while teaching. Things got worse, and I was stuck here. My first operation occurred in May of 1964 and knocked me out for over a year. In the summer of 1965 I revised the Yeats (slightly) and wrote the rest of Chapter VI. Then followed my last year of teaching, and I was still in bad shape. Last spring quarter I wrote the Introduction and the Introduction for the early poems and put the book of poems together. My eyes were bad, and I could not concentrate; the style was frightful; I had to revise repeatedly. But my mind started working on the book again, working faster than I could write. In three or four months I wrote III, V, and VII and revised the Cunningham. I went back to old habits: straight whisky and black coffee, starting often at 3 A.M. In Sept., or early Oct., I noticed the lump on my neck; I was pretty sure of what it was, and I knew that an operation would interrupt the book for a year, and perhaps for good. I wanted to finish it while my mind was working. I had a date with my surgeon for Dec. 5, and set that as a deadline. I finished almost a month before that, but Alan was already sending me galleys and I continued to work under great strain. My typing is erratic; I had to watch out for that. And I had to try to save my text from the printer, for I was pretty sure that Alan had not enough strength or presence of mind to be trusted. The whole business was a desperate race, here and in Denver. I am not very good at the subtleties of correct form, and I had not the strength to worry about them.

That is how the whole thing got dumped on you in that shape. If that short paragraph of appreciation for your help will embarrass you in your professional capacity, you may strike it out; but I owe you a great deal and I wanted to say so.

Yours, / Arthur

MS: Stanford

TO MARTIN P. MILLER

March 27, 1967 / 143 West Portola Ave. / Los Altos, Calif. 94022
Martin P. Miller, Attorney at Law / Littleton, Colorado
Dear Mr. Miller:

I have your letter of March 22 last, regarding the estate of Alan Swallow. Please forgive my typing. I have no secretary. Last Dec. 15 I underwent an operation for cancer on the right side of my neck, which removed nearly all of the muscle from the upper right hand corner of my torso; insofar as the muscle has been replaced it has been replaced by scar tissue. The scar tissue is crippling. This letter is hard to write.

I am glad that Mae has decided to go on; this is the first word I have had of the decision. I have the impression that James Laughlin of New Directions would like to buy her out. You probably know nothing of him; I wonder how much Mae knows. He is something of a scoundrel, I feel sure, and is wholly irresponsible; I have done business with him to my sorrow. I have never heard him well-spoken of. I can give you a good many stories should you be tempted to urge Mae to sell to him. I would fight his getting control of my work in any way at my disposal.

You invite questions: I have one. When Alan died, my book of criticism, *Forms of Discovery,* was set up in type, but very badly set. I had seen a set of galleys for nearly the entire book, and a "corrected" set for a large part; both were loaded with very bad mistakes. Gus Blaisdell has been working on the book, and he tells me that he brought it to "letter-perfect" condition, has finished paging and will send me page-proofs presently. I would be interested to know just how far along things have gotten. But there is another problem: Alan had not gotten around to sending me a contract; I have asked Gus to get me a contract, and he promises but does not get it. I have asked Mae to send me a contract, and she does not answer. Alan was my publisher for twenty years, and I want to stay with the firm; he did a great deal for me. But I am beginning to wonder if I am wanted, and would like to find out. Since I have no agreement, I could publish in England at any time. Two English publishers want the book, and a very intelligent young English agent has offered to act for me. I could easily get an American publisher. Mae would be very foolish to give this book up. The sales of my books have been increasing steadily and will be a source of considerable income ten years from now. This new book will outsell the others and will increase the sales of the others. You have never heard of me, but I am a great poet and critic and my books will last. There are dissertations written on me in India. And so on. I want to stay with Mae, but I want to know what she wants, and soon. And if she wants me to stay, I want a contract, and soon. And I want to know what is happening to my book.

I hate to seem improperly urgent, but I urge you to inform me nevertheless. I am an old man, and I could die at any time. I would like to leave my own estate in order.

Sincerely yours, / Yvor Winters.

MS: Stanford

Martin P. Miller: Lawyer for Alan Swallow's estate.

April 14, 1967 / 143 West Portola Ave. /
Los Altos, Calif. 94022

Mr. Martin P. Miller, Attorney /
2009 West Littleton Blvd. /
Littleton, Colorado

Dear Mr. Miller:

This morning's mail carried off my note to you dated April 13 and brought your letter dated April 10. We may cross again. This will be a long letter, and it may take me a couple of days to finish it. As I have told you, I am crippled. But please read this letter carefully from start to finish. I have the impression that you don't know very much and that Mae knows little if more. I will try to explain some of the facts of life.

First, let me rehearse briefly what has happened between us. When Alan died, my book was printed, but with many errors. Gus Blaisdell undertook the job of straightening out the proofs; he tells me that he is sure he has a clean book, and that he has paged it; he has done this very laborious job with no payment from the company and at considerable financial sacrifice to himself. He has done this out of admiration for Alan and myself and out of loyalty to Mae. In my opinion the company should reimburse him for what he has lost in wages but he tells me that he would refuse to consider this; so let it pass. For three months or so Gus kept promising me a contract and page proofs, but he never kept his many promises. I became pretty irritated with Gus; I now know that you and Mae were to blame and that Gus was covering for Mae. On March 27 last I wrote you that I wanted a contract in a hurry, and you sent one by return mail. It is customary, as you ought to know, for the publisher to sign the two copies of the contract before sending them to the author; Mae had not signed these, but you said that you would get her signature and return my copy. A contract is a two-way arrangement, and so far there is no contract between us. If I do not receive my copy within a very few days, I will arrange for immediate and independent publication in England; and if this involves litigation, there will be litigation, and no matter who wins, the reputation of the company will be ruined. Continue reading to find out why.

First of all, however, I will try to explain my own situation. In the past three years I have undergone two operations for cancer, the first for cancer of the tongue and the second for a rather large cancer on the side of my neck. Cancer spreads itself by dropping a microscopic fragment into the blood stream, a fragment which lodges somewhere and grows. Both of my operations were successful so far as anyone could tell. But the second cancer occurred close to the first, and it appeared within a six-months' period between examinations. A new cancer could appear anywhere at any time and progress rapidly. It would be the last.

The writing of this book was delayed by ill-health, including the first operation and the after-effects, and by the fact that I was teaching. I retired last June. During the spring quarter I had a light teaching schedule and began writing, and I wrote steadily through the summer and into the fall, often getting up at 2 A.M. to work. Alan regarded this book as the most important book in his publishing career, and he was sending me proof before I finished writing. I had an appointment with my surgeon for Dec. 5; I noticed the swelling on my neck in late summer; I decided to go on writing without advancing the appointment, for I knew that an operation would incapacitate me. I finished the book and read most of the very bad proof sheets. Alan died on Thanksgiving day just after sending me a card to the effect that he was about to mail the last proofs.

In brief I gambled with my life to finish the book. This is why I am goddamned serious about it. Deadly serious. I expect to wring no tears from you or Mae, but I mean business.

I doubt that you know anything about me or my reputation. In England I am regarded generally as the foremost living critic; in this country I am very famous. It has been known for years that I was working on this book; people have been waiting for it. Alan announced it as in proof on the cover of my *Early Poems*; it has been announced in the *Southern Review*. Some of Alan's novelists doubtless outsold me, but I am by all odds the most famous man on his list, and I am famous in literary and academic circles all over the world. People are expecting this book all over the world. You are being watched, and the ultimate reputation of the press will depend on your behaving or failing to behave like literate and civilized adults. If the word got out that you were trying to play footsie, to tease me along with no contract and then a contract that is not a contract, you would be finished. You would lose your best authors (nearly all of whom are my close friends) and you would get no more. Half a dozen of my friends in this region, all of them distinguished and in close touch with the most distinguished people in this country and in England, are fully informed of the progress of this business and are bothered by it.

I cannot understand what you think you are doing; you seem to practice deception and evasion for the pure pleasure of it. Money has been spent on the book; you can recover the money only by publishing the book; this will cost more money. But the book is not a gamble; it will sell 10,000 copies in less than two years, and you can arrange for British publication at a profit. Alan understood all this; Gus understands it. Are you and Mae so ignorant that you do not understand? If I should die before I have a chance to see this thing through, the whole story of incompetent little minds will be published, you may be sure; the company will be famous, but in the wrong way.

I expect prompt action from you or a prompt release. If I get neither I will go my own way without a release.

Yours, / Yvor Winters.

MS: Stanford

TO RICHARD ELMAN

May 11, 1967 / 143 West Portola Ave. / Los Altos, Calif. 94022

Dear Mr. Elman:

David Lamson has shown me your letter to him of May 2. Lamson is now past sixty and his wife is a little older; both are in frail health. A couple of years ago he had a coronary attack. Your letter upset him so that he might easily have another. Lamson went through hell for years; now, when his strength is almost gone, you propose to send him through more. Don't get the idea that you could clear his name, as the saying goes; you would merely stir up old gossip and old venom. There is a lot of both left around here, but it is quiet. Lamson's daughter is married to a very brilliant young engineer; they have four children of grade school and high school age. If you write your book,[1] even if it flops clear across the country, the book will send the reporters and photographers and TV men to Lamson's house in Los Altos, to his daughter's house in Palo Alto; you will have succeeded in putting the children through a torture that might mark them permanently. They will probably come to my house also, but if they do, I will meet them with a gun and a bulldog. For God's sake keep your hands off the Lamsons; they have been through enough.

Last Dec. 15 I had an operation for cancer on the side of my neck. It was what they call radical surgery. At present I have almost no muscle on the right side of my neck and right collar-bone; instead I have massive scar tissue which adheres constantly and has to be torn loose several times a day and which then burns like fire. My right shoulder flips out of control at no provocation. I cannot drive; typing is difficult and painful; this letter is an ordeal. This is why I have not answered your letters and cannot correspond with anyone. The operation got all of the cancer; but three years ago they got all the cancer in an operation on my tongue. It could start any time or something else could get me. It horrifies me to think that you are planning to destroy one of my few close friends and damage his family irreparably, when he and I are both so near the end of the line. Please stop and think.

Yours, / Yvor Winters.

MS: Winters

[1]Elman was planning a novel based on the David Lamson murder case.

TO GUS BLAISDELL

May 14, 1967 / 143 West Portola Ave. / Los Altos, Calif. 94022

Dear Gus:

I have now sent you more than half of the book, in three manila envelopes. Tomorrow I will send the rest; I have read all of it. I have the impression that corrections in page proof are expensive; I don't know how expensive; I don't know how much resetting is necessary to a page. But the book is not in good shape as it now stands.

I would make the following requirements:

1. That every error in the text of a poem be corrected. This is absolutely essential.

2. That everything that I have marked for deletion be deleted.

3. That everything that I have inserted (this was all in my copy) be inserted.

4. That any other error which might confuse the reader be corrected.

I would be satisfied to pass over all minor errors which anyone can correct for himself as he reads. This would reduce the number of pages to be corrected to a fourth. I don't know how much of this is your fault or my fault or Alan's fault or the printer's fault. If the cost is large let me know what it will be and I will try to cover it: the cost for the items listed above is essential.

The last galley I saw ended at the bottom of the present page 331. But the last line of the 2nd stanza of Janet's poem was missing, and I wrote it in to make sure that it got there. The line now appears twice in succession and ruins the poem. This is a very beautiful poem, one of the most expert I quote. It is by my wife. It will have to be printed correctly. In general, however, the book is worthless without accurate texts of the poems.

I shall have to ask you to send me the corrected pages—along with my present marked copies.

Yours, / Arthur

MS: Stanford

TO RICHARD ELMAN

May 17, 1967 / 143 West Portola Ave. / Los Altos, Calif. 94022

Dear Dick:

I have your letter; your wire came earlier. Many thanks for giving it up.[1] You say I exaggerated the local consequences; you are wrong; I have lived here for 38 years. A book of that sort would be news and it would be made news; republication of *We Who* in *Coronet* stirs up nothing. You cannot change these people. A couple of years ago I was walking past the open office door of Ackerman, our second-string philologist. His back was to me; he was discussing Lamson and I think my poems with some one else. His shoulders hunched and wiggled; I heard his low-pitched academic giggle; he said: "Of course everybody knows he was guilty as hell." That is it: everybody knows.

There is far more to it than you could find in your sources: a corrupt political boss who attempted extortion and then turned his machine on Lamson when he was not paid off (Rankin was one of his boys—you can see how innocent you were.) I cannot go into detail; I cannot type.

12 or 14 years from now it would do no harm. Lamson and his wife will be dead, the grandchildren grown up and scattered, and they have a different name. A brief discussion of the case in an essay on my poems would do no harm. Nobody reads poems or essays on poems.

I am sorry I hurt your feelings, but you startled us here. And you still don't understand what it would have meant.

Yours, / Yvor Winters

MS: Stanford

[1]Elman did not, in fact, give up on the novel. It was published four years later: *An Education in Blood* (New York: Scribner's, 1971).

TO GUS BLAISDELL

May 30, 1967 / 143 West Portola Ave. / Los Altos, Calif. 94022

Dear Gus:

I have not yet received the corrected page proofs, but yesterday the front material (minus only the table of contents) arrived, along with the colophon. I found two errors on one of the pages and enclose it herewith. The pages are very fine in appearance. I didn't think anyone could get this sort of thing out of that print shop.

It is an odd book; most of its readers will think it monstrous. But I think it will explode its way in.

Yours, / Arthur

MS: Stanford

TO GUS BLAISDELL

July 5, 1967 / 143 West Portola Ave. / Los Altos, Calif. 94022

Dear Gus:

You did not make me angry; neither did [Frank] Mahood. I appreciate the work that both of you have done. Maybe Mahood can do better in oil with a living model. But that was bad drawing and a bad portrait.

Consider: you are using "Time and the Garden" on the jacket. The final lines call for quite a portrait if there is to be one; and I have enemies and shall have more. The face that Mahood gave me was dead, self-satisfied, silly—everything that my enemies have ever claimed.

I prefer to portray myself in my own writing. This book is the major work in prose of my life. More than forty-five years of study, writing and rewriting have gone into it.

I am sorry about the grant. As to myself I have had no letter, no check.

Arthur

MS: Stanford

TO GUS BLAISDELL

Nov. 13, 1967

Dear Gus:

My last letter was so brief that I may have given the impression that I was blasting you. Far from it: the book is in print, which was mainly what I wanted: the errors obscure nothing. But there are so many and some are so absurd, that in connection with that colophon, they may cause a little ribbing. I am deeply grateful to you and Mahood.

But you are not a proof-reader and will never be one; you have other gifts. I hope the boys in Chicago[1] realize that Alan's Model-T methods will no longer work.

As to myself, I doubt that any of my young friends have the vaguest idea of my condition or more than half believe in it. I am disabled, and much of the time am almost blind in spite of a new pair of reading glasses.

A

With the glasses, I can sit up and read for short periods; sitting up increases pain without giving me the exercise I need; the pain blinds me, glasses or not.

MS: Stanford

[1]Swallow Press had been sold to Mort Weisman, the McClurg heir, of Chicago. YW's plural presumably encompasses Durrett Wagner, of the new Swallow Press.

SELECTED INDEX OF PERSONS

(Page references in italics indicate the recipients of letters.)

More, Paul Elmer, 153–54, 155, 200
Munson, Gorham, 105, 126
Nashe, Thomas, 201, 368
Nims, John Frederick, *273–74*

Perkins, Maxwell, *233–34, 234, 235, 236–37, 237–38, 238–39*
Peterson, Douglas, 339, 369–70, 370n
Peterson, Margaret, 336, 336n, 338, 339
Pinkerton (Trimpi), Helen, 308, 309, 309n, 312, 331, 336, 338,
Plato, 48
Poe, Edgar Allan, 12, 291
Polelonema, Otis, 112
Pope, Alexander, 180, 215, 220
Porter, Katherine Anne, *132–33*, 157–58, 158, 159, 162, *176–77*, 211, 331
Pound, Ezra, 3–4, 7, 9, 11, 11–12, 12, 19, 21, 24, 25, 34, 44, 47, 71, 72, 73, 79, 86, 91, 92, *115*, 116, 117, *118–20*, 160, 164, 174, 195, 204, 208, 209, 210, 213, 219, 281, 282, 322–23, 362n, 368, 372
Proust, Marcel, 148

Racine, Jean, 89, 93, 106, 115, 117, 147, 163,
Rago, Henry, *390–91*
Raleigh, Sir Walter, 188, 361–62, 362n, 376, 391n
Ramsey, Henry, *129–30, 135–36, 153–55, 165, 169–70*, 171, 175, 180, 194, 208, *321–22*
Ransom, John Crowe, 110, 111n, 114, *115–18*, 150, 151n, 173, 207–8, 212, 213, 255, 261, 281, 291, 293, 301, 309, 376, 379
Reeve, Paul Eaton, 189, 193–94
Richards, I. A., 104, 107, 281, 364
Riding, Laura, 110, 114
Rimbaud, Arthur, 43, 45, 82, 86, 89, 106, 117, 127, 189, 193, 206, 224, 279, 304, 373
Roberts, Elizabeth Madox, 3n, 29, 34, 37, 52, 62, 67–68, 72, 80, 82, 84, 85, 88–89, 94–95, 109, 128–29, 130, 133, 155–56, 241, 274
Robinson, Edwin Arlington, 49, 139, 168, 284, 356
Rodker, John, 21, 24, 44,
Roethke, Theodore, *257, 257–58, 262, 270–71, 322–23, 335*, 350, 351
Ronsard, Pierre, 32, 57, 66–67, 67n, 315
Rossetti, Christina, 306
Russell, Frances Theresa, 231, 233, 238

Sandburg, Carl, 7, 12, 18, 21, 24, 25, 27, 31, 39–40, 40, 41, 93, 219, 251, 357

Saroyan, William, 182, 183n, 190, 191
Sassoon, Siegfried, 15, 368–69
Schoell, Franck, 82, 83, 84
Scott, Winfield Townley, 194, 206, 210
Shakespeare, William, 12, 89, 106, 117, 163, 164, 202, 240,
Sheehy, Eugene, *374*
Shelley, Percy Bysshe, 12, 163, 167–68, 287,
Sidney, Sir Philip, 99, 188, 364, 371, 377, 391n
Smith, Maurine, 3n, 8, 9n, 26, 29n, 46, 47, 54, 56, 60, 89, 162
Smitter, Wessel (YW's brother-in-law), 218–19, 229, 325
Spencer, Theodore, 210, 216, 223, 226, 230–31
Spenser, Edmund, 12, 188, 292, 361, 362n, 377
Stafford, Clayton, 182, 183n, 209, 210, 212, 213, 222, 226, 258, 265
Stanford, Donald E., 202, 202n, 208, 210, 215, *216–17*, 218, 220, 225, *246–47*, 262, 271, 274, *277*, 338, 352, *365n*, 393, *395–97*, 400, 400, *402*
Stegner, Wallace, 279, 280, 315, 327, 332
Stephens, Alan, 355, 356n, 379
Stevens, Wallace, 7, 12, 24, 25–26, 30, 44, 45, 77, 92, 153, 164, 168, 175, 181, 182, 209, 255, 260, 262, 269, 284, 297, 305, 331, 348, 355–56, 359, 364, 373
Stone, Geoffrey, *247–48*
Swallow, Alan, 256, 256n, 279, 310, 311, 379, 391n, 396, *398*, 399, 400, 400–402, 402n, 402, 404, 406, 407, 408, 409, 411, 413
Swallow, Mae, *400–402*, 402, 406, 407, 409–10
Swett, Margery, 73, *75–76*, 76n, 84
Swinburne, Algernon Charles, 12, 117, 119, 209
Symons, Julian, *249–50*

Tate, Allen, *80–81, 81–83, 85–87, 87–88, 90–91, 93–97, 97–99, 99–101, 101–3, 103–6*, 106–8, *108–11*, 111, *113–14*, 115–116, 117, 118, 122–23, 124, *125–26, 126–27, 127–29*, 131, 134, *136–38*, 139, 140, 145, 149, 150, 152, 153, 155, 156, 161, 162, 166, 168, *172–74, 174–75*, 177, 181, *183–84, 184–85*, 187, *187–88*, 190, 192, *196–97*, 198, *201–3*, 204, 208, 210, 211, 212, 213–14, 215, 216, 219, 221, 222, 224–25, 242, 246, 255, 260, 275–76, *277–78, 278–80*, 280, 281, 282, 284, *288*, 297, 303, 309, *309–11, 318–19*, 321, 331, 334, *343–45*, 346, 347, 348–49, 352, 353, 355, 356, *358–59, 359, 359–62, 363, 363–65, 365–67, 367–69, 369–70, 371, 372, 373–74, 375–76, 384–85*, 386, 387, *394*, 396, *403*

Taylor, Edward, 295, 296, 297n, 298
Tennyson, Alfred Lord, 12, 306
Thompson, Sara Elizabeth (YW's grand-
    daughter), 385, 386
Thorpe, Jack, 23, 26
Traherne, Thomas, 193
Trimpi, Wesley, 277, 278n, 308–9, 312–13, 331,
    338, 339, 369–70, 370n, 391n, 396
Tuckerman, Frederick Goddard, 68n, 297,
    304–5, 306, 396
Turbervile, George, 368
Turbyfill, Mark, 24, 25n, 46, 49, 59, 84

Valéry, Paul, 84, 89, 106, 131, 156, 164, 305, 323,
    347, 351, 359, 360, 364, 367, 373
Van Doren, Mark, 128, *250–51, 256,* 261
Vaughan, Henry, 89, 100, 193–94, 295
Verlaine, Paul, 65, 89, 100
Very, Jones, 244, 304
Vielé-Griffin, Francis, *84–85,* 146

Warren, Robert Penn, 116, 122, 129, 207–8,
    212, 213, 223, 281, 309, 344, *343, 343–45*
Watt, Ian, *399*
Webster, John, 104, 110, 113, 220, 355
Wescott, Glenway, 3n, 5, 7, 9, 13, 15, 16, *19–20,*
    21, 22, 24, 25, 26, 27, 28–29, 29, 30, *30–31,*
    32, 33, *34, 35–37, 37–38,* 39, 40, *40–42,*
    42–43, 46, *47–48, 48–49, 52–53, 53–54,*
    54–55, 56, *57,* 58, *61–62, 63–64, 68–70,*
    70n, 71, 76, 87, 89, 94, 102–3, 128, 130,
    157, *162–63,* 204, 241, 274, 345, *386–87*
Westphal, Dorothy M., *265–66*
Wharton, Edith, 311, 318, 320
Wheeler, Monroe, 28, 29n, *32, 33,* 34, 37,
    38–40, 40, *46–47,* 47, 53, 54, 56, 58, 60,
    61, *62–63,* 69, 70n, 71, 89

Whitaker, Virgil, 288, 348–49, 365, 370
Whitehead, Alfred North, 107, 131
Whitman, Walt, 12, 96, 220, 304
Wilbur, Richard, 355, 356
Williams, John, 389–90, 390n, 390–91, 391n
Williams, William Carlos, 6, 10, 12, 24, 29n,
    47, 60, 61, 63, 64, 71, 77n, 79, 81, 82, 84,
    86, 88, 89, 92, 99, 100, 110, 112, 116, 117,
    121, 128, 139, 140, 156, 160, 164, 168, 194,
    195, *195n,* 208, 209, 249, 250n, 279, 281,
    331, 373, 374n
Wilson, Edmund, 126, 135, 150, 157
Wilson, Mrs. George Osborne, *231*
Wilson, T. C., *209–10,* 222
Winters, Daniel Lewis (YW's son), 321,
    321–22, 383, 385, 386, 388, 392
Winters (Smitter), Faith (YW's sister), 8, 10,
    18, 31, 33, 25, 43, 70n, 88
Winters, Faith Evangeline (YW's mother), 8,
    10, 15, 18, 61, 70n, 88, 102, 177, 241, 244
Winters, Harry Lewis (YW's father), 15, 18,
    19–20, 61, 68–69, 70n, 80, 88, 159, 170,
    176–77, 240–41
Winters, Joanna (YW's daughter), 177, 358,
    383, 385, 386
Wordsworth, William, 224, 304, 306
Wyatt, Sir Thomas, 188, 314–15, 377, 391n

Yamamoto, Hisaye, *315–16, 316–17, 317–18,*
    320, 325, 327–28, 332, 336
Yeats, William Butler, 7, 17, 25, 119, 128, 138,
    140, 168, 188, 220, 226, 230–31, 244,
    244–45, 313, 337, 358, 361, 362n, 405
Young, Pearce, 278, 307

Zabel, Morton Dauwen, 204–5, 403, 403n
Zukofsky, Louis, 195

SELECTED INDEX OF WORKS

BY YVOR WINTERS